T0354725

THE
FINAL CRISIS
THE PROPHETIC HISTORY OF THE WORLD

LENNOX F. HAMILTON

WESTBOW
PRESS®
A DIVISION OF THOMAS NELSON
& ZONDERVAN

WestBow Press books may be ordered through booksellers or by contacting:

WestBow Press
A Division of Thomas Nelson & Zondervan
1663 Liberty Drive
Bloomington, IN 47403
www.westbowpress.com
844-714-3454

Unless otherwise indicated, all scripture quotations are taken from the King James Version (KJV) of the Bible which is in the public domain.

Scripture marked (DBY) or (JND) taken from the Darby Bible.

Scripture marked (WK) taken from William Kelly's Translation of the Bible.

ISBN: 978-1-6642-6563-9 (sc)
ISBN: 978-1-6642-6564-6 (hc)
ISBN: 978-1-6642-6565-3 (e)

Library of Congress Control Number: 2022908333

Print information available on the last page.

WestBow Press rev. date: 05/27/2022

To my beloved wife, Paula, and the six children
my God has graciously given to me.

CONTENTS

Foreword.. ix
Acknowledgments xi
Introduction.. xiii

Chapter 1   Christ Takes the Book of Inheritance............................ 1
Chapter 2   The Four Main Antagonists in the Last Days 7
Chapter 3   Israel Protected by the USA according to Prophecy......... 26
Chapter 4   Geographic Egypt: The Terrorist King of the South 71
Chapter 5   Designated Egypt: The Land Shadowing with Wings..... 85
Chapter 6   The Dangerous Power That Shall Arise 116
Chapter 7   Designated Egypt: The Destruction 123
Chapter 8   The Mighty: The Powerful USA Challenged............... 130
Chapter 9   Designated Egypt: The Fallout after Its Destruction......157
Chapter 10 The Future Tyrus: The Commercial USA.................... 177
Chapter 11 The Future Assyrian: A Religious Kingdom..................183
Chapter 12 The Future Assyrian: A Terrorist Power 194
Chapter 13 Russia Strengthens the Terrorist Assyrian 205
Chapter 14 Israel: God's Earthly People 226
Chapter 15 The Trap...251
Chapter 16 The European Union and the Roman Prince............... 273
Chapter 17 The Wicked and the Antichrist................................... 306
Chapter 18 The Assyrian Conflicts 325
Chapter 19 Jordan: The Escape Route.. 337
Chapter 20 Christ's First Coming..344

Chapter 21   Christ Presented in Zechariah......................................351
Chapter 22   Christ Returns in Power and Glory.............................355
Chapter 23   The Prayer 372

Bibliography.. 375

FOREWORD

When Brother Lennox approached me about two years ago to read his manuscript, *The Final Crisis*, I immediately appreciated his serious approach to scripture, and I commend his efforts to the scrutiny of the readers. While I may not follow the author in every detail of his interpretations and conclusions, I believe the reader's personal endeavor to study this book and search the scriptures will be richly rewarded.

This is the promise we have: "Blessed is he that reads, and they that hear the words of the prophecy, and keep the things written in it; for the time is near" (Rev. 1:3 JND).

May the Lord bless the author, Lennox Hamilton, and each of the readers, according to this promise.

Alfred Bouter
August 8, 2020

ACKNOWLEDGMENTS

I hereby acknowledge the contributions of the following persons, who helped in the production of this book. Alfred Bouter was of special value to this project, since he read the book multiple times, providing editorial help and offering doctrinal suggestions. In the early draft, Franklin Langhorne was of great worth by offering much encouragement and helping immensely with the editing.

My sister, Juliet Higgins, was of particular help by encouraging and providing structural support. Her sacrifice cannot be expressed merely by words. Her editorial help and sequencing suggestions were of great value.

My friends David Roberts and Daniel Bubenzer were of particular support. They read the manuscript and offered suggestions that influenced the beginning of each chapter.

Finally, my wife, Paula, was of tremendous assistance. She provided comfort when I needed it the most, encouraging me when the project seemed to stall and offering editorial skills of a high order. I am forever grateful to her for the completion of *The Final Crisis*.

INTRODUCTION

The Final Crisis is unique. It is unlike any book one may have read about prophecy. It is the only book on Bible predictions that involves predictions of the past, present, and future. It enlightens us about prophecies that were fulfilled. It informs us about predictions that are being fulfilled today and those that will unfold in the future.

The Final Crisis doesn't indulge in speculations; it has no place for newspaper clippings but depends on only the specific utterances of God's word. This book begins with the present, how Israel will be restored to Palestine after a long exile. It enlightens us that when Israel becomes a nation in Palestine, a great power will protect and provide for her. According to the geography given in scripture, the country that will protect and provide for Israel is the USA. *The Final Crisis* shows this relationship from the word of God.

Moreover, *The Final Crisis* informs us that the USA will protect Israel for quite a while. During this protection, an incident will happen in the USA, called the "falling of the towers"—what we today call 9/11. It then informs us that after this incident, a new Islamic power will rise northeast of Israel. It explains to us that this power will be weak at its commencement. Afterward, a great nation will support this extremist power, and this power will then become very strong and restore the ancient Assyrian Empire. Once this power becomes strong, it will export terror to the world and come in conflict with the USA. This book gives us the history and result of that confrontation. *The Final Crisis* identifies the country that will embrace this terrorist power. It also shows how the world will change due to the support given to this extremist power.

Further, this book explains the revised Roman Empire in a way never presented before. It clearly shows from scripture that the European Union is the revised Roman Empire. It explains in detail how the European Union will shrink in size from the present twenty-eight nations to the prophetic number of ten countries. Furthermore, it shows how and why this European power will seek to protect Israel. It discloses the confrontations that will develop between the European countries and the terrorist government, which will be located in northeast Israel. It enlightens us as to the results of those confrontations.

Another important subject highlighted in this book is the trap. This book then informs us as to who will be entrapped. It explains the reasons for the two Muslim mosques on the temple site and what will become of them.

The Final Crisis identifies and explains in detail the activities of the three wicked men who will roam the earth: the Antichrist, the Roman Beast, and the Assyrian Leader. *The Final Crisis* outlines the Antichrist's role, the dealings of the Roman Prince, and the deeds of the Destroyer. We are shown the difference between these powers and where their governments will be located.

Furthermore, we are taught about the king of the South and the king of the North. We are, moreover, instructed on the difference between the king of the North and the Russian power called Gog. We are shown their diverse activities.

The Final Crisis instructs us about an Islamic kingdom that will rise in northern Israel and another extremist kingdom in the South. It gives us the histories of these kingdoms and describes the havoc they will cause on the earth. This book is the only book known to me that explains the king of the North and the king of the South in such detail.

The Final Crisis educates us about the prophecies concerning the Jews. It instructs us about the Assyrian captivity of the ten tribes. It teaches us about the Babylonian captivity of the two tribes and the Jewish wars with the Romans. It shows the importance of World War II to the Jews, according to scripture, and of their restoration to the land of Palestine.

Moreover, this book explains the tribulation and the battles that will ensue. It explains the revelation of Jesus Christ and the need for the Rapture of the saints. There is no exposition like this in all of Christendom. It gives the right place to the scripture, and it is comprehensive, enlightening, and exhilarating. If one wants to understand prophecies, he or she needs this book; if one desires to learn about future events, he or she must have it. May the truths of scripture unfolded in this book resound to the glory of God and the edification of the saints.

CHAPTER 1

CHRIST TAKES THE BOOK OF INHERITANCE

This first chapter addresses issues related to two objects, a person and a book. The person envisaged is a man whom God has chosen to rule the universe. Who will that man be who will govern the universe for God's glory? We are enlightened about this worthy one, who will rule over angels, men, and all creation. The honor given to this man will be far above all glories previously given to men.

Second, a book will be given to this man; this book will explain why this man was chosen above all others to rule the world for God's honor and praise. Moreover, the opening of this book will unveil the means the worthy one will use to take possession of the world. We must, therefore, know who will rule the universe and what this book will unfold. It is the opening of this book that will explain what will happen in this world. We all need to know, and God wants to teach us. Therefore, I will now unveil the secrets regarding the man and the book.

The book of Revelation asks a critical question: "Who is worthy to open the book, and to loose the seals thereof" (Rev. 5:2)? John was privileged to witness a scene in which there was a throne in heaven, and one was seated on that throne. In the right hand of the one seated on the throne was a book. This book was written on the front and back of the page. There was more. The book was sealed—not with one seal but with seven seals. What did this book signify? The scene was developed further. A strong angel proclaimed with a loud voice, "Who is worthy to open the book, and to loose the seals thereof" (Rev. 5:2)? We discovered that no one in the heavens, in the earth, or under the earth was found worthy to open the book. John, who was witnessing the scene, said, "I wept much, because no man was found worthy to open and to read the book, neither to look thereon" (Rev. 5:4). No one could open the book. No one could read the book, and no one could even look in the book.

While he wept, an elder spoke encouraging words to him, declaring, "Weep not: behold, the Lion of the tribe of Judah, the Root of David, hath prevailed to open the book, and to loose the seven seals thereof" (Rev. 5:5). Alas, there was a man found who would open the book and loose the seals thereof. Who was this man? Who was the only worthy one in the whole universe? We received a response to that question. The answer was the Lord Jesus Christ. He alone was declared worthy of all honor and glory.

This scene demonstrates that there is only one worthy in the sight of God. Though despised on earth, He alone is declared worthy in heaven. This scene is precious. This scene is unique, and it needs to be expanded.

Hebrews 1:1–3 declares that the Lord Jesus Christ has an exclusive right to this world in three ways. First, He has the right to it because He is the heir of it. We read in the passage, "His Son, whom he hath appointed heir of all things" (Heb. 1:2). God has given the whole universe to His Son, Jesus Christ. Second, He has the right to it because He created it. We read additionally, "By whom also He made the worlds" (Heb. 1:2). Christ is the Creator of the world; He is God, the Creator. Third, He has the right to it because He redeemed it. We are instructed that He, "when he had by himself purged our sins, sat down on the right hand of the Majesty on high" (Heb. 1:3). Christ is the only redeemer. This world belongs to Christ - not only because He is the Creator and the heir but also because He paid for it with His blood. It is this redemption we have developed in Revelation 5. If the world is His, then Christ will take it when He is ready. To take possession of the world, we have the scenes developed in Revelation 6. No one can divert Him from His purpose.

If Christ alone could open the book, what is the purpose of the book? We know this book must be quite important. What, therefore, is its content? We must find out. Therefore, from our meditation in Revelation 5:6-12, we learn the following truth: the book in the hand of the one seated on the throne is the book of inheritance - the rights to this world. God was about to give the rights to the universe to His Son, Jesus Christ. The Lord Jesus Christ, who will rapture His bride to heaven in Revelation 4, will take the inheritance from the one seated on the throne, in chapter 5, to share it with His bride, the church of God. He had paid the price for the world in His death as the Lamb of God, and He will redeem it by His power as the Lion of the tribe of Judah.

> As one writer stated, The inheritance is the Lamb's by purchase of blood; that blood sealed Him as the fully obedient One, and therefore God could thus highly exalt Him (Phil. 2), and that blood had also reconciled all things in heaven and earth. (Col. 1) And the inheritance being therefore thus purchased, He has now only to redeem it. His blood as the Lamb slain had given Him the title to it; His strength as the Lion of the tribe of Judah must now provide him with possession.

> In Israel, there was the ordinance of redeeming the inheritance by the heir or person. (Lev. 25) If either an Israelite or his possession had been sold, it was both his kinsman's duty and right to ransom him and it; now Jesus has approved Himself our kinsman in both ways ... the book taken by the Lamb is the title deed; and that it is so, and not a book of instruction to Him as the prophet of the church, or anything but this title deed that concerns the church's inheritance of the earth.[1]

---

[1] John G. Bellett, *Musings on the Apocalypse: Being Meditation on the Revelation* (London, UK: James Carter, 1895), 19.

3

Furthermore, Jeremiah 32:6–17 instructs us concerning the acquiring of the inheritance. In Jeremiah's transaction, we learned that the evidence of the purchase was written in two books: one open and one sealed. The open book represents the Bible, which we read today and typifies God's word, which deals specifically with the inheritance. Therefore, from God's word, we know that the Lord Jesus Christ has paid the ultimate price for the redemption of the inheritance. We learned that from the witnesses, those who have written on this matter in the New Testament. We also know the size of the inheritance; it encompasses the whole universe.

Furthermore, in Jeremiah 32 we learn another aspect of how the inheritance is transferred. The evidence of the purchase is also written in a sealed book. Moreover, the book of Daniel instructs us about the sealed book, which typifies what will be opened in the coming day when Christ will take the inheritance. We read, "But thou, O Daniel, shut up the words, and seal the book, even to the time of the end" (Dan. 12:4). The book in Daniel's day was sealed until a particular time - this action gives us the meaning of the closed book. The book in Revelation will be sealed until Christ takes the inheritance. What we learn from Revelation 5 is that Christ, as the lamb, has redeemed the estate by paying the price. However, in the coming day He, as the Lion, will redeem the inheritance by His power. Therefore, the redemption by power is what we find in Revelation 5, the twofold character of the Lamb and the Lion. The Lord Jesus will lay claim to the inheritance. He paid for it - that was in the past. In Revelation 5, He will take possession of it - that will be in the future.

The Lord Jesus Christ had the right of redemption, and He exercised that right. He was willing and able to redeem both the saints and the estate. He purchased the whole world by His death. Moreover, the witnesses subscribed to the evidence in the book. My God, who knows who has a right to the inheritance, was about to give it to His Son. However, before He gave it, He caused a proclamation to be issued to the whole world just in case another man thought he had a right. No one could come forward, not even the best of this world; only the Lord Jesus Christ could. He alone has the right to the universe. He alone paid the price. He alone is worthy. What is written in the book is the evidence of His claims to the inheritance. It describes how He sold all He had to purchase the world and how He died and paid the ultimate price to acquire it.

The seals that sealed the book are the means Christ will use to take possession of the inheritance. Therefore, what we have stated in Revelation chapters 6 through 20 are the means Christ would employ to take ownership of the world.

Christ is the center of all God's thoughts. Angels will be put under Him. Men will be placed under Him. The whole universe will be set under Him, and thanks be to God, the church will share it all with Him when He is thus exalted.

If, therefore, Christ will rule the universe, then Christ will destroy all aspects of man's power and be installed as the only potentate, the King of kings and the Lord of lords. No one will stop His exaltation. Earthly potentates won't give their kingdoms to Christ. He will subject and destroy all powers. According to 1 Corinthians 15, we know that day is coming "when He shall have put down all rule and all authority and power" (v. 24). Every rule Christ will put down. Every authority He will destroy. Every power He will eradicate. This subjection of authorities is what He begins to do in Revelation 6, so by the time we come to Revelation 20, Christ is in possession of the universe.

Nevertheless, this possession is no imagination; it is real. Christ will take possession of this world. Therefore, come with me up the mountain, my reader; let us observe the scenes that will unfold before us as the Lord Jesus Christ introduces the participants. Let us view the Antichrist, who will rule Israel, and the Roman Prince, who will preside over the European Union during the tribulation; let us stand in awe at the actions of the Destroyer, the leader of the Assyrian; we will be astonished. We will take note of Israel; we will observe the king of the North and the king of the South. The USA will come before us, the Assyrian operations will frighten us, and the European Union will interest us.

Come with me up to the tower, my friend, and let us observe Russia. We will call it the traitor; we will resent what Russia will do. We will view Iran with Russia as they set the world on fire. We will witness the destruction of Turkey, Syria, and Iraq; we will observe the rise of a destructive power. Nevertheless, we will see Christ, who will destroy all forces and reign supreme regardless of the storms.

This book begins with Christ in heaven and will end with Christ on earth. He is declared worthy in heaven, and all will worship Him on earth.

Every knee shall bow before my Lord. "Every tongue should confess that Jesus Christ is Lord to the glory of God the Father" (Phil. 2:11). Come with me; let us see Him shatter all powers and reign over all to God's glory.

Let us now begin this journey but wait. Before we do, I would like to introduce the concept of a difficulty scale. This scale will rise from one to ten, with ten being the most difficult and one being the least difficult. The subject presented in this chapter has a difficulty level of four on this scale. Therefore, it shouldn't have been too difficult to grasp. We will now systematically unfold the future, as presented in the word of God.

CHAPTER 2

THE FOUR MAIN ANTAGONISTS
IN THE LAST DAYS

The subject we are about to study is fascinating. We are about to observe the activities of the four main rivals in the last days. Which will be the first to rise and fall? Which will be displayed before the tribulation and which will be manifested during the tribulation? We are about to notice these antagonists. This subject has a difficulty level of eight on my scale. We, therefore, need to pay special attention to apprehend God's word.

Revelation 6 presents the introduction of seven seals. These seals bind the book together. Unless these seals are opened, the inheritance cannot be taken. However, these seals are only preliminary judgments and are followed by more severe judgments in the Trumpets. The first four seals represent the four central powers that prevent the taking of the inheritance. When the Lamb opens the first seal, we see a white horse ridden by a prominent rider. This white horse speaks of victorious power. The word *horse* in scripture depicts power in government. In Isaiah, we read, "Which bringeth forth the chariot and horse, the army and the power" (Isa. 43:17).

We learn from this verse that "chariot" portrays the army, and "horse" speaks of power. We, therefore, have four future powers depicted in the four horsemen. In the horse, we have portrayed the power, and in the man on the horse, we have presented the regime's ruler. The horseman is giving direction to the power. What we have depicted in the first four seals are four imminent powers in four different locations, headed by four individuals. These powers are so central that they are given a principal place after the Rapture. They will be the first four powers to be introduced on earth after the church of God is translated to heaven because they will dictate what will happen after the Rapture and during the tribulation.

Moreover, in these four horses and riders we have depicted four revived powers. These powers were here before but were destroyed. Yet, these powers will be revived in the last days. Furthermore, there is a close connection between the rider and the horse. The horse speaks of the power, the empire, and the rider speaks of he who will control the power. Therefore, the rider is seen as a dictator who will usurp the authority of the empire, or power. What the leader does is what the empire does. Moreover, both the power and the rider are identified by the same designation in the scripture.

It needs to be clearly understood that the scripture presents the Assyrian, for instance, as a power and a person; both are called the Assyrian; so, also, the first Beast of Revelation 13 is recognized. The head of the power is presented as superseding all the authority of the empire. He is an absolute ruler. The word of God is not making a mistake by presenting these powers in this way; as horse and rider, we cannot correct God's word; we have to interpret is as it is presented.

An important question must now be asked. Which power is depicted by the first horse in Revelation 6? The correct answer to this question can be obtained only when we learn that four rival powers will be jostling one another during the tribulation and that these horses represent those powers. Therefore, the white horse represents the Assyrian, an Islamic power that shall rise northeast of Israel, and the rider represents the Assyrian leader.

However, most Christians know very little about the Assyrian. What is even worse, they know practically nothing about the future Assyrian. Moreover, the scripture presents the Assyrian as a power and a person. In this book, when I speak of the person, I will use *he* and when I speak of the power, I will use *it*. Nevertheless, this book will enlighten us concerning this most important power.

The scripture speaks about the Assyrian more than any other power in the word of God; since he is the one that will bring all God's judgment to a climax. However, he is the least known in Christian circles but he is the most important personage in the scripture. Consequently, Christian writers mention the Antichrist, Israel's false king, and the Roman Prince, the future ruler of the revived Roman Empire, most in their writings. Yet, these two players are only two of the four horsemen presented in Revelation 6. Surely, without the other two powers, we will never understand the puzzle of the last days.

It is not surprising, therefore, that some think we might have the Roman Empire depicted in the first seal. But that isn't accurate. There are specific reasons why the Assyrian power is seen in the first seal, and the Roman Empire is represented later. Let us quickly evaluate the evidence.

One of my favorite writers, Edward Dennett, was one of the first to suggest that we may see the Roman Empire in the first seal: "Such is the divine portrayal of a mighty conqueror who will arise hereafter, as the blind instrument, like Nebuchadnezzar, of God's vengeance upon the nations of the earth. Who he will be it is impossible, spite of the pretensions of men, to forecast; but from indications given in this book, it may be that the picture finds its counterpart in the first 'beast' of Rev. 13; that is, the imperial head of the Western Empire."[2]

We need to ponder what Dennett said when he wrote, "Who he will be it is impossible, spite of the pretensions of men, to forecast."[3] What Dennett meant was that no one could say authoritatively who the picture represented without proof. He cannot mean it is impossible to know the power, since "those things which are revealed belong unto us" (Deut. 29:29), at the right time God will give the understanding; if not, the Bible is a sealed book. However, the Bible is not a sealed book. Therefore, we can give our views, but we must find scripture to advance our suggestion. In Dennett's opinion, the first horseman may be the ruler of the future

---

[2] Edward Dennett, *The Visions of John in Patmos: Being Notes on The Apocalypse* (London, UK: George Morrish, 1919), 121.

[3] Dennett, *The Vision of John in Patmos*, 121.

Roman Empire. There was a past Roman Empire, and there will be a future one.

The problem that has arisen in some minds since that suggestion is that *it may be* has become *it is* and that everything else *is wrong*. But we cannot interpret scripture that way; it is perilous. We must guard against that form of interpretation because God's word doesn't name the participant. We must study the scriptures carefully to get the right appreciation of the power. God hasn't written His word so we might not understand it. Despite this, we must accept that the future Roman Empire has a special place in the book of Revelation. The reason is real: the Roman Empire will be the "would be" protector (one who will endeavor to protect Israel but will fail) of the Jews during the tribulation. While in Isaiah we have two "would be" protectors of the Jews in the last days, when we come to Revelation, one of these protectors is already destroyed, and only the Roman Empire remains until it breaks the treaty. Therefore, the Roman Empire is prominent in the book of Revelation, and the other protector is famous in the book of Isaiah. This doesn't mean that every power in the Apocalypse is the Roman Empire.

It is essential to highlight that the expositor, Frederick Grant, puts it best when he wrote the following in his book on Revelation 6: "We naturally ask, Can we find no intimations elsewhere of this conqueror? It appears to me we may, and I hope to give further on what I think Scripture teaches as to it, not as pretending to dogmatize as to what is obscure, but presenting simply the grounds of my own judgment for the consideration of others. If it be not the exact truth, it may yet lead in the direction of the truth."[4] These words of Frederick Grant are indeed precious: "If it be not the exact truth, it may yet lead in the direction of the truth,"[5] and I would like to present the grounds for my judgment and allow others to judge which position is more scriptural.

William Kelly wrote,

Here, then, we have a series of providential judgments. The first is the white horse, the symbol of triumphant

---

[4] Frederick W. Grant, *The Revelation of Christ* (New York: Loizeaux Brothers, 1894), 62.
[5] Grant, *The Revelation of Christ, 62.*

and prosperous power. "He that sat on him had a bow" (Rev. 6:2). The bow is the symbol of distant warfare. His course is evidently that of unchecked victory. The moment he appears, he conquers. The battle is won without a struggle, and apparently without the carnage of the second judgment, where the sword, the symbol of close hand-to-hand fighting, is used. But this first conqueror is some mighty one who sweeps over the earth, and gains victory after victory by the prestige of his name and reputation. There is no intimation of slaughter here.[6]

Kelly doesn't name the rider. Darby doesn't identify the rider either. Still, what Walter Scott said about the second seal in his book is essential to this discussion and helps us identify the rider.

He wrote,

In all the Seal judgments, save the second, the Seer informs us that he was an eye-witness: "I saw." Then under the other Seals, the word "behold" precedes the description of the horse, whereas it is here omitted. Instead of "behold," the word "another" is added, not found in the other Seals. These may be termed trivial differences, but as we are firm believers in the verbal inspiration of the Holy Scriptures, we are satisfied that there is a divine meaning in these seemingly unimportant details. The occurrence of the words "I saw" and "behold" in the first Seal, and their omission in the second, may be accounted for by the fact that the word "another" in the latter connects the two Seals. Thus "I saw," and "behold ... another, a red horse."[7]

Walter Scott rightly identified the connection between the first and second seals. The word *another*, showed that connection between the

---

[6] William Kelly, *"Remarks on the Revelation: Being, Lectures on the book of Revelation,"* In The Bible Treasury, vol. 2, ed. William Kelly (London, UK: George Morrish, 1858), 101.
[7] Walter Scott, *Exposition of the Revelation of Jesus Christ* (London, UK: Pickering & Inglis, 1920), 148

seals. These two seals represent two similar powers: the king of the North and the king of the South, who are placed together. They will be Islamic kingdoms that will rise in the future. They will be similar in nature and character. Therefore, the difficulty becomes apparent; if the first seal is the Roman Empire, then with whom is it seen connected in the second seal? The word *another* shows that the power depicted in the second seal is of the same character as the power expressed in the first seal.

Now, let's tie what Walter Scott said to what Kelly indicates here:

> The difference is here marked. It is necessarily by bloodshed in the second Seal, which implies carnage if not civil war. The rider is not on a white horse, the symbol of victory, but mounted on another, a red horse, with a great sword, he has a commission to kill. Aggressive power which subjugates is meant by the horse in every color, but in the first case that power seems to subject men bloodlessly. He had a bow, typical of distant warfare, not close or hand to hand. The measures are so successful - the name itself carries such prestige with it - that it becomes one onward career of conquest without necessarily involving slaughter. However, in the second Seal, the great point is that the peace of the earth is taken away, and "that they should slay one another" (Rev. 6:4). It may be the horror of civil warfare.[8]

In the second seal, we have the king of the South (an Islamic Empire that will be established south of Israel) introduced with a violent civil war in Egypt, as is declared in Isaiah 19. This king of the South will eventually take the peace from the earth by being the first power to attack Israel during the tribulation. In his book *The Revelation*, F. B. Hole agrees with Kelly that it might be civil war in the second seal. Moreover, F. W. Grant states the following, "In the first and second seals we have correspondingly war - that of conquest and civil war."[9]

---

[8] William Kelly, *The Revelation Expounded* (London, UK: T. Weston, 1901), 97.
[9] Grant, *The Revelation of Christ, 58.*

The Roman Empire is seen here in Revelation 6, because it is prominent in the book of Revelation. Still, it is recognized under the fourth seal. We are sure there is a connection between the first two seals, as Walter Scott indicated; since that is so, then with whom is the Roman Empire connected if it is identified under the first seal? Its proper place would be in the fourth seal, because there it would be seen associated with Israel, which is the third seal, and the persecution of the saints in the fifth seal. Please note, also, that Kelly is more inclined to place the Roman Empire under the fourth seal. He wrote the following, "But it is important here to notice, that there is positive ground from the Apocalypse itself to deny the assumption that the horse means the Roman Empire...And here it appears to me that the fourth seal rises up conclusively against such a view, the four seals being providential judgments homogeneous in character but differing in form. The Roman earth may be the sphere, but this has nothing to do with the symbolic force of the horse in the passage."[10] The horse speaks of power and the horseman of him who is guiding or ruling the government. These horses represent not only events but also powers. It is these horsemen and their dealings that will cause the tribulation. Without these powers, there will be no tribulation.

The most reliable indicator that the first seal isn't the Roman Empire is the fact that after the Rapture, the Roman Empire is portrayed as first getting smaller before extending wider. Then during the tribulation, its influence extends to the "third part." This smaller size is why it is seen as the "fourth part" here (in Rev. 6) and not the customary "third part" (as in Rev. 8, 12) because in Revelation 6, it is seen as smaller. The "fourth part" is smaller than the "third part." How the Roman Empire will shrink from a larger body to a smaller one will be explained later. However, to grasp this development, we need to observe that the present European Union, which is the revised Roman Empire, is bigger than the ten nations that will comprise the empire during the tribulation. This current Roman Empire is pictured as the "feet," according to Daniel 2.

During the tribulation, the Roman Empire will be seen as the "toes," not the feet. After the Rapture, just before the tribulation, there will be a significant crisis in the Roman Empire, which will cause it to condense

---

[10] William Kelly, *"Remarks on the Revelation,* In The Bible Treasury, vol. 2, 135,136

from a larger number of countries to ten nations. It will shrink from the "feet" to the ten "toes," according to the prophecy of Daniel. Therefore, after the Rapture, the Roman Empire will not be seen as "conquering and to conquer" (Rev. 6:2) but as dealing with internal matters that will threaten the very existence of the Roman Empire. In Revelation 13, we read, "I saw one of his heads as it were wounded to death; and his deadly wound was healed" (Rev. 13:3). The empire will suffer a wound during the seventh head, which will nearly kill it. This wound didn't occur in the Ancient Empire but will take place in the future Roman Empire. This wound is what will engage the attention of the empire after the Rapture and not the adventure to conquer.

Moreover, the fourth seal's horseman is called the exact names by which the Roman Empire is called in Isaiah 28. The fourth seal is the Roman Empire. The scripture is so correctly written that one power is expanding, the Assyrian, while the other is contracting, the Roman Empire, to prevent misinterpretation. The expansion of one government and the contraction of the other are taking place after the Rapture and before the tribulation; this is to avoid confusion. It is the Assyrian who is presented as conquering and desiring to conquer, while the Roman Empire will be contracting.

Surely, apart from the Lord Jesus Christ, the only people the future Roman Empire is said to war against are the saints. It isn't presented as warring against anyone to conquer territories. If we try to make it a bloodless, ideological conquest, the Roman Empire is pictured as getting smaller before getting wider after the Rapture.

Therefore, to get the right interpretation of the seals, we need to grasp that there are four powers seen under the first four seals. These are the four leading players after the Rapture and during the tribulation. It is necessary to understand that as we have the four empires presented in the book of Daniel, so we have the four central powers after the Rapture, given in Revelation 6. These four powers in Revelation 6 are the king of the North, the king of the South, Israel, and the Roman Empire (in that order). These four adversaries will be contemporary powers and not successive powers as presented in Daniel 2.

We also need to comprehend that these powers aren't merely countries. Israel will remain a country; however, the Roman Empire will be composed of many nations. Furthermore, the king of the North and the king of the South will consist of many countries. The Roman Empire will be an empire in Europe, while the northern kingdom will be an empire in Asia. The king of the South will rise in North Africa. The last two empires will be located north and south of Israel, hence their designations: king of the North and king of the South.

In God's word, especially in prophecy, one can identify nearly every army or power God presents. He uses some keywords so one may recognize the participants. If one follows those keywords, he or she shouldn't make mistakes.

Therefore, in Isaiah we read, "In that day shall there be a highway out of Egypt to Assyria; and the Assyrian shall come into Egypt, and the Egyptian into Assyria; and the Egyptians shall serve with the Assyrians. In that day shall Israel be the third with Egypt and with Assyria, even a blessing in the midst of the land; Whom the Lord of hosts shall bless, saying, Blessed be Egypt my people, and Assyria the work of my hands, and Israel mine inheritance" (Isa. 19:23–25).

Also, we read, "And it shall come to pass in that day, that the great trumpet shall be blown, and they shall come which were ready to perish in the land of Assyria, and the outcasts in the land of Egypt, and shall worship the Lord in the holy mount at Jerusalem" (Isa. 27:13).

These scriptures, and many more, teach us that when the Lord comes, there will be a people called the Assyrians, and there will be a place called Assyria. However, both the power and the leader are called in scripture the Assyrian. We also learn that God will bless Israel, Assyria, and Egypt at the same time. Yet, there is no country called Assyria today, so the Assyrians must go forth and conquer that region and establish their empire. They will then seek to enlarge their domain. As a result, we read, "And I saw, and behold a white horse: and he that sat on him had a bow; and a crown was given unto him: and he went forth conquering, and to conquer" (Rev. 6:2). The Assyrian does what is stated in this passage; he must conquer the territory to establish his kingdom. The bow is the symbol of long-distance warfare, so the Assyrian will conquer territories far and wide. Moreover, a crown was given unto him. It will be shown that the Roman Prince, the ruler of the future Roman Empire, is never called a king; therefore, this power couldn't be Rome.

Now, consider what is presented in Isaiah 10 concerning the Assyrian. "O Assyrian, the rod of mine anger, and the staff in their hand is mine indignation. I will send him against a hypocritical nation, and against the people of my wrath will I give him a charge, to take the spoil, and to take the prey, and to tread them down like the mire of the streets. Howbeit, he meaneth not so, neither doth his heart think so; but it is 'in his heart' to destroy and cut off nations not a few" (Isa. 10:5–7).

We learn that in the heart of the Assyrian (the Assyrian is presented both as a power and a person, because the Assyrian Leader will usurp all the authority of the power) will be the desire to cut off nations and not a few. This desire to conquer is the same aspiration displayed by the power in Revelation 6:2. We don't read of this craving in the future Roman Empire which is the present European Union. The Roman Prince, the future head of the Roman Empire, is strengthened, but we don't read of him going out to conquer anyone. We need not be confused with the activities of the ancient Roman Empire and that of the future Roman Empire. The future in scripture is opposite the past. We are observing the rise of the future Roman Empire today, and we don't see any desire to conquer militarily. However, when the Assyrian arrives, he will display that quality.

Further, in Daniel 8, we read, "And his [the "his" here is the Assyrian] power shall be mighty, but not by his own power: and he shall destroy wonderfully, and shall prosper, and practice, and shall destroy the mighty and the holy people. And through his policy also he shall cause craft to prosper in his hand; and he shall magnify himself in his heart, and by peace shall destroy many: he shall also stand up against the Prince of princes; but, he shall be broken without hand" (Dan. 8:24–25).

The Assyrian destroys not only the mighty and the holy, but he also "shall destroy many" (Dan. 8:25). He will even venture to stand up against the Lord Jesus Christ, the Prince of princes, but he will be broken without hands in that confrontation.

In Daniel 11:40–43, the Assyrian enters many countries, overflows them, and passes over them. In verse 41 we read, "he shall enter also into the glorious land, and many countries shall be overthrown." We read further that the land of Egypt shall not escape. The more scriptures we read, the clearer it becomes that the Assyrian fulfills what is stated in the first seal of Revelation 6.

The Lord will use the Assyrian to chastise both Israel and the world as is presented in Isaiah 13:3–8. In verse 5 we read, "They come from a far country, from the end of heaven even the Lord, and the weapons of His indignation, to destroy the whole land. In Isaiah 13, the weapon of Jehovah's indignation is the Assyrian. Moreover, in Isaiah 13:9–12 we read that the Assyrian will be used to destroy the world. This is also confirmed in Isaiah 14:24–27. However, the Assyrian of the prophet Isaiah, is the king of the North of the prophet Daniel, and is presented in scripture both as a power and a person; therefore, we have both a "he" and an "it," the "he" is the leader and the "it" is the empire. In the same way, the Roman Beast of Revelation 13 is presented as a power and a person. In the last days the rulers of these empires will be dictators.

Therefore, the king of the North, or the future Assyrian, is seen under the figure of the first horse, and the Roman Empire is seen under the fourth horse. Thus, the four horsemen of Revelation 6 depict the four leading powers after the Rapture and during the tribulation, just as the book of Daniel depicts the four empires during the times of the Gentiles. God has not given His word so we might not understand it; at the right time, He will give us the understanding. Moreover, the reason the Assyrian is revealed as being on a white horse is that before the tribulation he will attain a significant victory over a mighty power. This victory will be expounded later.

The rider had a bow; that is, he carried on distant warfare. He was fighting battles in faraway lands. He had a crown; he was a king but not the King of kings; he was the king of the fierce countenance of Daniel 8. The crown isn't the main feature of this personage; it is the battles that he will fight that will thrust him into this position of dominance. Christ also comes on a white horse in Revelation 19:11. The saints are also seen on white horses in Revelation 19:14, since the white horse speaks of victorious power. However, the white horse in Revelation 6 isn't representative of Christ. It signifies the Assyrian or the northern kingdom, the last enemy of the Jews and the West. It will be an essential power during the last days.

Furthermore, the Assyrian will be the most influential of the major players to put in its appearance that is why it is put first. Hence, we have not only a horse but also an outstanding rider. It is important that we see the horse and the rider together, as presented in the scripture, since the rider is the ruler of the power. Therefore, what the rider does is what the power does; the rider directs the power.

Therefore, after the Rapture (because we are dealing with things that will happen hereafter), there will be a mighty, victorious power in Israel's northeast. This kingdom will defeat another mighty power before the tribulation. As a consequence, when this seal opens, the Assyrian is already seen as a white horse. This white horse depicts it as victorious over that significant power. The defeat of this mighty power could take place before the Rapture. Thus, the Lord Jesus Christ will allow the Assyrian kingdom to rise in Israel's northeast to accomplish His purpose. This power will be an enemy of the Jews. It will be the most dangerous and the greatest enemy the Jews will ever confront. It will rise in the northeast of Israel, with its seat in Syria.

When the second seal was opened, there was another horse. It was of the same character as the first, as we note in the word *another*. Still, it wasn't as powerful or victorious as the previous power. The term *another* used about this second seal shows that this power was similar in character and nature to the first power. Nevertheless, it wasn't white; it was red. We learned from this symbol of the red horse, as we have it in Zechariah that the energy of the government or power acted in opposition to God's people. In this red horse, we will have a second power, which will be an enemy of the Jewish people. However, it had no crown and wasn't as powerful as the first power. This power was shown with a sword and not a bow. The influence of this leader will not be as far reaching as the first horseman, since his impact will be localized. These events take place near Israel. Two essential features enable us to identify him. First, he takes peace from the earth; and second, there is great blood shedding, as in Isaiah 19, where we read of a civil war in Egypt, the central territory of the king of the South.

This antagonist will be the first of the two powers to attack Israel during the tribulation and thereby take peace from the earth. Thus, he will be the southern king and the next significant influence in the world after the Rapture. He will appear even before the Roman Prince and the Antichrist but after the Assyrian king, the king of the North. The king of the South will not be as powerful as the king of the North. However, he will establish his kingdom with bloodshed.

Thus, in His dealings to take possession of the universe, the Lord will allow the southern kingdom to rise south of Israel with its seat in Egypt. Therefore, these two powers, the king of the North and the king of the South, will be enemies of the Jews. This common characteristic is the reason Walter Scott indicated that these first two powers are connected.

When the Lamb opened the third seal, we saw a black horse. The rider had no sword. He had no weapon. However, we noticed the economic situation in the country. The rider wasn't seeking to extend his power near or far. He had no offensive intentions and no defenses either, but he presided over a significant country. This power was quite important; as a result, God noted the state of its commerce. A day's pay could buy only a measure of wheat or three measures of barley. The black horse represents Israel, the subject of prophecy. The leader was trying to stabilize the country's economic situation, but the food was scarce, and the financial crisis was deteriorating. Nevertheless, there was still oil and wine - the portion of the rich was still available - which means the rich were still able to purchase their needed supplies. Israel will be reduced to great distress after the Rapture of the church of God, with the poor struggling to survive, as presented in this seal.

As the Lord opened the third seal, we saw the state of Israel and its leader seeking to regulate commerce in the land. The ruler was trying hard to provide food for the people. He is not the Antichrist but his predecessor. Later on, when the Antichrist will be manifested, we find that through his policies the Jews won't be allowed to buy or sell unless they accept a distinctive mark.

In the third seal, we have highlighted Israel in the land of Palestine after the Rapture. However, she will be there in great distress. Her country will be constantly attacked by Islamic fighters who will reduce her to great difficulties in her territory. These attacks will be coming mainly from the king of the North but also from the king of the South. These attacks will center on Israel's food supplies.

In Joel 1, we read, "That which the palmerworm hath left hath the locust eaten; and that which the locust hath left, hath the cankerworm eaten; and that which the cankerworm hath left hath the caterpillar eaten" (Joel 1:4). The future attacks on Israel's territory are compared to attacks by destructive insects and are centered on her food supplies. These attacks will compromise Israel's food supplies and will force the future Roman Empire to station troops in Israel. Undoubtedly, the attacker is the Assyrian. The first two horsemen will be opposed to Israel and cause untold economic misery for her. Israel will be the center of all their hatred.

In Daniel 11:35–45, we have these three players grouped together. In verse 40 we read, "At the time of the end shall the king of the South push at him: and the king of the North shall come against him as a whirlwind, with chariots, and with horsemen, and with many ships; and he shall enter into the countries, and shall overflow and pass over." The willful king is the Antichrist in Israel. At the time of the end, the king of the South will attack him. The king of the South will have his headquarters in Egypt. However, his kingdom will extend over many African countries, as we observed in the passage. Soon after, the king of the North (the Assyrian) will also attack the Antichrist, the king in Israel. The king of the North will have his headquarters in Syria, but his kingdom will extend beyond Iraq and Turkey. The first three horsemen exhibit the king of the North, the king of the South, and the nation of Israel. Therefore, we have the final attack on Israel by these nations before the Lord comes. Thus, Revelation 6 presents the main antagonists after the Rapture and before the battle at the end.

Furthermore, we read similar words in Isaiah 7:17–20. We have presented the three powers again. First, Israel is seen under these terms: "thy people, and upon thy father's house" (Isa. 7:17). Second, the king of the South is presented under the figure of "the fly that is in the uttermost part of the rivers of Egypt" (Isa. 7:18). Lastly, we have the king of the North seen under the picture of "the bee that is in the land of Assyria" (Isa. 7:18). These are the first three powers introduced in Revelation 6.

Finally, when the fourth seal was opened, we saw a pale horse, and "his name [was] Death and hades followed" (Rev. 6:8 JND). We noticed in Zechariah 1 that the Spirit of God was using horses to represent the three empires - Persia, Greece, and Rome - that succeed Babylon. Again, in Zechariah 6, the word of God shows all four of these empires - Babylon, Persia, Greece, and Rome - under the symbols of chariots and horses. However, in Revelation 6, we find that the rider was very prominent. He had a name, not a bow or sword, called Death and hades followed. In Isaiah 28, we read, "Therefore hear the word of Jehovah, ye scornful men, that rule this people which is in Jerusalem. For ye have said, We have made a covenant with death, and with Sheol [Hades] are we at agreement; when the overflowing scourge shall pass through, it shall not come unto us: for we have made lies our refuge, and under falsehood have we hid ourselves" (Isa. 28:14 -15 JND).

Notice that this power seen under the fourth seal takes the same names given to the Roman Empire in Isaiah 28. It is necessary to comprehend that the Death and Hades of Revelation 6 are developed from the names given in Isaiah 28. These names are not just introduced in Revelation 6, they were introduced before. More so, the power, in Isaiah 28 and Revelation 6, is called by these names at the same epoch. Therefore, the power in Revelation 6, must be the Roman Empire.

In Isaiah 28:14 -15, we see Israel will be in a covenant with Death and an agreement with Hades because she will be afraid of the Assyrian or the king of the North. This pale horse, therefore, of the fourth seal is the Roman Empire. It bears the same names in both Revelation 6 and Isaiah 28. Israel will make a covenant with this government, which is called Death and Hades because of its ties to the Dragon (the Devil seen as cast down from heaven) who will give the Roman Empire and its leader his power. We further read of the "fourth part," which also tells us it's the territory of the Roman Empire. Still, the area isn't as extensive as the "third part," which is the usual designation as in Revelation 8.

This "third part" is what the future Roman Empire will become during the tribulation since the empire after the Rapture will shrink from "the feet" to "the toes," according to Daniel's prophecy. It is during this shrinking that the Roman Empire will be described as the "fourth part." Then after the shrinking, the Roman power will be strengthened by Satan; then it will become the "third part," which is well known in the book of Revelation. Moreover, this power will kill with the sword, hunger, and death. The killing with the sword will be the attacks, by the Roman Prince, on the remnant of Israel, who will not be able to buy or sell because they will not accept the mark of the Beast.

Additionally, we find this power is said to also kill with the "beasts of the earth" (Rev. 6:8)—that is, the Antichrist and the Roman Prince. This expression, "the beasts of the earth" (Rev. 6:8), further ties this power to the Roman Empire. Israel will seek the protection of this imperial power against the government that will rise in the North, called "the Assyrian." The Roman Empire or the European Union will try to protect Israel from the Assyrian.

The first two horsemen have war-like powers; they have a spear and sword, and their desire is to destroy Israel with their weapons. These authorities are the king of the North and the king of the South. The third horseman is concerned with the maintenance of the state; this power is Israel. The last entity is called "death and Hades" following death, this power shows its connection to the underworld. This power is the Roman Empire strengthened by Satan, the Dragon.

Therefore, as we contemplate these four horsemen, we are introduced to the four rivals during the tribulation. These are presented early in the book of Revelation; everything that will happen afterward will hinge on these players. These will be the central powers during the tribulation. The Great Tribulation will occur because of the activities of these powers. The first two powers will seek to destroy Israel, and the last one will attempt to protect her. The actions of these powers are developed in the book of Revelation and the prophecies in the Old Testament. At the end of it all, the Lord Jesus Christ will use these powers to chastise Israel. Then, when the chastisement period is over, the Lord Jesus will turn and save Israel and will destroy the very forces He employed.

According to the passage in Daniel 11, we find that at a particular time, called "the time of the end" (Dan. 11:40), the final crisis will take place. The king of the South will attack the Antichrist in Israel. The king of the North will also swoop down with his mighty army against the same opponent—here called "the king," the Antichrist of the scriptures. We further read that when the king of the North shall "come to his end" (Dan. 11:45), it will be when Christ returns in glory and destroys the Assyrian. The Roman Empire is conspicuously absent here, because the Roman Prince will break the treaty with Israel and will leave Israel to fight the king of the North alone.

These are the main antagonists in the last days. First, a powerful terrorist kingdom (we will later prove that the Assyrian is a terrorist empire), will rise in the northeast of Israel, called the king of the North or the Assyrian. It will have its headquarters in Syria. It will be the most dangerous of the terrorist groups. It is the first power presented here; it is the main antagonist. Second, another terrorist kingdom will rise south of Israel, called the king of the South, and it will have its headquarters in Egypt. It isn't as powerful as the first terrorist kingdom, but it will still be a menace to society. Already, we saw ISIS seeking to establish an empire north of Israel in the Syria/Iraqi area. More so, at the same time, we noticed ISIS attempting to install another one, this time south of Israel, in the Libya/Tunisia area. In God's word, we are told that these are the very places where these kingdoms will rise, and these are the very people who will establish these empires. Let me state clearly that these kingdoms will be resuscitated, and no power on earth will prevent them from being resurrected. In Daniel 8, we read, "in the latter time of their kingdom" (Dan. 8:23). Therefore, these kingdoms will reappear just as the Roman Empire, the present-day EU, has reemerged.

I will demonstrate from God's word, what no evolutionist can counterfeit, that an all-wise and almighty God directs and allows what is happening in this world. He will take this world and give it to His Son, our Lord Jesus Christ, to rule in righteousness. When given this position of glory, the Lord Jesus Christ will order the affairs of this world for the glory of God and God only. I will clearly show this from the Bible, which was written by the Jews, whom I believe are God's earthly people. Still, before God establishes them as the head of the nations, He will carry them through an extreme trial. Their prophets wrote about these things many years ago; I am only endeavoring to interpret their writings while I depend on the Lord for guidance.

Additionally, there will be two other essential players in the last days. Still, they aren't found here in the book of Revelation, which is primarily occupied with events after the Rapture. One player will appear before the tribulation, and one will come after. One will rise and fall before the Great Tribulation, and the other will rise and fall after the tribulation. These players are the land shadowing with wings of Isaiah 18, and Gog, the land of Magog, of Ezekiel 38–39. The land shadowing with wings has been very prominent since Israel became a nation, but it will be destroyed before the tribulation begins. Additionally, Gog, the land of Magog, will be active even before the tribulation, but the Lord Jesus Christ will demolish it after the great tribulation.

Likewise, we will have some critical smaller players when the Assyrian will attack Israel and God will make a way for her to escape. These nations will be Moab, Ammon, Edom, Gaza, and Tyrus. How these nations will treat Israel as she tries to survive will be very important. We will also see this development from scripture.

Moreover, as we carefully study the Bible, we observe that from the future Assyrian power will emerge the Destroyer, the most significant terrorist the world will ever see. We see further that from Israel both the Christ and the Antichrist will appear. Then from the future Roman Empire will emerge the Roman Prince, the Beast, the leader of the revived Roman Empire, who is often confused with the Antichrist, by Christian writers. However, the Beast is very distinct from the Antichrist.

Do you think that when Christ comes to establish His kingdom here on earth, man's response will be welcoming? Do you believe the leaders of this world will step down from their positions of authority and power, and relinquish their thrones to Him? If they killed Him the first time, for sure, they will try to kill Him again. However, this time He will destroy all these powers and reign as King over all. This time He will announce His arrival with devastating judgment on this world and take His great strength and rule. No potentate will give Him power; He will destroy them all, and then He will rule as the only potentate, the King of kings and the Lord of lords.

We must cover one more important event in this book; that is, "the trap," our Lord Jesus Christ spoke of. The trap is a pivot as to how the events will unfold in the tribulation. It is one of the most critical developments in prophetic happenings. We must understand "the trap" if we will understand the events of the last days.

Is the Bible God's word? If it is, then events are about to happen that will cause the bravest of men to tremble. Let us, therefore, seek His help in understanding the events Christ, our Lord, will introduce. God will begin by escalating the crisis, then take possession of this world. He will then reign supreme over all. We will endeavor to take these subjects in order so we can lay hold on divine truth. We, therefore, desire God's help as we seek to understand His revealed mind.

Though much has been said and will be said that the reader may have never heard before, please don't despair; these things will be explained later in the book. I will show from scripture what is said about the Assyrian, the king of the South, Israel, and the Roman Empire. Russia's role will also be explained in God's scheme of things. The European Union will be described with its associated leaders. Moreover, the role of the United States will also be explained. All events and subjects will be presented in their right contexts.

I will now end this chapter with quotes from two excellent Bible teachers. The first is from the writings of W. H. Westcott in 1924:

> May I say that it is of the utmost importance that we should all be saved from looking to man, in the things of God, neither can we accept untruth that a good man says because it is he that says it, nor can we reject a true thing because we think he is a bad man that says it. A good man like Job has to confess in self-judgment that he had spoken things that he understood not, and a bad man like Balaam was forced to say true things in spite of himself, by the power of God.[11]

Therefore, my first desire is that the truth presented in this book will be comprehended and accepted, not because of the writer but because you have judged it to be God's word.

Second, William Kelly wrote in his exposition on Colossians 1, "Real truth, even when new, never sets aside the old, but on the contrary, supplies missing links, deepens the foundations and enlarges the sphere."[12]

The purpose, therefore, before me is specific - not to set aside the old but to deepen the foundation and enlarge the sphere. May my God help me as I endeavor to accomplish such a task and glorify Him in the process.

---

[11] William H. Westcott, *"A letter on New Birth and Eternal Life,"* In Scripture Truth Magazine, vol. 16 (London, UK: Central Bible Truth Depot, 1924), 17.

[12] William Kelly, *"Notes on the Epistle to the Colossians,"* In The Bible Treasury, vol. 6, ed. William Kelly (London, UK: George Morrish, 1866), 8.

CHAPTER 3

ISRAEL PROTECTED BY THE USA ACCORDING TO PROPHECY

God has given us, in grace, the prophetic history of His earthly people, Israel, that highlights significant events from the days of Abraham to the coming of Christ; even to the end of the kingdom. He has done this that we might be assured that the Bible is the word of God, as we behold the fulfillment of His prophetic history. I will, therefore, endeavor to outline just a sample of this history. In this prophetic history, the prophecies concerning the past have been completely fulfilled. The prophecies relating to the present are being fulfilled before our eyes and those of the future will be fulfilled. The subject I will now undertake is a prophecy concerning the present, it is being fulfilled in our day and before our eyes. I hope this current focus will open our understanding so that we might believe God and receive His salvation, since our eternal destiny is at stake.

This present topic is intriguing. We will begin to see God's hands providentially controlling everything. We will see that when Israel returns to Palestine, after being dispersed by the Roman Empire, a mighty power scripture calls "the land shadowing with wings" will protect her. As we study this topic, we will be fascinated to discover the identity of this country. We will now begin our study on this most influential country. We need to pay special attention to the dissertation, since this topic has a difficulty level of eight.

First, we need to seek divine help in understanding what the expression "shadowing with wings" means. Second, we need to know the significance of "the land shadowing with wings." Third, we must find out the association between Israel and "the land shadowing with wings." Fourth, we must seek to identify the location of this land. The answers to these inquiries will prove that God's word is being fulfilled even in our day before our eyes.

Scripture informs us that Judah (called Israel by the nations) was to be restored to the land of Palestine after the Romans destroyed her city and state. This restoration has been accomplished. Israel is now an independent country. The scripture further asserts that Israel was to be restored to Palestine after a long exile. That restoration was to become a reality after the Roman destruction but after a long interval. Israel (mainly the tribes of Judah and Benjamin but called Israel by the nations) was to be out of the land of Palestine for a long time; then afterward, she was to return. What is written in the scriptures has been accomplished. The scripture then predicted that a great nation would protect Israel after she was restored to the land. This protection should be happening at this moment, since Israel is in the land.

Therefore, if the Bible is God's word, we should be currently observing a mighty power actively protecting Israel and providing for her. This unfolding relationship should be happening before our eyes. What is distinct about Isaiah 18 is that we aren't dealing with something that happened in the ancient past, and so gives one the excuse of saying that he or she wasn't there and therefore doesn't know if that is true. We are talking about something that should be happening today. Yes! We are talking about something that should be happening now - right before our eyes - for all to see. That is what I would like the evolutionist to match for me. Show me something present: show me a dog-cow, a pig-goat, and a tiger-elephant so I may see evolution in action. The evolutionists may talk much but they will never be able to deliver. Yet, I will show you what the scripture says should be happening now, and we will look together to see whether it is developing as it was prophesied.

Yet, before I proceed, I will set down some rules, some of which are very stringent. First, I won't quote from any book on prophecy that was written more recently than seventy years ago. Why? The answer is simple. Then no one can say I am writing about events because I know these incidents have occurred, or are unfolding, and am trying to tie them to scripture. For example, the Bible declares that Israel would become a restored nation in the land of Palestine. This declaration became a reality in 1948.

In addition, I won't quote from any Christian writer who interpreted the scriptures and declared that Israel would become a restored nation unless that writer died long before that event. I will endeavor to prove that although that writer wrote more than seventy years ago, his prediction was fulfilled long after he wrote about it. The writer didn't see it happen, but because the Bible is the inspired word of God and it is precise and detailed, the writer wrote about the event, and it came to pass just as it was written.

Second, I want to list three of my favorite Bible teachers who dealt with these subjects so your research can convince you that they lived and died more than one hundred years ago. The teachers I will quote from are William Kelly (May 1821–March 1906), who died more than 110 years ago; John Nelson Darby (November 18, 1800–April 29, 1882), who died more than 130 years ago; and Edward Dennett (1831–1914), who passed more than one hundred years ago.

Third, I will quote from my favorite Christian magazine, the *Bible Treasury*. This former periodical incorporates a series of Christian articles written between 1856 and 1920 by well-taught believers. These article quotations have to do only with the prophetic matters I intend to develop. I will quote from later writers to show that the prophecies have been fulfilled. Having now set up my limits, let us now go through the word of God, see the person of the Christ, and see whether the things prophesied in the scriptures haven't happened as they were communicated. This phenomenon, I assure you, is what we will certainly observe.

Fourth, and most importantly, I absolutely believe the Bible is God's word. Surely, it is indeed and in truth the word of God. Consequently, it gives prophecies concerning some of the most famous countries of this world. These prophecies concern Europe, Russia, America, Syria, Jordan, Israel, Iraq, Egypt, Turkey, Iran, Ethiopia, Libya, and Lebanon, just to name a few. This writer has no hidden agenda when he writes about these countries. He is expressing only what the Bible says will happen to them. He has no personal view or bias against any country, he only writes about the declaration of scripture. Today, for instance, terrorism is rampant, but because the Bible is God's word, it has a lot to say about this terrorism. The Bible, moreover, gives the future destruction of some of these elevated countries listed above. The writer has nothing to do with these troubles but only to instruct and warn people about God's impending judgment. Therefore, by God's help, I will seek to show what is about to happen in this world. May the Lord help me and give me guidance in this endeavor.

Nevertheless, before I deal with this fascinating country called "the land shadowing with wings," I will endeavor to put the subject in its right context. Thus, I will give a short outline of Israel's history from the days of the kings to the time of "the land shadowing with wings." I will show that the history books written by man have entirely vindicated the Bible.

One of the primary features of Revelation 2–3 is the presentation of the prophetic history of the church of God. However, in the book of Revelation, the church isn't seen in its unique relations to Christ: as the body of Christ, the bride of Christ, or the house of God. Instead, the church of God is seen as a testimony on earth from the apostles' days until the Rapture. No believer familiar with the church's history will doubt that the church's history as a testimony on earth has precisely occurred as it is written in Revelation 2–3. This prophetic history isn't meant to deny that they were seven literal churches, situated in present-day Turkey, in the conditions highlighted in these chapters. However, what is being said is that one of the main features of these seven churches is the prophetic significance. It doesn't take much to behold this manifestation. Though these churches disappeared a long time ago, God's word describes them as "the things that are," as indicated in Revelation 1:19. If they had no prophetic significance, they would have never been so defined.

Moreover, when they shall cease to be, God's word introduces what will come after them as "the things that will be hereafter" (Rev. 1:19). At present, these churches have ceased to be real, historical churches. Yet the things listed to begin after their passing haven't yet commenced, because these churches have greater prophetic significance.

In the same way, Leviticus 26 emphasizes the prophetic history of the ten tribes of Israel. It states that the Assyrian will take these tribes into captivity. However, they will never be restored to the land, as a unit, until the Lord Jesus Christ returns in power and glory. Just as the word of God stated, these ten tribes have been outside the land of Palestine since the days of the Assyrian Empire.

Identically, Deuteronomy 28 primarily gives us the prophetic history of two tribes, Judah and Benjamin. This prophetic history covers the period from the days of Moses until the bewilderment of "Israel" in World War II - just before she became a nation in 1948.

Moreover, in contrast to the ten tribes, who will not be restored to Palestine until Christ returns, the two tribes (Judah and Benjamin) were going to be taken captive by the Babylonians. After that captivity, they were going to be restored, then dispersed again, this second time by the Romans, and finally, they were going to be seen in their bewilderment during World War II. It needs to be clearly stated that just as in Revelation 12, the prophetic word blends past, present, and future events into one picture, so Deuteronomy 28 goes with Daniel 9 -12 and Matthew 24.

Therefore, in Deuteronomy 28, we have outlined the history of the two tribes from the days of Moses to World War II. Israel's blessings were dependent on her obedience. In Deuteronomy 28:36, we find that Israel was going to suffer the first of two exiles. Nebuchadnezzar, the king of Babylon was going to take her to Babylon. Nevertheless, one may ask, How do you know the captor? The answer is simple. God gives signposts in His word so we may not make mistakes. In the first exile, Israel had "a king," as we read. "The Lord shall bring thee, and thy king which thou shalt set over thee, unto a nation which neither thou nor thy fathers have known; and there shalt thou serve other gods, wood and stone" (Deut. 28:36). Did this happen? Yes, it did, just as the word of God stated. Judah was taken captive with her king. At that time, Zedekiah was the king in Jerusalem; just as the word of God predicted, so it happened.

Moreover, in the second instance, when Judah was taken captive, there was no king mentioned. This situation was manifest when the Romans took the two tribes captive; at that instant, there was no king in Jerusalem.

The fulfillment of these scriptures displays only the truth of God's word, and the history books by men only confirm these facts.

In Deuteronomy 28:49–58, we are enlightened further to the degree that no man who is acquainted with history could challenge the accuracy of what is stated there in Deuteronomy. These things not only happened but also did so precisely as stated here. In the Jewish war against the Romans, the Jews put up such a fight that the Romans were discouraged and had to decide on a future course of action. Three considerations were before them. One, storm the city immediately. Two, raise the banks. Three, build a wall around the city and starve the Jews into subjection.[13] They chose the third and so fulfilled the word of God. They decided to build a wall around the city and starve the Jews until the city was subjugated. The historical events happened precisely as they are presented in the word of God.

We read further, "And he shall besiege thee in all thy gates, until thy high and fenced walls come down, wherein thou trustedst, throughout all thy land: and he shall besiege thee in all thy gates throughout all thy land, which the Lord thy God hath given thee" (Deut. 28:52). We must confess that it happened exactly as was stated in this text.

Nevertheless, when was Deuteronomy written? Deuteronomy was written in 1450 BC, nearly 1520 years before the event. Oh, what a unique book is the Bible! Even the location of the enemy is specified.

Therefore, we read, "The Lord shall bring a nation against thee from far, from the end of the earth, as swift as the eagle flieth" (Deut. 28: 49). The scripture informs us that the enemy was coming from far. He was coming from a different continent. This enemy came from Western Europe. This nation was the Roman Empire. It was coming from the end of the earth, where the sun ended its journey, not east where it began but west where it ended. This enemy was coming from the direction across the Mediterranean Sea. What a barrier he had to cross, yet he was coming. In the first captivity, the Babylonians came from close. In this second captivity, the Romans came from far. They were as swift as the eagle, the very symbol of the Roman Empire.

---

[13] Flavius Josephus, *War of the Jews*, Book 5, Ch. 12, Para. 1, 2 in Whiston's translation (Carol Stream, IL: Tyndale House Publisher, 1980)

The Romans used the "Aquila" or "the eagle" as their prominent symbol. This symbol was explicitly used in ancient Rome as the standard of their legions. They had an eagle bearer who carried this standard. It was a common practice that each brigade took one eagle. How could it just happen as it is stated in the Bible? Why did it happen as it was prophesied? Let us hear the critics of the Bible cry, "Coincidence!" However, we don't deal with coincidences. We read further, "Which shall not regard the person of the old, nor shew favor to the young" (Deut. 28:50). This action characterized the behavior of the Romans toward the young and the old they had captured. They put them all to the sword.

Moreover, we read, "And he shall eat the fruit of thy cattle, and the fruit of thy land until thou be destroyed" (Deut. 28:51). The Romans surrounded the city of Jerusalem, locked the Jews in, ate the fruit of their land and the fruit of their cattle, and starved the Jews until they were destroyed. Who can say this didn't happen as was recorded? I didn't outline these incidents. The Jews did. In verse 53 the word of God declared, "And thou shall eat the fruit of thine own body, the flesh of thy sons and of thy daughters, which the Lord thy God hath given thee." Josephus, the Jewish historian, reported with tears in his eyes that the Jewish women ate their children during the Roman siege. Yet men talk today as if there is no God and as if it is a proven fact that man came from evolution. What nonsense!

Man needs to be told what God plans to do to those who reject His Son. The word of God declares, "For this cause God shall send them strong delusion, that they should believe a lie: that they all might be damned who believed not the truth, but had pleasure in unrighteousness" (2 Thess. 2:11–12). This delusion is primarily real for those who will give up the truth and will be swallowed up by the Antichrist. God will also see to it that this will happen to the wise, who will reject God for their evolution. The word of God states, "For it is written, I will destroy the wisdom of the wise, and will bring to nothing the understanding of the prudent. Where is the wise? Where is the scribe? Where is the disputer of this world? Hath not God made foolish the wisdom of this world?" (1 Cor. 1:19–20).

God will laugh at them in that day. Where are the writers who promoted evolution? That is what God will ask, when God, whom man says doesn't exist, puts in His appearance. Where are they who told us everything came from nothing? According to the evolutionists, we had a vacuum, and over time it became a universe. That is the religion of the wise. God plans to destroy their wisdom. He gave them understanding, and they used it to deny His very existence. Understand my position. I love science, and no exact science that is repeatable will ever contradict the Bible. The problem isn't science but the so-called science that cannot be repeated or tested. This so-called science is the fiction of man's imagination. So is evolution, which states there is no God.

The word of God further declares, "And even as they did not like to retain God in their knowledge, God gave them over to a reprobate mind, to do those things which are not convenient" (Rom. 1:28). God knows that people don't want to retain Him in their knowledge. That is the main reason men advance evolution. They desire no God; they crave no restraint. They want to be responsible to no one; they want to do what they want to do. Nevertheless, what they don't know is that God had already planned for that eventuality.

We need to get sober because we will soon start dealing with the place called "the land shadowing with wings." When we do, we will see that God's determined counsel and foreknowledge is directing everything in this world. This view will cause us to realize we have no excuse to reject our Creator. I hope it will make us own Him as our Savior before we close our eyes and disappear into a lost eternity.

Now, we need to ask ourselves a few questions. When was this book of Deuteronomy written? It was written fifteen hundred years before this event. How can a book written fifteen hundred years before an event describe that event so extensively and clearly? This clarity reminded me of a series of wars recorded in Daniel 11. These wars were fought between the king of the North and the king of the South—that is, two parts of the empire of Alexander the Great in the hands of his generals after his death: the segment of Alexander's empire around Syria and the element around Egypt. Moreover, these wars were described in such detail that no schoolboy acquainted with the history of those times will doubt the antagonists' identities.

Now, when we compare the same history written by man, what do we find? The narratives are so similar that they will astound any student of history. The best historians gave up a long time ago in their quest to find an error between the word of God and secular history. Instead, they sought to prove at all costs that the book of Daniel wasn't written by Daniel but by some later writer. Why? What was at stake? Daniel was written three hundred years before the events, and man's history books were written after the events. Therefore, to believe Daniel wrote the book could mean only one thing: there is a God, and man doesn't want to entertain that conclusion.

Moreover, those wars spanned a long time, with many different players and intricate details. How could the Bible record all this history so accurately before the events? To acknowledge the date of Daniel's book meant one had to believe in God. No other explanation was possible. Yet, man won't accept God. Therefore, man concluded that the book of Daniel must have been written after those events. This behavior is what man exhibits; he closes his eyes and rejects God. What did God do to counter man's late-date theory of the book of Daniel? He caused another book to be written. God saw to it that a monarch in Egypt would commission a book called the Septuagint, which is the translation of the Hebrew Bible into Greek, about three hundred years before Christ.

In this Septuagint is found the translation of the book of Daniel. It is common knowledge that the Greek king of Egypt, Ptolemy II Philadelphus, asked seventy-two Jewish scholars to translate the Old Testament's biblical text into Koine Greek for inclusion in the Library of Alexandria. This translation was done in the third century BC. Therefore, Daniel had to have been written before the translation to be included in the Septuagint. That monarch was no Christian; he just wanted to have the best literature known at that time in his library. He got the best, the word of God.

However, it is necessary to state that just as men disagreed with the dates and reject the declared writers of the books of the Bible, so they disagree with the history of the Septuagint. What is very glaring, is that men will reject everything written on the Bible, but accept anything written by the critics. They do the same today, reject the Bible for their evolution.

"Then the Lord will make thy plagues wonderful, and the plagues of thy seed, even great plagues, and of long continuance, and sore sicknesses, and of long continuance" (Deut. 28:59). We need to see the excellent care God took in this passage in Deuteronomy. He made sure there was no doubt that it was the Roman captivity under discussion. Before the event, God listed the first captivity; then he said their plague would be of a long duration after the Roman captivity. God said that after the Roman wars with the Jews, their afflictions would be of long continuance and sore sickness. It happened precisely so; after the Roman wars, Israel was under judgment for a long time and was out of Palestine for approximately nineteen hundred years—a very long time indeed.

Thus, as verses 64 - 65 state, Israel was scattered all over the world. We read, "And the Lord shall scatter thee among all people, from the one end of the earth even unto the other; and there thou shalt serve other gods, which neither thou nor thy fathers have known, even wood and stone. And among these nations shalt thou find no ease, neither shall the sole of thy foot have rest: but the Lord shall give thee there a trembling heart, and failing of eyes, and sorrow of mind" (Deut. 28:64–65). I didn't write these things; the Jews did. I am only showing you what they wrote, and it is accurate.

We now come to World War II in Deuteronomy 28:66, where Israel's life would hang in doubt; in the morning she would wish it was evening, and in the evening, she would wish it was morning. This development could be expanded further if we bring in other scriptures. Nevertheless, at the end of World War II, Israel will again become a nation. This nationhood is stated not in Deuteronomy but in other portions of the Bible.

Further, as we meditate on the prophetic books of the Bible, we notice that Israel would be restored to the land of Palestine after a long time of wandering. This time, her restoration will be primarily by two means.

First, she will return by herself, as is stated in Zephaniah. We read, "Gather yourselves together, yea, gather together, O nation not desired; before the decree bring forth, before the day pass as the chaff, before the fierce anger of the Lord come upon you, before the day of the Lord's anger come upon you" (Zeph. 2:1–2). Israel was to return to Palestine in unbelief before the Great Tribulation of Zephaniah 2:2. This return happened exactly as was prophesied. The great trial hasn't yet come, but Israel is back in the land. According to the word of God, Israel had to return before the fierce anger of the Lord. The "fierce anger of the Lord" (Zeph. 2:2) is the Great Tribulation. Therefore, everything is right on schedule.

Now, observe that the Lord doesn't give her a command to return but says that she will return by herself. Israel has returned, but still, not believing that the Lord Jesus Christ is her Messiah. She has returned to the land in unbelief.

Second, she was to return because of World War II:

> Therefore, behold, the days come, saith the Lord, that it shall no more be said, The Lord liveth, that brought up the children of Israel out of the land of Egypt; But, The Lord liveth, that brought up the children of Israel from the land of the north, and all the lands whither he had driven them: and I will bring them again into their land that I gave unto their fathers. Behold, I will send for many fishers, saith the Lord, and they shall fish them; and after will I send for many hunters, and they shall hunt them from every mountain, and every hill, and out of the holes of the rocks. (Jer. 16:14 -16)

Israel was to return to the land of Palestine as a result of fishers and hunters. The fisher's sense implies that Israel would be lined up as a fish at the end of a line. She was to be hunted down and lined up; these events happened precisely so during World War II. As a result of that horrible ordeal, Israel returned to her land. Three years later, she was established as a nation after the war. The historical events confirm the scriptural directive.

Once Israel was restored to Palestine and became a nation, the word of God declared that a mighty nation, unknown in the days of Isaiah the prophet, was going to seek to protect her. Thus, Israel's security as a nation would be tied up with the safety of the land shadowing with wings. Therefore, what is being communicated is that when Israel was restored to her country, a mighty power would seek to protect her. This power would be the most significant power on the earth during that time. This power is called here "the land shadowing with wings." We have outlined the context in which the land is found. Now this land of protection will become the subject of our study.

We will now peruse the passage where this prophecy is found. This matter is taken up in Isaiah 18. There are seven verses in this chapter, but they are of the utmost importance. These verses are symbolic but clear. We will break the passage into three sections for simplicity.

> Woe to the land shadowing with wings, which is beyond the rivers of Ethiopia: that sendeth ambassadors by the sea, even in vessels of bulrushes upon the water, saying, Go, ye swift messengers, to a nation scattered and peeled, to a people terrible from their beginning hitherto; to a nation meted out and trodden down, whose land the rivers have spoiled! All ye inhabitants of the world, and dwellers on the earth, see ye, when he lifteth up an ensign on the mountains, and when he bloweth a trumpet, hear ye.

> For so the Lord said unto me, I will take my rest, and I will consider in my dwelling place like a clear heat upon herbs and like a cloud of dew in the heat of harvest. For afore the harvest, when the bud is perfect, and the sour grape is ripening in the flower, he shall both cut off the sprigs with pruning hooks, and take away and cut down the branches. They shall be left together unto the fowls of the mountains, and to the beast of the earth: and the fowls shall summer upon them, and all the beasts of the earth shall winter upon them

> In that time shall the present be brought unto the Lord of host of a people scattered and peeled, and from a people terrible from their beginning hitherto; a nation meted out and trodden under foot, whose land the rivers have spoiled, to the place of the name of the Lord of host, the mount Zion. (Isa. 18:1-7)

My dear reader, after reading these seven verses, did you understand anything? If your answer is no, you are not alone; I felt the same way many years ago when I read them. Nevertheless, these brothers, John Nelson

Darby and William Kelly, helped me to understand the passage. This subject, as was stated before, has a difficulty level of eight, so it is difficult. Therefore, we will need to tread slowly and carefully, but once God gives us the understanding, it will be clear. We need to pray for this understanding. I need to emphasize that passages of this nature have distinguished Bible teachers like Darby and Kelly from other expositors. Many have written on this passage, but their interpretations were found to be wanting and were discarded over time.

Nevertheless, the writings of Darby and Kelly have stood the test of time. These men wrote, about one hundred and fifty years ago, yet what they wrote is coming to pass just as it was stated. Why is this so? This is so because they were rightly dividing the word of God. Do you believe in the Rapture and the return of Christ in glory? If yes, then you have embraced the teachings found and taught in scripture, discovered again, and expounded by Darby and Kelly.

Therefore, before I unfold this passage, I will let John Darby (1800–1882) help us with its interpretation. I will also allow William Kelly to do the same. Please bear with me here with the old writings. Still, I intend to show that the way I interpret the passage is the same way it was interpreted one hundred and fifty years ago. The difference, however, is that what was future then is all coming to pass today, and it is declaring loudly that the Bible is the word of God.

J. N. Darby wrote the following in 1880,

> It is needful to remember the position of the land of Israel. The rivers of Ethiopia (Cush) are the Nile and the Euphrates, which represent the two nations on the frontiers of Israel that had oppressed them, Egypt and Babylon. The country here summoned, "shadowing with wings" (Isa. 18:1 JND), is beyond those rivers. It was a country unknown at the time when the prophet lived and was consequently in no connection as yet with Israel, but it will be so in the last days. To shadow with wings is an expression often employed in the word of the Lord for marking protection. It will be a powerful nation, outside their ordinary limits, undertaking to protect Israel.

The great nations of those days occupy themselves with the Jews (v. 2). From the time the nations begin to be the object of God's judgment, they will be crushed (Zech. 12:1–3 JND). "All ye inhabitants of the world and dwellers on the earth" (Isa. 18:3 JND). God summons attention to that which He is going to do. "See ye when he lifteth up an ensign on the mountains; and when he bloweth a trumpet, hear ye" (Isa. 18:3 JND).

For so Jehovah said unto me, I will take my rest, and I will consider in my dwelling- place like a clear heat upon herbs, and like a cloud of dew in the heat of harvest" (Isa. 18:4 JND). We see what God will do when the nations, following their own policy, will have restored the Jews to their land. He lets them act and keeps quiet; but He keeps His eye on His dwelling-place.

For afore the harvest, when the bud is perfect, and the sour grape is ripening in the flower, he shall both cut off the sprigs with pruning hooks, and take away and cut down the branches" (Isa. 18:5 JND). It isn't yet judgment, so all come to nothing, whatever the promise, as in all human things where God is concerned.

They shall be left together unto the fowls of the mountains, and to the beasts of the earth: and the fowls shall summer upon them, and all the beasts of the earth shall winter upon them" (Isa. 18:6 JND). The people are brought back to their land to be given over as a prey to the nations, like wild beasts in winter or ravenous birds in summer. Such will be their fate when anew they return to Palestine, for God is not yet putting His hand to it. Jerusalem will again be the central object of political schemes for the world, though the world despises God's people, and never occupies itself with them but to exalt itself. The Jew will be oppressed by the Gentiles once more in their land; but deliverance is at hand.

In that time shall the present be brought unto Jehovah of hosts of a people scattered and peeled, and from a people terrible from their beginning hitherto; a nation meted out and trodden under foot, whose land the rivers have spoiled, to the place of the name of Jehovah of hosts, the mount Zion" (Isa. 18:7 JND). A present is to be brought of Israel and from Israel to Jehovah. They will bring an offering, and themselves be as it were an offering, to Jehovah, who will manifest anew His abode in Zion (after all the long sorrows and desolations), but also His hand in judgment of the nations. After this will begin His relationship with Israel for everlasting blessing under Messiah and the new covenant.[14]

We will now interpret Isaiah 18 since it is a most crucial portion of God's word, and what is stated here is taking place today. The fulfillment of the events recorded in this passage, when expounded by Darby, was still in the future, but now this fulfillment is taking place in our days before our very eyes, so let us pay special attention.

However, we need a second testimony. The scripture says that "in the mouth of two or three witnesses shall every word be established" (2 Cor. 13:1). What we are about to uncover is too important a matter for travesty and carelessness. Isaiah 18 speaks about a great nation that will undertake to protect Israel and will do so for a while. Still, an unknown enemy will come up and destroy this great country, and Israel will again be exposed as prey to the hostile nations. Please bear with me as I give you the interpretation of another brother, who wrote over one hundred years ago.

William Kelly (1821 - 1906) expressed the following, in his commentary on Isaiah 18, in January 1865. I will break the passage up into sections for clarity:

---

[14] John N. Darby, *"Thoughts on Isaiah the Prophet,"* In The Bible Treasury, vol. 13, ed. William Kelly (London, UK: George Morrish, 1880), 120.

The true reference to Egypt and Ethiopia is in Isa. 19, 20, which accordingly have the title prefixed, "The Burden of Egypt." It is not so here. Neither is the chapter called a "burden," nor should the opening exclamation be rendered "Woe" as it often is, but "Ho!" as the context shows. It is a call to a land designedly unnamed, quite outside the bounds of those which Israel knew, and characterized at the time of the action by sentiments of friendship, in contrast with the usual animosity of Gentiles, which here breaks out once more. The last verse intimates that the time when these events occur is the closing scene marked subsequently by Jehovah's interference on behalf of His people, and in full grace their re-establishment in Zion, to which prophecy as a whole points.

Our chapter seems thus to be distinguished from the overthrow of the nations, predicted at the close of the preceding section, "the Burden of Damascus," and so forms a scene sufficiently distinct to be treated separately. It is a deeply interesting episode, and it is plain that the new "burden" opens Isa. 19, and distinguishes the judgment of Egypt from the subject before us. This it is well to notice distinctly, because Jerome and Cyril, Bochart and Vitringa, among many more, have fallen into the error of supposing that Egypt is the "land shadowing with wings," addressed in verse 1, and that the Egyptians or the Ethiopians are the people to whom the message is sent in ver. 2, some of them being even brought to the grateful worship of God in ver. 7.

Others again are no less confident that Ethiopia is meant, as Calvin, Piscator, Michaelis, Rosenmller, Gesenius, Ewald, Delitzsch, Drechsler, and Driver. Yet Jerome and Calvin agree with the more famous Jewish authors that the people spoken of in verses 2 and 7 are the Jews. All must be confusion where this is not seen. And a nation is here distinguished by favor to the Jew in its own way, but in vain. There follow nations hostile as usually of old. But the main issue is God, Who observes all, at length accomplishing His gracious purpose in Israel.

The reader need not be surprised at confusion, alas! Too common in commentators ever so erudite and otherwise eminent. For there is hardly a portion of Isaiah which has given rise to greater discord and more evident bewilderment among men of note, from Eusebius of Caesarea (who saw in it the land of Judaea in apostolic times, sending Christian doctrine to all the world, an interpretation founded on the ἀποστέλλων ... ἐπιστολὰς βιβλίνας of the LXX) down to Arias Montanus, who applied it to America, converted to Christ by the preaching and arms of the Spaniards!

Plainly the right understanding of the chapter depends on seeing that the Jewish nation are those intended in verses 2 and 7, and this, not in the days of Sennacherib, save perhaps as a historic starting-point, but for the future crisis, and its glorious issues. A few expressions, especially in verses 1 and 2, may be obscure, but the general scope is remarkably clear and of exceeding interest. It is true, as Henderson says in common with very many, that the chapter is not a "woe" (as the Sept., the Vulgate, and the A.V. translate), nor yet like the preceding or following "burdens," but rather a call summoning attention - "Ho!" - to the land unnamed, which is to be described. The contrast seems plain between Isaiah 17:12 -14 and Isaiah 18:4 - 6.

One nation whose name is not given will seek to befriend the Jews in the time and way spoken of; while others break out into their old jealousy and hatred, and wreak their vengeance on them all the more. But that the friendly protector is Ethiopia seems wholly without and against the tests of the chapter. According to this idea, when Tirhakah in alarm summons his troops, the Jews send swift messengers to acquaint him with the destruction of Sennacherib's host when it seemed to threaten, not only Jerusalem but Ethiopia. But this dislocates the chapter, making the Ethiopians the prominent figure instead of the Jews, and terminating ineptly with a present offered by the Ethiopians to the God of Israel.

It is enough to examine the words of the prophet with care, in order to refute any such speculation. "Ho! Land shadowing (or, whirring) with wings, which [art] beyond [the] rivers of Cush" (Isa. 18:1 WK) (i.e. beyond the Nile and the Euphrates). It means a country outside the sphere of those nations, which up to the prophet's day had menaced or meddled with Israel. Usually firm against mere tradition, and careful of scriptural truth, even Dr. Kay has failed to notice the true force of this remarkable expression found here only and in Zephaniah 3:10. The object is not at all to direct attention to the country adjoining the Nile, nor even to combine with this the land adjacent to the Euphrates. The call is expressly to a land beyond either limit. Egypt and Assyria had been the chief of those powers, for there was an Asiatic as well as an African Cush.

The land in question lay (not by any means contiguous to, but perhaps ever so far) beyond these well-known countries. Here is the first indication; and it is of the highest importance, but neglected by most. It expresses a country far away. This comparatively distant land espouses the cause of Israel; but the protection would be ineffectual in result, however loud the proffer and the preparation. The use of "wings" to convey the idea of a cover for the oppressed or defenceless is too common to

43

need proofs. "Ho! land shadowing with wings, which [art] beyond [the] rivers of Cush; that sendeth ambassadors by the sea, even in vessels of papyrus upon [the] face of [the] waters, [saying,]" (Isa. 18:1, 2 WK).

The second verse shows, in addition to the previous characteristics of this future ally of the Jews, that it is a maritime power, for it sends its ambassadors over the sea, and in vessels of bulrushes (i.e. of "papyrus") on the face of the waters, Israel is the object of their interest. "Go, swift messengers, to a nation scattered (or dragged) and peeled, to a people terrible from their beginning and onward, to a nation meted out and trodden down, whose land the rivers have spoiled" (Isa. 18: 2 WK).

The attempt to apply this description to the Egyptians, or the Ethiopians, has largely affected the view taken of the epithets here applied, e.g., "tall and smooth," and "that meteth out and treadeth down"). The mistake of not a few is to introduce Christianity into the chapter; whereas it is really a question of earthly things and the earthly people in presence of a friendly effort, but also of enemies before God's time comes to deliver them Himself.

The learned may enquire whether "boats" are really intended by "keli-gem" in verse 2. Here only is the word so rendered in all Scripture. It occurs very frequently for an ornament, implement, or utensil; even for sack, stuff, or any such thing in general; for armor, or weapons; for instruments of music, or furniture, etc. Hence the Seventy here translate by "paper letters," which we can well understand requisite for ambassadors sent on their errand. It is the more worthy of careful consideration, as this phrase more than any other has misled the commentators. Otherwise, there is but little difficulty in the chapter.

The country therefore to which the prophet calls is characterized as one which in the days of the completion of this prophecy should be a great maritime and commercial power forming remote alliances making distant voyages to all parts of the world with expedition and security and in the habit of affording protection to their friends and allies. Where this country is to be found is not otherwise said than that it will be remote from Judaea and with respect to that country beyond the Cushean streams. But, in fact, there seems no sufficient reason to question the general accuracy of our authorized version, which, as predicating Israel in ver. 2 yields the sole clear and good sense. Above any, they are a nation whose hope is indeed long deferred, and who have suffered indignity beyond all; yet marked by portents from their existence and thenceforth. Upon them has been exactly measured divine judgment, as none other had. Who else trodden down as they? Nor had their land escaped the desolating ravages of powers overwhelming like rivers, as we find the same figure used of it in Isa. 8 and elsewhere.

The difference between the land in the first verse which sends out its messengers and ships, and the dispersed people from all time marvelous or hitherto formidable, but of late ravaged by their impetuous enemies, stands on no minute points of verbal criticism, but on the general bearing of scripture history as well as the context, which the English-reading Christian is quite able to judge. This is the weakest point in Bishop Horsley's (Bible Crit. ii. 162) otherwise able investigation of the chapter: "The standard of the Cross of Christ; the trumpet of the gospel. The resort to the standard, the effect of the summons, in the end will be universal." But it is the prevalent bane of theologians to bring in the gospel or the church into the prophets, where the dealings of divine government and ultimately of Messiah's kingdom are really meant.

Thus far we have seen the intervention of this unnamed land, described as the would-be protector of Israel actively engaging with their swift ships; it would seem on a friendly mission in quest of that scattered people to plant them again in their own land. But another enters the scene who puts an arrest on the zeal of man. Universal attention is demanded. Great events tremble in the balances. Signs are given visibly and audibly.

> "All ye inhabitants of the world, and dwellers on the earth, see ye when an ensign is lifted up on the mountains; and when a trumpet is blown, hear ye. For thus, Jehovah said unto me, I will take my rest, and I will observe in my dwelling-place like a clear heat upon herbs, like a cloud of dew in the heat of harvest" (Isa. 18: 3, 4 WK). God is contemplating this busy enterprise. Man is active, Jehovah, as it were, retires and watches. It is like a clear heat in the sunlight, like a cloud of dew in the heat of harvest. It is a moment of deep stillness and suspense, where He allows apparent advantage of it but does not act Himself, while immense efforts are made to gather in the Jews by the patronage of the maritime nation of verses 1 and 2.

> All then seemed to flourish: but what is man without God? "For before the harvest, when the bud is finished (or, past), and the blossom becometh a ripening grape, he shall both cut off the sprigs with pruning-knives, and take away and cut down the branches" (Isa. 18:6 WK).

> Thus, total failure of the friendly plan ensues. Everything in appearance betokened a speedy ingathering of good to Israel, and their national hopes seemed to be on the eve of being realized when God brings all to naught by letting loose once more the old passions of the Gentiles against His people. The effect is that "they shall be left together unto the birds of the mountains and to the beasts of the earth; and the birds shall summer upon them, and

all the beasts of the earth shall winter upon them" (Isa. 18:6 WK).

It was not for that power to interfere, nor was it Jehovah's time; and yet it was for Himself in the end. The shadow of God's wings is the true resource of His people's faith (Ps. 57: 1). For "in that time [a period of course, not an epoch merely] shall be brought unto Jehovah of hosts a present of a people scattered and peeled, and from a people terrible from their beginning and onward, a nation meted out and trodden under foot, whose land the rivers have spoiled, to the place of the name of Jehovah of hosts, the mount Zion" (Isa. 18:7 WK).

Thus, will the presumptuous help of man be rebuked, as well as the renewed wrath of the nations once more preying on the poor but loved people of Jehovah? For as surely as they turn again to rend Israel, He will appear in the midst of the desolation, and with His own mighty hand accomplish that which man as vainly seeks to effect as to frustrate. The Jewish nation, at that very season, shall be brought a present to Jehovah; and they shall come not empty-handed but emptied of self, with lowly and grateful hearts to Jehovah in Mount Zion, after their final escape from Gentile fury in His mercy which endures forever. They bring the present, and they are the present to Jehovah. Here, as ever, the dealings of God in judgment result in the blessing of His ancient people; and Zion accordingly is the place where His name is manifested in connection with them.

We also see how unreasonable it would be to imagine that the church, called to heavenly glory, is concerned as God's object in the chapter. It is Israel only, destined to pass through renewed and bitter trouble, most of all at the close, before Jehovah does His work of establishing

them in the seat of royal grace under Messiah and the
new covenant. He has never abandoned this purpose of
His for the earth.[15]

We observed from the writings of Darby and Kelly how distinguished
Christian writers in their days struggled to interpret Isaiah 18. We note
how Darby and Kelly explained it, and we will seek God's help to do the
same. However, before we do, we will highlight 8 points from each writer
to enhance our interpretation.

First, Darby stated these eight points. One, the rivers of Cush are
the Nile and the Euphrates. Two, the country shadowing with wings was
unknown during the life of the prophet. Three, the land was previously in
no relationship with Israel but will be so in the last days. Four, to shadow
with wings was to offer protection. Five, the land shadowing with wings
will be a powerful country outside the Nile and Euphrates corridor. Six,
the nations following their own policies will restore the Jews to their land.
Seven, God will allow man to act but He will keep quiet and observe.
Eight, the Jews will be brought back to their land to be given over as prey
to the nations.

Second, Kelly observed these eight points. One, the Jewish nation are
those intended in verse 2 and 7 during the future crisis. Two, verse 1 is a
"Ho," summoning attention and not a woe. Three, an un-named land will
seek to befriend the Jews. Four, "beyond the rivers of Cush" expresses a
country far away from the Nile and the Euphrates. Five, this comparatively
distant land will espouse the cause of Israel but the protection will be
ineffectual in result, however loud the proffer and preparation. Six, the
future ally of the Jews will be a maritime and commercial power. Seven,
total failure of the friendly plan will ensue. Eight, the presumptuous help
of man will be rebuked.

Now, if we asked college students on any continent which country
protects Israel today, nearly all of them would answer, "The USA!" That
there is a protector of Israel, we cannot doubt; even the average man is
acquainted with this relationship. The word of God declared that there will

[15] William Kelly, *"Notes on Isaiah,"* In The Bible Treasury, vol. 5, ed. William Kelly (London, UK: George Morrish, 1865), 195.

be a protector of Israel after she becomes a nation. In the texts, we observe that both Darby and Kelly affirmed the same long before Israel became a nation. They wrote concerning these events nearly one hundred and fifty years ago. Today we are privileged to see this relationship unfolding, but they never saw it. We observe America protecting Israel as the word of God declared.

Nevertheless, could the Bible depict this association and portray it with such clarity that none would be in doubt as to the participants? Could it give us the direction to this land that would remove all uncertainty? These questions we will seek to answer. This is a critical study, because it's not a past prophecy that has been fulfilled. It's not a future prophecy that will be fulfilled; it is a prophecy that is currently being fulfilled. Therefore, we will interpret the passage using the information we have gathered from those two eminent Bible teachers, Darby and Kelly.

"Woe to the land shadowing with wings, which is beyond the rivers of Ethiopia" (Isa. 18:1). We learn from Kelly that the first word in Isaiah 18 should be translated "ho" instead of "woe." The reason given was that the word for "ho" and the word for "woe" are the same Hebrew word. It is the context that must determine which word is used in English. In this passage, the word *ho* is more appropriate. This is a call summoning attention. It isn't a "woe"; it is a "ho."

We will now endeavor to understand what the term "shadowing with wings" in this passage means. In Isaiah 25, we read, "For thou hast been a strength to the poor, a strength to the needy in his distress, a refuge from the storm, a shadow from the heat, when the blast of the terrible ones is as a storm against the wall" (v. 4). In Psalm 17, we read, "Keep me as the apple of the eye, hide me under the shadow of thy wings" (v. 8). Psalm 36 states, "How excellent is thy lovingkindness, O God! Therefore, the children of men put their trust under the shadow of thy wings" (v. 7). Again, in Psalms, the word of God declares, "Be merciful unto me, O God, be merciful unto me: for my soul trusteth in thee: yea, in the shadow of thy wings will I make my refuge, until these calamities be overpast" (Ps. 57:1). Also, in Psalm 61, we are instructed, "I will abide in thy tabernacle forever: I will trust in the covert of thy wings" (Ps. 61:4). Psalm 63 affirms, "Because thou hast been my help, therefore in the shadow of thy wings will I rejoice" (v. 7). Also, Psalm 91 relates, "He that dwelleth in the secret place of the most High shall abide under the shadow of the Almighty" (v. 1). One more verse should suffice. Psalm 91 declares, "He shall cover thee with his feathers, and under his wings shalt thou trust: his truth shall be thy shield and buckler" (v. 4).

We must conclude, from the way the scriptures use the term "to shadow with wings," that this expression means to offer protection to the oppressed. Consequently, we have highlighted in the land shadowing with wings a mighty nation protecting other nations.

What we have learned until this point is that when Israel is restored to the land of Palestine in the last days, a powerful country will seek to protect her. This country will protect not only Israel but also other countries. It shadows with wings; that is, it protects its allies. As yet, we don't know the name of the country or its location, but we know what the government does. First, it is seen protecting other countries before it is seen defending Israel. In verse 1, Israel isn't yet in the picture. All we see is the land's activities. Second, God then gives the location of the country. He says it is beyond the rivers of Cush. The vital point to note is that God says that the protective land is there. The land is there - beyond the rivers of Cush. The word for "Cush" in this verse is the word for "Ethiopia."

We know the USA protects Israel. We now know from the Bible that when Israel becomes a nation, in the last days, a mighty country was going to protect her. What we must find out is whether the geography given to locate this country corresponds to the location of the United States, for if that is so, then this unfolding relationship will be a powerful testimony that the Bible is the word of God. Who in his right mind could doubt such a deduction? No man will be able to say that Isaiah 18 was written after the event.

We need to observe, from the given geography, that it isn't "river" but "rivers" of Cush. The Hebrew word for *river* is in the plural. We learn from both Kelly and Darby that the "rivers of Cush" are the Nile and the Euphrates, because there was both an Asiatic Cush as well as an African Cush. We learn about these two settlements of Cush from the book of Genesis.

What we have learned thus far about the location of this land is that it is outside the countries between the Nile and the Euphrates. We also know the land is beyond these two rivers; that is, if one tried to get to this nation by going toward the direction of the Nile, this land is beyond the Nile. One must cross the Nile and keep going. Moreover, if one tried to get to this country by going toward the direction of the Euphrates, this land is beyond the Euphrates; one must cross the Euphrates and keep going. What is emphasized is that one can get to this land by not merely going toward the Nile, but one must go beyond that river. Furthermore, one can also get to this country by going not merely toward the Euphrates but beyond that river, because the scripture says it is there, beyond the rivers of Cush. What the word of God has also just indicated is that the earth is round and that one can get to this land by going in opposite directions.

At this point, we see that Europe is eliminated and consequently England, since these lands are not beyond the rivers of Cush but are in a different direction from Cush. The focus is given southwest/northeast and not northwest/southeast. Therefore, countries toward the northwest are eliminated, and lands toward the southeast are also excluded. Furthermore, the word for "beyond" in Hebrew is the word *eber*; it means a region across or on the opposite side. The emphasis here is that one must cross the rivers and go on the opposite side.

Therefore, the idea of "beyond the rivers of Cush" is not only a matter of limits but also of direction and location. The land is there, beyond the rivers of Cush. We will see in a moment how accurate the Bible is - it is more than one can imagine; therefore, we will go to verse 2 and find this unnamed land. We read, "That sendeth ambassadors by the sea, even in vessels of bulrushes upon the waters, saying, Go, ye swift messengers, to a nation scattered and peeled, to a people terrible from their beginning hitherto; a nation meted out and trodden down, whose land the rivers have spoiled" (Isa. 18:2).

In this verse, we are told that the land shadowing with wings sends its ambassadors over the sea to this nation scattered and peeled. We learn that this great land gets involved politically with this nation scattered and peeled - which is Israel. When God speaks of a country and gives specific economic conditions or mentions great upheaval without naming the location, that place is usually Israel. This observation is true because God's eyes are ever on Israel. We see the same thing in Revelation 6:5, 6 when the third seal was opened. It was the economic reality that made us know the identity of the country. We must conclude that when we read of this country, "scattered and peeled" without being told which country was so designated, we know we are dealing with Israel because of the many examples given in the scriptures.

The land shadowing with wings not only seeks to protect Israel but also gets involved in her politics to establish her and solve her difficulties. It sends its ambassadors to help solve Israel's political problems. Let us meditate on this verse because it is most informative, and it will enable us to find the land. It states, "That sends ambassadors by the sea, even in vessels of bulrushes upon the waters, saying, Go, ye swift messengers, to a nation scattered and peeled, to a people terrible from their beginning hitherto; a nation meted out and trodden down, whose land the rivers have spoiled" (Isa. 18:2).

The land shadowing with wings is depicted as courting Israel's friendship to protect her but only after she became a nation. God doesn't play with words; He says what He means and means what He says. Please note that Israel was already a nation when this protective country became involved with her to protect her. The fact that Israel was already a nation when she was being protected is a significant point. It's not seeing this point that has caused some excellent Bible teachers to suggest that the land shadowing with wings might be England. It was England that helped Israel immensely before she became a nation. However, the land shadowing with wings was seen as protecting Israel *after* Israel became a nation until it could protect her no more.

Moreover, this is how it happened historically, because this country didn't want to offend the Arabs. Consequently, this country didn't align itself with Israel to protect her even years after Israel became a nation. After Israel became a nation and quite a while after that, "the land shadowing with wings" got involved in her protection. The history of that period also corroborates the biblical record.

Besides, it is not only the people this country was getting involved with; it was also getting involved with the country. It was sending its ambassadors to a specific nation. Israel was already a nation when it sought to protect her. The help was intended not only to help Israel get back into the land that was before the prophet's eyes, but it was also for the protection of this country once she was established as a nation. In Isaiah 18:2, twice we read that she was "a nation," and once she was referred to as a "land." Therefore, Israel was an independent nation in Palestine when this powerful country sought to protect her.

In verse 2, God's word gives us one more critical piece of direction to find the "land shadowing with wings." Nevertheless, excellent Bible teachers haven't grasped this vital information. However, it is difficult to see this essential piece of geography because of how the King James Version (KJV) translates this verse. Therefore, we will read this verse in J. N. Darby's translation. It says, "That sendest ambassadors over the sea" (Isa. 18:2 JND). Also, when we read what Kelly wrote (as an excellent Hebrew scholar), we see that he translated this part of the verse as "that sendest ambassadors across the sea" (Isa. 18:2 WK). We need to note that the ambassadors are sent over the sea or across the sea. The "crossing of the sea" is an essential piece of geography. Three crucial geographic features are now given: 1) the land, 2) the rivers, and 3) the sea. With these three geographic features, we are now in a position to find the country.

What is even more critical is that in verse 2, the geography is given from the position of the land shadowing with wings, not from the perspective of Israel as in verse 1. In verse 1, the land is viewed from without; while in verse 2 it is viewed from within. The way this is presented in verse 2 helps us to understand and prevent confusion. It clearly states that from this land to the Nile, one had to cross a sea and then proceed straight to the Nile. Similarly, from this land to the Euphrates, one had to cross a sea and then proceed straight to the Euphrates. Moreover, it is clearly stated that there was no way to get to the Nile from the land shadowing with wings without crossing the sea. Furthermore, there was no way to get to the Euphrates from the land shadowing with wings without crossing the sea. Therefore, this land is located at a point where there is a sea on opposite sides of the country, not as is typical, with a sea on one side only.

Verse 1 states that the land was beyond the rivers of Cush, and we know that the rivers of Cush are the Nile and the Euphrates. We were advised that we can get to this land if we go in the direction of the Nile. However, to get to the country, we must go beyond the Nile; that is, we must cross this river and keep going. We were also told that we can get to this land if we go in the Euphrates's direction, but we must go beyond the Euphrates; that is, we must cross the Euphrates River and keep going. Now, we are given the final piece of geography. We must go until we get to the sea; then we must cross the sea, and we will get to this land. If we go in the Euphrates's direction, the sea we must cross is the Pacific Ocean. If we go in the way of the Nile, the sea we must cross is the Atlantic Ocean. We need to emphasize that we read the word *sea* four hundred times in God's word, but we never read the word *ocean*. Therefore, from the standpoint of the Bible, the Atlantic Ocean is a sea, and the Pacific Ocean is another sea. The Bible never mentions the word *ocean*; this is a human designation.

Here scripture tells us that the earth is round and that we can get to this land by going west or east. We must go from Israel, from which land the direction is taken, to the Nile River, then cross that river. Once we cross the river, we must continue on the latitude at that point (we must not change direction) to the Atlantic Ocean and cross the sea; then we will get to this land. Alternatively, we can go from Israel to the Euphrates, cross the river, go along the latitude at that point (we must not change direction) to the Pacific Ocean, and cross the sea. Then we will arrive at this land. This direction is specific.

We need to stress that the direction in verse 1 puts us on the opposite side of the rivers of Cush from Israel. We need to cross the Nile River and stop there. We also need to cross the Euphrates River and stop there - beyond the rivers of Cush - on the opposite sides of the rivers of Cush. There is now a change in the point of reference in verse 2, direction is now given from the side of the land shadowing with wings. As a result, from the opposite side of the river, we need to go along the latitude at that point and across the sea to the land shadowing with wings. As indicated by verse 2, we need to change prospective from the side of Israel to the side of the land shadowing with wings. This change in reference suggests that once one is on the opposite sides of the rivers of Cush, the latitude to the land shadowing with wings from these points doesn't change.

There is one other point of importance to arrive at the stated land, and that is that we must understand how the scripture deals with directions. We must get a reference point. In scripture, the direction is taken from Israel. We are all aware of the truth of that statement. Nevertheless, we cannot just reference any arbitrary place in Israel; it must be the center of Israel. There are two centers in Israel: the administrative center and the geographic center. The geographic center is the center of Israel, from which direction is taken. The administrative center is Jerusalem, which is Zion, where Christ will reign and administer this world's affairs. However, that isn't the geographic center. The geographic center is another point. We need to prove this statement. We must not only say things about the Bible, but we also must give proof.

We know from scripture that Jerusalem is the administrative center of the world. This statement isn't in dispute, yet Jerusalem isn't the geographic center. According to the word of God, Zion is north and not center. One verse will suffice. Psalm 48 declares, "Beautiful for situation, the joy of the whole earth, is mount Zion, on the sides of the north, the city of the great King" (v. 2). Here we are told that Zion, which is Jerusalem under royal grace, isn't in the center but in the North. Therefore, when dealing with direction, we must start from the center of Israel, not from Jerusalem. Once we find the center, we can then wear a blindfold, draw a line through the center of Israel, through the Nile and the Euphrates, and across the sea along the correct latitude. Then we will arrive at the land shadowing with wings. This description is unambiguous. Let us now present the proof.

We need to find where the geographic center is located. It must be close to the center of Israel but not at any random point; this center is a specific point. How do we find this point? God's word will show us. God's word is too accurate and precise not to teach us. Let us now locate this center and locate the land.

To locate the territory, we must go to a world map with longitude and latitude. However, because we are going across the Nile and the Euphrates, the latitude is essential in this instance; those are the horizontal lines, or imaginary horizontal lines, on a map. Let us first locate Jerusalem, which is stated on any map to be below latitude 31.77 degrees. It is said to be north, not center. Therefore, we must go a little south to get to the geographic center. This center will be close to Hebron, which is at just about latitude 31.53 degrees. If you are wondering why I selected Hebron, I will now give you the reason. When Lot separated from Abram, the Lord came to Abram, spoke to him, and gave the geographic center. That information is found in Genesis 13:14 -18.

First, God waited until Abraham was in a particular place before He gave him the geographic direction. He then told him to look east, west, north, and south from that location. I didn't say this. God did. Henceforth, from this place, we observe the direction east, west, north, and south.

This point in Israel is the geographic center. In nearly every country, the geographic center is different from the administrative center. Second, the location to which Abram moved after this encounter was Mamre, which is in Hebron. Therefore, we know or can conclude that it is close to Mamre from which the geographic direction is given.

Having been given our point of reference, we need to observe on the world map that the Nile River goes down from the horizontal plane of Hebron while the Euphrates River goes up. God designed it in this fashion. What we need now is a straight line that goes from Hebron to the Nile and to the Euphrates. When this line is drawn, it slopes upward from the Nile. When we check the coordinates, we will see why. Hebron or Mamre is slightly up from the Nile River. This clearly states that no part of the Nile River is on the same latitude with either Hebron or Jerusalem. Therefore, to get to Hebron, and for that matter Jerusalem from the Nile, we need to go at an angle. We cannot cross horizontally from the Nile to Hebron, since they don't lie on the same horizontal plane. The same applies to the Nile and Jerusalem. Therefore, to go from the Nile to Hebron or Jerusalem, we must go at an angle. Hebron's latitude is given as 31.52 degrees, while the latitude of the Nile is given as 30.6 degrees. As a result, when we draw a straight line from the Nile River, and it passes through the city of Hebron all the way to the Euphrates River, it intersects the Euphrates River at about latitude 34 degrees.

We need to perceive that in Isaiah 18:2, the direction is changed from Israel's side to the side of the land shadowing with wings. That means that once we cross the rivers of Cush, we must remain on that latitude to the land shadowing with wings. In verse 1, the direction is given from Israel to the rivers of Cush, which are the Nile and the Euphrates. Once we get to these rivers, as directed in verse 1, and go to the other side - which now is beyond the rivers or the other side of the rivers - the reference point then changes to the side of the land shadowing with wings as we go across the sea. It needs to be emphasized that verse 1 deals only with the rivers, while verse 2 deals with the sea. Therefore, there is a slight change of direction once we cross the rivers of Cush. We must go from the land shadowing with wings along the appropriate latitude to the points where we cross the Nile and the Euphrates; from these points, we go to the center of Israel.

It is needful to see that the latitudes on the other side of the rivers must be the same latitudes to the land shadowing with wings. This is why the instruction is changed at these points from Israel's side, in verse 1, to the side of the land shadowing with wings, in verse 2. There is a straight line or no change in direction from the land shadowing with wings to the Nile River or from the land shadowing with wings to the Euphrates River. There is no change when we cross the sea from the land shadowing with wings to the rivers of Cush. It is also needful to observe that both Hebron and Jerusalem are at an ascending angle from the Nile River.

We need to use this latitude, just about 30.6 degrees, where the straight line from the Euphrates River passes through the city of Hebron and intersects the Nile River. We must then proceed to the sea along the latitude at the intersection. We proceed across the sea, which is the Atlantic Ocean, and arrive at the USA. Again, we will use the second latitude, about 34 degrees, where the straight line from the Nile River passes through the city of Hebron intersects the Euphrates River. Next, we go to the sea using that same latitude and then cross the sea, which is the Pacific Ocean. Where are we now located? The answer is inevitable: the United States of America. The Bible is impossible if it isn't the word of God. Therefore, please look at the map on page 59 so we can go through the sequence.

We need to notice that the Hebrew word for "sea" is in the singular, while the word for "river" is in the plural. Therefore, we must draw three straight lines to establish this location. The first straight line runs from the Nile, passes through Hebron in Israel, to the Euphrates. Since verse 1 deals with two rivers, the first straight line must pass through two rivers. The second straight line connects from the point where the first straight line intersects the Nile. Nevertheless, Hebron is the pivot. Therefore, once the first straight line passes through Hebron, it can only cross the Nile close to its mouth or else it won't intersect the Euphrates. The second straight line then runs along the latitude at that point, continuing across the sea to the land shadowing with wings. Verse 2 deals with "one sea" from the land shadowing with wings; thus, the latitude from the land shadowing with wings to the Nile River doesn't change but crosses one sea.

The third straight line connects from the point where the first straight line intersects the Euphrates River. It then runs along the latitude at that point, continuing across the sea to the land shadowing with wings. This path is taken because only one sea is between the land shadowing with wings and the Euphrates River. Once we observe these details, we will find the right country. We cannot go in a straight line from Israel to the land shadowing with wings. As we have indicated in verse 2, directions must change once we cross the rivers of Cush. Consequently, there are three straight lines - one from Israel to the rivers of Cush and the other two from Cush's rivers to the land shadowing with wings across one sea.

Take a careful look at this geography and tell me this. Who could have given us a better geographic description than Isaiah did in 760 BC, when America was unknown? For Isaiah to have given us these directions from Israel to the USA nearly three thousand years before the establishment of their relationship is astonishing. Nevertheless, it is even more incredible when we realized that the directions to this country are given from Israel going in opposite directions. Scripture states that "in the mouth of two or three witnesses every word may be established" (Matt. 18:16). This is the reason the direction is given from two sides - to establish His word. This fulfillment testifies to the word and work of an omniscient God. He placed the USA in the middle of two seas. The geography is perfect.

We cannot just draw a straight line from Hebron through the Nile and through the Euphrates to the land shadowing with wings. That endeavor is too simplistic; we will never get it right. One direction is given in Isaiah 18:1, which deals with the rivers - from Israel to Cush's rivers. The other direction is shown in Isaiah 18:2, which deals with the sea - from the land shadowing with wings to the points across the sea. We must observe these changes.

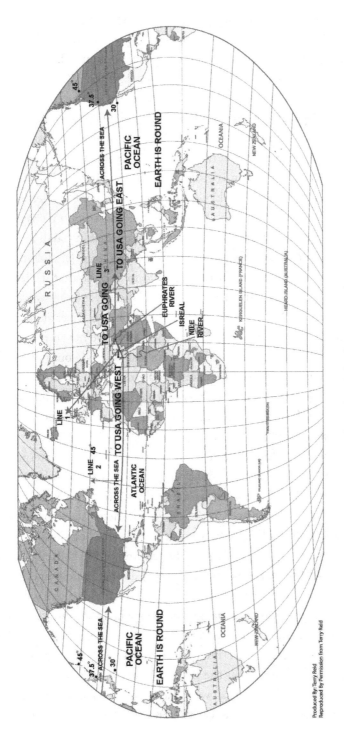

Location of the land shadowing with wings

Produced By: Terry Reid
Reproduced By Permission from Terry Reid

I need to explain that we would have obtained the same results if we had drawn the line from Jerusalem instead of Hebron to the Nile and the Euphrates. On the Nile side, our latitude would be about 30.2 degrees. The Euphrates side would now be about 36 degrees latitude. When we cross the sea on the Euphrates side at this new latitude, we will arrive at the same destination. Regardless of the location we use, when we cross the sea on the Nile side, we come to the southern USA, while when we cross the sea on the Euphrates side, we arrive at the northern USA. However, I haven't used Jerusalem because Jerusalem is geographic north, not center as we read in God's word. Later in this book, we will notice that if we use Jerusalem as the geographic center, we won't be able to interpret certain passages.

Jerusalem is the administrative center, as is evident in Isaiah 2:3 - 4 and Jeremiah 3:17. Jehovah will administer the world from Jerusalem during the thousand-year reign of Christ. We need to also see that if Hebron or Jerusalem were on the same latitude as the Nile River, we wouldn't have arrived in the USA. If we had to go from the Euphrates River along latitude 30.84 (the Nile River) across the sea, we would arrive not in the USA but in Mexico. We would get to the USA from the Nile side but not from the Euphrates side. Moreover, if we take Jerusalem or Hebron's latitude to go horizontally toward the Nile, we won't get to the Nile River, since the Nile River is below these latitudes. Therefore, the scripture gives the correct geographic location.

Nevertheless, before we can satisfy ourselves that this interpretation is correct, we need to ask an important question. Does the USA protect Israel? Is the USA politically seen in a friendly relationship with Israel? We must confess that the answer to these two questions is a resounding yes. These descriptions highlight the accuracy of the word of God. Please also note that whenever we quoted J. N. Darby and William Kelly, we were quoting men who wrote about these events approximately one hundred and fifty years ago, men who had never seen this land engaged with Israel. Furthermore, there was no Israel in existence when they wrote. However, because their writings were based on God's word and they were rightly dividing the scripture, their interpretation had to come to pass. This fulfillment demonstrates that the Bible is God's word.

Now, take a closer look at what Kelly said over one hundred years ago. He declared, "The country, therefore, to which the prophet calls is characterized as one which in the days of the completion of this prophecy should be a great maritime and commercial power forming remote alliances making distant voyages to all parts of the world with expedition and security and in the habit of affording protection to their friends and allies."[16]

How could Kelly have written that about America over one hundred years ago? How could he have written with such accuracy? There is only one answer; this book, the Bible, is the word of God.

Nevertheless, we don't depend on this one passage to say conclusively that the USA is the land shadowing with wings, even though we have proven it. We must hold ourselves to a higher standard. We must find other passages that deal with the same matter and see whether they all agree. Then and only then can we conclusively say that this nation is the land shadowing with wings. We must have other scriptures that declare the same thing. We must have two or three witnesses. These other scriptures we will advance shortly. The Bible explicitly states that "in the mouth of two or three witnesses every word may be established" (Matt. 18:16). We now know the country; let us seek to understand the relationship so we may learn what is about to take place.

Therefore, we must continue our interpretation of this chapter. We must know the future of this relationship, because men are boasting of great things. Will they be able to accomplish their boast? This matter is too important to neglect. We will proceed with our interpretation of verse 2, but we will read from the new translation by J. N. Darby. It translates the verse this way: "That sendest ambassadors over the sea, and in vessels of papyrus upon the waters, [saying,] Go, swift messengers, to a nation scattered and ravaged, to a people terrible from their existence and thenceforth; to a nation of continued waiting and of treading down, whose land the rivers have spoiled" (Isa. 18:2 JND).

First, the ambassadors go "over the sea"; that is, by flying. Second, they also travel "upon the waters"; that is by sailing. Please tell me quietly whether that isn't true. Yes! Every word is correct. The ambassadors consult with Israel concerning her political affairs and bring their big ships for her protection. It's important to note that the verse gives us the attention the USA is paying Israel and not vice versa. In another passage, we will

---

[16] Kelly, *"Notes on Isaiah,"* In The Bible Treasury, Vol. 5, 195.

see where Israel is showing the land shadowing with wings great interest. Moreover, Israel is already a nation when this country gets involved with her. Twice in this verse we read that Israel is a nation.

Consequently, we read about both "over the sea" (Isa. 18:2 JND) and "upon the waters" (Isa. 18:2 JND). "Go, swift messengers" (Isa. 18:2 JND); the swift messengers carry messages to Israel from the land shadowing with wings, using their different vessels. The nation "scattered and ravished" (Isa. 18:2 JND) is Israel. When the USA got involved with Israel, she was said to be scattered and ravished. Israel was still scattered all over the world and ravished. The USA protected her from that condition to become a powerful nation. We read further, "To a nation of continual waiting" (Isa. 18:2 JND); she was waiting for her Messiah, who will establish God's kingdom. Still, in ignorance and unbelief, she had already killed Him. Therefore, she didn't acknowledge Him as her Messiah, so she is seen as continuously waiting for Him.

We read more. "Whose land the rivers have spoiled" (Isa. 18:2 JND). Here, the land represents Israel, and the rivers have spoiled her. Observe that it is the plural form of the word *river* that is used; the rivers have spoiled her. The first river that had spoiled Israel was the Nile, which represented Egypt, to the south of Israel; Egypt had broken her. The second river that had spoiled Israel was the Euphrates, which represented Babylon north of Israel. Here, the scripture uses the term *rivers* to represent the countries through which the rivers passed.

Isaiah 18:3 is most important. We will read from the New Translation by J. N. Darby to help us with the understanding. "All ye inhabitants of the world, and dwellers on the earth, when a banner is lifted up on the mountains, see ye, and when a trumpet is blown, hear ye" (Isa. 18:3 JND). First, we must perceive that God is calling the whole world to observe two signs but one event. In the previous verses, we were occupied with two lands: the land shadowing with wings, which we found out was the USA, and the land of Israel.

In verse 3, God's word summons us to pay particular attention. This passage now directs us to see and hear. The word *ensign* is the word *nes* in Hebrew. It means "flag," "banner," "standard," or "signal." When a flag or banner was lifted on the mountains, we are all called to see. Moreover, when the trumpet is blown, we are all called to hear. We aren't told who will lift the flag or blow the trumpet. What is indicated is the event when Israel would become a nation in the last days after the Roman dispersion. In our interpretation of verse 2, we said Israel was already a nation when the land shadowing with wings got involved with her to protect her; here we are told when she became a nation. We are admonished to observe this event. Then, after Israel becomes a nation, the land shadowing with wings would build a relationship with her to protect her. Have you seen this development? Please take a closer look, because this relationship is developing right before your eyes. You do not have the luxury to declare you do not know.

Therefore, when Israel will raise her national flag and blow her trumpet, declaring her independence to the world, that event will be a vital sign. The occasion is the declaration of the state of Israel. According to God's word, this manifestation would occur when Israel, by political influences and helped by the land shadowing with wings, attained statehood. On that momentous occasion, she will raise her national flag and blow her trumpet, announcing to the world her independent status. The declaration of the state of Israel is the event the whole world is called to see and hear.

That event is most important, since after that event, the land shadowing with wings will be associated with Israel's protection. We read, "See ye when he lifts up an ensign" (Isa. 18:3) and, "When he blows a trumpet, hear ye" (Isa. 18:3). Therefore, this lifting of the flag was when the Israeli flag was hoisted high at her independence. This blowing of the trumpet was when her independence was announced to the world. Have you taken notice of that event? It's not that we don't have evidence of God's presence; it's that we don't care to observe it. God said Israel would become a nation again. Why when it happens, do we not acknowledge God? As we see here, it's not how important a country is in this world that causes it to be mentioned in the word of God, but it's how that power relates to Israel. In the scripture, the importance of a country is directly related to its dealings with Israel.

Second, as Christians, we don't look for signs, for we are a heavenly people; yet we are the only people on earth who can understand the significance of these events. This sign that God calls the world to observe has gone entirely unnoticed, and only to the church does Israel's restoration to her land have importance. To the world, the thought of a people out of Palestine for nearly two thousand years, now being restored, has no meaning whatsoever. Instead of believing in God, who said He was going to restore Israel to her land, and acknowledge that He accomplished it in our day, before our eyes; man forgets the event and pursues his belief in evolution. He is looking to find aliens on exoplanets instead of looking for Christ. What folly! The restoration of Israel, as a nation, has happened right before our eyes, and yet we haven't understood it. We continue to behave as if there is no God. What a sad state man is in.

Therefore, we have noticed God calling the world to observe that significant event when Israel became a nation. You are urged to hear; I am called to understand, and all are invited to listen. This development is momentous. Israel, exiled from her land by the Romans, was once again a nation in Palestine. This event was prophesied in the word of God. Our God accomplished this event in our day before our eyes. Is there not a God? Sure, there is a God.

Darby and Kelly informed us, and I will quote them at the appropriate stage; when they wrote that Israel had to return to the land of Palestine, no other Christian group embraced their teaching. "Where was Israel at that time?" people asked. She was nowhere to be found. Darby and Kelly and others from their group stood alone. Still, their clear understanding of God's word was something that distinguished their writings as rightly dividing the word of God. They wrote not from what they were seeing but from what the word of God said. Israel became a nation on May 14, 1948. Have you noted that development? Please carefully consider what I say.

However, "the land shadowing with wings" along with other nations helped to produce an independent Israel. When that was achieved, God then called the whole world to observe that event. Furthermore, He told us what He will do concerning this relationship. This unfolding is what we have next. He told the prophet a secret: he wasn't part of the political arrangement, as we read in the next verse. The prophet declared, "For so the Lord said unto me, I will take my rest, and I will consider in my dwelling place like a clear heat upon herbs, and like a cloud of dew in the heat of harvest" (Isa. 18:4). What God stated in the verse was that all man's effort will be transient and impermanent. A cloud of dew in the heat of harvest doesn't last long.

Man was very active, and God was inactive though observant, but the two powers' relationship was transient. We now have Israel restored to Palestine in unbelief and under the primary influence of the land shadowing with wings. Man was busy, but God was silent and just observed. God said He would take His rest and consider, and this He does. God will wait for a while without doing anything and just watch on. However, please note that God uses the pronoun "I" so we won't confuse the "I" with the "he" of the next verse. The "he" is critically important, as we will explain immediately.

We now come to verse 5, which is most significant, so we must pay particular attention to what is about to happen. Let us read this verse. "For afore the harvest, when the bud is perfect, and the sour grape is ripening in the flower, he shall both cut off the sprigs with pruning hooks, and take away and cut down the branches" (Isa. 18:5). If, in your mind, I am quoting the word of God too much, please forgive me, but I won't do otherwise; I will stick to the word of God, because it is the only sure resource. I don't want to entertain speculation. I don't need newspaper clippings to strengthen my points. All I need is the word of God. I don't need man's thoughts, for the word of God has given me all the details.

Please permit me to share the explanations of J. N. Darby and William Kelly before I proceed with the interpretation, because the consequences are too severe to indulge in travesty. We will start first with Darby. He wrote the following, "It is not yet judgment, so all come to nothing, whatever the promise, as in all human things where God is concerned … The people are brought back to their land to be given over as a prey to the nations, like wild beasts in winter or ravenous birds in summer. Such will be their fate when anew returned to Palestine, for God is not yet putting His hand to it."[17]

If Darby's interpretation of the scripture is correct (and he has been correct until this point), then this relationship between the USA and Israel will end in total disaster, and Israel will be exposed to her enemies again. Can you believe that? Oh no! No! No! Darby wrote, "The people are brought back to their land to be given over as a prey to the nations, like wild beasts in winter or ravenous birds in summer."[18] We will shortly see whether God's word will stand or whether man's boast will prevail.

---

[17] Darby, "*Thoughts on Isaiah the Prophet,*" In The Bible Treasury, Vol. 13, 120.
[18] Darby, "*Thoughts on Isaiah the Prophet,*120.

Please take a moment to observe the time the Lord gives us in this verse. "For afore the harvest, when the bud is perfect, and the sour grape is ripening in the flower, he shall both cut off the sprigs with pruning hooks, and take away and cut down the branches" (Isa. 18:5). In this verse, we are told that the land shadowing with wings will suffer a two-fold destruction, and we are even given the time. The time is stated to be "before the harvest." In Matthew 13, we get the time of the harvest. We read, "The enemy that sowed them is the devil; the harvest is the end of the world, and the reapers are the angels" (v. 39). In Joel 3, we read, "Put ye in the sickle, for the harvest is ripe: come, get you down; for the press is full, the fats overflow; for their wickedness is great" (v. 13).

We learn from Matthew 13 that the harvest is at the "end of the age" or "completion of the age." We understand further from Joel 3 that the harvest is said to be full during the Great Tribulation. Nevertheless, the destruction of the land shadowing with wings is stated to be "before the harvest." God's word clearly says that before the harvest, before the end of the age, "he shall both cut off the sprigs with pruning hooks, and take away and cut down the branches" (Isa. 18:5). Therefore, before the tribulation and before the end of the age, a great event will take place. The same way Israel was going to become a nation before the tribulation, so another significant event will occur before the tribulation. This momentous event will be the destruction of the land shadowing with wings.

Thus, William Kelly wrote,

> This comparatively distant land espouses the cause of Israel, but the protection would be ineffectual in the result, however loud the proffer and the preparation. Thus the total failure of the friendly plan ensues. Everything in appearance betokened a speedy ingathering of good to Israel, and their national hopes seemed to be on the eve of being realized, when God brings all to naught by letting loose once more the old passions of the Gentiles against His people. The effect is that they shall be left together unto the birds of the mountains and to the beasts of the

earth, and the birds shall summer upon them, and all the
beasts of the earth shall winter upon them.[19]

Here, William Kelly, like J. N. Darby, says the same thing; all man's
activities will end in total and absolute failure. How, I ask, will Israel be
suddenly exposed again to the nations' wrath, as Kelly stated? The answer
to that question is terrifying. The land shadowing with wings will be
destroyed. The time of its destruction is before the tribulation—both its
army and land. This is why Israel will sign a protection treaty with the
Roman Empire; her first protector will disappear. It is a twofold judgment
God will inflict on her protector. Israel's protection will then cease. Israel
will then be exposed again to the wrath of the nations. This destruction
is problematic for me to develop in this book in the atmosphere in which
we live today; I can attempt only to outline the events simplistically. It is
one thing to write about the rise of a country, it is a completely different
thing to write about its fall.

To understand the coming crisis, we need to grasp who the "he" of verse
5 is, who will accomplish this destruction. Some, without careful observation
will say the "he" is the Lord. However, we need to pay special attention to
scripture. We know that in verse 4, the "I" is the Lord. How then does the
"I" become the "he"? That isn't a wise way to interpret scripture. The "I"
doesn't become the "he." In verse 5, the "he" is another person and he is the
head of the Assyrian, and this interpretation will be established presently.

This verse must be explained further because we haven't been taught
much about the Assyrian. This interpretation isn't speculative; this is clear
scripture. What we find in Isaiah 18:3 is that "all ye inhabitants" - that
speaks for itself - are addressing all. If we notice verse 3 in the J. N. Darby's
translation, we see there is no "he" in the verse. Then in Isaiah 18:4, we
have the "I" twice, which speaks of the Lord. It wasn't "I" and "he" but "I"
and "I" alone. Observe how carefully the Lord speaks of Himself as the "I."
However, when we come to Isaiah 18:5, the "I" of verse 4 gives way to the
"he" of verse 5; therefore, it couldn't represent the same person. How could
the "I" and the "he" be the same person? Note carefully that the "I" of verse
4 was going to take His rest and only observe. He wasn't going to intervene.

---

[19] Kelly, *"Notes on Isaiah,"* The Bible Treasury, Vol. 5, 195.

Why does God say in verse 4 that He will take His rest and observe, then immediately after (the next verse) do the opposite? That doesn't make sense. The very thing God says He won't do He does in the next verse - that is, if the "I" is the "He," as some think. If I say I will not do something and in the next moment, do it, what would you say about me? You would think very poorly of me. That is why God does nothing in this chapter. You cannot find one verse in this chapter that shows God is active. The reason is, God said He will take his rest and observe from His dwelling place. If one is resting and observing, what is he or she doing? That statement is expressed in that way for a reason. There is no evidence to interpret the "I" of verse 4 as the active "he" of verse 5. There is no evidence that the "I" of verse 4 has stopped observing and has become involved in verse 5. That view goes against the quick movement of the chapter.

We have "all" (all humanity) in verse 3, "I" (Jehovah) in verse 4, "he" (the Assyrian head) in verse 5, and "they" (Israel) in verse 6. The Lord isn't seen as active in this chapter. Nothing is attributed to Him in these seven verses. It has been stated that there is more written about the Assyrian than any other power in the word of God, yet we know so little about it.[20] We must, therefore, seek to widen our knowledge of the Assyrian and recognize this most critical player.

This destruction explains why in Revelation 6, when we read about the first horse, which represents the Assyrian, it is seen as the white horse - a victorious power - because it was the one who had just inflicted this decisive blow on the land shadowing with wings. Let those who think this is impossible consider what Josephus, the Jewish historian, wrote about Rome after he saw their military might, he told the Jews, "That they must know the Roman power was invincible."[21] Today we all know differently.

We need to discern what verse 5 declares. "When the blossoming is over, and the flower becomes a ripening grape" (Isa. 18:5 JND), a great event will occur. That means that, as time passes, things will look good. There will be blossoms, there will be the flower, and there will be ripening grapes - then suddenly, destruction. We learned from this verse that "the land shadowing with wings" would be protecting Israel for quite a while.

---

[20] William Kelly, *Notes on the Book of Daniel* (London UK: George Morrish 1865), 141
[21] Josephus, War of the Jews, book 5, chap. 9, para. 3.

Also, when everything seems to be going according to plan, suddenly, a "he" appears and "cuts off the sprigs with pruning knives." The "sprigs" are the armed forces of the land shadowing with wings. The "he" is the head of the Assyrian, an Islamic kingdom, which will destroy the armed forces of the country shadowing with wings.

However, it must be observed that the land shadowing with wings is seen as a tree before its destruction. This symbol in prophecy speaks of worldly magnificence and power (see Dan. 4 and Ezek. 31). Therefore, instead of a land, this aspect of a tree is when this mighty country begins to glory in its greatness. We read here of "sprigs" and "branches"; these are the components of a tree, not a land. This aspect will be explained later.

Next, we read in Isaiah 18:5, "Take(s) away," but what is "taken away" isn't stated. What is here taken away? Israel's protection is what is taken away. The USA, Israel's protector, has been shadowing with wings, but then the USA will cease to shadow with wings. Israel's protection will be taken away after the armed forces of the land shadowing with wings will be destroyed. Israel will then be left defenseless; hence, the next verse will subsequently be fulfilled. We have seen that Isaiah 18 has been fulfilled from verse 1 to verse 4. The next part that will be accomplished is verse 5; that is, the destruction of the land shadowing with wings. If God is currently fulfilling the first part of the relationship, then indeed, He will also fulfill the latter part. We will need God's help with the confusion that will ensue after the fulfillment of verse 5. Is there a God? Please take warning, my friend. There is a God, and He has stated what He will do, and He will do it.

Nevertheless, it is important in divine things to give hope. For one may ask, isn't it possible to avert this destruction. The answer is no. Once God utter His word, it will be accomplished. It may be delayed, if one repents, but God will fulfill His word.

The scripture gives further insight. "And cut down the branches" (Isa. 18: 5 JND). The Assyrian then attacks "the land shadowing with wings" at home and destroys this country in the second part of the attack. A question then arises. Where will the armed forces of the land shadowing with wings be destroyed? The answer is by the Euphrates River, which will become the Assyrian territory; this destruction will be seen later. The Assyrian territory will include Syria, Iraq, and Turkey; the countries through which the Euphrates River passes. In response to terrorist attacks that will be launched by the Islamic kingdom, called the Assyrian, against the USA, the land shadowing with wings will attack the Assyrian in the Syria/Iraqi area to disband the terrorist. However, in that future encounter when the USA invades the area, the result will be different. It will not be like the time when the USA entered the Syria/Iraqi area after the Bin Laden's attacks. In the future assault, when the USA returns to the region after the Assyrian attacks, the USA will not be successful. Russia and Iran will support the Assyrian, and together, they will unleash on the USA the most potent terror attacks the world will ever see. What Bin Laden did was just a shadow of what will happen in the future. This encounter will be developed later in the book.

We will now end this chapter with some thoughts from William Kelly in 1860. He wrote,

> Population does not in itself make a nation strong. Some of the nations greatest in masses of men have been politically weak before a small energetic kingdom. Look at Darius's power, as opposed to Alexander and his Macedonians. The last appeared contemptible. Did it not seem the greatest folly for these few adventurers to invade Asia, and face the enormous armaments of Persia? Yet the he-goat with his horn was too much for the myriads of the great king, and the second empire collapsed ... so as to America, I conceive that the young giant power which has grown so fast will sink still faster ... but assuredly somehow before that day comes.[22]

Therefore, the land shadowing with wings will be destroyed before the tribulation. This protective land is one of the many powers the Assyrian will destroy. If the scripture says so, it will undoubtedly come to pass, regardless of the thoughts of men.

---

[22] William Kelly, *Lectures on the Minor Prophet: Joel* (London, UK: George Morrish, 1860) 207.
https://www.stempublishing.com/authors/kelly/1Oldtest/joel.html

CHAPTER 4

GEOGRAPHIC EGYPT: THE TERRORIST
KING OF THE SOUTH

I n this chapter, I intend to continue our study on the land shadowing with wings. I desire to gather more information on this unfolding relationship between the USA and Israel. However, the land shadowing with wings is called by different names in Isaiah. As a result, we will look for this land under other names, because we desire to be enlightened further concerning these unfolding events.

Therefore, we will begin our search for the land shadowing with wings under the name of Egypt. This chapter will unfold to us the first of the two powers called in the word of God - Egypt. We will observe the future activities of the country we know today as Egypt. We will then notice that this geographic Egypt will become the headquarters of the king of the South. We will endeavor to understand the composition, nature, and role this power will play in the last days. We will also see the connection between the king of the South and the king of the North.

Then we will be introduced to another Egypt found in the word of God. This second Egypt we will identify as the land shadowing with wings. We will call this mysterious Egypt "designated Egypt." Therefore, we must learn the teachings concerning geographic Egypt so we may differentiate between the two depictions of Egypt. We cannot understand designated Egypt unless we first understand geographic Egypt. We will then see that designated Egypt is the land shadowing with wings, which is viewed as Egypt, while geographic Egypt will become the headquarters of the king of the South. This subject of geographic Egypt has a high difficulty rating; thus, we must pay particular attention. May the Lord help us in the understanding of His word.

We read the following in Daniel 11: "And at the time of the end shall the king of the south push at him: and the king of the north shall come against him like a whirlwind, with chariots, and with horsemen, and with many ships; and he shall enter into the countries, and shall overflow and pass over" (v. 40). Here we are told that at the time of the end, a power called the "king of the south" shall attack the Antichrist in Israel. The expression "the time of the end" signifies just after the middle of the tribulation. Therefore, we must know who is represented by the term "the king of the south," for we see him in Daniel 11 attacking Israel during the tribulation.

Nevertheless, we don't need to look far to identify the king of the South, since Daniel 11:5–35 gives us a series of wars between the king of the South and the king of the North, which were well documented in secular history. These wars clearly define the players. We aren't ignorant concerning their separate identities. The king of the South was part of the empire of Alexander the Great; south of Israel, with its headquarters in Egypt. In contrast, the king of the North was equally part of Alexander the Great's empire; north of Israel, with its headquarters in Syria. The king of the North isn't Russia. Russia is another power found in Ezekiel 38–39. The designations of the king of the North and the king of the South were given to the kingdoms north and south of Israel after the death of Alexander the Great.

Therefore, what the scriptures teach us is that the Lord Jesus Christ will allow a power to rise south of Israel. This power will be called the king of the South. This southern kingdom will be an Islamic empire in the Egyptian area. However, it will be more of a nuisance than a real threat to Israel. This power is also termed "the fly" in Isaiah 7:18. It is, therefore, essential for us to identify this player and view its activities. This topic is a nine on my scale of difficulties. Consequently, it is a complicated subject, but it can be grasped. Therefore, we will now seek to comprehend this subject to be better positioned to solve the puzzle of the last days.

It was said that the Assyrian destroyed the land shadowing with wings. Furthermore, I indicated that this destruction took place by the Euphrates River. However, those details were not found in Isaiah 18. In that chapter, we saw that "the land shadowing with wings" was destroyed by a "he" (the head of the Assyrian) and was inflicted with twofold destruction. First, the army of "the land shadowing with wings" will be destroyed in the Syria / Iraqi area. Then, second, "the land shadowing with wings" will be attacked at home and destroyed. Therefore, I need to find additional scriptures that deal with "the land shadowing with wings" to establish what I say. I cannot speculate with scripture.

When I was a young Bible student, I asked, Why is the USA not in the book of Revelation? I was told that the USA might become part of the Roman Empire during the tribulation. The Bible teachers who gave me that answer were trying to help me according to their knowledge. I know that was their intention. However, as the Lord opened my eyes, I began to see differently. I began to notice from many scriptures that the Assyrian will destroy "the land shadowing with wings" and that the land shadowing with wings is one of the most significant powers that will be devastated by the Assyrian. This same Assyrian is the reason Israel will sign the protection treaty with the Roman Empire. Also, the Assyrian power is the reason the Roman Empire will break the treaty of protection after being relentlessly attacked. I know many consider the destruction of "the land shadowing with wings" by the Assyrian to be impossible. However, I believe God. It is so ironic that men could believe that a little country, on a small planet, orbiting a tiny star, would defeat the counsels of the Creator of the universe.

Up to this point in our study, we can identify "this protective land" by what it does, by its activities, and by its peculiar functions - it shadows with wings; that is, it offers protection to many nations, Israel included. Nevertheless, in my present endeavor, I need to find the name by which "the land shadowing with wings" is called in other passages in the Bible, since the word of God says, "That in the mouth of two or three witnesses shall every word be established" (Matt. 18:16). The word of God states plainly in 2 Peter, "Knowing this first that no prophecy of the Scripture is of any private interpretation. For the prophecy came not in old time by the will of man: but holy men of God spoke as they were moved by the Holy Ghost" (2 Peter 1:20–21). We must have other scriptures that deal with the land shadowing with wings, or else we must be silent.

Furthermore, in Isaiah 28, we read, "For precept must be upon precept, precept upon precept; line upon line, line upon line; here a little, and there a little … but the word of the Lord was unto them precept upon precept, precept upon precept; line upon line, line upon line; here a little, and there a little" (Isa. 28:10, 13). Even here, we find each item repeated - it must be two or three - for every word to be established. We see a little in Isaiah 18; we need to find a little somewhere else. When we see that little, we must identify that land as the USA, as we did in Isaiah 18; then we will know for sure whether the Assyrian chief will destroy this protective land.

It is said that the book of Isaiah is comprehensive. It speaks of different subjects in a complete way so one may have a fair understanding of what is to take place. When it mentions Israel, for instance, it speaks of her nearly one hundred times. When it identifies Assyria, it indicates it almost forty times. When it mentions the Assyrian, it suggests it nearly ten times. When it speaks about Egypt, it mentions it over forty times, and it refers to the Egyptians over ten times.

However, when it mentions Gog of Ezekiel 38, it indicates it under the names of the "treacherous dealer" and "the spoiler," and it refers to Gog multiple times by those names. Moreover, the same thing happens when it mentions the future Roman Empire; it sees it not as a Beast, as in Daniel or Revelation, but it gives it a name. For instance, the Roman Empire is seen in Isaiah under Babylon in chapters 13-14 and also under the names "death and Hades" in chapter 28. These future adversaries are given names. Moreover, a name given to a former power may be reused to represent a future but different power. For instance, we see this where Babylon was used to describe the future Roman Empire in Isaiah 13-14.

We need to remember that Isaiah was written around 760 BC, approximately 165 years before Ezekiel. Hence, the name Isaiah gave to Gog could be different from that Ezekiel gave to Gog. Moreover, Daniel was written around 607 BC, more than 150 years after Isaiah was written, so the name Daniel used to refer to Rome could be different from what Isaiah used to refer to Rome. This information isn't presented to say that God couldn't have used one name throughout - God can do anything - but He chose to give different names according to His purpose. Therefore, we have to study to understand what He has written. We need to remember that names change as time changes. Why am I emphasizing this point? I am doing so because the land shadowing with wings is developed again in Isaiah, but it is seen under another name. We must find the next name given to the land shadowing with wings.

When the Assyrian attacked Judah in the days of Hezekiah, the Assyrian thought Hezekiah was trusting in a specific power for his protection, a power as great as the Assyrian; that power was called Egypt. In Isaiah 36, we read, "Lo, thou trustest in the staff of this broken reed, on Egypt; whereon if a man lean, it will go into his hand, and pierce it: so is Pharaoh king of Egypt to all that trust in him" (v. 6). Again, in Isaiah 36, we read, "How then wilt thou turn away the face of one captain of the least of my master's servants, and put thy trust on Egypt for chariots and for horsemen" (v. 9)?

Therefore, "Egypt" is the name "the land shadowing with wings" is called. Why? This is so because Egypt represented the most powerful country in Isaiah's days, and Israel wasn't going to trust in any other power except the most significant power on earth at that time. It needs to be pointed out that the Egypt I am talking about isn't Egypt in Africa. We will coin a new name for this Egypt; we will call it "designated Egypt," for God so designates it. We now see that God speaks of another Egypt in His word that is entirely different from Egypt in Africa.

Carefully note that Hezekiah didn't trust in Egypt; he believed in Jehovah. However, to the Assyrians, Egypt was the most significant power. It was only natural that if anyone was going to trust in a powerful country, it had to be in Egypt. We are now made aware that this human reasoning will characterize Israel in the last days. As a result, Israel will believe in Egypt - not Egypt in Africa but in a new Egypt, which we will identify as "designated Egypt."

Permit me, therefore, to show you that God's word speaks of two depictions of Egypt. I will call the first Egypt, "geographic Egypt." That Egypt is the one south of Israel, where Moses was born. Joseph took our

Lord Jesus Christ there to shelter him from Herod. Nevertheless, I will also reveal, as clear as day, another Egypt hidden in the word of God; unless God opens our eyes, we will never see it. I call this hidden Egypt the "designated Egypt" because God so designates it. Therefore, we will learn that the first Egypt, geographic Egypt, will become the headquarters of the king of the South, while the second Egypt, designated Egypt, is the land shadowing with wings.

When I give the topic of "designated Egypt" a level of difficulty, I must confess that it is a ten out of ten. When it comes to difficult scriptures, the understanding of Egypt as the land shadowing with wings is the most challenging topic I have ever encountered; yet this extreme difficulty has caused me to believe in God's word 100 percent, irrespective of human reasoning. This portrayal of Egypt is too complex for man to have conceived; only an all-wise God could have designed such a description.

This topic's difficulty level is why respectable and knowledgeable Bible teachers haven't introduced any other passage that deals with the land shadowing with wings in more than 150 years since Darby and Kelly advanced Isaiah 18. The understanding of "Egypt" is complicated, and as a consequence, we know only Isaiah 18. Hence, this limited knowledge causes us to speculate on many subjects, and we say some of the things we say in the absence of truth. Remember, there can never be only one scripture that speaks on a matter. Therefore, once we grasp "designated Egypt," many of our speculations will disappear, if we are willing to accept the truth. Therefore, we will seek God's help to understand this mysterious Egypt. Nevertheless, before we can appreciate designated Egypt, we must understand geographic Egypt.

In Isaiah 18, we have the land shadowing with wings, and immediately after that, God introduces Egypt in Isaiah 19 - 20. We are introduced to the burden of Egypt. Nevertheless, under the burden of Egypt in Isaiah 19, we have Egypt's history in the last days as the headquarters of the king of the South. Moreover, in Isaiah 20, we find the attack by the king of the North on the king of the South during the tribulation, as is presented in Daniel 11:42-43.

Isaiah 19:1- 4 further gives us the reason we have the king of the South in the second seal of Revelation 6, since here we have this violent civil war.

Nevertheless, this civil war will not only rage in Egypt but also ravage the nations close to Egypt to produce the king of the South.

In Isaiah 19, the Bible gives us the process whereby Egypt will change from a secular state to a religious terrorist body. In this chapter, God will act (unlike Isaiah 18, where He is seen as inactive), and his actions will be disastrous for Egypt. He declares that He will visit Egypt; as a result of His visit, there will be a civil war in Egypt, and everything in which Egypt will take pride will be overthrown. Even though it will look like a normal occurrence, it is God who will do this, and no one will be able to stop Him. Then two terrorist leaders, called here "a cruel lord" and "a fierce king," will eventually have dominion over Egypt.

We need to note that, as a result of the future civil war, Egypt's spirit will fail. God will destroy their counsel. This destruction will result in Egypt seeking the idols and charmers, those who have familiar spirits and wizards. Geographic Egypt will then embrace a mixed religion with also a Jewish element. The religious leaders are also introduced; the Egyptians will I give over into the hand of "a cruel lord," and "a fierce king" shall rule over them.

Therefore, according to Isaiah 19, a religious body will hijack and overthrow geographic Egypt. Then a fierce king will be set up as the ruler in Egypt. This is the ruler that has the great sword in the second seal of Revelation 6. This ruler will be the head of the king of the South. It is also needful to notice that the Egyptian will be given into the hand of a cruel lord. The cruel lord here is the Assyrian head. The time when the Egyptian will be delivered into the hands of this cruel lord is highlighted in Isaiah 20. This is in the future, when the Assyrian will attack and conquer Egypt during the Great Tribulation, as stated in Daniel 8:42- 43.

I don't doubt that there might have been a cruel lord in the past, but the cruel lord here will be in the future. The fierce king will also be in the future and he is contemporary with the cruel lord. The fierce king will arrive on the scene after the Lord visits Egypt and during the raging civil war in the country. Moreover, he will be present during the time of the cruel lord, who is the head of the Assyrian. Furthermore, the time during the event is short, since the Lord comes and puts an end to the king of the South. Therefore, Isaiah 19–20 develops Egypt's activities from the moment the Lord visits Egypt to produce the king of the South until the coming of Christ, when Egypt will become a blessing in the land.

Therefore, we read, "The princes of Zoan are become fools, the princes of Noph are deceived; they have also seduced Egypt, even they that are the stay of the tribes thereof. The Lord hath mingled a perverse spirit in the midst thereof: and they have caused Egypt to err in every work thereof, as a drunken man staggereth in his vomit" (Isa. 19:13- 4). Two things will characterize the period; one will be deception, and the other will be seduction. As a result of this religious deception and seduction, Egypt will err in everything. She will then be entirely in the hands of the fierce religious king, and all the steps of Egypt will be as a drunken man.

It is needful to say that, because Christian teachers haven't fully developed the king of the North and the king of the South as future powers to the same extent as that to which the Roman Empire has been expounded; we may have difficulty understanding these two powers. As a result, it is easy to misinterpret the Roman Empire for the Assyrian in a passage. Nevertheless, it must be understood that the king of the North and the king of the South make their appearance early and create extreme havoc in the world.

Thus, the whole area, not only Tunisia and Libya but also Egypt to Ethiopia, will become a terrorist enclave, as we will see in future passages. Egypt will become the head of this terrorist kingdom in the South. This is what Isaiah 19 develops - Egypt as the head of the king of the South. Once we see the future of the first Egypt and then notice that the future of the second Egypt is entirely different from that of the first Egypt at the same period in time, then we know we are dealing with two different depictions of Egypt.

Therefore, geographic Egypt is destined to become the head of a southern terrorist empire. This terrorism is Egypt's future history - not written by man but determined by God. I need to tell you truthfully that if there is no God, this will not happen. On the other hand, if there is God, and it is the correct interpretation, it is sure to come to pass. I know there is God, and I know this will happen because I believe His word. Let those who believe in evolution prevent it if they can.

It is for this reason that we read, "The Lord hath mingled a perverse spirit in the midst thereof: and they have caused Egypt to err in every work thereof, as a drunken man staggers in his vomit" (Isa. 19:12–14). As a result of the perverse spirit the Lord was going to mingle in Egypt, the nation will err. The erring here is religious. Her religious identity was going to cause her to err. In another place, we will be given another reason for the erring. Nevertheless, Egypt will be identified with religious terrorism. She will be deceived and seduced. Carefully note what is stated: "I will destroy the counsel thereof; and they shall seek to the idols, and to the charmers, and to them that have familiar spirits, and to the wizards. And the Egyptians will I give over into the hand of a cruel lord; a fierce king shall rule over them, saith the Lord, the Lord of hosts" (Isa. 19:3-4).

We are here told that Egypt will embrace a mixed religion composed of different religious elements; this belief would borrow extensively from the Jewish faith. Egypt will become a terrorist nation but not by its own will. Still, the country will be hijacked by those who have another plan. Then two religious leaders, here called a "cruel lord" and a "fierce king," were going to subjugate Egypt. The "cruel Lord" is the head of the Assyrian, in whose hands the Egyptians will be given. This will be accomplished when the Assyrian attacks Egypt during the tribulation. Egypt will then be associated with a religion embracing different components.

On the other hand, the "fierce king" will be the terrorist leader in Egypt, called the king of the South. This ruler will be a religious dictator. However, observe that it is God who will bring this on Egypt. Man may say Arab Spring, but he has no idea what God plans to spring.

However, according to Isaiah 19:16-7, things will change further, and instead of Egypt being a terror to Israel, which she will be during the tribulation, Israel will become a terror to Egypt. This change will take place when Christ comes and destroys the armed forces of the king of the South. The appearing of the Lord Jesus Christ will bring this terrorist power to an end. Note: for the first time, the word *terror* is introduced in the passage. This word for "terror" is used only here in the whole Bible.

We read further,

> In that day shall five cities in the land of Egypt speak the
> language of Canaan, and swear to the Lord of hosts; one
> shall be called, the city of destruction. In that day shall
> there be an altar to the Lord in the midst of the land of

Egypt and a pillar at the border thereof to the Lord. And
it shall be for a sign and for a witness unto the Lord of
hosts in the land of Egypt: for they shall cry unto the Lord
because of the oppressors, and he shall send them a saviour
and a great one, and he shall deliver them. (Isa. 19:18-20)

This passage clearly establish that the events discussed are future since
it is the Lord's coming that end the distress in Egypt. Moreover, it is of
great interest to see that an altar and pillar will be established in Egypt
to show the connection between the God of Israel and Egypt's people.
This altar will become a witness to Egypt that the Lord is God, as the
two and a half tribes similarly established in Joshua 22. This is in contrast
to the Muslims who will claim nearness to Israel's God. Moreover, the
oppressors are the "cruel lord" and the "fierce king" who will suppress
Egypt. The people will cry to the Lord for deliverance, and He will send
them a Deliverer. The Deliverer is the Lord Jesus Christ. He will be sent
as a Savior to Egypt, a great Savior; this deliverance is when the Lord Jesus
Christ returns. He will deliver Egypt from the terrorist caliphates, called
the king of the South and the northern king. Egypt will then become a
place where the Lord Jesus Christ is praised and glorified. This situation
doesn't exist today. It will be so tomorrow.

Moreover, we have a delightful sequence in Isaiah 19:21–25. "The Lord
shall be known to Egypt, and the Egyptians shall know the Lord in that
day and shall do sacrifice and oblation; yea, they shall vow a vow unto the
Lord, and perform it" (Isa. 19:21). A change will occur in Egypt from being
a Muslim nation to a nation that will worship and serve the Lord. We read
further, "And the Lord shall smite Egypt: he shall smite and heal it: and
they shall return even to the Lord, and he shall be entreated of them, and
shall heal them" (Isa. 19:22). The Lord will smite Egypt when Egypt will
be the king of the South; then He will heal Egypt when He returns and
establishes His kingdom.

It is indeed astonishing that the Lord will use these two powers - Egypt
and Assyria - to chastise Israel in the last days; afterwards, He will make
them a blessing in the land. Here God will bless, saying, "Blessed be Egypt
my people, and Assyria the work of my hands, and Israel mine inheritance"
(Isa. 19:25). These two powers, which will become the king of the South

and the king of the North respectively, the enemies of Israel, will eventually become a blessing in the land. Therefore, these verses give us the future of geographic Egypt and set the stage for us to understand designated Egypt; where we will see another Egypt's future during the last days, just before the Lord returns. This new Egypt will be entirely different.

What we observe is that Egypt and Assyria will both be blessed simultaneously with Israel. Only God can conceive such a plan. We are further taught that Egypt, located south of Israel, will become the king of the South, an enemy of Israel before the Lord comes. Moreover, when the Lord appears, we will also have a land called Assyria in the North of Israel; yet today we have no such nation. Therefore, the future of these regions is fascinating and pertinent for the display of God's purpose. These regions will change, and will change drastically.

In Isaiah 19, we have Egypt's prophetic history from the time the Lord will visit Egypt to Christ's coming. We have presented, Egypt in her land in the last days. In verse 1, the Lord will visit Egypt, not for good but for judgment. In verse 2, we have an ensuing civil war. We will know when the Lord visits Egypt, for there will be a civil war, and things won't get better but worse. The counsel of Egypt will be destroyed in verse 3, and they will become religious, or a religious identity will be thrust on them. In verse 4, they will be given over into the hands of a cruel lord, and a fierce king will rule over them.

This fierce king is the head of Egypt, who is the head of the king of the South and is seen on the red horse of Revelation 6. Nevertheless, he isn't an Egyptian but a foreign terrorist. He is the fierce king in the South. There is another fierce king who is in the North. He is the king of the North or the Assyrian, and he is seen on the white horse of Revelation 6. This word for "fierce" here is the same word used in Daniel 8, and it means "vehement" or "harsh." These kings are fierce; they are driven by ideology. In Daniel 8, we have the king of fierce countenance. He is the ferocious king of the North, the Assyrian; both of these kings are heads of terrorist empires. Explore the happenings in our world today and tell me whether this won't soon happen; the situation is already taking shape. Very shortly, there will be two significant changes in the world; one to the North of Israel will produce the king of the North, and another to the south of Israel will produce the king of the South.

The king of the North and the king of the South will be allied as terrorist kingdoms, only as far as their hatred toward Israel is concerned. Moreover, present-day ISIS attempted to do what the scripture says will be done. She tried to revive the king of the North and the king of the South. Moreover, we notice that ISIS, north of Israel by the Euphrates River, is in an alliance with ISIS south of Israel in North Africa. However, as time passes, the terrorist empires will become bitter enemies as they were of old.

"Where are they? Where are thy wise men? And let them tell thee now, and let them know what the Lord of host hath purpose upon Egypt" (v. 12). We learn from this verse that, Egypt's wise men don't know what will be; only the believers know. The geniuses and experts of the world have no clue as to what will be happening. As we look at the news on television, we are often reminded about this verse. We observe the announcers constantly introducing their experts to give their points of view and try to make sense of what is happening globally. However, if you listen carefully, you will hear their contradictions as they struggle to interpret the future. Nevertheless, they clearly show that no one knows the future but the God of the Bible.

Therefore, these events in the last days will cause the nations to err. Just as Israel was blinded when Christ came (and they rejected Him), so will the nations be blinded. The professing Christians will apostatize, the mass of the Jews will also apostatize, and both will embrace Antichrist. Islam will be radicalized, and evolution will be the blindest of the lot. When a man rejects the Son of God, his eyes are blinded, and he cannot see the truth, so he embraces delusions.

However, there is a change in Egypt (v. 16) when the Lord Jesus returns in glory: then and only then will things change in Egypt, Assyria, and Israel. It is interesting to observe that Assyria will return in the last days and is there when Christ comes. What ISIS was seeking to do was to redefine the Euphrates area. Instead of these separate countries, as are known today, the whole region will be renamed Assyria. There will no longer be Iraq, Turkey, and Syria but only Assyria. Consequently, these countries by the Euphrates River will be overthrown, and a terrorist power will occupy them. This development will be explained in detail as we proceed.

In verse 20, Egypt cries to the Lord, and the Lord sends them a Savior. This Savior is the only Savior, the Lord Jesus Christ. It is when Christ returns that this verse will be fulfilled. We should observe that Assyria will be a country when Christ returns, as we see in verses 23-25. The understanding of this future Assyrian is fundamental. We must learn about the Assyrian if we are going to be serious Bible students. Nevertheless, those who aren't well informed biblically will say the Assyrians are dead and gone. The old Assyrian Empire is dead and gone, but be sure that a future Assyrian Empire is coming.

Nevertheless, just as the Roman Empire will be revived and restored, so will the Assyrian Empire be revived and restored. Consequently, we find the Assyrian here when Christ returns. That is, the terrorist empire north of Israel will conquer all the countries along the Euphrates River and restore the Assyrian Empire - this is, the future Assyrian; this is the king of the North. This development is what ISIS was trying to accomplish. This fulfillment will come to pass at the right time.

Furthermore, we need to stress the importance of Isaiah 20. It presents the future attack of the king of the North, the "cruel lord," on the king of the South. This attack will occur just after the king of the North will invade Israel during the Great Tribulation. For three years, just after the middle of the tribulation, the northern king will have the upper hand on the king of the South. Nevertheless, when the king of the North will hear the tidings of Christ's return, he will leave Egypt to go and fight against the Lord Jesus Christ. However, during this encounter, the Lord Jesus Christ will destroy the king of the North. This teaching will be developed in the appropriate place.

This passage also emphasizes the delusion of some, who will flee from their dwelling places to hide in the nearby islands, not believing that the Assyrian will attack Egypt, only to wake and find the Assyrian has taken Egypt and Ethiopia as captives. They now exclaim, "How shall we escape" (Isa. 20:6)? Also, this time of three years here is essential because it shows that the attack on Israel will occur just after the middle of Daniel's seventieth-week prophecy, since the Assyrian will attack Israel before it attacks Egypt, according to Daniel 11. The fact that Ethiopia is brought in here demonstrates that we are indeed speaking about the king of the South, of which Ethiopia will be a part.

I must emphasize that as a Christian I can never be part of terrorism or encourage it. The problem is this. I have three options: I tell my readers the truth, I lie to them, or I keep quiet. However, I cannot keep quiet when I know people will be lost forever, since I know the Bible is true. I cannot lie to you and preach to make money; that is the worst evil. Therefore, I must tell you the truth. What is presented here will be accomplished.

The Bible is factual, and once it is correctly interpreted, one will see that what is happening today is just what God declared will happen. Believers in Christ will never be involved in terrorist activities. This goes against the grain of Christianity. However, the Bible isn't evolution; it isn't speculation. It is indeed and in truth God's word; therefore, it gives us the future history of the world.

I don't want to write about such terror; nevertheless, I must explain the scripture. I owe the world the explanation of the word of God. Perhaps some of my readers may turn to Christ and be saved. As a result, though I disagree with terrorism, I need to tell the world what will come to pass. I cannot change God's mind or His plan. I can only warn you about what is to come. I desire that you might repent and accept the Savior, our Lord Jesus Christ, before it's too late. Soon Christ will return, and the church of God will be raptured away to glory, and those who will remain will face the brunt of what is here prophesied. Where will you spend eternity, my friend? Where will you spend eternity? Christ is your only hope. Christ died for your sins upon the cross, accept him before it is too late.

CHAPTER 5

DESIGNATED EGYPT: THE LAND SHADOWING WITH WINGS

I n the previous chapter, we studied the future of Egypt in Isaiah 19-20, because we were seeking to find the land shadowing with wings under the designation of Egypt. Subsequently, we learned that the Egypt of Isaiah 19-20 is geographic Egypt and that this topographical Egypt is slated to become the headquarters of the king of the South in the end-times. We also learned from Isaiah 20 that the Assyrian will attack and subjugate Egypt during the Great Tribulation, according to Daniel 11, just before the Lord returns.

We will now study the mystical Egypt found in Isaiah 30-31, which will give us the prophetic history of another Egypt in the last days, just before the Lord returns in glory. However, this history is entirely opposite the history of geographic Egypt in Isaiah 19-20. It is also important to say that similarly Darby and Kelly unfolded a mystical Babylon in Isaiah 13-14 and declared that that Babylon was the Roman Empire, even though scripture calls it Babylon. These mysterious powers, though difficult to understand, are true. They are the Jewish protectors in the last days, but they are given Old Testament names, contemporary with the ancient Assyrian Empire, since the future Assyrian will engage them.

On my scale of difficulty, this subject of designated Egypt is a ten. There is nothing in God's word I have encountered that is more difficult than this subject. It is very complicated and only the writers of the *Bible Treasury* make mention of it. There we read the expression when speaking of Egypt: "whoever that Egypt might be." There the writer recognized that the Egypt of Isaiah 30-31 was different from geographic Egypt. Still, he didn't unfold who that Egypt represented. Nevertheless, we need to understand the subject because it is happening in our day before our eyes. This focus will put the Bible where it belongs - in a class all by itself, above everything ever written by man.

Nevertheless, as we study Isaiah 30-31, we will learn much more concerning the land shadowing with wings, seen under the picture of Egypt. We will then be fascinated to see in scripture the correlation between the land shadowing with wings and 9/11- the falling of the towers on Tuesday, September 11, 2001. Further, this chapter gets even more interesting, since we will also see a connection between the land shadowing with wings and the Muslim mosques on the temple mount. We will then close off the chapter with the introduction to the Assyrian.

We will now pause to read Isaiah 30-31, since I desire to put every verse in its context. I don't want anyone to accuse me of taking verses out of context. As a result, we will read God's word repeatedly to present the right context. I desire to convey not my thoughts but the precious word of God.

If we read Isaiah 30-31 casually, we will think we are reading about Egypt in Africa. However, as we study the passage carefully, we will realize the passage isn't as simple as it appears. Therefore, we will first seek to obtain the context of the passage. As we study this portion of scripture, we find that the Assyrian is introduced in both chapters. We read, "For through the voice of the Lord shall the Assyrian be beaten down, which smote with a rod" (Isa. 30:31). Nevertheless, though I quoted verse 31, verses 27-28, 30, and 33 all speak about the Assyrian. Also, in Isaiah 31, we read, "Then shall the Assyrian fall with the sword, not of a mighty man; and the sword, not of a mean man, shall devour him: but he shall flee from the sword, and his young men shall be discomfited. And he shall pass over to his strong hold for fear, and his princes shall be afraid of the ensign, saith the Lord, whose fire is in Zion, and his furnace in Jerusalem" (Isa. 31:8-9).

We note that it will be the time when the future Assyrian is destroyed. "Then shall the Assyrian fall" (Isa. 31:8). However, a person might say this was in the past. How can you prove to him or her that this is in the future? We can prove this destruction is future, because Christ is the one who will fight and destroy the Assyrian, as we read. "So shall the Lord of hosts come down to fight for mount Zion, and for the hill thereof. As birds flying, so will the Lord of hosts defend Jerusalem; defending also he will deliver it, and passing over he will preserve it" (Isa. 31:4-5). This never happened in the past, where the Lord came down, defend, and deliver Jerusalem. This will be in the future when Christ returns as Jehovah of host. Further, after Christ destroys the Assyrian, He will reign as is presented in chapter 32.

We need to remember that the Bible wasn't written with chapters and verses. These were put in the Bible for easy reference. Therefore, after the fall of the Assyrian, the Lord Jesus will reign in power and glory. It becomes evident that after the destruction of the Assyrian, Christ's kingdom will be established for a thousand years. This sequence didn't happen in the past when the former Assyrian was destroyed; this will happen in the future. When the future Assyrian will be defeated, Christ will reign. Therefore, the passages in Isaiah 19–20 and Isaiah 30-31 speak of the same period. In Isaiah 19, after the destruction of the king of the South, the Lord reigns. In the same manner, in Isaiah 30, after the collapse of the Assyrian, the Lord reigns.

Furthermore, in the introduction to his translation, Darby wrote the following on page xiii: "In [Isaiah] chapter 28-33, a series of special prophecies portray the last assault of the Gentiles against Israel, in which the Edomite and the Assyrian are conspicuous, but each of these prophecies ends with the full blessings of Israel and the presence of the king." Therefore, Darby tells us these chapters are future and are the Gentiles' last attack against Israel. These chapters end with the presence of the Lord Jesus Christ as king in Israel.

One may ask, Why is Egypt in Isaiah 19 not identical to Egypt in Isaiah 30-31? The answer is that Egypt in chapter 19 is an enemy of the Jews, while Egypt in chapters 30–31 is a friend, a protector. What strength does the geographic Egypt of today have to protect Israel? Israel is already stronger than geographic Egypt; hence this Egypt in Isaiah 30-31 is different.

Let us now explain the two depictions of Egypt, and then we will develop the passages. In the book of Jeremiah, we learn the secret to understanding the two aspects of Egypt. We learn that Israel was going to be exiled in Babylon for seventy years. We acquired that knowledge in Jeremiah 25:8-14. Those pronouncements God accomplished. Those prophecies were fulfilled.

In Ezekiel, we learn that Egypt also was going to be taken captive, not for seventy years but for forty years. Nevertheless, when Egypt emerged from exile, some specific things were going to happen to her for the duration of her future. We learn these truths in Ezekiel 29:

> I will make the land of Egypt desolate in the midst of the countries that are desolate, and her cities among the cities that are laid waste shall be desolate forty years: and I will scatter the Egyptian among the nations, and will disperse them through the countries. Yet thus saith the Lord God, At the end of forty years will I gather the Egyptian from the people whither they were scattered: And I will bring again the captivity of Egypt, and I will cause them to return into the land of Pathros, into the land of their habitation; and they shall be there a base kingdom. It shall be the basest of the kingdom; neither shall it exalt itself again above the nations: for I will diminish them, that they no more rule over the nations. And it shall be no more the confidence of the house of Israel, which bringeth their iniquity to remembrance, when they shall look after them; but they shall know that I am the Lord God (Ezek. 29: 12-16).

What the scripture states first is that Egypt was going to go into captivity for forty years and not seventy years as Israel did. She was going into captivity after the other countries around her were already in captivity. Second, at the end of forty years, she was going to return to her land. Third, from the time she returned, she was going to be there as a base kingdom. It is important to note that she will be "there," in geographic Egypt - a base kingdom. Fourth, she will be the basest of the kingdoms. Fifth, she shall not exalt herself any more above the nations. She will never again exalt herself over the nations. Sixth, the Lord will diminish her.

Therefore, from the time Egypt emerged from the Babylonian captivity, we observe that she will never be strong again - forever. That is why the king of the South, which would be headed by Egypt, is seen only as a fly, an annoyance, while the king of the North is called the bee - it will swarm Israel and sting her.

The seventh and most crucial point is that Egypt would no more be the confidence of the house of Israel. We need to grasp that, from the moment Egypt returned from the captivity of Babylon, Israel will never again confide in it. However, what we find in Isaiah 30-31 is an Egypt, in the last days, that is very strong. This country isn't base like geographic Egypt; this country is exalted.

Moreover, this Egypt is protecting Israel and Israel is confiding in her, and this is happening in the last days, long after the Babylonian captivity. The things Ezekiel 29 said would never happen again concerning geographic Egypt were all happening regarding the Egypt of Isaiah 30-31. Therefore, this Egypt must be different, or we would have to accuse the scripture of contradiction—an impossible thought.

Moreover, as early as Isaiah 1, we are informed that we will have only two protectors of the Jews in the last days: the land shadowing with wings and the Roman Empire. One will be before the tribulation, after Israel returns from the Roman dispersion. The other will be during the tribulation. One protector will be destroyed, and the other will break the treaty of protection, so it won't be destroyed. There is no other protector. Therefore, this Egypt must be the land shadowing with wings since Israel is trusting in its protection. Moreover, it is present before the tribulation.

Nevertheless, lest men debate; there was one defining moment in Isaiah 30 that proves without a doubt that the Egypt there was the land shadowing with wings, the USA. That defining moment was 9/11, the attack on the World Trade Center.

Now, we will grasp that the Bible is the word of God, not fiction. In this land called Egypt, which was going to protect Israel, an incident was going to take place called the falling of the towers. That incident won't need any explanation; all will know because all will see. It was going to happen in our day, before our eyes. The towers were going to fall in Egypt. Did the towers fall in geographic Egypt or designated Egypt? The towers fell in the USA, which is designated Egypt. The place where the towers fell proves that Egypt in this passage is the USA and further confirms that the land shadowing with wings is the USA.

Therefore, let us read this verse. "And there shall be upon every high mountain, and upon every high hill, rivers and streams of waters in the day of the great slaughter, when the towers fall" (Isa. 30:25). Rivers and streams of water are what characterize the terrorist attacks. Assyria was located on a river. God uses these symbols - rivers and streams of water - to describe the character of the terrorist attack. The mountains and hills are major cities and smaller cities in the world. These symbols will be expounded on later.

Consequently, every major city and the lesser-known cities will come under terrorist attacks in the day of the great slaughter (or multiple slaughters) when the towers fall. The great slaughter hasn't yet arrived, but the day had come. The falling of the towers didn't usher in the day of the great slaughter, but it was an event that declared to us that the day had arrived. The towers' falling should reassure the believer that the church's Rapture is imminent, since real terror is just around the corner.

The falling of the towers was a sign from God that the day of the great slaughter (many slaughters) had come, just like the signs He gave in Isaiah 18 when He called all to observe the rebirth of the Israeli nation. In Isaiah 30, God gave another sign - this one, in the land of Israel's protector—the falling of the towers. God in His grace has given this world two signs, in these last days: one in the land of Israel (Isaiah 18), and the other in the land of Israel's protector. Please turn away from sin before it is too late, since you have no excuse.

A point of vital importance is that even though Christians don't look for signs, they are the only ones who understand them. When the great slaughter will take place isn't stated, but its day had come. Who will be slaughtered isn't indicated either. However, according to the passage's context, it will be a slaughter on the land shadowing with wings.

Nevertheless, it also has an application to the world as a whole; major cities and minor cities are going to come under terrorist attacks. This great slaughter will begin in earnest, as we will see later when Russia embraces the terrorist group called the Assyrian. This embrace by Russia will strengthen the Assyrian appreciably and cause it to attack the world and inflict spectacular devastation.

This attack will be on everything in which man prides himself, as is declared in Isaiah 2:12–17. The writer isn't inventing these things. I didn't write these words; the Jews wrote these words in the book we know as the Bible, which I believe with all my heart is the word of God, inspired by God Himself. The Bible infers that Iraq will fall, Turkey will fall, and Syria will eventually fall. Russia will be infuriated with the West and will support the terrorist group, the Assyrian, against the West. What the passage in Isaiah 30 indicates is how the attacks will unfold. However, exactly when all of this will unravel, I cannot say. How many more twists and turns will occur before this happens? I don't know. I watch, as the word of God instructs me to watch.

The scripture didn't have to elaborate on the falling of the towers. Once the towers fell, the event spoke for itself. It was an event the whole world witnessed, confirming scripture. Nevertheless, to unbelievers, the thought that scripture mentions 9/11 is beyond belief. For this reason, we first needed to extensively study the land shadowing with wings, regardless of the challenges, so we may better understand what is happening in the world today. Even some Christians have a hard time apprehending the fact that this verse speaks about 9/11. The Bible skeptics cannot believe that things are happening in their day that demonstrate such a profound biblical basis, especially when they are glorying in their evolution. We must also emphasize that the word for towers in Hebrew is in the plural, not the singular or dual. Who therefore could deny that more than two towers came down at that event? The wise men of our day can never argue that this was written after the event.

On the other hand, some boast about the theory of evolution, which has no consistency and foundation. Yet they believe it is the basis of everything, despite all the discrepancies associated with evolution. They believe that nothing created everything. What folly! The fulfillment of this event, on the other hand, proves without a doubt that there is a God and that He is entirely in control of what is happening in this world. Sadly, to the world's dismay, this event is only a foreshadowing of bigger and bolder attacks, which will take place in the near future.

Nevertheless, be assured, everyone, that the prophet is speaking about 9/11; because we aren't dealing with man's book; we are dealing with God's word. It could speak of no other time because we have already proven that this Egypt is a future Egypt. We need to underscore that both Darby and Kelly predicted that this Egypt, as well as the events highlighted in the prophecy will take place in the future.

Moreover, it can be proven by any standard that John Darby died in 1882, and William Kelly died in 1906. The towers were going to fall in Egypt after their deaths, since they said that Isaiah 30-31 presents future events. Moreover, the events were going to take place after Israel was restored to Palestine, but during the time when designated Egypt will be protecting her.

We need to stress that Isaiah 30 begins with Israel being protected by designated Egypt, but that protection did not start until after 1960. Israel became a nation in 1948; the towers were going to fall after Israel became a nation but during the time the land shadowing with wings will be protecting her. Moreover, the towers were going to fall at a time when Israel was depending on the protection of that land, as we find in the early verses of Isaiah chapter 30. Moreover, this Egypt in Isaiah 30 is only seen in relation to future events; commencing with the protection of Israel, and concluding with the casting into hell of the Antichrist and the Assyrian leader, by the Lord Jesus Christ. During the protection of Israel by the land shadowing with wings, an event was going to take place in Egypt, called the "falling of the towers." Did the event happen as prophesied? We know for sure it did happen as stipulated, but more than that, it happened in our day and before our eyes. We have no excuse regarding the presence of a holy God. Nevertheless, we have taken no notice of the presence of an omniscient God. What did this event prove? It proved without a shadow of a doubt that the Bible is God's word. What about man's conspiracy theories about the event? Absolute nonsense.

To further convince you that these passages speak of the future, let us consider the thoughts of William Kelly. He wrote, "Israel, when threatened by the Assyrian, sought the help of Egypt: I am speaking now of the literal fact when this prophecy first applied. Though it did bear on the days of Isaiah, yet the character of the prophecy shows that it cannot be limited to that time: only a small part of it was accomplished then."[23] Obviously, this Egypt has a future manifestation; Kelly said that over one hundred years ago, and so did Darby in the introduction to his translation.

Therefore, if the remainder of the prophecies of Isaiah 30-31 need to be fulfilled in the future, the question must be asked. Where on earth geographically will these prophecies be fulfilled? We have the answer in designated Egypt, a protector, since geographic Egypt will be an enemy of the Jews.

In Revelation 11, we read, "And their dead bodies shall lie in the street of the great city, which spiritually is called Sodom and Egypt, where also our Lord was crucified" (Rev. 11:8). Israel (more specifically, Jerusalem) is called "spiritual Sodom" as in Isaiah 1 and spiritual Egypt during the tribulation. We therefore know that more than one name can be assigned to a given place. Consequently, we have a spiritual Egypt, geographic Egypt, and designated Egypt. Spiritual Egypt is Israel, geographic Egypt is Egypt in Africa, and designated Egypt is the land shadowing with wings. Having been enlightened that Isaiah 30–31 speaks of the land shadowing with wings, let us now find out what further information is given about this power by interpreting these two chapters; we must remember that it must agree with Isaiah 18, or our interpretation is wrong.

However, some say America isn't in prophecy. They say, by interpreting Daniel 9:24–27, which speaks of Daniel's seventieth week, that all predictions have been suspended. Nevertheless, could they be so bold? Please show me the scriptures that expound that the USA isn't in the Bible; I will be the first to bow to the authority of God's word. If one says the church is a parenthesis lodged between the sixty-ninth and seventieth weeks of Daniel's prophecy, I will say, "Sure." If one says that all prophecies are suspended, I will say, "Show me the verses."

I have clearly shown that Deuteronomy's verses deal with the war between Rome and Israel. The time of that battle was during the church period. Even more, Israel's return to the land in unbelief, described in Zephaniah and Jeremiah, occurred during the time of the church's presence on earth. Furthermore, the establishment of the state of Israel, described in

---

[23] Kelly, *"Notes on Isaiah,"* The Bible Treasury, Vol. 5, *353*.

Isaiah 18, also happened during the time of the church of God's presence on earth. We can multiply the scriptures, if need be, but there is no need.

Nevertheless, we must address what is suspended. These verses in Daniel 9 address the suspended items. Daniel 9 declares that "seventy weeks are determined upon thy people and upon the holy city to finish the transgression, to make an end of sins, to make reconciliation for iniquity, to bring in everlasting righteousness, to seal up the vision and prophecy, and to anoint the most holy" (Dan. 9:24). All the events in Israel's calendar were moving to the fulfillment of verse 24 and the introduction of the Messiah. These events have been suspended because of the death of the Messiah. These events cannot be fulfilled now but will await the return of our Lord Jesus Christ, since the church occupies the period between Daniel's sixty-ninth and seventieth weeks.

Nevertheless, the scriptures clearly state that the Romans were going to put Israel out of the land of Palestine and that she was going to return in unbelief before the tribulation. Darby and Kelly state the same, and I believe what they said because it is God's word rightly divided. Moreover, these events were fulfilled during the period of the church's presence on earth. These events haven't been suspended. They are already fulfilled. They occurred in our day before our eyes. Darby and Kelly, sound Christian expositors, wrote that Israel was going to become a nation again and that a powerful land would protect her after she became a nation. These events are happening during the sojourn of the church on the earth. These events are happening in our day before our eyes. This great power is the USA, as we have proved in this book. I am clear that the USA is in prophecy and that prophecy hasn't been suspended.

I can multiply the examples, for none of those expositors I have quoted have been so bold to declare that the USA isn't in prophecy. What is even more striking is that a country so tied up with Israel's security would be said not to be in the scriptures. When Darby and Kelly interpreted the scriptures, they declared that when Israel would be restored to the land, she would be protected by a great power. We know the protector, they never saw him.

Therefore, as we analyze Isaiah 30:1–3, we need to appreciate that the passage in Isaiah 30–31 opens with the same word as Isaiah 18. However, we said that in Isaiah 18, the word was better translated "ho" than "woe."

We noted that the specified land was protecting Israel. Here in Isaiah 30, the perspective is different, and the word is better translated "woe." It is one thing for a man to show interest in a woman who is already married. Still, it is an entirely different matter when a married woman shows interest in a man who isn't her husband.

Similarly, this is the exact situation presented before us in Israel's relationship with the land shadowing with wings. In Isaiah 18, we see the picture from the side of the land shadowing with wings (the man), showing interest towards Israel. Still, here in Isaiah 30–31, we see the picture from the side of Israel trusting in the land shadowing with wings. This aspect of the relationship is what is developed before us. In Isaiah 18, the land shadowing with wings (like the man) is showing interest towards Israel, though she is married to the Lord. In Isaiah 31, Israel (the married woman) is wooing the land shadowing with wings (the man), who isn't her husband. This relationship is destined for disaster. It must bring out a woe. This disaster must be so, because the Lord clearly stated in Jeremiah 3:14 that He was married to Israel.

"Woe to the rebellious children saith the Lord" (Isa. 30:1). We immediately see that the "woe" here isn't addressed to the obedient children but to the rebellious. Judah, called Israel by the nations, is the one on whom the "woe" is pronounced. God was in a relationship with Israel, but at the same time, Israel was carrying on a relationship with the land shadowing with wings.

The second thing we observed is that Israel takes counsel but not from Jehovah. We must remember the "swift messengers" of Isaiah 18:2; the land shadowing with wings was courting Israel's affection. The swift messengers carried messages from the land shadowing with wings to Israel. Israel was taking the counsel of the messengers and refusing God's word. She was taking advice from designated Egypt and forgetting God. We observed that Israel's actions were responsible for the woe. "Cover with a covering" (Isa. 30:1) is better translated "who make leagues," as J. N. Darby translated it. Israel was in an alliance with the land shadowing with wings. This association was an ungodly alliance. God's people should never be allied with the world, so this alliance was doomed for judgment.

We read next, "Who walk to go down into Egypt, and have not asked of my mouth,—to take refuge under the protection of Pharaoh, and trust in the shadow of Egypt" (Isa. 30:2 JND). We should observe that God doesn't waste words by putting it this way; He was also giving us a time frame of the last days. When the remnant of Judah went down to Egypt in the days of Jeremiah after Nebuchadnezzar had taken them captive, they asked counsel of the Lord, but they refused the counsel. Regrettably here, in this case, they simply didn't ask, as the history of this relationship clearly demonstrated.

Moreover, in Hoshea's day, there was a sense of urgency, and there was a reason for the sending of messengers; there was an enemy at the gate, the Assyrian. However, in Isaiah 30–31, there isn't that sense of urgency. They walk to go down to Egypt - there is leisure; there is no enemy, at least not yet. Later, the enemy will appear - again, it is the Assyrian but the future Assyrian.

There was a reason Israel went to Egypt; it was "to take refuge under the protection of Pharaoh and to trust in the shadow of Egypt" (Isa. 30:2 JND). The protection of Pharaoh gives us Egypt's side, while the trust in the shadow of Egypt gives us Israel's side. Moreover, the "shadow of Egypt" brings us back to the land shadowing with wings of Isaiah 18. Here Israel accepts this protection and seeks to deepen it. She is now trusting in this protection for her defense. She finds comfort in a friendly nation. Once again, we see further confirmation that Egypt here is the land shadowing with wings of Isaiah 18, not Egypt in Africa, because that Egypt is an enemy. Here, Israel depends on Egypt's protection. It isn't merely Egypt offering protection to Israel as Isaiah 18, but Israel trusting in the protection of Egypt.

Moreover, in verse 3, we are informed of what will happen to the protection. "For to you the protection of Pharaoh shall be a shame and the trust in the shadow of Egypt a confusion" (Isa. 30:3). The expression "for to you" specifically addresses God's concern for Israel. The other nations may trust in that protection but not Israel. Here for the first time, like in Isaiah 18, God tells us that this protection will be ineffective. Israel will be ashamed of this protection, and her enemies will laugh at her. Also, she will be confused when this protection is no more, and her enemies will mock her.

Here we observe that this chapter is consistent with Isaiah 18, but it gives us more details. Furthermore, it is noticing events from the side of

Israel instead of the side of the land shadowing with wings, as in Isaiah 18. Moreover, we observe that this land is protecting Israel, and Israel is trusting in its protection and obeying its counsels.

In Isaiah 30:4, we find that there are two critical places mentioned in this land shadowing with wings. We read, "For his princes were at Zoan, and his ambassadors came to Hanes" (Isa. 30:4 JND). The princes are the leaders, since there is no king as yet, and the ambassadors are the political representatives of Israel. In Isaiah 18, it was the ambassadors of the land shadowing with wings who were active; here is the reverse. Zoan was the capital, and Hanes was central Egypt. One was the capital, and the other was the world's political center, like the United Nations.

In verse 5, God again gives the result of this protection, but He sees it as already accomplished. "They were all ashamed of a people [that] did not profit them, nor were a help or profit, but a shame, and also a reproach" (Isa. 30:5 JND).

God saw their shame, even though it hadn't happened as yet. He saw the embarrassment that would result from that relationship. Here we are told about their humiliation, because the land shadowing with wings won't profit them. Instead, their help will become a shame and a reproach. The enemy will laugh at them and reproach them. Let men ponder these words, who think this defeat isn't possible.

Some believe the destruction of the land shadowing with wings is impossible. Consequently, Christian writers tie the protective land to Rome during the tribulation. However, this interpretation would be entirely against scripture, but they cannot believe otherwise, because the destruction of this great power is too outrageous to be believed. How can a superpower with such nuclear capabilities be defeated? This country is a superpower, men say, but God says this power isn't a god. God now tells us what He will do to this protective land. What is important here is what God says He will do; therefore, if there is no God nothing will happen since only God can accomplish this defeat. It is of great interest that in Isaiah 18 God does not act, while in Isaiah 30-31 He is active. We are presented with the two sides of the matter.

The word of God then switches focus and looks at this matter from the side of the land shadowing with wings. We read, "The burden of the beasts of the south: into the land of trouble and anguish, from whence come the young and old lion, the viper and fiery flying serpent, they will carry their riches upon the shoulders of young asses, and their treasures upon the bunches of camels, to a people that shall not profit them" (Isa. 30:6). We need to see why God placed this land in this location in the geography of this world. Even as He spoke of the beast of the South, He still had the land shadowing with wings in mind. Let us also get some help from the J. N. Darby's translation. "The burden of the beasts of the south: through a land of trouble and anguish, whence cometh the lioness and lion, the viper and fiery flying serpent, they carry their riches upon the shoulders of asses, and their treasures upon the bunches of camels, to the people that shall not profit [them]" (Isa. 30:6 JND).

The land of trouble and anguish is Israel, like the nation scattered and peeled of Isaiah 18. The lioness and the lion represent Christ, while the viper and the fiery flying serpent represent the Antichrist. We need to be careful that we don't interpret the fiery serpent as the devil but notice that both the lion and the serpent come from Israel's land. You cannot say Satan comes from Israel's land; it is Christ, the rejected Messiah, and the Antichrist, who is received as Messiah. The scripture in verse 6 changes the vantage point from Israel to the land shadowing with wings, as it did in Isaiah 18:2. It brings in these two personages to show that it is still speaking of the same place. These two personages come from that land. Christ came first, but He was rejected; afterward the Antichrist will come, who will be accepted. The majority of the people rejected Christ, but a remnant received Him. In the future, when Antichrist comes, the situation will be reversed. The majority of the people will receive the Antichrist, and a remnant will refuse him. Christ came first, and the Antichrist will come later.

In Genesis 49, we are told, "Judah - [as to] thee, thy brethren will praise thee; Thy hand will be upon the neck of thine enemies; Thy father's children will bow down to thee. Judah is a young lion; from the prey, my son, thou art gone up. He stoopeth, he layeth himself down as a lion, and as a lioness: who will rouse him up?" (vv. 8–9 JND).

It is Christ who is the Lion of the tribe of Judah. He is the Lion from the prey from the moment that battle takes place, where He destroys him who had the power of death, who is the devil. Christ is declared to be the Lion of Judah's tribe. However, He isn't a Lion to the saints, though He prevails as a Lion; when John sees Him in Revelation 5, instead of being seen as the Lion, He is seen as the Lamb, the one who died for the saints. As a Lamb, He redeemed us by His blood. As the Lion, He will redeem us by His power.

The scripture then identifies the place where the Antichrist will appear. In the same passage in Genesis 49, we read, "Dan will judge his people, as another of the tribes of Israel. Dan will be a serpent on the way, a horned snake on the path, which bites the horse's heels, so that the rider falleth backward. I wait for thy salvation, O Jehovah" (Gen. 49:16–18 JND). We need to observe that the Antichrist in Genesis 49 is this same snake we read about in Isaiah. 30:6. Genesis tells us not only the country from which the Antichrist will come but also from which tribe—the tribe of Dan. However, because of the Messiah's rejection and crucifixion, when the land shadowing with wings will be destroyed, Israel will fall into the hands of the Antichrist. It is a strange teaching indeed that many believe that the Antichrist will be the head of the Roman Empire. How can a Roman Prince be the long-expected Messiah of the Jews? He must be a Jew for them to be deceived, the Israelites knew that from their scripture. However, this mistaken identity between the Antichrist and the Roman Prince shows our poverty in Christendom when it relates to prophetic matters.

Scripture also indicates that "they carry their riches upon the shoulders of asses, and their treasures upon the bunches of camels, to the people that shall not profit [them]" (Isa. 30:6 JND). Here, we learn that Israel uses the transportation available at the time to carry her wealth and invest in designated Egypt. They are putting their money in the place of their protection. All these things you know are true; Israel invests heavily in the USA. This investment wasn't so in the past, since during the wars, both with Babylon and Rome, Israel had no treasure to invest.

Here in verse 7, God clearly shows us why He is calling this place Egypt. However, we cannot obtain that information from the King James Version. We need J. N. Darby's translation to help with the Hebrew. It reads, "For Egypt shall help in vain, and to no purpose; therefore, have I named her, 'Arrogance,' that doeth nothing" (Isa. 30:7 JND). J. N. Darby's translation helps us further with a note on "Arrogance," which says *Arrogance* can be translated "Rahab," and Darby notes that Rahab is a name for Egypt.

Moreover, he gives us the meaning of the word; it is "the boaster." He boasts, but he cannot fulfill what he says. He says, but he cannot do what he says. Here God's word clearly states that this country isn't geographic Egypt, but I call it Rahab; I call it Egypt because it says and cannot do. That is why I call it Egypt. These are similar words to what Rabshakeh said to Hezekiah about Egypt. In Isaiah 36, we read, "Lo, thou trustest in the staff of this broken reed, on Egypt; whereon if a man lean, it will go into his hand, and pierce it: so is Pharaoh king of Egypt to all that trust in him" (Isa. 36:6).

Therefore, we are dealing with a country called Egypt, but it isn't geographic Egypt; it is the land shadowing with wings - but it is now given a name; that name is Egypt. We will also shortly see that this Egypt is found all over the prophetic word, and we will be given another reason the land was called Egypt.

Further, we note in Isaiah 30 that a momentous event was about to occur, and it could take place in our day if we are still here. However, one may ask, "What are you saying? We will be raptured long before these events take place. Do you not believe that the church can be raptured at any time?" Sure, I do. That is elementary.

Concerning the Rapture, I am sure that the only thing the scriptures affirm is that we are raptured before the tribulation and intimates that we can be raptured at any time. Scripture doesn't say anything else. That is, we can be here until just before the Tribulation, unless we believe there is a considerable gap between the Rapture and the tribulation. That seems not to be so, since we are very close to the Lord's coming, and we are still here. We will deal with this matter more in depth shortly, and we will see what the scripture declares.

Isaiah 30 reminds us that these events are in the future. "Now go, write it before them in a table, and note it in a book that it may be for the time to come forever and ever" (v. 8). It may be for "the time to come"- the time isn't now, not in the prophet's day, but a day to come. Furthermore, we see how the Lord was rejected in verses 9-11.

In Isaiah 30:12–14, we observe that Jehovah's word was rejected. In contrast, the words of the land shadowing with wings were trusted - to Israel's destruction. Jehovah's word would have shown Israel how to behave herself; instead, she confided in oppression and willfulness, which she learned from the land shadowing with wings.

In Isaiah 18, we read, "For before the harvest, when the blossoming is over, and the flower becometh a ripening grape, he shall both cut off the sprigs with pruning-knives, and take away [and] cut down the branches" (Isa. 18:5 JND). We said earlier that the "he" in Isaiah 18:5 is the Assyrian. The Assyrian head inflicts "two-part" destruction on the land shadowing with wings.

We will prove this destruction in another passage, but we will strengthen it here. In Isaiah 30:12-14, we notice that Israel's actions are causing problems for her protector. Israel, having returned to the land after the dispersion by the Romans, should have trusted in God's word. But instead, she follows the pattern of the land shadowing with wings and displays the show of strength. She believes in oppression and perverseness. As a consequence, God now declares that this iniquity will be as a breach ready to fall. It immediately became clear that the way Israel was dealing with the nations nearby was causing a problem for the land shadowing with wings. The high wall was Israel's protection, but Israel's actions regarding her neighbors were causing radicals to target her wall. The wall here is the land shadowing with wings seen under another figure.

Consequently, the breach was swelling out in the high wall; that is, the attacks on the wall were getting bigger and bigger and were causing problems to the wall - until the wall was going to be broken suddenly. The Assyrian will attack the land shadowing with wings with vicious terrorist attacks. These attacks will cause the land shadowing with wings to advance to the Euphrates River to engage the Assyrian in battle, but it won't be successful. The land shadowing with wings will fall. The moment the wall is broken, God's word says this: "he" shall break it. "He" shall not spare. This "he" is the same "he" of Isaiah 18:5. The "he" here isn't the Lord; it is the head of the Assyrian, as we will see shortly. This destruction is so complete that afterward, the wall is good for nothing. The leader of the Assyrian inflicts this judgment on the land shadowing with wings. "He" shall cut down the sprigs with pruning knives; here, "he" breaks down the wall. The "he" is just introduced into the passage because he is identified in Daniel 8 and other passages.

In Isaiah 25, we read, "For thou hast been a strength to the poor, a strength to the needy in his distress, a refuge from the storm, a shadow from the heat, when the blast of the terrible ones is as a storm against the wall" (Isa. 25:4). It was the terrible ones - the Assyrian - that attacked and destroyed the wall. The terrible ones is the terrorist king of the North, who is the Assyrian.

God declared in Ezekiel 13:10–15 that He was going to break the wall. Nevertheless, Ezekiel clearly indicates that it is the Assyrian who will break the wall. "Overflowing showers" and "stormy wind" are metaphors for the Assyrian. That is how it is continuously described in Isaiah as an overflowing storm. God says more; He says He will destroy this wall, as God said in Isaiah 31:3 "The Lord shall stretch out his hand." Here He says, "I will even rend it with a stormy wind in my fury, and there shall be an overflowing shower in mine anger, and great hailstones in my fury to consume it. So will I break down the wall that ye have daubed with untempered mortar, and bring it down to the ground" (Ezek. 13:13–14).

The daubing with untempered mortar was Israel's boast of her mighty protector, but God would destroy her wall of protection. Israel boasted here in the same manner as she did in Isaiah 28 about the security of the Roman Empire. Little did she realize that her protector was going to be destroyed. However, we need to notice one other point: Jehovah's wrath was going to be on the wall and on those who daubed it with untempered mortar - on the land shadowing with wings and on Israel. The two are again placed together, and the order is also reiterated.

There is a remarkable sequence to notice here. There is a breaking down, and afterward, there is a defiling. The wall is broken first, and then comes the defiling - the Assyrian breaks down the wall. Israel then defiles the two Muslim mosques on Mount Moriah and casts them out. The land shadowing with wings is destroyed first; then the two Muslim mosques are defiled and subsequently broken down, according to the sequence in Isaiah.

Thus, the Jews, having returned to their land, should have put their trust in Jehovah for their salvation and protection. On the contrary, they put their trust in natural strength, as symbolized by the horse, but that reliance will be detrimental to Israel. Nevertheless, Israel declares, "We will flee upon horses" (Isa. 30:16); they think they will escape by natural strength. She reiterates, "We will ride upon the swift" (Isa. 30:16). The swift is seen associated with the land shadowing with wings, which is equipped with fast-moving military machines. Nevertheless, with all this military might, they will not prevail.

We will escape, and we will be sustained, Israel thinks. In Isaiah 30:16, the enemy is the Assyrian, which God was introducing slowly. We now read, "Therefore, shall ye flee." Also: "Therefore, shall they that pursue you be swift" (Isa. 30:16). Here we discover that the Assyrian will become equal to the land shadowing with wings - both in strength and power. This increase in strength will happen when Russia strengthens the Assyrian. What will unfold in that day is that as America will cause a waning of relationship with its former allies, Russia will expand its relationship with its new allies: the Assyrian and Iran. This new shift in the relationship will have a profound effect on this world.

We are introduced to more. "One thousand shall flee at the rebuke of one; at the rebuke of five shall ye flee: till ye be left as a beacon upon the top of a mountain, and as an ensign on a hill" (Isa. 30:17). As we said before, we didn't see Egypt in conflict with Assyria in the past, except in one battle where Nebuchadnezzar intervened. We must recognize that all the present-day enemies of Israel will be part of the Assyrian in the future.

We now see the wisdom in waiting on Jehovah. "Therefore, will the Lord wait, that he may be gracious unto you, and therefore will he be exalted, that he may have mercy upon you: for the Lord is a God of judgment: blessed are all they that wait for him" (Isa. 30:18). Here Jehovah waits that He may be gracious, not to act on the law that cannot save Israel. We now read, "Therefore, will he be exalted, that he may have mercy upon you" (Isa. 30:18). It is Christ who is Jehovah and "waits" and "is exalted." Nevertheless, not Christ alone is Jehovah. The Father is Jehovah, the Son is Jehovah, and the Holy Spirit is Jehovah. Here it is Christ who is presented as Jehovah, and we read, "Blessed are all they that wait for him" (Isa. 30:18). Now we know that Jehovah is coming, so the remnant is waiting for Him. Moreover, when He comes, He is going to act in grace toward Israel.

Furthermore, between Isaiah 30:19–26, we have a series of contrasts between the day of the great slaughter and the day when the Lord binds up the breaches of His people. There is a distinction between these two days. We read, "For the people shall dwell in Zion at Jerusalem: thou shalt weep no more: he will be very gracious unto thee at the voice of thy cry; when He shall hear it, He will answer thee" (Isa. 30:19). Zion represents the place of royal grace, so Zion takes precedence over Jerusalem because God deals with His people not according to the law but according to His grace, not according to what they had done but according to the goodness of His heart. Jerusalem answers to Mount Sinai, where the law was given (Gal. 4:25). Therefore, (Isa. 30:19) speaks of the day when the Lord will bind up His people's breaches. Moreover, they are "His people;" He now owns them. It is the day when the Lord comes.

In the first part of verse 20, we read, "And though the Lord give you the bread of adversity, and the water of affliction" (Isa. 30:20), this is during the day of the great (or many) slaughter(s). In the latter part of verse 20 through verse 21, we are told, "Yet shall not thy teachers be removed into a corner any more, but thine eyes shall see thy teachers: and thine ears shall hear a word behind thee, saying, This is the way, walk ye in it, when ye turn to the right hand, and when ye turn to the left" (vv. 20–21). Israel will walk aright during the day when the Lord binds up the breaches of His people.

In verse 22, we have a solemn event - it is when Israel defiles the two Muslim mosques on the temple mount. This defiling, as we will see later, has an important place in scripture. These mosques will be defiled and destroyed after the destruction of the land shadowing with wings. It is only after the protective land will be destroyed and Israel becomes vulnerable to her enemies that she will nominally seek the protection of her God. This nominal return, coupled with other factors we will disclose later, influences her to defile and destroy the mosques and rebuild her temple. Once the land shadowing with wings is present, Israel will never rebuild her temple. She will seek Jehovah's protection only when the protection of the land shadowing with wings will be no more.

We therefore read, "Ye shall defile also the covering of thy graven images of silver, and the ornament of thy molten images of gold: thou shalt cast them away as a menstruous cloth; thou shalt say unto it, get thee hence" (Isa. 30:22). What the prophet is writing about is the destruction of the two Muslim religious buildings on the temple mount. These two buildings are the Al-Aqsa Mosque and the Dome of the Rock. These two buildings, which form the Noble Sanctuary of the Muslims, make Jerusalem the third holiest city of Islam after Mecca and Medina.

The translation by J. N. Darby gives us a better understanding of the text. We read, "And ye shall defile the silver covering of your graven images, and the gold overlaying of your molten images; thou shalt cast them away as a menstruous cloth: Out! Shalt thou say unto it" (Isa. 30:22 JND). We need to clearly see that these are the Muslim religious buildings that are destroyed here. We stated earlier that two things were destroyed in this passage: first is the wall, which we said represented the land shadowing with wings. The second is the destruction of the two Muslim mosques on the temple site.

We must now prove that the two mosques on the temple site are the same objects mentioned in this scripture. We cannot afford to speculate on matters of such importance and seriousness. Here we are told that Israel will defile two religious objects, seen together so that polluting them will be seen as one act. Second, she is seen as casting out these images from a specific place, and these images are viewed nearby, so close that we read, "Thou shalt cast them away as a menstruous cloth" and "Out! Shall thou say unto it" (Isa. 30:22 JND). In one act, Israel, acting together, will defile and then cast out two religious objects simultaneously and from the same place. The next thing we notice is that one of these two sacred objects is said to be of silver covering, and the other is said to be of gold overlaying. Israel will so act after her wall of protection is broken down. It is clearly stated that it's not the objects that are made of silver and gold but only their coverings. Moreover, one covering is said to be graven, and the other is said to be molten. If this isn't the most precise indication of the mosques on Mount Moriah, then no proof will be sufficient.

What is stated here is so accurate; it is challenging to contest the facts. What more could be said? The dome of the Al-Aqsa Mosque is made of silver - it is called the silver-domed mosque - while the Dome of the Rock Mosque is made of gold. These two mosques are just a few hundred feet apart, so they are seen together. The word for "covering," *tsipuy* in Hebrew, is used only five times in the Bible. It is used twice in Exodus and twice in Numbers concerning the tabernacle. Finally, it is used here for another religious building. Moreover, the word means to cover, to overlay, or to encase with metal. The metal that covers the building here is silver. Additionally, the word translated in the KJV for "ornament" or "overlaying" in Darby's translation is the Hebrew word *ephuddah*. This word is used only three times in the Bible: twice in Exodus and finally here. In Exodus it is used of the ephod, and it means a plating of metal. The metal plated here is gold. These words are used concerning religious objects.

The word *dome* means the covering, ceiling, or roof of a building in the form of a hemisphere. These coverings are indicated explicitly as they are stated here - one is a silver dome, and the other is a golden dome. What is even of greater significance is that the Hebrew words used to describe the images in the same verse are different. One word is for "graven," and the other is for "molten." The dome of the Al-Aqsa Mosque is of graven silver, while the roof of the Dome of the Rock Mosque is of molten gold. As usual, the word *image* speaks of representation; therefore, the Muslim religion is represented by these images. These religious objects are in Israel on her temple mount, and for some reason, not given here, Israel will defile them, then destroy them after her protector is destroyed.

We also need to see that the destruction of these mosques is going to take place in the day of the "many" slaughters, or the "great" slaughter in contrast to the day when the Lord binds up the breach of His people. In that day, when the Lord binds up the violation of His people, we read in Isaiah 31:7 what will happen regarding their idols. "For in that day every man shall cast away his idols of silver and his idols of gold, which your sinful hands have made unto you" (Isa. 31:7). We note that every man shall do this to his idol. He made those idols; he will destroy them when the Lord comes.

However, what we have in verse 22 is "Ye" - not what everyone will do but what he or she will do together. Furthermore, the word in this verse isn't "idols" but "images" - objects that represent another religion in the land of Israel, on Mount Moriah. We need to note the precise language: as a menstruous cloth (a cloth used by women in the olden days during their menstruation), something defiled and needing to be discarded. We have these two images taken as one - "a menstruous cloth" and "Out! Shall thou say unto it." The two mosques are separated by only a few hundred feet. More than that, the actions are seen as one because they are in one place and are both owned by one religion. We therefore read, "Out! Shall thou

106

say unto it." The mosques will be destroyed together; the actions will be recognized as one. The mosques here are called an "a" and an "it" because they are in one place, are of the same character, and are destroyed together.

Why is the defiling of the mosques, or Islamic religious buildings, put here? The defiling is placed here because scripture is now giving us the sequence of two most important events: the destruction of the land shadowing with wings and its correlation to the destruction of the mosques on Mount Moriah. We now know that the temple is only rebuilt after the land shadowing with wings is destroyed. Then, after the destruction of the land shadowing with wings, the Jews will first defile and then destroy the mosques and rebuild their temple. This destruction of the mosque will initiate the holy war.

When I was a young Bible student, I was told that maybe an earthquake might destroy the Dome of the Rock to allow the Jews to rebuild their temple. We knew they have to rebuild their temple, according to 2 Thessalonians 2, but we didn't know under what circumstances. Today I know Israel will destroy these mosques after the destruction of designated Egypt. Moreover, there were many earthquakes during the history of those mosques. The reality is that Israel will destroy both mosques after the destruction of the land shadowing with wings. Israel's destruction of these mosques will introduce jihad, something she won't anticipate.

The Jews will believe the answer to their many problems is the rebuilding of their temple. They will think God destroyed the land shadowing with wings because He wanted them to return to Him. They will surmise that the only way to validate their sincerity of walk with Him is to rebuild their temple and restore their worship. Consequently, they will defile the Muslim mosques, then break them down and rebuild their temple. These actions, however, will lead to grave consequences. They cannot foresee that destroying the mosques will introduce many new complications and the eventual destruction of Israel.

Moreover, as we will see later, when the temple's rebuilding doesn't solve their difficulties, they will then apostatize and fall into Antichrist's hands. Here we have the sequence of how the Jewish apostasy is realized. Israel will turn back to God nominally but will not find Him. God won't come to their deliverance at that time; thus, they will then apostatize— giving up all they believed about God.

Christendom will also apostatize after the Rapture of the church takes place. What will then be left of Christianity will be only an empty profession but no reality. What will be left will only be church goers and no born-again Christian. The Antichrist will then come and sweep the apostate Jews and professing Christians into the worst idolatry and blasphemy. It will be noted later that both the Christian apostasy and Jewish apostasy coincide; this shows that the Rapture takes place close to the tribulation. Therefore, Isaiah 30:23–24 will be fulfilled when the Lord binds up the breach of His people at His return.

However, the importance of verse 25 is universal. There is the attack on the twin towers in the USA, which people today call 9/11. Regardless of man's theories about this attack, it is God's word that gives us the reason for the attack. The attack on the towers announced that the day of the "great, or many" slaughters had come. It didn't introduce the day; it announced that it had arrived. "And there shall be upon every high mountain, and upon every high hill, rivers and streams of waters in the day of the 'great' slaughter, when the towers fall" (Isa. 30:25).

The falling of the towers, therefore, announced two momentous events. One, it informed us that the day of the multiple slaughters had arrived. Two, we are now notified that the Assyrian terrorist group, which will perform the many slaughters, was about to be unfolded. The day had come, and the power to darken the day is about to be manifested. In verse 25, we have the falling of the towers, and in verse 27, we have the coming of the Assyrian, with the bright day of the Lord's coming in between.

To understand verse 25, we need to translate the word *great*, which is translating the Hebrew word *rab* into "many." This word *rab* is translated 190 times in the KJV as "many" and only 118 times as "great." There is no need to change it from its customary meaning of "many" to "great," which is its less ordinary meaning. Once we get this right, we see that the falling of the towers announced a particular day, here called the day of the "many" or "multiple" slaughters. This day of the many slaughters is the day when the Assyrian - who reappears in the place of the ancient Assyrian Empire as a terrorist power - will inflict on the land shadowing with wings and this world, multiple slaughters on their cities and armies.

The Assyrian is the rod of Jehovah's anger, and the staff in the Assyrian's hand is Jehovah's indignation, according to Isaiah 10:5. Moreover, it is during the indignation that we will have multiple slaughters. Therefore, if we keep this word *great* in mind, it will give us the magnitude of the attack on the land shadowing with wings. However, the Bible gives us the magnitude of the attack and the frequency. More than that, "great slaughter" will provide us with a one-event scenario. At the same time, the word of God unfolds multiple simultaneous attacks. No country in this world will be spared.

Let us open the curtain a little wider, for even Christians will say that you cannot pronounce from one verse on so grave an issue, and I agree. The problem is that they are astonished at the accuracy of scripture.

Therefore, I will elaborate a little on the topic. I will do so from Daniel 8. Let us now pause and read Daniel 8:23–25. First, we read, "At the latter time of their kingdom" (Dan. 8:23 JND), as is stated by God's word, the two kingdoms must be revived. These empires are the kingdom of the king of the North and the kingdom of the king of the South. Therefore, what ISIS was trying to accomplish when that power first rose was the resurrection of these two empires. We are next given the time: "when transgressors are come to the full" (Dan. 8:23 JND). That is when Israel fully embraces the sinful lifestyles of the land shadowing with wings; the Assyrian head will come. We now read that "he shall destroy marvelously" (Dan. 8:24 JND). He will destroy spectacularly, terrorist attack after terrorist attack.

Moreover, this king is bold; he takes on the world. Alas! It must be remembered that just as we have a fierce king in the North, there is another fierce king in the South. One is the king of the North, and the other is the king of the South. Together, there are two terrorist empires bent on inflicting maximum casualties on this world in their countries and cities. Nevertheless, why is this so? This is allowed because man has embraced every form of evil God had condemned in His word, and they won't repent. Moreover, they seek to penalize those who sought to warn them.

Another question may now be asked. Why is the Assyrian not captured and destroyed? The answer is because Russia will protect him. Just as America protects Israel today, so will Russia protect the Assyrian. The Assyrian power will develop in the Syrian and Iraqi area under the protection of Russia. Therefore, to get to the Assyrian, one will need to invade Syria under Russia's control. Notice on the world scene that Russia has already gone down into Syria, which is by the Euphrates River. This isn't by chance; we will show you later that Kelly wrote over one hundred years ago that Russia will support the Assyrian and that the Assyrian will come out of Syria.

Please note that Russia hasn't gone into Syria empty handed, but it has armed itself with sophisticated weapons. Soon Russia will support the terrorist group, and the world will change forever. Soon we will see who is right: what the evolutionists say or what the word of God says. The Assyrian empire will develop under the protection of Russia in Syria. No man will prevent this manifestation.

Alas! Note that "he shall prosper and practice" (Dan. 8:24). No one can kill the Assyrian but the Lord himself. Please remember that both the power and the person are called the Assyrian. Therefore, I have to say what the scripture says. When I speak of the *he*, I have the leader in focus, when I speak of the *it*, I have the empire in mind. What this means is that the head of the Assyrian usurps all the authority of the empire. He is a complete tyrant, what he says is what the empire says, what he does is what the empire does.

Moreover, he will prosper and practice his destruction in this world. Most distinguished Bible teachers agreed that the "he" here in Daniel 8 is the head of the Assyrian. Furthermore, he is one man from the beginning to the end. He isn't of a succession as with the king of the North or the king of the South of Daniel 11. This passage in Daniel 8:23–25 presents one man and one man only—the Assyrian leader. Bin Laden was a type of this man; that is why 9/11 is placed in Isaiah 30. This man, when compared to Bin Laden, makes Bin Laden look like an altar boy. The Assyrian is the Destroyer. All the Assyrian does is destroy, as we read: "He shall destroy wonderfully" (Dan. 8:24). He will unleash terrorist attack after terrorist attack on this world; these are the many slaughters Isaiah 30:25 details. He is a Muslim because he understands dark sentences, the teachings of his religious book. The falling of the towers is placed explicitly in Isaiah 30:25, because the late Bin Laden was a type of this Destroyer, who will rain terror in this world, exceeding that of the late Bin Laden.

Moreover, in Psalms, we are confronted with even worse: the magnitude of the terrorist attacks. We read further, "O thou enemy, destructions are come to a perpetual end: and thou hast destroyed cities; their memorial is perished with them" (Ps. 9:6). The "enemy" is also a name for the Assyrian. Here he destroys cities, not just towers. Imagine that you wake up one morning, and the city you once knew is no more. It is gone forever. This situation is what is about to happen to this world, which has rejected God and restrains believers from speaking against evil. God will allow another religion to deal with man because of his rebellion. Let me comfort you, my reader; if there is no God, this will not happen. However, if there is a God, take heed. Remember that it isn't Christians who will do this, but they will be members of another religion. We cannot influence their actions; only God can bring this about.

Permit me to give a word of caution, for many will say I am just another doomsday preacher. I am not a doomsday preacher; I am a preacher of righteousness. I am explaining to you that God is about to take this world and give it to His Son, our Lord Jesus Christ, who will rule it for God's glory and blessings for mankind. Therefore, instead of the corruption and violence that characterize the world today, God will be glorified in His world, and man will be blessed. In that state of things, sin won't be rampant and normal as is displayed today, but righteousness will reign. To bring this about, God will destroy all that encapsulates the pride of man and will use the Assyrian to accomplish His task; then when He is finished using him, He will destroy the Assyrian and rule in righteousness.

Therefore, as a result of those terrorist attacks, mostly directed against "the mighty, or the mighty ones" - the land shadowing with wings - those attacks will provoke similar responses as with the Bin Laden attack on the World Trade Center. Therefore, "the mighty" will then invade the kingdom of the Assyrian, located by the Euphrates River to fight against it, but the Assyrian will destroy "the mighty." We saw a similar picture with Bin Laden after the attack on the World Trade Center. The land shadowing with wings will go to fight the Destroyer, as the USA went to battle against Bin Laden, but unfortunately, the result this time will be different. Therefore, it is because of these similarities that the falling of the towers is placed in Isaiah 30.

Furthermore, after the destruction of "the mighty," this bold king, the Assyrian's chief, will then destroy the people of the saints or "the holy." "The holy" is Israel. The Assyrian leader cannot destroy the holy unless he destroys the protector first. The Assyrian will destroy "the mighty" before the tribulation. He will then destroy "the holy" during the tribulation. Finally, he will stand up against the Prince of princes after the tribulation. The Prince of princes is the Lord Jesus Christ. As a result, these events will take place just before the Lord comes, because it is the coming of Christ that puts an end to the adventure of the Assyrian.

Interestingly, once the land shadowing with wings is destroyed, the man who destroys it will still be alive when Christ comes. Therefore, these scenes will take place just before the Lord comes and establish His kingdom. Once this man is manifested, Christ will come during his life. Consequently, if as Christan teachers we cannot differentiate between the Antichrist and the Roman Prince, we will be completely lost when we speak of the Assyrian and the land shadowing with wings. However, the scripture declares the activities of four horsemen; not one or two; hence, we must seek to understand these revealed truths.

Accordingly, as King of kings, He reigns, but as Prince of princes, He will soon reign. It is when the Lord Jesus comes a second time that He will destroy the Assyrian before He reigns as King of kings and Lord of lords. We thus observe that these events are in the future, and they are just before the Lord comes. There is a particular order in scripture.

However, before we return to Isaiah 30, let us note with great care that it is the "he" that will destroy "the mighty" and "the holy"; this is the same "he" of Isaiah 18 and Isaiah 30, the head of the Assyrian. It isn't "the holy" that is first destroyed but "the mighty" and then "the holy." This order shows that it isn't the Roman Empire that is here destroyed. Here, "the mighty" is destroyed before "the holy;" while with the Roman Empire, "the holy" is destroyed before the Lord destroys the Roman Empire.

We need to forge a clear understanding of Isaiah 30:25, so we will now explain the first part of the verse. "And there shall be upon every high mountain, and upon every high hill, rivers and streams of waters in the day of the great slaughter, when the towers fall" (Isa. 30:25).

Only scripture can interpret scripture. We cannot interject our views into scripture. Every symbol presented in God's word must be interpreted by the use of that symbol in scripture. We cannot bring our ideas into scripture. In Psalm 48, we read, "Great is the Lord and greatly to be praised in the city of our God, in the mountain of his holiness" (Ps. 48:1). Here the city is associated with the mountain. Also, in Daniel 9, we read, "O Lord, according to all thy righteousness, I beseech thee, let thine anger and thy fury be turned away from thy city Jerusalem, thy holy mountain: because for our sins, and for the iniquities of our fathers" (Dan. 9:16). Here the same thing that is said about the city is said of the mountain. The city is seen as the mountain. In Joel, we read, "Blow ye the trumpet in Zion, and sound an alarm in my holy mountain: let all the inhabitants of the land tremble: for the day of the Lord cometh, for it is nigh at hand" (2:1). Yes! The same we read in Joel 3: "So shall ye know that I am the Lord your God dwelling in Zion, my holy mountain: then shall Jerusalem be holy, and there shall no strangers pass through her any more" (v. 17).

In Isaiah 2:2–3, we notice again that the word *mountain* is identified with the word *city*. Yet it must be appreciated that a "mountain" is not only seen as "a city" in the word of God, but the context determines the meaning. In this latter passage, we find the word *hills*. "The mountain of the Lord's house shall be established in the top of the mountains, and shall be exalted above the hills" (Isa. 2:2). Here hills are minor cities, so mountains are more famous cities. What we now have communicated to us are that popular cities, less popular cities, notable cities, and less favorite cities will become the objects of terrorist attacks.

The final part of verse 25, which we need to grasp is, "rivers and streams of water." These metaphors we said previously represent the attack of the Assyrian. Let us now establish that imagery. In Isaiah 18, we read, "Whose land the rivers have spoiled" (Isa. 18:2). Here the rivers are said to have spoiled the land of Israel. The rivers attacked and destroyed Israel. Again, in Isaiah 18, we read the same thing: "In that time shall the present be brought unto the Lord of hosts of a people scattered and peeled, and from a people terrible from their beginning hitherto; a nation meted out and trodden under foot, whose land the rivers have spoiled" (Isa. 18:7). Here they are meted out and trodden under foot, spoiled by the rivers. The rivers here represent Egypt, Babylon, and Assyria.

Finally, in Isaiah 8:6–8, "the waters of the river, strong and many" (v 7) are said to be the king of Assyria, who is the Assyrian leader. God will bring him against Israel. With strong attacks and many attacks, he will confront Israel and the whole world. Some countries will suffer rivers some will suffer streams but all will be inundated with water. I must interject here to show that the word translated "many" in this verse (Isa. 8:7) is the same word translated "great" in Isaiah 30:25. There was no need to change it from "many" to "great" in the Isaiah 30 passage.

Having gone through every segment of Isaiah 30:25, let me now give the meaning of the verse. There shall be, "not might be," in every major city and every lesser-known city of this world many simultaneous terrorist attacks in the day of the many slaughters when the towers fall. Some cities will have rivers, while others will have streams, but all will come under terrorist attacks. The slaughters will be the results of the attacks. This verse shows how this day will unfold with many terrorist attacks all over the world. This description is no delusion. This destruction is no game. The scripture says, man will seek death but death will flee from them. The reality is, if there is a God, we cannot live in sin without severe consequences. God destroyed the world with water, then He destroyed Sodom and Gomorrah with fire and in our day, he will use terrorism to chastise this world. Who can tell Him He cannot do it?

God doesn't need to prove that He exists. God doesn't need to ask for permission to do what He intends to do. He doesn't need to ask for my approval either. God will destroy most of humanity in hell forever, not because He wants to but because of man's unbelief. If we reject His Son, God will also reject us. Therefore, it isn't by chance that we have terrorism today; it is all by design. Nevertheless, the proud ones will say, "What kind of God is this?" Somehow, they feel that they can judge God. Somehow, they believe they must be allowed to do all the wickedness of their hearts and be blessed. Nevertheless, others will humble themselves and beseech God for mercy.

In His word, God said He destroyed the world with a flood; men say today that it didn't happen. God said He destroyed Sodom and Gomorrah with fire; again, men say that event didn't occur. Instead, men say, "Do not believe the Bible. Believe in the teachings of evolution." What do you think God will do? I plead with my fellow men to repent, for disaster is ahead. The day is coming when the Lord will unleash the Assyrian; it will be worse than the flood. That day will be worse than the destruction of Sodom and Gomorrah. In Daniel 12, we read, "And there shall be a time of trouble, such as never was since there was a nation even to that same time" (v. 1). In Matthew 24, we read similar words: "For then shall be great tribulation, such as was not since the beginning of the world to this time, no, nor ever shall be. And except those days should be shortened, there should no flesh be saved" (vv. 21–22). My friends run to Christ for rescue.

Today it is all about political correctness. I desire to offend no one; however, I want all to know that God respects no man. He will act, and we cannot stop Him. He gave His Son to save us from a lost eternity; if we reject His Son, we will be lost forever. If we disobey God's word and replace it with our own thoughts, then we must be prepared for the consequences, since "God is not a man, that he should lie; neither the son of man, that he should repent" (Num. 23:19). The coming day is all about God and what He has determined. Nothing will change that perspective. We need to believe and receive Christ as Savior and Lord before it is too late. I cannot stop you from doing what you want to do; neither can I force you. I cannot make you believe what you don't wish to consider; neither do you need to listen to me. However, remember that nothing changes the word of God. If all that was prophesied has come to pass, the other predictions will also be fulfilled. This reality is indisputable.

Nevertheless, just as was predicted, the day of the many slaughters has come. However, for the comfort of the saints, if we see the Destroyer - the head of the Assyrian - then we know that during his lifetime, we shall be raptured to heaven; God will save us from the impending disaster. This fact will be proven shortly.

We now have a beautiful contrast in verse 26. We read, "Moreover the light of the moon shall be as the light of the sun, and the light of the sun shall be sevenfold, as the light of seven days, in the day that the Lord bindeth up the breach of his people, and healeth the stroke of their wound" (Isa. 30:26). This day is when Christ returns; it is contrasted with the day of the many slaughters. The day of the many slaughters is before He arrives, while the day when He binds up the breach of His people is after He comes. We need to note carefully that when Christ comes, He will bind up the breach of His people and heal the stroke of their wound. The breach and the stroke are inflicted by the Assyrian. I hope you will be there to enjoy God's kingdom for a thousand years and the new heaven and the new earth for eternity. I surely will be there.

CHAPTER 6

THE DANGEROUS POWER THAT SHALL ARISE

I n chapter 6, we will deviate slightly to notice in an elementary way the power that will confront the land shadowing with wings and the world. We will then resume our study of the land shadowing with wings, as seen under Egypt's picture, to chronicle its destruction. We aren't moving from Isaiah 30–31, but we will deal with the Assyrian separately, who is uniquely introduced in these chapters.

We have been instructed that a dangerous power shall arise called the Assyrian. This power will be the worst nightmare this world will ever experience. It will be a power that shall rise from the northeast of Israel. This power will rise while Israel is being protected, but after the towers fall, it will cause real chaos in this world. We will now get a glimpse of this power. This topic is an eight on my scale of difficulty. Therefore, to obtain the foretaste, we will return to the passage in Isaiah 30, but we will focus our attention on verse 27.

This passage says, not that the Lord comes, but that the name of the Lord comes. What we have is a religious group making war in the name of religion. This power rises after an incident the Bible calls the falling of the towers in Isaiah 30. In verse 25, we have the incident called the falling of the towers, and in verse 27, we have the arrival of the Assyrian, with the blessed day of the Lord's coming between. Therefore, before the Lord gives us the horror of the day of the Assyrian, He gives us the blessings of His day. The Assyrian will arrive just after the falling of the towers. First, we need to observe that the Assyrian, according to man's definition, is a terrorist kingdom. Second, it will conquer, occupy, and rename the territories through which the Euphrates River passes. That is, the names men have given to these countries along the Euphrates River will be changed. This area will then be called "Assyria." Third, the Assyrian will sift the nations with the sieve of destruction; it is going to inflict vicious terrorist attacks on the nations. Fourth, and most importantly, the Assyrian also represents a religious body, but it is a religion that borrows parts from the Jewish faith. The prophets of the Bible are said to be their prophets. They claim the God of the Bible to be their God. Hence, the Assyrian God is the God of the prophets.

The Assyrian is such a central part of the puzzle in the last days that we need to obtain a fuller picture of the scope of its activities. We must understand the Assyrian; if not, we will be deficient in our appreciation of prophecy. Let me now introduce Isaiah 10, where we will study the Assyrian. Therefore, we will pause to read Isaiah 10:3–33.

We have presented in Isaiah 10 that God will bring the Assyrian against Israel to accomplish His righteous indignation. The destruction of Israel here is the destruction of "the holy" of Daniel 8. After the task given to the Assyrian is performed, God will then destroy the Assyrian. On the other hand, what we have in Isaiah 30:27–33 is how God will bring the same Assyrian against the nations, but in this particular instance, it won't be against Israel but against the land shadowing with wings, to destroy the mighty. At the same time, He lets us know that He alone can, and will, finally destroy the Assyrian. At first, God will use the Assyrian to accomplish His purposes; then, after He is finished, He will crush the Assyrian.

Nevertheless, God gives us a time when the Assyrian is going to be introduced. He declares, "And what will ye do in the day of visitation, and in the desolation which shall come from far? To whom will ye flee for help? And where will ye leave your glory? Without me they shall bow down under the prisoners, and they shall fall under the slain. For all this his anger is not turned away, but his hand is stretched out still" (Isa. 10:3–4).

The Romans inflicted the destruction that was to come from afar. Nevertheless, that destruction didn't end God's anger. We read, "For all this his anger is not turned away, but his hand is stretched out still" (Isa. 10:4). Just think about what the Romans did to the Jews, yet that did not end God's anger. The destruction that ends His anger is the destruction the Assyrian will execute. Therefore, the Assyrian devastation will be executed after the conquest by the Roman Empire. More so, the Assyrian destruction will be worse than the destruction by the Romans, which could not end His anger. The question is also asked: "And where will ye leave your glory?" (Isa. 10:3). Israel's glory was the Messiah; they had left Him, as far as they were concerned, in the tomb. They had crucified Him. Nevertheless, without Him they would only get disaster. We read, "Without me they shall bow down under the prisoners and they shall fall under the slain" (Isa. 10:4). As a result, we see the time of the coming of the Assyrian: after the death of Christ and after the destruction the Romans inflicted.

God now introduces the Assyrian in a passage that has to do with Egypt. Why is the Assyrian suddenly introduced in that passage? To the casual reader, it looks out of place and incomprehensible. Yet to the man taught of God, it is the most necessary introduction of the Assyrian. Understanding this lies in the fact that in the days of Isaiah, God presented a contemporary power to the Assyrian to represent a future power that will confront the future Assyrian in the last days. For this, therefore, to be understood, God directed the events related to ancient Egypt and Assyria in such a way that there was no recorded attack by Assyria on Egypt in the past.

There was one confrontation between Egypt and Assyria, but in that confrontation, Egypt attacked Assyria and not the reverse. Moreover, when that confrontation took place, Nebuchadnezzar intervened in the war and destroyed Pharaoh. That intervention was necessary to prevent any results from that war between Egypt and Assyria, and to become a type of the future war so we may not err in the comprehension of Egypt and the future Assyrian.

It is necessary to see that Egypt in Isaiah 30 is designated Egypt, which like geographic Egypt in the days of Nebuchadnezzar, will attack Assyria by the Euphrates River. Still, Russia, like Nebuchadnezzar, will help destroy Egypt. Take note that the Lord then said that He alone was going to crush the Assyrian. This statement lets us know that the land shadowing with wings wasn't going to accomplish that feat. Therefore, by God declaring that He would destroy the Assyrian, He lets us know that the land shadowing with wings was going to lose the war and be utterly destroyed.

A similar situation repeats itself regarding Babylon in Isaiah 14. There again we see the Assyrian introduced without explanation. Why? Because Babylon, the Roman Empire, would be attacked by the Assyrian, since it, like the land shadowing with wings, would also endeavor to protect Israel. In Isaiah 14, the Roman Empire is identified under the name of Babylon, another contemporary power to the Assyrian. Please note that I'm not the only one saying that Babylon in Isaiah 13–14 has its future component in the Roman Empire; both Darby and Kelly said the same over one hundred years ago, and I will quote them in the appropriate place. This isn't the religious Babylon of Revelation 17 we are talking about but political Babylon.

Again, there was no recorded war between Assyria and Babylon; that was done to prevent confusion, since there would be a future war between the future Assyrian and future Babylon. Isaiah 14:25 also stated that the Lord will destroy the Assyrian. It says it that way because Babylon, the future Roman Empire, will lose the fight and run. This book, called the Bible, is beyond human authorship. The Bible is the word of God.

Someone could now ask, "Why only concerning these two powers, Egypt and Babylon, was the Assyrian introduced without explanation?" The answer is because these two powers represent the two protectors of the Jews in the last days, but they are given names contemporary to the Assyrian of old. Consequently, the future Assyrian will attack them. One will be destroyed, and the other will break the treaty to prevent its destruction.

In Isaiah 30, the Assyrian attacks Egypt. Still, God purposefully refrains from using the name Egypt but speaks in such a way to include the attacks on the other nations. However, in Isaiah 10:24, we read that the Assyrian will lift up its staff against Israel after the manner of Egypt.

This smiting couldn't be when the Assyrian attacks geographic Egypt in the future, because the Assyrian will attack Egypt after it attacks Israel, the inverse of what is stated in Isaiah 10:24. In the future, geographic Egypt will be attacked after the attack on Israel. If we didn't know about designated Egypt, the land shadowing with wings, we would need to interpret this verse in this way: as Egypt smote Israel, so will the Assyrian. This interpretation would have to mean that this smiting took place in the days of Moses. Nevertheless, this isn't what is declared.

Therefore, it's essential to note that the Assyrian of the future will defeat both geographic Egypt and designated Egypt. Geographic Egypt will be destroyed, according to Isaiah 20 and Daniel 8, and designated Egypt will be destroyed according to Jeremiah 46 and Isaiah 30–31. However, our focus now is on designated Egypt, not geographic Egypt.

There is an absolute necessity that we examine Isaiah 30 a little closer. "And his breath, as an overflowing stream, shall reach to the midst of the neck, to sift the nations with the sieve of vanity: and there shall be a bridle in the jaws of the people, causing them to err" (v. 28).

The Assyrian will sift the nations with the sieve of destruction - not one nation but many. Note that the destruction is going to be against the nations, not merely Israel. However, we are told again that there will be a bridle in the people's jaws, causing them to go astray. If it was Jehovah who came when we read, "Behold, the name of the Lord cometh from far, burning with his anger, and the burden thereof is heavy: his lips are full of indignation" (Isa. 30:27), then the erring that engulfed the nations wasn't possible, because when Jehovah comes, the people shall see clearly. The coming here is of the Assyrian making war in the name of religion to rid the world of its evil practices.

We need to translate the word *people* into its plural form *peoples*, as stated in the J. N. Darby's translation, since so it is in the original Hebrew. When this word is in the singular, it means Israel; it means the nations when in the plural. Here in this passage, it means the nations. We therefore read, "There shall be a bridle in the jaws of the peoples, causing them to err" (Isa. 30:28). The destruction of the land shadowing with wings will cause the Gentile religious world to err. This erring will produce chaos in the world.

We need to grasp what scripture is unveiling. The Assyrian, the religious terrorist power, will inflict a devastating defeat on the land shadowing with wings while calling on its god, Allah. Nevertheless, it will be God who will cause this rout, using the power of the Assyrian backed by the Russians. When this supposedly smaller power, calling on Allah's name, defeats this acclaimed superpower, the religious world will err. The world will now believe that the Assyrian's god is the real God, and the Assyrian will rise and attack and destroy the land shadowing with wings in its homeland. This act will accomplish the twofold destruction of Isaiah 18:5. This erring of the Assyrian will also cause the increase of the Assyrian armed forces many times over, for people from all nations will now join in. The Muslim world will now believe for sure that their god is the right God and that their teachings of the Koran are the correct teachings. This belief will then create a severe crisis in the world.

The same will happen regarding the king of the South. In Isaiah 19, we read, "The Lord hath mingled a perverse spirit in the midst thereof: and they have caused Egypt to err in every work thereof, as a drunken man staggereth in his vomit" (Isa. 19:14). The king of the South will err; so also, the king of the North. They will both think that their religion is right because they embrace the same religion. However, they both will err, as stated by God's word, and only so it will happen. The world will suffer because of this erring.

This erring will also be true of the Antichrist, who will introduce his own religious teachings. We read, "And for this reason God sends them a working of error that they should believe what is false, that all might be judged who have not believed the truth, but have found pleasure in unrighteousness" (2 Thess. 2:11 JND). After the Rapture, what is false will be on display. We now clearly see that the erring the scripture is speaking about is religious erring. The whole world will err.

Finally, the last three verses of Isaiah 30 declare that the Assyrian will be destroyed through the voice of the Lord. This wasn't the case with the Assyrian of the past, which was destroyed by an angel, a type of Christ. The historical Assyrian was destroyed by an angel, whereas in the future encounter, the Lord Jesus Christ's coming in glory will destroy the

Assyrian. Furthermore, we are told that Tophet, or the place of burning, is ordained of old, "for the king also it is prepared." We need to have the word *also* in this verse as in Darby's translation - for the king, "also." The Bible is teaching that Tophet was prepared for "the head of the Assyrian" and for "the king," who is the Antichrist. When the Assyrian of the future is destroyed, he will be cast into hell with the Antichrist. Nothing of this sort ever happened in the past. Therefore, this destruction also proves that the passage addresses future events when the Lord will come and cast both the Antichrist and the Assyrian head into the lake of fire.

In Revelation 20, we read, "And the Beast was taken, and with him the false prophet that wrought miracles before him, with which he deceived them that had received the mark of the Beast, and them that worshipped his image. These both were cast alive into a lake of fire burning with brimstone" (Rev. 19:20).

The Beast is the head of the future Roman Empire, and the False Prophet is the Antichrist. In Revelation 20, these two will be cast alive into the lake of fire. However, in Isaiah 30, we notice that both the Assyrian head and the Antichrist will be cast into the lake of fire. Therefore, three persons will be cast alive into the lake of fire together: the Assyrian leader, called the "Destroyer"; the Roman head, called the "Beast"; and the Jewish head, called the "Antichrist." These three men will be the worst of humankind the world will ever know. When they appear on the scene, no man will kill them; only the Lord Jesus Christ will destroy them. Only God can help those who will be present on earth when those men will be revealed, and they will appear very soon.

CHAPTER 7

DESIGNATED EGYPT: THE DESTRUCTION

The destruction of the land shadowing with wings is seen under two names: "Egypt" and the "mighty." Here we will begin with Egypt. This topic is again a ten on my scale. This matter of the "land shadowing with wings" and its destruction, seen under Egypt's name, is more meat than milk. This complication is evident because we know of the Egypt of the past. However, in the future, we will have two contemporary powers called "Egypt"; these are geographic Egypt, the Egypt of the past; and designated Egypt, the land shadowing with wings. Therefore, the destruction of designated Egypt is the destruction of the country shadowing with wings.

According to Isaiah 18:5, a "he" was going to inflict two-part destruction on the land shadowing with wings; this destruction will cause Israel to be exposed again to the ravages of the nations. In Isaiah 31:1–9, we are given the reasons God will cause the land of protection to be destroyed with Israel. We are taught that to leave God to trust in human strength was an insult to God. This is the behavior Israel is now displaying. God, therefore, pronounces woe on her. Israel was trusting in horses, which represented human power. She was confiding in chariots, which meant military power. She abandoned God to believe in Egypt's strength and military power. The horses were many, representing many branches of institutional power. The chariots were many, representing many branches of military power. The country was great, and the army was powerful.

These are the factors that cause many to think the destruction of this country isn't possible. We say the country is a superpower. Israel believed the land shadowing with wings was invincible; consequently, they won't look to the Lord; neither will they seek His face. God now tells Israel that if Egypt is wise, He also is wise. God says that He will bring evil and will not change His mind. We are next told that God Himself is going to rise against the house of evildoers and the help of the workers of iniquity. If Christ is going to rise against these two powers, can we say they will not be destroyed? That is why we read in Daniel 8 that He shall destroy "the mighty and the holy," the same two powers presented here in Isaiah 31.

The "house of evildoers" is presented as Israel. The "help of the workers of iniquity" is identified as the land shadowing with wings. Note carefully, it is when these countries become really wicked that God will act. Presently, God is watching the development. Man thinks only of money, he does not realize that his relationship with a holy God is a moral one. If he becomes wicked God will destroy him. God Himself will rise against Israel and her protector. He isn't going to leave this destruction to someone else. We need to note the time. The time is when Israel becomes "the house of evildoers," when she will deteriorate to this moral state. It is the same time and same moral condition as Daniel 8: "when the transgressors are come to the full" (Dan. 8:23). It is Israel's association with the land shadowing with wings that will bring her to this evil state. Israel will now be in her worst moral condition; this is what the association of God's people with the world brings. Instead of being the house of Israel, she will deteriorate to the house of evildoers. Instead of being the house of God, she will decline into the house of evildoers.

Meanwhile, Egypt will also deteriorate morally. Instead of being the help of Egypt, it will become the help of "the worker of iniquity." Egypt will be the worker of all kinds of evil. It is evident that at the beginning of this relationship between these two powers, all this evil wasn't present. However, over time evil will ripen, and God will be ready to judge.

We need to reemphasize what God said. "The Egyptians are men, and not God, and their horses flesh, and not spirit; and Jehovah shall stretch forth his hand, and he that helpeth shall stumble, and he that is helped shall fall, and they all shall perish together" (Isa. 31:3 JND).

How ironic that when Egypt was ripe for judgment, men began to regard Egypt as a superpower. God had to remind Israel that the Egyptians were men and not God. God knew this power was going to become mighty; as a matter of fact, it was so established by His determined counsel. God made Egypt great, but he began to regard himself as God; a dangerous assumption. God will show that designated Egypt is not God. What a confrontation.

However, in Israel's eyes, Egypt was so strong that she was mistaking this power for God. It's the same mistake the nations of the world are making today. Men see this land as God when they designated it a superpower - above all powers. If it is above all powers, then it is God, but God says Egypt it not God. It is this designation of superpower that God is addressing. This nation's strength showed that it couldn't have been geographic Egypt before the eyes of the prophet. This evaluation is evident because when geographic Egypt returned from the Babylonian captivity, it would be a base kingdom; it was never going to rise above the nations. It was never going to be so strong as to ever be regarded as God - superpower.

Israel would have to learn the hard way that designated Egypt was not God; they were misguided in their judgment. Egypt's power was only human. God now tells them how He will accomplish this destruction. "The Lord shall stretch out his hand," [God says] "and he who helpeth shall stumble and he that is helped shall fall, and they all shall perish together" (Isa. 31:3 JND).

Here we find the secret of the destruction of designated Egypt and Israel. God was going to intervene directly in the war, to accomplish this destruction. This country was so mighty that God had to intervene himself for its destruction. There are three things God said He will do. 1) He will bring evil and not call back His words. 2) He will arise against the house of the evildoers and against the help of them who work iniquity. 3) He will stretch out His hand, and he who helped was going to stumble, and he who was helped would fall, and they both would perish together.

If God said He would do these things and Egypt and Israel's destruction was assured, how can we say that this won't happen? If God cannot destroy designated Egypt, how will He raise the dead? Today God has allowed a little coronavirus to warn mankind about the impending disaster. This has brought terror to mankind. I can assure you that God will accomplish His word. The destruction of Egypt was sure. This destruction will prove there is a God and that He has acted in judgment. He is going to stretch out His hand on designated Egypt, as He did to geographic Egypt in Exodus when He destroyed Egypt with Pharaoh. In that incident, all knew that God had intervened on behalf of Israel in Egypt's destruction.

However, here in Isaiah 31, it is different. This isn't God acting for Israel against Egypt but God acting against both Egypt and Israel, as if He acted for the Assyrian. This action of God is what will cause the nations to err. The nations will think it is the God of the Muslims who has acted against designated Egypt and Israel. When God stretches out His hand this time, designated Egypt will stumble, Israel will fall, and they are both going to perish together. It is like a horse and its rider; the horse stumbles, and the rider falls. Egypt carries Israel, Egypt will stumble, and Israel will fall.

Please note the order of this event, for it has never happened so in history. Egypt never carried Israel in the past. Moreover, it never transpired in that manner, in that Egypt stumbled first, then Israel fell; neither did they perish together, especially against the Assyrian. Examine the Babylonian captivity; for instance, Egypt was taken into captivity thirty years after Israel. Egypt didn't stumble first; neither did Egypt and Israel go into captivity together. This is how God ordered the events of the past to prevent confusion in the future.

Moreover, we need to note that "perish together" has the sense that both of them will perish at the same time. In the war by the Euphrates River, these two powers will go down together to fight against the Assyrian; thus, they will stumble and fall and perish together. The land shadowing with wings will cause a rift between itself and its allies through its foreign policies. It will then wage war with Israel, against the Assyrian, and both of them will perish in that war.

In Daniel 8, the emphasis isn't on the war by the Euphrates River but on the attacks on the homelands of Egypt and Israel. Daniel clarifies that it is the spectacular attacks of the Assyrian in foreign countries that are presented in chapter 8. There we see that the Assyrian head shall destroy spectacularly, and then he shall destroy "the mighty" and then "the holy." The mighty and the holy are tied together. The mighty is going to be destroyed first. In the past, Egypt was never destroyed first, neither by the Assyrian nor by the Babylonians. Therefore, what is presented here isn't history; it is the future, and it will have its climax just before Christ returns, because it is the coming of Christ that will destroy the Assyrian. Neither is this the future geographic Egypt since we saw geographic Egypt's history in Isaiah 19–20, and it tells a different story.

It now needs to be emphasized that concerning the war by the Euphrates River, the expressions are "stumble," "fall," and "perish together." These words express the destruction of the armies of designated Egypt and Israel. However, we must remember that we are dealing with two-part destruction of both the land shadowing with wings and Israel.

Therefore, in Daniel 8, when the Assyrian's head shall destroy the mighty and the holy, that destruction is against their countries, not merely against the armies. The armies perish together in the war; this is the first-part destruction. The countries are destroyed one after the other; this is in the second-part destruction. These two acts complete the two-part destruction of the land shadowing with wings and Israel. Israel will suffer the same fate as the land shadowing with wings, which she follows. The only difference is that Israel will be delivered during the second-part destruction.

In Isaiah 31, designated Egypt and Israel will attack the Assyrian by the Euphrates River, while in Daniel 8, it is the Assyrian who will attack both designated Egypt and Israel in their homelands. The land shadowing with wings will be destroyed first before the tribulation, while Israel will be destroyed after, during the tribulation. To accomplish this destruction, the attack on Israel's homeland will not happen until after the middle of the seventieth week of Daniel's prophecy. The Assyrian will destroy designated Egypt first and then Israel, while their armies will perish together by the Euphrates River.

We are now confronted with a mystery again. Why does God introduce the Assyrian in this chapter as He did in the previous one? Why is the Assyrian here again? The Assyrian is here in Isaiah 31:4–8 because the

Assyrian will accomplish Egypt's destruction in the last days. Christ will then appear and destroy the Assyrian. The Lord enlightens us that He will have to come down and fight for Mount Zion, because Egypt is going to help in vain (Isa. 30:7). Instead of helping, Egypt will need help, because it will be defeated.

Subsequently, in our next passage, God will call Egypt by another name, "the mighty," and link this new name to Egypt. God will then show the future battle and how Egypt will stumble and fall. When God connects "the mighty" to Egypt and we see that Egypt is "the mighty," then we will comprehend Daniel 8, where the Assyrian head destroys "the mighty" and "the holy" of that scripture. Again, we will see that the "he" in Isaiah 18:5 is the head of the Assyrian.

We are now further told, "As birds flying, so will the Lord of hosts defend Jerusalem; also defending he will deliver it; and passing over he will preserve it" (Isa. 31:5). We have the Lord fighting, defending, delivering, and preserving Jerusalem against the Assyrian. Here the Lord will have to do what Egypt couldn't do. Egypt talked much but was unable to perform; Christ alone can save.

In Isaiah 31:6–7, God tells Israel to turn now because in the future their idols will be useless for deliverance. "In that day" is the day when Christ comes. "Then shall the Assyrian fall with the sword, not of a mighty man; and the sword, not of a mean man, shall devour him: but he shall flee from the sword" (Isa. 31:8). He says, "Then" - that is, when the Lord comes - "then" shall the Assyrian fall. "With the sword" - it is the Lord's word that is the sword, which tells us that the Lord will be present. The Lord will come at that moment, not to rapture the saints but with the saints to destroy Israel's enemies and establish His kingdom.

Please note how the Lord, when speaking of the Assyrian, gives a beautiful contrast. He says the Assyrian will fall "with the sword, not of a mighty man" (Isa. 31:8). The mighty man is the land shadowing with wings, but it couldn't accomplish the destruction. The Lord will do what "the mighty man" couldn't do. Only the Lord is going to defeat the Assyrian. In the expression "and the sword, not of a mean man" (Isa. 31:8), the mean man is the Roman Prince; he runs and leaves the battle to Israel alone. The Roman leader is the mean man, in that he isn't willing to pay a high price for Israel's deliverance. Here the "he" is the remnant of the Assyrian army, which the Lord allows to escape; he shall flee from the sword. The Lord will destroy the Assyrian army, and a terrified remnant will be allowed to escape. Moreover, to show that this passage is in the last days, the moment the Assyrian is destroyed, the Lord will reign.

Therefore, in Isaiah 32:1–4 we read of the reigning of Christ. The Lord Jesus will then come and reign as King of kings and Lord of lords. The kingdom will then be established for a thousand years. The Lord will be the hiding place from the wind, the covert (shelter) from the tempest. The wind represents the Assyrian. The tempest prefigures the Assyrian. The Lord Jesus Christ will be the shadow of a great rock. He will be the protection of Israel. What the land shadowing with wings couldn't do, the Lord Jesus Christ will do. Finally, instead of the river of judgment, He will be a river of comfort and provision.

CHAPTER 8

THE MIGHTY: THE POWERFUL USA CHALLENGED

This chapter highlights how the powerful country called the "land shadowing with wings" will be challenged by another power, which will rise from Israel's northeast. We will identify the place where this battle will take place. We will also explain what will happen during this confrontation. Now, let us seek to understand this confrontation. The level of difficulty of this topic is ten out of ten. We will need to meditate on the scriptures that will be unfolded.

In Isaiah 30–31, we studied the land shadowing with wings under the name of Egypt. We saw Israel trusting in that land. We observed that Israel was investing heavily in that land, but God pronounced a woe on Israel. Nevertheless, Israel didn't hear and didn't care. God told us further that the towers were going to fall in that land. That incident was fulfilled. He said that their wall of protection will be broken down. That event will soon be fulfilled. He then lets us know that after the wall is broken, Israel will break down the two Muslim mosques on the temple site. God's word then informed us that that action by Israel was going to introduce jihad which they did not anticipate.

We also learned that Egypt will stumble, and Israel will fall. We were further told that designated Egypt will perish, but we weren't told who will be the author of that destruction. We discovered further that a new name was given to the land shadowing with wings. The new name was "the mighty." However, at the same time, while it will be called "the mighty," it will be destroyed. God will intervene in the war and show that He alone is "the mighty."

Therefore, we will now pause to read Jeremiah 46, for it is here that we will find the two-part destruction of the land shadowing with wings. We saw in Isaiah 30–31 that the land shadowing with wings of Isaiah 18 was presented as Egypt. We are now going to see in Jeremiah 46 that the land shadowing with wings, which we identified as Egypt, is also presented under another name - "the mighty." I will not fool you; it is baffling, but these complex scriptures are what make us assured that this book is the word of God. A man could never have written such a book. This Bible is God's word. Once we understand that the land shadowing with wings is seen as "the mighty," then all the difficult scriptures will be unlocked. We will then be able to appreciate Daniel 8. Nevertheless, as we saw in the previous chapters when we discussed Egypt, we can understand the subject once we are guided. We should note that until now I haven't given you what might happen: what I think, what I feel, what I suggest. I have given you only the unadulterated word of God. I now seek to continue in that same channel.

We must emphasize that with many Old Testament prophets, God's word blends the past with the future. Jeremiah 46 is no exception to this rule; it is a specific example of the rule. A past war with Nebuchadnezzar is used here as a type of a more significant war that will occur in the future. More than that, we have the reason the word of God merges two wars together: one outside the land and the other within the land of Egypt. These two wars are combined to present Egypt's twofold destruction: once by Nebuchadnezzar and then the other by the future Assyrian.

In Jeremiah 46:1–28, we have the two-fold destruction of Egypt by Nebuchadnezzar, which was used as a type of the future two-fold destruction of the land shadowing with wings, as mentioned in Isaiah 18. If we meditate on these matters, we will notice how the writer moves from the past war with Nebuchadnezzar to the future Assyrian conflict. God didn't highlight a war between the ancient Egypt and Assyria as the type of the future war between designated Egypt and Assyria. It would have confused the reader. We would have struggled to differentiate between the past war and the future one. Therefore, God used a war between Nebuchadnezzar and Egypt as the type. This is now easier to grasp.

We learn in Isaiah 18 that Israel will return to the land of Palestine and become a nation again. We also understand that God will sit back and observe for a while, as the land shadowing with wings embraces Israel politically, provides Israel's security, and transfers its immorality to Israel. That protective land will do all it can for Israel. For a time, everything will look hopeful and flourishing as this powerful land protects Israel. Israel is upheld financially and strengthened, but she is also becoming immoral because of her connection with this protective land. Men do not think much about morality, they think only about money; however, our relationship with God is a moral one.

Nevertheless, as the relationship between the land shadowing with wings and Israel develops, an enemy will appear, as if out of the blues, and will destroy the land shadowing with wings. This enemy wasn't there before; he wasn't part of the regular nations. This foe just seems to come up, as if from nowhere, and will shower the world with terror. We observed in Isaiah 30 that it is after the falling of the towers that this power will appear. At first, the power won't be strong but relatively weak. Nevertheless, the relationship between the West and Russia will deteriorate to such a point that Russia will find in the Assyrian an ally and will strengthen it. This terrorist power will then become strong and menacing.

We need to grasp that though the Assyrian will be a religious terrorist power, America's enemy will become Russia's friend. This unlikely association will develop because the West's relationship with Russia is going to deteriorate. As a result, Russia will embrace the terrorist empire as a countermeasure against the West. This Assyrian power, with Russia's military might, will become very strong. We are instructed from God's word that when this power becomes strong, it will attack the land shadowing with wings, as the late Bin Laden did. These attacks will cause designated Egypt to go down to fight the Assyrian by the Euphrates River. God will then intervene, and the result that men thought was impossible will become a reality.

What men are sure will happen, won't happen. Instead, the Assyrian, supported by Russia and Iran, will inflict a devastating defeat on the land shadowing with wings. This defeat will happen because God will fight against the land shadowing with wings. When this event unfolds, the whole world will be stunned. The entire world will be terrified. The Assyrian will then rise, assured that God will be on its side, and will attack and destroy the land shadowing with wings at home. The land shadowing with wings, also called designated Egypt, will be attacked at home; because, it will have no defense, since its army would have been defeated by the Euphrates River.

It must be accentuated that the land shadowing with wings is changed in its identification from being a land to being a tree before its destruction. When it was seen as "a land," the emphasis was on protecting other nations. In the prophet's days, the country had no name. However, when it was presented as "a tree," that was when it was seen as glorying in its greatness. We see this same change with Nebuchadnezzar when he was about to be judged. We read about Nebuchadnezzar as a tree in Daniel 4:20–22. As a tree, it meant he had grown and had become strong and was now occupied with his greatness. As a consequence, destruction wasn't far away. Daniel had a piece of good advice for Nebuchadnezzar, which he shared with him in Daniel 4:27–31. However, he didn't listen.

Therefore, when Nebuchadnezzar enjoyed his most incredible honor and began to glory about his greatness, judgment came. In like manner, the same character of judgment will befall the land shadowing with wings. Note the boast: "I have built" for "the might of my power" and "the honor of my majesty" (Dan. 4:30). This boast sealed his fate. This boast will also seal Egypt's fate.

Observe that it won't be as a land but as a tree that the land shadowing with wings will be destroyed. We read, "He shall both cut off the sprigs with pruning hooks, and take away and cut down the branches" (Isa. 18:5). We know "sprigs" and "branches" are the components of a tree. Similarly, when designated Egypt is described as "the mighty," a name reserved for God, it indeed is about to be destroyed. This is what we will see in Jeremiah 46 and Ezekiel 31.

In Jeremiah 46:1–12, we have the sprigs being cut off. In Jeremiah 46:13–28, we have the branches cut off. We need to keep in mind that there was a partial fulfillment of this prophecy in the prophet's days. This prophecy is similar to the utterances concerning the seven churches of Revelation 2–3, which both have a historical component and a future element. This isn't easy to understand. This matter concerning Egypt is complicated but accurate and very authentic.

I am often appalled when Christian men give a date for Christ's coming, because Christ will never come according to men's calculations. I have read the Bible many times and I have never found a verse where one can calculate the coming of Christ. It is all a delusion from the Devil. This practice by Christian men only brings the Bible into disrepute and heaps dishonor on a holy God. For one to know the future, he must study the Bible intensely.

Prophecy is different from other doctrines: it is either true or false. If it is true, it will come to pass, as Darby and Kelly have proven, though they had endless critics; until now, their books are still read, while their critics' books have disappeared. This I will say; if we prayerfully consider what is presented here, we will find that it agrees entirely with God's word. It is difficult, yes, but it isn't erroneous. Don't reject it because of a misunderstanding. Study it carefully; you will be rewarded.

Therefore, in Jeremiah 46, we read, "The word of Jehovah that came to Jeremiah the prophet concerning the nations. Of Egypt: concerning the army of Pharaoh-Necho king of Egypt, which was by the river Euphrates at Carchemish, which Nebuchadnezzar king of Babylon smote in the fourth year of Jehoiakim the son of Josiah, the king of Judah" (Jer. 46:1–2 JND).

The way this is presented is similar to Revelation 1:19, where we read about three things. However, in J. N. Darby's translation, we seem to have more in the original. We seem to have the topic with which the prophet would like to engage our attention: 1) concerning the nations, 2) Egypt, and 3) the army of Pharaoh-Necho king of Egypt. What we are occupied with is Egypt.

In Jeremiah 46:2, we have a war between Pharaoh-Necho, king of Egypt, and Nebuchadnezzar, king of Babylon. We have the time of this war; it is in the fourth year of Jehoiakim, the son of Josiah, king of Judah. We have the place of this war. It was by the Euphrates River. Finally, we have the result of this war: who Nebuchadnezzar slew. What more do we need to know about this war? We have all the information on the war.

Moreover, according to 2 Chronicles 35:20–21, Pharaoh-Necho didn't want to fight against Josiah: neither did he want to fight against Nebuchadnezzar. He tried to fight against Carchemish. He wanted to fight against Assyria. Here he went against a particular place.

No! No! God won't have a war between Assyria and Egypt, that would complicate the understanding of the war between the future Assyrian and Egypt, therefore, Nebuchadnezzar slew him. We need to appreciate that any conflict between Egypt and Assyria would have complicated further the understanding of the future encounter between the Assyrian and designated Egypt. Such a war couldn't have taken place; God wouldn't allow it. We noticed how Josiah first tried to stop Pharaoh, but Josiah couldn't represent the war between Egypt and the Assyrian. That type couldn't fit. Pharaoh, therefore, killed Josiah, and Pharaoh's plans were stalled for a while. Four years later, Pharaoh went again, but this time Nebuchadnezzar slew Pharaoh; this then becomes the type of the future encounter between Egypt and Assyria, where Nebuchadnezzar, like Russia, will fight on the side of Assyria and defeat designated Egypt.

Besides, we read in 2 Kings 23, "In his days Pharaoh-Necho king of Egypt went up against the king of Assyria to the river Euphrates: and king Josiah went against him; and he slew him at Megiddo, when he had seen him" (2 Kings 23:29). Here Pharaoh-Necho slew Josiah, the king of Judah, who tried to stop him.

We are told in Jeremiah 46 that Pharaoh-Necho persisted and went up against the king of Assyria four years after his encounter with Josiah. To fight the Assyrian, Necho went by the Euphrates River. The person he wanted to fight was the king of Assyria. This war wasn't to take place at any cost. Consequently, Nebuchadnezzar, the king of Babylon, changed all Pharaoh's plans. This war then became a type of the future engagement between Egypt and the Assyrian. The land shadowing with wings, like Pharaoh, will go to fight against the Assyrian by the Euphrates River. Still Russia, like Nebuchadnezzar, will fight on the Assyrian's side and change the outcome.

We need to note also that though the scripture says Pharaoh-Necho went against the king of Assyria, there was no report (who won or who lost) of that war. What we are told instead is that another power came and helped in Egypt's destruction. This is the historical event, but it now helps us to understand the future encounter.

However, what we will read next isn't about a short war, and the result is entirely different. Therefore, it is a very different war before the eyes of the prophet Jeremiah; this we will now see. "Order ye the buckler and shield, and draw near to battle. Harness the horses; and get up, ye horsemen, and stand forth with your helmets; furbish the spears, and put on the brigandines" (Jer. 46:3–4). In these verses, we have excellent preparation for war; nothing is left to chance. Moreover, we have a great emphasis on defense. This is definitely not the war with Pharaoh-Necho, since Necho felt he could beat the Assyrian, the reason he left Egypt and ventured to the Euphrates River. Pharaoh's emphasis wasn't on defense but on attack; in this scene, the focus was on defense. The past is opposite the future all the time.

We need to take a careful look at what we already see today; Russia, the betrayer, has gone down by the Euphrates River and has established its presence there in Syria. Russia has taken with it its weapons of war. Moreover, after verse 2, we don't read any more about Pharaoh-Necho; he has completely disappeared from the narrative. Neither do we learn of such preparation from Pharaoh-Necho. "Order the buckler and shield" (Jer. 46:3) - that is, make ready the buckler and shield. That tells us this battle is in the future. It's not what just happened previously. "Draw near to battle" (Jer. 46:3) indicates that this is a future engagement.

The attacker here is Egypt; it wasn't when Nebuchadnezzar attacked Pharaoh–Necho but when designated Egypt will attack the Assyrian. "Draw near to battle" shows future action; there is excellent preparation for war when designated Egypt goes down to fight by the Euphrates River. The "buckler" and "shield" are both defensive weapons. We have a typical shield and specific shield - a lot of emphasis on defense. Today we are dealing with missile defense systems. There is much emphasis on protection, because Russia will be there, and one will need to penetrate its radar detection systems to avoid being attacked. There is no mention of the word *sword* in this passage, which indicates close warfare, but we have a spear, which indicates long-distance combat. It is all technological warfare.

Moreover, we observe in Jeremiah 46:5 that instead of Pharaoh-Necho, whom Nebuchadnezzar slew, we have a prominent army, and it is called by the name of their "mighty ones." This army is familiar. The "mighty ones" are the army of the land shadowing with wings, but the expression "their mighty ones" lets us know it is Israel who is viewing the land shadowing with wings as "his mighty ones," a dangerous assumption. We need to appreciate that the expression "their mighty ones" is the same one we read about in Daniel 8, where we learned that this bold king would destroy "the mighty" or "the mighty ones" and the "holy people" or "the people of the saints," as Darby asserted in his translation.

J. N. Darby helps us in his translation of this verse. "Why do I see them dismayed, turned away back? And their mighty ones are beaten down, and take to flight, and look not back? Terror [is] on every side, says Jehovah" (Jer. 46:5 JND). Again, in J. N. Darby's translation, we note that it is the army that is beaten down instead of Pharaoh being slain. In the past engagement, the emphasis was on the destruction of one man - Pharaoh, whom Nebuchadnezzar slew - but this isn't so in this encounter. There is no indicator that a leader like Pharaoh is in the battle in this engagement. The leader will be at home, and the army will be engaged in the fight. The identity of "their mighty ones" is Israel's mighty ones, the one she will put all her confidence in, designated Egypt. She will be sure designated Egypt cannot be defeated. However, remember, according to Isaiah 1:24, Jehovah is called the "Mighty one of Israel," but Jehovah is now replaced by the land shadowing with wings in the dealings of Israel. Designated Egypt is now Israel's mighty ones. This replacement will bring disaster.

Please take time to notice how J. N. Darby rightly introduces a new word in his translation; instead of the word *fear* as in the KJV, he uses the right word in the passage: *terror*, which is the correct translation. He was writing this over one hundred years ago when he never saw terrorism. Terrorism now characterizes the counterattack of the enemy. We need to observe these expressions: "dismayed," "turn away back," "beaten down," "take to flight," and "look not back." It is a five-fold consternation. Terror takes hold of them. It is the zenith of the terrorist attack. God brought terror upon them. Terror to that extent was never displayed before, as will be displayed when the land shadowing with wings will attack the Assyrian by the Euphrates River.

We knew about 9/11, but this will be worse. We will then learn about terror. It isn't the prophet who sees this; it is Jehovah. He saw it, and He spoke about it. The question was, "Why did I see them run?" The answer was then given: "terror on every side" (Jer. 46:5 JND). No one else saw this reaction because it is in the future. The Lord, who saw the conflict, is the one who spoke about the encounter. He saw them run from the terror. There was no terrorism in the war with Nebuchadnezzar; terrorism will characterize the future war with designated Egypt.

We need to observe that, according to Isaiah 30:25, when the towers fall, the day of the multiple slaughters had come. What we don't know is how long it will take to get to the day of the many simultaneous terrorist attacks. Furthermore, before the falling of the towers, the Assyrian wasn't present. It was after the falling of the towers that he appeared on the scene. The day of the great slaughter had come, but the Assyrian, who would provide the carnage, hadn't yet arrived. The Assyrian will come from the Syrian, Iraqi, and Turkey corridor, the territories along the Euphrates River, the old Assyrian regional zone. As a result, none of the terrorist networks mentioned before the fall of the towers are the Assyrian. Al-Qaeda isn't the Assyrian. Hezbollah isn't the Assyrian. Boca Aram isn't the Assyrian. However, ISIS could be the Assyrian because of the timing of its rise and geographic location. We will later see the role Russia will play in all this development.

We need to observe what is taking place by the Euphrates River today - that is, in Iraq, Syria, and Turkey. Russia has already gone down into Syria. The USA doesn't want to get caught in the quagmire, so it stays out, but it has its faction it is supporting. We have all kinds of factions there: the Russian's faction, President Assad's forces, the side of the Curds, ISIS's side, the side of the rebels, the Iraqi forces, Turkey's side, and the Iranian's side. Now, look at the verse again. It says, "Terror on every side" (Jer. 46: 5 JND). Russia has its side, Turkey has its side, Iran has its side, and Saudi Arabia has its side, but all these sides will eventually be controlled by the Assyrian who will rain terror on its attackers.

Therefore, the land shadowing with wings will find no friend to work with, only enemies. The protective land will make a critical mistake, and that will be to go to the war with Israel against the Assyrian. The presence of Israel will cement the Muslim world against designated Egypt. Nevertheless, God will order the event; designated Egypt will be doomed.

We must remember that the land shadowing with wings will not go to the Euphrates River willingly. The president will try to stay out of the quagmire, but he will be drawn into the quicksand. His presence by the Euphrates River won't be by desire but due to the Assyrian attacks on his territories. These future attacks will lure the land shadowing with wings to engage the Assyrian in battle by the Euphrates River. Nevertheless, when the protective land will go to that battle, it will stand alone. All the sides will be against it. That is why we have the expression "terror on every side." Designated Egypt will have no friends because Israel will go with it. The protective land's traditional allies will not go with it, so its coalition will be small. As a result, this mighty superpower will run from the battle; after all, the land shadowing with wings is only flesh and not spirit, as the word of God declared in Isaiah 31.

It should be emphasized that if believers are still here when this event is unfolding, they will know when the Assyrian has come, even though they don't look for it; they look for the coming of the Lord Jesus Christ. The believers will know, because once the Destroyer comes, he will rain terror - simultaneous, multiple terrorist attacks worldwide. Once Russia aligns itself with this terrorist kingdom, things will move quickly. Once we see these attacks, we will know the Assyrian has come. Once we see the protective land going down to fight the Assyrian by the Euphrates River, we will know the Assyrian chief is present.

Therefore, we must plead with the US president not to go to this war; we must use every persuasive word in the dictionary. However, he won't listen to us; he will go to his destruction. We must beg him not to go to this conflict, but he won't respond to our plea. How can he not go, when the man in Syria is attacking his country with terrorist attacks? The president must go to rid this world of such terror. He is the guardian of the world, yet he will be defeated. Once he is beaten, the Assyrian has come. The vital point for believers is this: if we see the head of the Assyrian during his life, we will be raptured to heaven before the tribulation.

Those who are not taught about the Assyrian may object to a lot that I say, but I am comfortable with their criticism. Prophecy will either come to pass or not. When it comes to pass, all mouths will be stopped. Therefore, please study these scriptures purposefully and see whether this isn't what God's word is unfolding.

The next verse will conclusively prove that there is more here than the war with Pharaoh-Necho. It will prove that the battle is with the land shadowing with wings, seen as designated Egypt but now called "the mighty." Therefore, we read, "Let not the swift flee away, neither let the mighty man escape! - Toward the north, hard by the river Euphrates, they have stumbled and fallen" (Jer. 46:6 JND).

Once we examine this verse carefully, we will immediately notice a significant problem. We unexpectantly read, "They have stumbled and fallen" (Jer. 46:6 JND). We must identify whom the word *they* refers to. We must remember that according to the war with Pharaoh-Necho, Nebuchadnezzar slew Pharaoh. Nothing was said about the army; nothing was said of any other person. No other person was seen associated with him, yet now we have "they have stumbled and fallen." However, lest men say the army is meant by the word *they*, note what verse 12 indicates, "The nations have heard of thy shame, and thy cry hath filled the earth; for the mighty man stumbleth against the mighty, they are both fallen together" (Jer. 46:12 JND). We need to tread softly here, for these scriptures are complicated.

This scenario didn't happen in the war with Pharaoh-Necho. Instead, we read that Nebuchadnezzar slew Pharaoh. Only two persons were mentioned there: Pharaoh and Nebuchadnezzar. Here, on the other hand, we find two persons connected, and both are destroyed together. We, therefore, read about the battle, and we are told that "they are both fallen together" (Jer. 46:12 JND). The "they" here is the land shadowing with wings and Israel. That is the identity of the "they" in this passage. Israel and the USA will go to war against the Assyrian, and they will both suffer the same fate. Note carefully the names of the two participants in Jeremiah 46:6; one is called *the swift* and the other is called *the mighty*.

Isaiah 3 makes this clear, "And it shall come to pass, that instead of perfume there shall be rottenness; and instead of girdle, a rope; and instead of well-set hair, baldness; and instead of a robe of display, a girding of sackcloth; brand instead of beauty. Thy men shall fall by the sword and thy mighty in the fight [KJV uses the word war]; and her gates shall lament and mourn; and, stripped, she shall sit upon the ground" (Isa. 3:24-26 JND). We are here told that Israel's men were going to fall by the sword and "her mighty" - the power she boasted about was going to fall in the war. The war by the Euphrates River will bring great distress upon Israel, as is highlighted in these verses.

We read the identical thing in Isaiah 31. "He that helpeth shall stumble, and he that is helped shall fall, and they shall perish together" (Isa. 31:3 JND). Here in Jeremiah 46, we find the same thing. "They are both fallen together" (Jer. 46:12 JND). In Isaiah 1, we read the same thing. "The destruction of the transgressors and of the sinners shall be together" (Isa. 1:28). The scripture asserts that "in the mouth of two or three witnesses, every word may be established" (Matt. 18:16). I am not pushing my views; this is what the scriptures consistently declare. I, therefore, know what will happen, even if others refuse to accept it.

In Isaiah 31:3, the relationship is looked at from the standpoint of Israel trusting in Egypt. As a result, Egypt will stumble, Israel will fall, and they will perish together. Here in Jeremiah 46, it is being looked at from the standpoint of the war, so we read "they" have stumbled and fallen. In Isaiah 31, we read, "He that helpeth shall stumble, and he that is helped shall fall, and they all shall perish together" (Isa. 31:3 JND). It is a consistent testimony throughout the scriptures. In Jeremiah 46, we read, "They are both fallen together" (Jer. 46:12 JND); there was no need for additional words. In Isaiah 31, we notice that they are going to perish together. There Jehovah is going to stretch out His hand, and he who helps is going to stumble, and he who is helped is going to fall. Isaiah 31 doesn't say where this "stumble," "fall," and "perish together" are going to take place. The answer is found in Jeremiah 46. Here we are told that both of them will stumble and fall by the Euphrates River. This chapter clearly states that it's at the home of the Assyrian that the land shadowing with wings will slip and fall.

We notice that Israel will become vulnerable once this battle takes place because her protection will be removed. The truth of Isaiah 18 will then be realized. "They shall be left together unto the fowls of the mountains, and to the beasts of the earth: and the fowls shall summer upon them, and all the beasts of the earth shall winter upon them" (Isa. 18:6). Israel will then be exposed to the king of the North (the bee), the king of the South (the fly), the Beast, the Roman Prince, and the Antichrist. These antagonists are what Israel will face for trusting human power instead of God. However, things are going to get even worse.

We are being enlightened to the future consequences of the association of Israel with the protective land. As in most relationships, romance is sweet; however, it isn't the romance that is the origin of the problem but the living together. We read, "Let not the swift flee away, neither let the mighty man escape! - Towards the north, hard by the river Euphrates, they have stumbled and fallen" (Jer. 46:6 JND).

In this verse, we see the ones who will stumble and fall. One is called "the mighty," which is designated Egypt, and the other is called "the swift," which is Israel. Remember, as early as Isaiah 18, we learned about the swift messengers of the land shadowing with wings crossing the sea and giving instructions to Israel. Therefore, the swift is seen associated with their ships and aircrafts - which are big and quick - that can cross the sea and carry their messengers. In Isaiah 18, the swift is the land shadowing with wings, which can cross, not only the river or the Mediterranean Sea, but also the Atlantic and Pacific Oceans. Moreover, Egypt, in Isaiah 30, with its military might is the swift.

Nevertheless, Israel is seen as riding the horse, the swift, in the figure; she is held up by the horse. Thus, she is regarded as one with the swift. Their relationship is so closely aligned together that either may be considered as most prominent. Israel has declared what she is going to do. Israel says, "We will ride upon the swift" (Isa. 30:16).

"Let not the swift flee away" (Jer. 46:6 JND). The swift here is Israel, the rider. "Neither let the mighty man escape" (Jer. 46:6 JND). This name "mighty" is the new name by which designated Egypt is now called. The "mighty" or "mighty man" represents Egypt. We have the two in the war.

Consequently, we read, "Towards the north, hard by the river Euphrates, they have stumbled and fallen" (Jer. 46:6 JND). We now see a clear picture of the association. We have designated Egypt and Israel in the war. There are two of them; it now makes sense. They have stumbled and fallen. Finally, we learn that he who is to carry Israel cannot carry himself. What is of even greater importance is that we have established that "the mighty" is the land shadowing with wings, the Egypt of Isaiah 30–31; this connection enables us to interpret Daniel 8, where the Assyrian will destroy "the mighty" and "the holy."

Now, as early as Isaiah 1, we read about two protectors of the Jews: two and no more. The language in Isaiah 1 is symbolic like in Isaiah 18, but it is clear. The first protector is called by the name "sinners," and Israel is called by the name "transgressors." The Gentiles are sinners, and the Jews are transgressors. Here, as in other passages, we read that the destruction of the transgressors and the sinners "shall be together." Israel will be destroyed with the land shadowing with wings. "For they shall be ashamed of the oaks which ye have desired, and ye shall be confounded for the gardens that ye have chosen" (Isa. 1:29). They are "ashamed of the oaks which ye have desired." Oaks speak of strength; gardens speak of provision or sustenance. Israel will be ashamed of both of her protectors the ones she had chosen. There are two of them in Isaiah 1, as we will later see: the land shadowing with wings and the Roman Empire. Israel will be ashamed of both of them - the same thing scripture asserts in Isaiah 30.

We need to observe that as "the mighty," the land shadowing with wings wages war, and as "Egypt," it is regarded as the boaster. It speaks much, but it cannot deliver. The deliverance it promised it couldn't accomplish. However, this mighty was to give way to another mighty, as we see in verse 12. "The mighty stumbles against the mighty." This is the same as we have in Daniel 8. "His power shall be mighty ... and he shall destroy the mighty and the holy."

We now read, "Who is this [that] riseth up as the Nile, whose waters toss themselves like the rivers? It is Egypt that riseth up as the Nile, and [his] waters toss themselves like the rivers" (Jer. 46:7 JND). The rivers here are the Tigris and the Euphrates, where the Assyrian will be located. Egypt will want to act like the rivers and attack the Assyrian at its homeland, just as the Assyrian attacked Egypt at home, but that will be a mistake. We now hear its boast. "I will rise up, I will cover the earth; I will destroy the city and the inhabitants thereof" (Jer. 46:8 JND). Egypt thinks much of its greatness. It is all the power of man. It is only what I will do; there is no thought about God, and as far as Egypt is concerned, God has no say. Egypt is "the mighty"; it is all about its power, but it is wrong. God alone will speak.

However, unknown to man, God has another plan. It should be emphasized that the city Egypt plans to destroy will be the capital of the Assyrian caliphate, the city the Assyrian will declare as its capital in Syria. The land shadowing with wings will want to attack and destroy that city, because the Assyrian head, which will attack designated Egypt, will be located there. The Assyrian leader doesn't run and hide; he feels safe at home, because the Russian force is there in Syria as his support. Therefore, he is bold and fierce; he isn't afraid of "the mighty." "This mighty" will need to invade Syria under Russia's protection to get to him. This invasion will cause his demise.

We need to observe something important in Daniel 8. We read, "He shall destroy wonderfully" (Dan. 8:24). We need to discern that before the Assyrian destroys "the mighty," it destroys spectacularly; whom he destroys spectacularly is undoubtedly the land shadowing with wings, but other countries are included. He will attack the mighty with vicious terrorist attacks; the word of God is clear. The attacks on the land shadowing with wings will cause the protective land to go down by the Euphrates River to fight the Assyrian. God is concerned with Israel, and He lists those in association with her. As a result, He mentions the mighty and the holy, and He combines Israel and her protector together.

The religious terrorist group, called the Assyrian, will take possession of Syria, Turkey, and Iraq - the countries along the Euphrates River. The Assyrian will be able to do this because Russia will support it. The head of the Assyrian will destroy those governments and establish its empire, called the "Assyrian Empire"; then when he becomes strong, he will inflict unimaginable, presumptuous, and destructive terrorist attacks on the world.

These terrorist acts will provoke the land shadowing with wings to invade Assyria by the Euphrates River. The Assyrian is confident that once he attacks designated Egypt, that strategy will initiate a response. This development happened before, so it will prepare for the encounter. The Assyrian will remember what unfolded after the attack of the late Bin Laden, so he will know what to expect.

I am sorry to relate this future event so vividly; I mean no harm to anyone or to any country, but the Bible is God's word, not fiction. Just as Darby and Kelly could have related what would have happened and it is all coming to pass, so it can be done today, because the Bible is the word of God, and it will come to pass, once rightly divided. Please accept the revelation of the precious word of God before it is too late. The evolutionists predict how this world will end, and we hear them gladly. Please permit a Christian to tell you what the future holds so you might assess what is true. I know what will be; God's word will triumph every time.

It must be understood that if the Lord doesn't stretch out His hand, the destruction will not occur. This power cannot be defeated without the Lord's intervention. God is the one who will act against both Israel and her lover. The alliance will be small, so we will have "the mighty and the swift" in the battle. Consequently, we have the expression "they are both fallen together" (Jer. 46:12 JND). Therefore, we read that they shall "perish together."

I'm sure this account is far removed from anything the evolutionists are likely to say about the future. They know nothing at all; they are the blind leaders of the blind. Perhaps their stories may include the collision of two galaxies because of their mathematical calculations, but before any such thing can happen, Christ will come and rule the whole universe. He made the world. He will rule it.

Therefore, when you see the USA going with Israel to fight the Assyrian by the Euphrates River, you must beg the president of the USA not to go to war. God will fight against him. Use all your influence to persuade him to do otherwise. This isn't a joke; this will happen! Nevertheless, the president will not listen, for as far as he will think, you are but a religious fanatic. He will reject such idle thoughts. Nevertheless, he will be wrong. He will be trapped, and the world will never be the same. Already, Russia, the betrayer, is in Syria. Already, ISIS a new terrorist group is there. Already, Russia has threatened to leave the West. Soon, very soon, he will embrace the terror. The world is doomed.

However, the president will have a response to your pleadings: "I will destroy the city and the inhabitants" (Jer. 46:8 JND). Therefore, God says to him, "Go up," but he did not know that disaster awaited him. "Go up, ye horses, and drive furiously ye chariots; and let the mighty men go forth" (Jer. 46:9 JND). Horses are human power, and chariots are military power. In this passage, the first mighty is told to "go up" while the second mighty is told to "go forth." The first mighty is seen attacking, while the second mighty begins to counterattack. As a result of his coming with Israel, we also find an infusion of terrorists from the southern kingdom, who will come to support the Assyrian in the North; they have one purpose: crush the mighty and the swift. We have both the Asiatic Cush and the African Cush battling with the Assyrian against the land shadowing with wings.

What the land shadowing with wings doesn't know is that it will be going to its own sacrifice. The Lord will stretch forth His hand. The word of God doesn't tell us how God is going to stretch out His hand. Clearly, God's intervention is what will bring about the defeat of Egypt. God will act against Egypt to accomplish a great slaughter. What man alleges is impossible will become possible. The whole world will then be catapulted into chaos and disarray. This chaos isn't what I say but what I believe God's word is saying; I am only explaining it. "For this is the day of the Lord Jehovah of hosts, a day of vengeance, that he may be avenged of his adversaries; and the sword shall devour, and it shall be sated and made drunk with their blood" (Jer. 46:10 JND).

God will then take control of the battle, and Israel will realize that Egypt, "the mighty," cannot be compared to God. This event never happened in the past; this will happen in the future. This war isn't the war with Nebuchadnezzar; this is the war between designated Egypt and the Assyrian.

Moreover, we read, "For the Lord, Jehovah of hosts hath a sacrifice in the north country, by the river Euphrates" (Jer. 46:10 JND). This conflict is stated to be in the future. However, the war with Nebuchadnezzar passed, and we know the result, but this war is said to be in the future. It is important to note one other thing: "the adversaries" are avenged but not yet the enemies. The time for the enemy's destruction will come as soon as the Lord returns. In the incident by the Red Sea, when Egypt pursued Israel, we read about God's intervention in Exodus 14:21–25. That intervention will be similar to what will happen with the land shadowing with wings.

In Exodus the Lord took off the wheels of Pharaoh's chariots amid the sea. We then discover that the chariots were useless without wheels. The Egyptians knew God was fighting against them. In the future battle, I wonder what God will do. What a disaster will ensue.

I know that when this book is read, many may think these events will never happen. They may say that this is just another churchman predicting what will certainly not happen, but this time they will be wrong, because I am only giving you the scriptures - nothing but the word of God. Nevertheless, they will see. They will see the Islamic Empire north of Israel rise under the protection of Russia. They will see the Islamic kingdom south of Israel rise. Then they will see the activities of those powers.

Further, they will see the battle with the land shadowing with wings. Sadly, they will see the defeat, which they won't be able to comprehend. As Isaiah 18 says, "Afore the harvest ... he shall cut down the sprigs with pruning knives" (Isa. 18:5). The harvest is the end of the age. The *he*, the Destroyer, is the head of the Assyrian. He will defeat the land shadowing with wings just before the tribulation. This defeat could even be before we are raptured to heaven. We might see the upheaval, but we will wait for Christ who will come and save us before the great tribulation.

We now need another passage to help us with this study. Needless to say, we will suffer a significant deficiency if we don't grasp the significance of Ezekiel 32:7-10 concerning this destruction. Therefore, we need to pause and read Ezekiel 32.

God declares for all to hear that He will vex the hearts of many people. God says He will make them horribly afraid. God affirms that they shall tremble at every moment. If God says so, it will be so. Many people will then become Muslims, and the army of the Assyrian will become innumerable. The Gentiles will then become blinded religiously as the Jews are blinded today. These nations will, therefore, err completely.

God warned the Gentiles in Romans 9-11 that they stood by faith. The Jews were blinded so the Gentiles might come in; now the Gentiles will be blinded, and the Jews were about to be grafted back in. We learned that the Jewish branches were broken off so that the Gentiles might come in; now the Gentiles will be "cut off" so the Jews might come back in. God in His grace offered His Son, but man rejected Him. We clearly see that the Gentiles were going to err as the Jews had erred. They hadn't continued in God's goodness. They wanted something new, and that new thing was to bring blindness to their eyes. What a horrible judgment awaits all who reject the Son of God.

We observe, further, that this war lasts for quite a while. Therefore, it's not the war with Pharaoh-Necho, which happened within a year. "Go up into Gilead, and take balm, O virgin, daughter of Egypt: in vain shalt thou use many medicines; for thou shalt not be cured" (Jer. 46:11). We are shown that Egypt will try many established military tactics, but none will work. Designated Egypt will use all the different military strategies, but none of its remedies will be successful. Here God toys with the superpower, telling it to try other medicines. It is like Elijah and the prophets of Baal. Here God tells it, "Thou shalt not be cured" (Jer. 46:11); it was doomed. This desperation displays a picture of man's helplessness against a holy God. My friend, turn from your sins. You cannot escape either when God rises in judgment; you are doomed.

Whose words were going to stand - what Egypt told Israel or what God told her? It doesn't matter what man says and how impossible things look; God's word alone will stand every time. "The nations have heard of thy shame, and thy cry hath filled the earth; for the mighty man stumbleth against the mighty, they are both fallen together" (Jer. 46:12 JND). "They are both fallen together" doesn't mean "the mighty" and "the mighty" fall together, but Israel and "the mighty" fall together. The Assyrian becomes even stronger, so strong that by the time we come to the middle of the book of Revelation, the Assyrian has an army of two hundred million fighters.

The scripture puts it this way: "the mighty stumbleth against the mighty" (Jer. 46:12), because one should have been following the line upon line, the precepts upon precepts, the here a little and there a little. The mighty that will stumble is Egypt. The mighty against whom it will stumble is the Assyrian. When "the mighty" will stumble, Israel will fall, and both of them will perish together. Israel is pictured as riding the horse, the horse stumbleth and the horse and rider falls. This event will then be fulfilled.

Moreover, just as God said in Isaiah 30, "Therefore shall the strength of Pharaoh be your shame, and the trust in the shadow of Egypt your confusion ... they were all ashamed of a people that could not profit them, nor be a help nor profit, but a shame, and also a reproach" (Isa. 30:3, 5); accordingly, He will bring this to pass.

God said Egypt would be a shame and a reproach, the world didn't believe it; however, so it will come to pass. In this scene before us, Israel won't be able to endure the experience; her cry will fill the earth, not merely the land. "The mighty" of whom Israel boasted about will then be destroyed, and Israel's army will also be destroyed with it; she will then cry bitterly. All her boasts will come to naught. The nations will hear about her shame. Then one mighty will supersede the other mighty. The Assyrian will now be the only mighty. However, this name, "mighty," is reserved for God. The Assyrian, by having this name, will also be destroyed, since there is only one mighty God. Soon we will read about a "strong," but that designation is reserved for the Roman Empire.

In His design, God will allow Israel as a nation to be spared for a while, but not the land shadowing with wings. God will then cause the Assyrian to target the land shadowing with wings at home with devastating results. This second attack concludes the twofold judgment of Isaiah 18:5.

This second part, the judgment at home, is now seen in Jeremiah 46:13–28. However, I want to be very clear that I cannot develop these verses to the extent that they could be developed, because of the environment in which we live today. It would have been better if this book were written thirty years ago before the times in which we live. I say no more.

We now read, "The word that Jehovah spoke to Jeremiah the prophet, concerning the coming of Nebuchadnezzar king of Babylon to smite the land of Egypt" (Jer. 46:13 JND). We need to appreciate a partial fulfillment in the past, just as in the earlier part of this chapter. However, nothing in history comes even close to what we are reading in this passage. As a result, we need to be careful in differentiating between the past and the future. We will notice only some salient points when we deal with this attack on the homeland of the land shadowing with wings.

We are first confronted with the devastation of the nations around Egypt. Those nations came under severe judgment. The sword had devoured round about Egypt. As a result, we read, "The sword devoureth round about thee" (Jer. 46:14 JND). This destruction around Egypt was fulfilled in the days of Nebuchadnezzar, all the nations around Egypt were destroyed. However, God speaks about that destruction here because He will show a contrast between the days of Nebuchadnezzar and the future day. We then move from the past to the future in the narrative. The attention is then turned to Egypt, and a question is, "Why are thy valiant swept away?" The answer is given; it is because the Lord thrust them down. We notice that this attack was seen as coming from the Lord, though He was using another power. "Jehovah did thrust them down; he made many to stumble" (Jer. 46:15 JND). However, there was no more the expression "the mighty." Thy valiant are swept away; that is, the defense force and paramilitary organizations, which will be trying to prevent the disaster at home, are here brushed aside, since the army will be already defeated by the Euphrates River.

Moreover, the people call for a strange occurrence. "Let us return to our own people and to the land of our nativity" (Jer. 46:16 JND). If this battle was against Nebuchadnezzar, this couldn't have been possible, since the nations around Egypt were already destroyed. That is why the destruction around Egypt was first mentioned; that is why verse 14 was first introduced. What is clearly evident is that this Egypt here is a land of immigrants. As a result, the immigrants voluntarily wanted to return to their own people and country when attacked. Immigration is a big issue today, and people don't want to voluntarily leave the USA, but that could change tomorrow. However, if it was only in Nebuchadnezzar's time, then there was no such movement of people. Additionally, they couldn't have returned because Babylon had already destroyed those cities; all around was destruction.

God destroyed the nations around Egypt first before He destroyed Egypt. That was the history of past Egypt. In the future encounter, He will destroy Egypt first so there will be places to which the people can migrate. This scenario is what is explained in Ezekiel 29. "And I will make the land of Egypt desolate in the midst of the countries that are desolate, and her cities among the cities that are laid waste" (Ezek. 29:12). As we read in Ezekiel 29, there would have been no place to go if this was the historical destruction; these countries and cities were already destroyed.

We note further, "No foot of man shall pass through it nor foot of beast shall pass through it, neither shall it be inhabited forty years" (Ezek. 29:11). Therefore, no one could have returned to those cities. They were all completely destroyed. However, there are places to go, for designated Egypt is one of the first to be destroyed in the future. In the days of Nebuchadnezzar, Egypt was one of the ultimate powers to be destroyed. Egypt was destroyed thirty years after Israel. In the future judgment, designated Egypt will be one of the first powers to be destroyed, while Israel will be one of the last. The future is opposite the past. We must keep in mind that the destruction takes place just before the Lord comes and establishes His kingdom. Once the destruction of the protective nation takes place, Christ will come during the days of the Destroyer. We are dealing with how God will remove all these powers on earth to deliver the world to Christ.

We read further, "There did they cry, Pharaoh, king of Egypt is but a noise; he hath let the time appointed go by" (Jer. 46:17 JND). We noticed again that the passage above speaks of the verbal power of the leader of designated Egypt. He boasts much about what he intends to do and can do, but he fails to deliver at the appointed time. Moreover, the words here for "let the time appointed go by" (Jer. 46:17 JND) are very interesting. They mean to cross a line that was set—like one president, who set a line in the sand for President Assad. He said that if Assad used chemical weapons, that was a line he wouldn't allow Assad to cross, and he would attack him. However, when it was proved that chemical weapons were used, he didn't attack Assad. When Russia saw the president didn't have the will to fight the war, President Putin went into Syria. His entrance changed all the dynamics in Syria. The American president didn't carry through with the commitment he had made; something like that was now blamed, in this verse, for all the problems. Perhaps if the president had invaded Syria, that move would have kept Russia out of the country. That action could have brought a different result. Nevertheless, God was the one directing the show; not the speculation of man.

We need to see that not only is Pharaoh's name dropped from the rest of the narrative, but a familiar "he" comes up. "For [as] I live, says the King, whose name is Jehovah of hosts, surely as Tabor among the mountains, and as Carmel by the sea, so shall he come" (Jer. 46:18 JND). The "he" was going to come. Nevertheless, you may say that the "he" here is Nebuchadnezzar, but I will say no more.

We observed further in Jeremiah 46:19–21 that those who went to the protective land only to make money couldn't face the destruction. They were fat; they were rich and proud. Nevertheless, they turned back; they ran away. They wanted the money, but they couldn't stand the destruction. More is declared: "They shall march with an army, and come against her with axes, as hewers of wood. They shall cut down her forest, saith Jehovah, though it is impenetrable; for they are more than the locusts, and are innumerable" (Jer. 46:22–23 JND).

The Assyrian will be coming with its army, but what will happen to the military of designated Egypt? The Assyrian will already have destroyed the military of Egypt by the Euphrates River. Whereas the Assyrian army will gain in strength and numbers, the weapons they have will be inferior to Egypt's. The Assyrians have numbers but less sophisticated weapons. Yet their simple weapons, coupled with their numerical strength, secure them a significant victory in the homeland of designated Egypt. Simple weapons of war, like swords and spears, are absent from their arsenal. What they have are axes for destruction. They use all kinds of improvised weapons they use. Therefore, it was God who made the difference.

The forest of Egypt represents Egypt's defense. Nevertheless, the Assyrian penetrates Egypt's defense even though its security is impenetrable from the eyes of man. Egypt will implement impossible security checks, but these will be infiltrated with devastating results. The word here *chaqar*, translated in the KJV as "searched," means "to penetrate." Therefore, it isn't their numbers, nor their weapons, since the security will be impenetrable. However, God will use the Assyrian to accomplish His purpose, and His purpose will be accomplished.

In which other war in the Bible do we find such language? This language is unique to this event; now look at the Assyrian army's size, "more than the Locusts" (Jer. 46:23 JND) - this is the expression of scripture. Scripture also uses another word called "innumerable," which clarifies that this couldn't be Nebuchadnezzar's army. Impossible! What we have here is the fact that all the so-called moderate Muslims join in this attack. This is what will happen to Egypt. A terrorist attack on a scale never seen before is depicted in the Assyrian attack on this Egypt. We also notice that their weapons aren't conventional weapons of war but improvised weapons. Every possible thing is made into a weapon, and Egypt suffers a terrible destruction. The branches are then destroyed; that means the different states. This country is made up of other states, and all are attacked and destroyed. I didn't imagine this; the Bible says this. I didn't write this; the Jews did, and they know what they have written is God's word.

Yet there is more. "The daughter of Egypt is put to shame; she is delivered into the hand of the people of the north" (Jer. 46:24 JND). This time it is Egypt that is put to shame. Here, it is delivered into the hands of the people of the North, not into the hands of Nebuchadnezzar. Again, it isn't just an attack; it is Jehovah who does this. He said He would punish 1)

Amon of No, 2) Pharaoh, 3) Egypt, 4) her gods, 5) her kings, 6) Pharaoh, and 7) those who confide in him. If this is just another war, then show me something similar in another place. Pharaoh was to be punished and also another group - those who trust in him. Those who trust in Pharaoh can easily be identified as Israel.

Finally, the last two verses, (Jer. 46:27, 27), clearly show that this event is in the last days. When will the Lord save Israel? "I will save thee." This is accomplished when the Lord returns. We have three things here: 1) "I will save thee from far," 2) "and thy seed from the land of their captivity," 3) "and Jacob shall return." That is all Israel, not a partial return. This restoration is when the Lord returns, so this attack is in the last days.

We have stated that the land shadowing with wings is seen as designated Egypt. However, is it unprecedented that a country called one name in scripture is clearly representative of another country? The answer is no. Babylon is also seen as the Roman Empire in Isaiah 13–14. If it were unprecedented, we would have to question our interpretation, since two or three witnesses must test everything.

Both Kelly and Darby said that Babylon in Isaiah 13–14 represents the Roman Empire of the future. Thus, though the word of God expressly uses the name Babylon, the content of the passage shows that it couldn't in its totality apply only to Babylon by the Euphrates River but also to Rome in the last days. Thus, Babylon represents the future Roman Empire.

Therefore, we will now read what William Kelly and J. N. Darby wrote about Isaiah 13-14. First, we will start with Kelly, who wrote:

> Thus, the fall of the first great power of the Gentiles is a type of the doom of the last, when Israel will have been finally set free, a converted people, being delivered spiritually as much as nationally, and thenceforward made to express the glory of Jehovah upon the earth...The overthrow of Babylon involves the emancipation of Israel. It has thus much greater importance than the history of any ordinary power; and the past Babylon is simply a type of the fall of the greater power, its final heir, which is to the last the enslaver of the Jews, the would-be protector but master of the holy city.

The king of Babylon sets forth no other than the last head of the Beast, just as Nebuchadnezzar was the first of that line. We must distinguish the imperial chief of the last days from the religious head of the antichrist; and the more carefully, because, having a similar policy and being confederates in evil, they are very generally confounded by ancients and moderns. Although the king of Babylon typifies the person who will finally have the Jews as his vassals, it would be a great mistake to conceive that it is to be a king of the Babylon in Shinar. We refer to this now merely to show that it rests upon a wrong principle. Some have the thought that there will be a re-establishment of oriental Babylon in the last days. They suppose there will be a literal city in the plain of Shinar. This appears to be fundamentally false.

While the Spirit of God speaks of the Assyrian subsequently to Babylon, it is certain that in past history the Assyrian fell first in order, then Babylon afterwards. By-and by Babylon will be smitten in the last holder of the Beast's power, and this in connection with the Jews; while the power then answering to the king of Assyria will come up after that, when God occupies Himself with the ten tribes of Israel. The Babylonian despot and the Assyrian, then, are two distinct enemies of the Lord, and types of two different powers in the last days, the one before, the other after, the Jews are in recognized relationship with Jehovah.

To restrain this scene to the past judgement of Babylon is to limit the word of God, and make the Spirit seem to be unreliable. But this is merely our own evil misconception and irreverent error.[24]

Second, J. N. Darby wrote the following:

---

[24] Kelly, *Notes on Isaiah*, The Bible Treasury, Vol. 5, 147.

Babylon is not only the capital of Nebuchadnezzar and of the habitable world; it is Babel, signifying confusion. It is there men are united to exalt themselves and make themselves a name and a reputation in the world.

From verses 3–23 there is a beautiful picture of the fall of Babylon's king in its last representative - the Beast of the close. The prophet takes occasion from events at hand in that day; but no prophecy of Scripture is made to be of its own interpretation, none has been fully or entirely accomplished. And the reason is that the Holy Spirit has always Jesus and His kingdom in view. God has always the second Man in His mind. Even the first prophecy, that the woman's Seed should crush the serpent's head, is not yet fulfilled. All that there is in God's word points onward to the glory of Christ.[25]

Therefore, in Isaiah 13-14, we have first an attack by the Assyrian on the Roman Empire because they will seek to protect Israel, and after they will break the treaty, the destruction of Rome by the Lord Himself. Similarly, some of the passages where the word *Egypt* is mentioned can be referring only to the land shadowing with wings.

William Kelly wrote these words about the Egypt of Isaiah 30: "Israel, when threatened by the Assyrian, sought the help of Egypt: I am speaking now of the literal fact when this prophecy first applied. Though it did bear on the days of Isaiah, yet the character of the prophecy shows that it cannot be limited to that time: only a very small part of it was accomplished then."[26]

Therefore, God's word explicitly teaches that God uses two contemporary powers to the Assyrian, Egypt and Babylon to illustrate the future wars between the two protectors of the Jews (Egypt and Babylon) against the future Assyrian. Future Egypt, the land shadowing with wings, and future Babylon, the Roman Empire, will both be defeated by the future

---

[25] Darby, *"Thoughts on Isaiah the Prophet,"* The Bible Treasury, Vol. 13, 118.
[26] Kelly, *Notes on Isaiah*, The Bible Treasury, Vol. 5, *353.*

Assyrian. It must be clearly stated that this distinction between geographic Egypt and designated Egypt isn't open to guessing. You will never get this right by conjecture. This can be understood only by serious meditation; as one studies the passages, God, the Spirit, makes them apparent.

Therefore, in the next chapter, we will develop one last portion of scripture on Egypt, which will unite all the passages on Egypt and show the terrible consequences that will befall this world because of the destruction of the land shadowing with wings. Moreover, we will also notice that when the Lord Jesus Christ will slay those who will be involved in the terror, when they enter into death; then and only then will they be confronted with the sad realization of their errors.

CHAPTER 9

DESIGNATED EGYPT: THE FALLOUT AFTER ITS DESTRUCTION

I n the previous chapter, we noticed that the land shadowing with wings will be destroyed. We saw that the Assyrian was going to destroy that power. In this chapter, we will investigate the chaos that will ensue due to that destruction. This topic is again a ten on my scale of difficulties.

We will now study a collection of four chapters on Egypt. In these chapters, we will observe that the scripture differentiates between the past Egyptian wars with Nebuchadnezzar and highlights the future wars involving Egypt as the headquarters of the king of the South. It will further develop the destruction of Egypt as the land shadowing with wings and will highlight the countries that will export terrorism according to the Bible. We will observe how Russia will betray the West and join the terrorist Assyrian to defeat the land of protection. Finally, we will witness the confusion that awaits the terrorists when they die and enter Hades.

Therefore, the topic we are about to enter into is challenging, because it has to do with designated Egypt. We note that anything that has to do with designated Egypt demands profound meditation. Nevertheless, as we saw before, it can be understood. As we enter into the fallout, as a result of this destruction of the land shadowing with wings, the subject becomes even more complicated. Nevertheless, all this complexity will only convince us that our interpretations of these scriptures are correct. Although the topic is involved, our knowledge of God's word will increase significantly due to this study. Nevertheless, the writer's greatest desire is that God will use this understanding to energize us into a godlier and more faithful walk so our Lord Jesus Christ may be glorified in our lives as we wait for God's Son from heaven. Let us now seek God's help in understanding this subject as presented in God's word.

Between Ezekiel 29–32, we have four chapters on Egypt. As we study them, we observe that the scripture divides these chapters into three main components: 1) the Egypt in the days of Nebuchadnezzar, 2) the Egypt that heads the king of the South in the future, and 3) the Egypt that prefigures the land shadowing with wings. Furthermore, we also detect the dreaded fallout that would occur due to the destruction of the land shadowing with wings.

In Ezekiel 29:1-3, Pharaoh is called a monster amid his rivers. "The river" represents what sustains. Pharaoh, king of Egypt, supported other economies, but he was a monster. He was not only a beast who didn't submit to God but also a monster; that is, he was big and powerful. This picture presented of Egypt depicted him as the most significant power on the earth until he was deposed. We see a very boastful Pharaoh, king of Egypt: "my river is mine, and I made it for myself" (Ezek. 29:3 JND), he declared. It was all about his country; he saw his country's blessings for himself alone. Nevertheless, the word of God proclaims, "God resisteth the proud and giveth grace to the humble" (1Pet. 5:5).

Therefore, in Ezekiel 29:4-5, God tells us what he would do to Pharaoh. We are told that God would bring Pharaoh and his army out of Egypt and destroy them in the open field. This war was in the past. This is the war with Nebuchadnezzar by the Euphrates River when Pharaoh was destroyed. "I will bring thee up out of the midst of thy rivers" (Ezek. 29:4 JND); this expression tells us this battle would be fought outside of Egypt.

Moreover, in Ezekiel 29:6-7, God gives us the reason for the destruction of Pharaoh by the Euphrates River. It was because of how Pharaoh dealt with Israel, when Israel in the past looked to Egypt to deliver them from their enemies.

Moreover, Ezekiel 29:8–10 gives us a second war. This war wasn't outside of Egypt, like the first, but it was within Egypt. Note the language: "I will bring a sword upon thee, and cut off man and beast from thee. And the land of Egypt shall be a desolation and a waste" (Ezek. 29:8–9 JND). Egypt itself was destroyed instead of when God said He was going to cast Pharaoh on the open field. This is the twofold destruction God was going to inflict on geographic Egypt so she would become a type of designated Egypt, which will be destroyed with two-part destruction, as we read in Isaiah 18. The first destruction of Egypt was when Nebuchadnezzar destroyed it near the Euphrates River. The second destruction was when Nebuchadnezzar destroyed Egypt at home as a reward for Nebuchadnezzar's labor against Tyrus. This two-part destruction of Egypt was to be a type of the two-part destruction of designated Egypt.

Moreover, the information provided in Ezekiel 29:11-16 is critical to understand designated Egypt. Israel would have already been in captivity when Egypt entered captivity. The nations around were already in captivity when Egypt entered captivity. There was desolation all around; this desolation was so great around Egypt that no foot of man or beast would pass through it. It was under those circumstances that Egypt went into captivity; also, Egypt was to be in captivity for forty years. However, when Israel returned from captivity, the two-fold destruction of Egypt had already taken place. Observe that Egypt wouldn't be in captivity as long as Israel since Israel was already in captivity. Nevertheless, what is emphasized is the situation that would exist after the Egyptian captivity.

First, the Egypt of Ezekiel 29 was going to be a base kingdom, but the Egypt in Isaiah 30 is not a base kingdom. Second, it was going to be the basest of all kingdoms, but the Egypt in Isaiah 30 isn't the basest of all kingdoms. It is the greatest power. Third, it was not going to exalt itself again above the nations, but in Isaiah 30, it is elevated above the nations. Fourth, the Lord was going to diminish it, but the Egypt in Isaiah 30–31 isn't reduced but increases in power and glory. Fifth, it was no more going to rule over the nations, but the Egypt in Isaiah 30–31 has dominion over the nations, so much so that it is protecting friendly countries from hostile foes. Sixth, it was no more going to be the confidence of the house of Israel, but in Isaiah 30, Egypt is the confidence of the house of Israel. Israel is trusting in Egypt for her protection. Therefore, designated Egypt displays all the scripture says geographic Egypt will not represent. We must conclude that the Egypt of Isaiah 30–31 is different and is the land shadowing with wings, since it is also a protector of the Jews.

We gain further insight into this matter in Ezekiel 29:17-21. First, the land of Egypt was going to be given into the hands of Nebuchadnezzar. Second, Nebuchadnezzar was going to carry away the multitude of Egypt. Third, Nebuchadnezzar was going to seize her spoil. Fourth, he would take her prey, and fifth, that would be the wages for Nebuchadnezzar's army. Vitally, the time of this war was given; it is said to be after the attack on Tyrus, so this is a different war from the one by the Euphrates River. However, we should carefully notice that this wasn't the destruction of Tyrus; that feat was left to Alexander the Great to accomplish. The inhabitants of Tyrus escaped Nebuchadnezzar's wrath and fled to an island about a half mile out at sea, with all their riches. Nevertheless, this action by the Tyrians did set up one of the most stunning fulfillments of God's word ever recorded.

Moreover, it displays the accuracy of God's word with incomparable splendor when Alexander the Great conquered the new Tyrian City. The word of God declared that Nebuchadnezzar's army got no pay for its work. As a result, the Lord was going to give him Egypt as his wages. The scriptures set this up beautifully; God first gave us the past events so He might unfold the future events. God first revealed the twofold destruction by Nebuchadnezzar and made us aware that those destructions were accomplished. We are then put in a position to understand the future Egypt.

The prophet then begins the next chapter by immediately putting us in the future. The word of God introduces the day of the Lord. The day of the Lord is in the future; we know this. Therefore, we are now transported from the past to the future in Ezekiel 30:1–9.

The day of the Lord here isn't the time of Jacob's trouble but the time of the nations. It is at the same time as Jacob's trouble, but the emphasis is on the other countries. It isn't seen here regarding Israel; it is seen concerning the Gentiles. It is no more the two-fold judgment by Nebuchadnezzar, but instead, it is a future judgment. It is the Assyrian that will execute this judgment on Egypt during the tribulation. Nevertheless, as you will notice, it is Egypt as the head of the king of the South, and the nations that make up the king of the South are here named. The sword here isn't associated with anyone, since it's the Lord's sword. The Lord Jesus Christ delivers this judgment, but He uses the Assyrian to accomplish it. That is why it is called the "day of the Lord."

Here there is judgment on Egypt, but it isn't associated with the past judgment by Nebuchadnezzar. Therefore, to establish this point, the scripture now brings in verse 10. "Thus saith the Lord Jehovah: I will also make the multitude of Egypt to cease by the hand of Nebuchadnezzar king of Babylon" (Ezek. 30:10 JND). The word *also* is significant; it shows that this attack on Egypt is distinct from what Nebuchadnezzar executed. One judgment was executed by the sword of Nebuchadnezzar, and "also" another judgment came by an unknown sword. Nebuchadnezzar couldn't introduce the day of the Lord; that day is in the future.

We should observe that this judgment isn't on Egypt *outside* the land but on Egypt *in* the land. This is very significant because we will notice that Egypt isn't alone in its suffering; Ethiopia is there, so also is "Put," which is Libya. So too are Lud and Chub, two other North African nations. "Cush, and Phut, and Lud, and all the mingled people, and Chub, and the children of the land that is in the league, shall fall with them by the sword" (Ezek. 30:5 JND).

What we have here is a league of nations. These countries close to Egypt form this league. Therefore, what the scripture is bringing before us at present is the king of the South headed by Egypt, the terrorist kingdom in the southern part of Israel. It is called the "fly." It isn't as bad as the terrorist empire, called the king of the North or the Assyrian.

Nevertheless, compared to our normal society today, it is horrible. Perceive how the scripture is accurate; observe how the Bible is organized. It wasn't written to confuse but to edify. This chapter is, therefore, different from the previous one. Here is the king of the South headed by Egypt, seen in association with other nations in Africa. In the preceding chapter, we witness geographic Egypt suffering from a specified two-fold judgment at Nebuchadnezzar's hands. The first chapter speaks of the past; the second chapter speaks of the future.

We are also introduced to a new expression: "They also that uphold Egypt shall fall, and the pride of her strength shall come down" (Ezek. 30:6 JND). Instead of Egypt protecting Israel, as we have in Isaiah 30–31, we have Egypt being upheld. This is a reversal of the situation we had in Isaiah 30–31, and thus it also confirms what was said of geographic Egypt in Ezekiel 29. It wouldn't be exalted again but would need helpers. Therefore, what we have here is the king of the South, who is very distinct from designated Egypt. Designated Egypt is strong, while geographic Egypt is weak. This is further confirmed by the expression in verse 8. "All her helpers shall be broken" (Ezek. 30:8 JND). Again, instead of Egypt helping others, it is being helped. Instead of shadowing with wings, it is being shadowed. Therefore, by no correct interpretation of scripture can these two Egypts be the same. One is geographic Egypt, while the other is designated Egypt. One is Egypt in Africa, while the other is the USA.

Nonetheless, this Egypt in Africa wasn't seen alone; it was seen allied with other nations. Those who helped it were the nations in the alliance with Egypt because it was a base kingdom—it needed helpers. Egypt will then be established as the capital of the South's king, a terrorist empire in the south of Israel, which will be formed by the alliance of many African nations in the last days.

Finally, we have a message being sent to Africa from the Lord Jesus Christ when He returns. "In that day, shall messengers go forth from me in ships, to make careless Ethiopia afraid; and anguish shall come upon them, as in the day of Egypt: for behold, it cometh" (Ezek. 30:9 JND). We need to note the time of this - "in that day"; it is when the Lord Jesus returns. We are told that when the Lord Jesus comes and delivers this terrible destruction on the southern kingdom, the Lord Jesus will send messengers to Ethiopia, who will make them afraid.

"I will also make the multitude of Egypt to cease by the hand of Nebuchadnezzar king of Babylon. He and his people with him, the terrible of the nations, shall be brought to destroy the land" (Ezek. 30:10–11 JND). First, we again have the word *also*, which shows that Nebuchadnezzar's destruction would be a different destruction. We have before us how the Lord was going to make the multitude of Egypt cease by Nebuchadnezzar's hand but not only by the hand of Nebuchadnezzar. Second, he and his people with him, the terrible of the nations, would be brought to destroy the land. They would fill the land with the slain. That is what Nebuchadnezzar was going to do.

Despite that information, we have in the next verse what was going to be done by "the terrible of the nations." It now becomes clear why Nebuchadnezzar and his people - "the terrible of the nations" - became a type of the Assyrian. Accordingly, in Jeremiah 46, Nebuchadnezzar is the one seen as the representative of the Assyrian. What we have presented here is Nebuchadnezzar as the "terrible of the nations." This is consequently seen in Jeremiah 46, representing a new expression, the "strangers, the terrible of the nations." We will shortly observe why the Assyrian is described as the strangers, the terrible of the nations.

Next, the language here in Ezekiel 30:12-19 is very similar to that in Isaiah 19, where we read about Egypt in the last days. We need to see the time of this fulfillment. God said, "There shall be no more a prince out of the land of Egypt" (Ezek. 30:13 JND). The time of this fulfillment is when God visited Egypt in Isaiah 19, when the fierce king shall rule Egypt and the cruel Lord shall conquer Egypt. These rulers won't be of Egyptian descent; they will be foreign terrorists, as was noted. "There shall be no more a prince out of the land of Egypt" (Ezek. 30:13 JND).

We then read, "I will make the rivers dry, and sell the land into the hand of the wicked" (Ezek. 30:12 JND). This is very informative. The land was to be sold into the "hand of the wicked;" the wicked here is the head of the Assyrian. The land will be sold into the hand of the wicked when the cruel Lord of Isaiah 19 will conquer Egypt. This will be accomplished when the Assyrian attacks Egypt during the tribulation and conquers it. "I will make the land desolate, and all that is therein, by the hand of strangers" (Ezek. 30:12 JND). It is informative that the destroyer of Egypt isn't now seen as Nebuchadnezzar, but strangers, the Islamic terrorist north, the Assyrian.

The country of Egypt will be taken over by terrorists and made into an Islamic state in alliance with other countries in the south of Israel. Egypt will then head this Islamic state. Egypt's land will suffer devastating destruction during the process of changing from a secular state into this caliphate. There will also be a fallout between the king of the North and the king of the South, which will bring further devastation by the Assyrian, and finally the judgment on Egypt by the hands of the Lord when He returns. However, the Lord will be gracious to Egypt and make her a blessing in the land. The wicked here is the Assyrian head. The land will be sold into his hands. He will control and direct what will happen there during the Great Tribulation. All the scriptures now agree, and there is no contradiction.

We also need to perceive that the captivity here is the captivity inflicted on Egypt by the Assyrian, as in Isaiah 20:3-6. Moreover, we need to stress the importance of the encounter of Egypt with Nebuchadnezzar; as a result of that encounter, Egypt was going to be made weak, and Babylon was going to be made strong, but also Egypt wasn't going to be strong anymore. Until that encounter, Egypt was strong, but it shall be strong no more but weak - a base kingdom after that encounter. Those verses now set the stage to introduce designated Egypt in the following chapters. The prophet now brings back Pharaoh to establish the separation between geographic Egypt, the king of the South, and designated Egypt.

In reading Ezekiel 31:1-9, it becomes clear that God's word is now presenting an Egypt that is strong and mighty; yet this is Egypt in its final stages, since it is seen as a tree. This isn't geographic Egypt, which was presented in chapters 29-30 but designated Egypt. The scripture uses Assyria as a type of this power; the time also is different. Moreover, the message is not only to Pharaoh but to him and his multitude. He is great, and who can be compared to him? God now compares him to Assyria, the only contemporary power, to whom he could be compared. No one was like unto him.

Assyria was a cedar in Lebanon. "Cedar" in scripture speaks of strength. It was also a famous tree of Lebanon. Thus, this Egypt was strong; it was famous; everyone knew it. Egypt had "fair branches" and far-reaching influences. Egypt was also "shadowing" but not with wings, as Isaiah 18 says, because he wasn't seen here as a bird but with shrouds because he was seen as a tree, a cedar of Lebanon.

Egypt here is still protecting others as the land shadowing with wings did, but it is more occupied with its own glory. It is of "high stature," an imposing country. Egypt is the top nation. The waters made it great; it is excellent, and it is well nourished. In verse 5, it is so strong; it is "exalted above all the trees of the field" (Ezek. 31:5 JND).

The field is said to be the world, according to Matthew 13. The conclusion is that Egypt was the greatest power on the earth - greater than any other country in the world. It was a superpower. We read further. "His boughs were multiplied, and his branches became long" (Ezek. 31:5 JND). Egypt became bigger and bigger; it became more and more powerful as time passed. People were comfortable living and bringing forth their young in this land. They were citizens of a great country. We are now able to ask our question. Is this not the accurate description of only one country in this world? One cannot deny it; he or she might not like God's word, but he or she cannot doubt its accuracy. There is no book like the Bible in the whole world.

Moreover, "The great nations dwelt under his shadow" (Ezek. 31:6 JND); they were comfortable under its protection. Here we find Egypt shadowing with wings as in Isaiah 18. These weren't small countries under his protection but great countries he protected. We see that he protected countries just as in Isaiah 18 and Isaiah 30–31. "He was fair in his greatness, no tree in the garden of God was like unto him" - "everyone envied him" (Ezek. 31:9 JND). What a picture of an exalted nation! In the history of humanity, there was never a country so exalted.

Which country, therefore, does this elevated power represent? Is this geographic Egypt in Africa? Never! It is designated Egypt, the USA. We were provided with three chapters on Egypt, but the subjects are entirely different. The order is remarkable.

In Ezekiel 31:10–14 we are given the reasons for the destruction of Egypt. The first reason is its pride - because it has lifted up itself since its heart was lifted up. That was why Egypt was seen as a tree. The Bible declares that "pride goeth before destruction, and a haughty spirit before a fall" (Prov. 16:18), so God was going to destroy Egypt because of its pride. The destruction was affected when the country began to glory in its greatness. The second reason given for his destruction was his wickedness. "I have driven him out because of his wickedness" (Isa. 31:11 JND). This same reason was given in Isaiah 31. "I will arise against the help of the workers of iniquity" (Isa. 31:2). The same is true in Isaiah 1. "The destruction of the transgressors and of the sinners shall be together" (Isa. 1:28). Moreover, the same reason is given in Daniel 8. "When the transgressors are come to the full" (Dan. 8:23). The word of God declares the same thing everywhere.

Most essentially, God now gives the name of the one who will destroy designated Egypt. The Destroyer is none other than "the mighty," who is the Assyrian. We read, "I have given him into the hands of the mighty, he shall surely deal with him" (Ezek. 31:11 JND). Why not Babylon? Why not Alexander the great? Why the mighty? Then, again note also that the "he" comes back: the "he" of Isaiah 18, the "he" of Isaiah 30, and the "he" of Daniel 8. But now the "he" is identified as "the mighty," the Assyrian.

It is necessary to remember that the word *mighty* was attributed to both the land shadowing with wings and the Assyrian, as recorded in Jeremiah 46, where we read that "the mighty" would stumble against "the mighty." The "he" is the head of the Assyrian, the Destroyer. "He shall surely deal with him" (Ezek. 31:11 JND) are the very words the Lord spoke. Therefore, this destruction is certain to happen, since God says so. If God says the "he" will deal with him, how can I say otherwise? If God says that the strangers, the terrible of the nations have cut him off (Ezek. 31:12 JND), how can I then say that I don't know how this country will be destroyed? I surely know: the Assyrian will destroy the land shadowing with wings.

We need to notice that the future two-fold judgment was also combined in the text here presented. The passage declares that one devastation was to be executed *out of* the land, while the other destruction was to be executed *in* the land. The purpose for all of this is now stated.

"To the end that none of all the trees by the waters exalt themselves in their stature, nor set their top amidst the thick boughs" (Ezek. 31:14 JND); that "no flesh should glory in His presence" (1 Cor. 1:29) is what the scripture teaches and what is applied here.

We must appreciate the scope of the new expression introduced; this unique expression is the "strangers ... the terrible of the nations." This expression appears four times in five chapters, Ezekiel 28–32. The first time it is introduced is regarding the city of Tyrus in Ezekiel 28. "Therefore, behold, I will bring strangers upon thee, the terrible of the nations; and they shall draw their swords against the beauty of thy wisdom, and they shall tarnish thy brightness" (Ezek. 28:7).

We know who was going to attack Tyrus. First, Nebuchadnezzar, the king of Babylon, was going to attack it; then second, Alexander the Great was going to finish the job. Hence, Tyrus was going to suffer two-fold destruction, like the land shadowing with wings. Therefore, Tyrus will also have a future component, and that component will represent the USA in its commercial activities. Tyrus, therefore, represents the land shadowing with wings in its economic supremacy. The same people who were going to destroy Tyrus were going to destroy designated Egypt. "No prophecy of the scripture is of private interpretation" (2 Pet. 1:20).

In these Ezekiel passages, instead of Nebuchadnezzar and Alexander, who should have been seen attached to Egypt and Tyrus's destruction, we have this new expression - "strangers ... the terrible of the nations" - associated with their destruction. The expression "strangers ... the terrible of the nations" represents the Assyrian - not the past Assyrian but the future Assyrian. They are termed "strangers" because they don't belong to Israel but are claiming rights to Israel's prophets, rights to Israel's place of worship and Israel's God.

The word *strangers* is introduced as early as Isaiah 1. We read, "Your country is desolate, your cities are burned with fire: your land, strangers devour it in your presence, and it is desolate, as overthrown by strangers" (Isa. 1:7). The strangers here are Muslims, but they are claiming nearness to Israel's God, like the Samaritan woman at the well in John 4. The "terrible" brings us now to the terror of the last days, as will become very evident in Ezekiel 32. This is what troubles men today: terrorism.

We will now confirm what has been explained concerning the strangers in Psalm 54:3–7. In Psalm 54:3, we have the strangers, but the word for "oppressors" is the same word in Ezekiel 28-32 translated "terrible." It is "mine enemies" (Psa. 54:5), the king of the North and the king of the South, primarily: the strangers and the terrible. They are not only strangers but also terrible.

Let it be clearly stated that the expression "the strangers, the terrible of the nations" is all over the prophetic books. Take, for instance, Isaiah, where the Lord Jesus Christ destroys the Assyrian capital, which the land shadowing with wings attempted to do, but its attempt resulted only in his destruction. In this portion of scripture, Isaiah 25:1-8, we read, "For thou hast made of a city a heap; of a defensed city a ruin: a palace of strangers to be no city; it shall never be built. Therefore, shall the strong people glorify thee, the city of the terrible nations shall fear thee" (Isa. 25:2–3).

What, we see in Ezekiel 31 that is associated with *the mighty,* is the "strangers, the terrible of the nations" (Ezek. 31:12). This is the Assyrian of the last days, of which Nebuchadnezzar and his people were but a type. Moreover, in Ezekiel we read that Nebuchadnezzar was called "the terrible of the nations" (Ezek. 30:10,11) when he had to do with Egypt's destruction. This explains why in Jeremiah 46, it was Nebuchadnezzar's two-fold attack on geographic Egypt that represented the Assyrian attacks on designated Egypt. This group, the "strangers, the terrible of the nations," (Ezek. 31:12) is going to rain terror on this world, unlike anything the world had ever seen. In the next chapter, we will see the main countries that would be involved in the "terror" of the last days.

In Ezekiel 31:15-18, we are given a preview of the world's response to the destruction of designated Egypt. We detect that this judgment is very different from what we saw before in Ezekiel. Once this judgment is inflicted on designated Egypt, it doesn't reappear; instead, it will go into Sheol. It will be dead and buried. There will be nothing else to be added. This is so unlike what we saw in Ezekiel 29. There will be no future component. This is not the same Egypt. This is designated Egypt judged in the last days. It shall rise no more. Instead, in Ezekiel 32, we will read about Egypt in Sheol and not reappearing. What was said before about geographic Egypt, after it was destroyed at home by Nebuchadnezzar, is entirely different from what is presented here; after that destruction by Nebuchadnezzar, geographic Egypt was to return after forty years.

However, in Ezekiel 31 after the destruction of designated Egypt, it will be found in Sheol. Designated Egypt will never rise again; it wasn't coming back after forty years; it wasn't coming back at all since it will be in Sheol. This Egypt isn't a blessing in the land, as the future geographic Egypt, with Israel and Assyria, will be, as was stated in Isaiah 19; this Egypt will be dead and buried. It is not a base kingdom; as a matter of fact, it is not a kingdom at all. Therefore, these two depictions of Egypt can never be the same, because the same things aren't said about them. Consequently, the events aren't the same. One is in Nebuchadnezzar's days, while the other is in the last days before the harvest - which is the end of the age. One is Egypt in Africa, and the other is designated Egypt.

There will be great mourning for designated Egypt. The trees will faint for it. The nations will tremble at the sound of its fall. This couldn't have happened during the destruction of Egypt by Nebuchadnezzar, since all the surrounding nations were already in captivity and couldn't have mourned its destruction. They were mourning their own demise. However, here the world will not believe what just happened.

Moreover, as we find in Isaiah 18, the protection will be removed due to this destruction. The same we see in verse 12. "All the peoples of the earth are gone down from his shadow, and have left him" (Ezek. 31:12). Designated Egypt cannot protect itself; how could it protect others? This is certainly not the Egypt in Africa.

The impact of chapter 32 is too significant to miss. We must carefully notice the description God gives of this power. We are presented with an Egypt here, depicted as a young lion, strong and majestic. On land, it is like a lion; in the seas, he is like a monster. He is strong both on land and on the sea. He is a mighty power – a super power. Who could give us this correct description of this country except God Almighty? We are told that he is strong not only in the river but also in the waters - whether the Atlantic Ocean, Pacific Ocean, or Indian Ocean. In the world, he is strong. How could this be geographic Egypt? One will have to accuse the scripture of exaggeration. However, Egypt goes to the wrong place; it fouls "their rivers." "Their rivers" are the Euphrates and Tigris Rivers. His river, as Egypt, is the Nile. He will go to the wrong battle. He will go by the Euphrates and Tigris Rivers to fight, but this will be the wrong fight.

It is vital to observe, as God said in Isaiah 31, that He is going to stretch out His hand, so He says here, "I will also spread out my net over thee" (Ezek. 32:3 JND). We need to realize that it's not Nebuchadnezzar who will take Egypt in his net but an assemblage of many peoples. The expression "the assemblage of many peoples" (Ezek. 32:3 JND) shows that the Assyrian is composed of fighters worldwide. "They shall bring thee up in my net" (Ezek. 32:3 JND). Egypt is going to be trapped. Moreover, the Lord said, "I will water with thy blood the land" (Ezek. 32:6 JND). This is all what God is going to do. There will be no escape; God determined this destruction both outside and inside the land.

In Ezekiel 32:7-8, we have further description of the world's response to this destruction. In Genesis, we read, "Let there be lights in the expanse of heaven … to give light upon the earth" (Gen. 1:14-17). We are told that when Egypt is put out, God will cover the heavens and make the stars black. The world rulers won't know what to do, since the source of their light will be extinguished; they will be without light. They won't know what direction to take to move their country forward. In Genesis 1:14, we are told that the greater light was to rule the day, and the lesser light was to rule the night, but now there was no light at all. For a time, no ruler knew what to do. The greater light, the smaller light, and the subordinate lights were all in a state of total confusion; they didn't know how to rule. These lights represent rulers in the earth; they were then without answers.

The effect of Egypt's destruction was a violent convulsion of the whole structure of man's society. Every form of the established order and every form of proven government - supreme government as seen in the sun, derivative government as seen in the moon, and subordinate governments as seen in the stars - will cease to give direction for a time. This will be the state of the world after the destruction of designated Egypt.

Every class of society and every power, from the palace to the pit, was filled with present and sustained terror. People were making themselves happy without God but only for a while, like the last king of Babylon; they were feasting with their wicked enjoyments, but then the whole framework of man's order, on which he had been reposing in fancied security, was smitten and shattered. God says in Isaiah 18, "I will take my rest and I will consider in my dwelling place" (Isa. 18:4). God does that now. God watches on, as man behaves as if there is no God; but when He rises in judgment man will shiver.

In Isaiah 24:16-21, we notice this destruction from the side of Russia. Here Russia, called "the treacherous," the betrayer, will support this terrorist kingdom and inflict this stunning defeat on the land shadowing with wings. As a result of this defeat, we see what will then face Israel in verses 17-18 and what will happen to the world in verses 19–20. We also see Satan cast out of heaven in verse 21 and the judgment of the earth's kings when Christ comes. Here we have the sequence. Therefore, in both Ezekiel and Isaiah, we see the absolute chaos that will overtake the world.

That is why we read in Isaiah 24 the following: "The earth is utterly broken down, the earth is clean dissolved, the earth is moved exceedingly. The earth shall reel to and fro like a drunkard, and shall be removed like a cottage; and the transgression thereof shall be heavy upon it; and it shall fall, and not rise again" (vv. 19-20). These circumstances are the result of the destruction of the land shadowing with wings.

Nevertheless, in Ezekiel 32:9-10, God says he will vex the hearts of many people. People will be vexed; people will be angry. God said He is going to make them vex and angry at the destruction of Egypt. The world won't be able to comprehend how such a mighty power will be destroyed. Every country knew Egypt, even though Egypt didn't care to know many of those countries. However, they knew Egypt, and the response to its destruction will be overwhelming. The people will be amazed. How could this have happened? They will be astonished by the destruction, but then fear and terror will overtake them in the face of the Assyrian. They will then reason that if Egypt couldn't defeat the Assyrian, then who could? If the greatest power on the earth couldn't defeat the Assyrian, then the nations are doomed. The governments will be terrified. The Assyrian will be the one used of the Lord to brandish the sword. The nations will tremble. They will be in constant terror, shaking at every moment, each for its existence. They will then be afraid because the established order will be wrecked.

If designated Egypt were destroyed today, just imagine the confusion that such an event would introduce. God opens the curtain a little so we may see one of the strokes of His hands. Yet it would not be the last. Not only is the mighty God going to judge designated Egypt, but all are going to come under His judgment. This protective land is only discussed first, because it is seen today as protecting Israel, and as a consequence, God gives us its history. Designated Egypt is the first major power to be judged. Let it be clearly established that the Bible shows what will happen in Europe, Russia, Turkey, Iran, Iraq, Jordan, Israel, and all the other nations; God will judge them all, as we will shortly see.

Verse 11 states a fact. "For thus saith the Lord Jehovah: The sword of the king of Babylon shall come upon thee" (Ezek. 32:11 JND). Yes, this is true; this has happened; yet it is fascinating to see how it avoids saying that this destruction came from the *king* of Babylon. Instead, it clearly states in verse 12 that by "the mighty" was the multitude of Egypt going to fall. The word of God declares this in Daniel 8, asserts it in Jeremiah 46, affirms it in Ezekiel 32, and proclaims it everywhere. I definitely know how designated Egypt is going to be destroyed; the Assyrian will destroy it. This is not what I want; I don't want the destruction of any country. This is what I am taught in God's word, and I believe God.

We read in Ezekiel 32:12 that by the swords of "the mighty," God will cause the multitude of Egypt to fall. He then states that "the mighty" was "the terrible" of the nations. Therefore, the scope of "the mighty" is too extensive to underestimate. It is vital to observe that the destruction is presented here as accomplished by "the mighty;" then God's word brings in a fascinating explanation: it states, "the terrible of the nations, are they all" (Ezek. 32:12 JND). Both Nebuchadnezzar and the Assyrian were "the terrible" of the nations. This is very important because Ezekiel 30:11 clearly states that the "terrible of the nations" were Nebuchadnezzar and his people.

However, when it speaks of the future, the passage brings in another expression to avoid confusion with the past. The new term is the "strangers, the terrible of the nations." (Ezek. 31:12) The "strangers" aren't seen associated with Nebuchadnezzar, not even once; only with the future Assyrian will the strangers be associated. Here it declares that "the mighty" is also "the terrible of the nations;" the "terrible of the nations are they all" (Ezek. 32:12 JND). The people from around the Euphrates River are here "the terrible of the nations." In the last days, everything is about terror. They are the ones who were going to spoil the pride of Egypt. However, after the destruction of Egypt, the Lord states that He will destroy the beasts. We need to note the order: after the destruction of designated Egypt, we have the destruction of the beasts, the Roman Empire and the Antichrist, the beasts of Revelation 13, will be destroyed after the destruction of Egypt. This Egypt is the first power consumed. After that, the beasts will be destroyed.

In this destruction of designated Egypt in Ezekiel 32:17-21, there was no thought of captivity, nor of being revived. Egypt instead goes into Sheol; it is dead, buried, and will never rise again. Moreover, others join Egypt in Sheol, since Christ will come and destroy the other powers. Then scripture opens our eyes to what will happen in Sheol. This is informative; it is fascinating. Those who say there is no life after death, take warning.

In Ezekiel 32:22-23, we have amplified that the Lord, having come and put an end to the excursion of men, will destroy these different powers; having used the Assyrian to destroy these nations, the Lord will then destroy the Assyrian. We know the Assyrian will be destroyed after the Lord comes. Then the Assyrian will enter death like Egypt, it and all those who followed it. We see from the passage that the Assyrian of the last days is a terrorist unit. The word of God declared that Assyria caused its terror in the land of the living. The Assyrian is the first to be mentioned, and it will be the most notorious terrorist group. It will be the mighty and the first of these terrorist powers in the last days. It will have a large following, then be revealed in death with Egypt. The scriptures clearly state that Assyria will cause terror in the land of the living.

Nevertheless, designated Egypt isn't said to cause terror, but this terrorist power is said to follow designated Egypt in death. This sequence has no parallel in the past; Assyria was destroyed first, then Egypt long after. Yet now Assyria is said to follow Egypt. This whole scene is in the future.

Moreover, in Ezekiel 32:24-25, another country is seen identified with this terrorist body—that power is Elam, which is modern-day Iran. Elam is seen as an associated country. This country will also export terrorism, but there is something more. Not only will these countries cause their terror in the land of the living, but they will bear their confusion with them that go down to the pit. Instead of their famed seventy virgins, which their religion promised, they will find confusion in death. They will then realize their whole teaching was wrong, and they will have to bear their confusion. They will also realize that they injured and killed so many people for nothing and that they will have to answer to God for their actions. They will then be in total confusion and consternation; they will be deluded. This confusion is what awaits the Assyrian in its religious war, but it is the same confusion that awaits all those who reject the Son of God.

Man thinks everything ends at death, but he is wrong. In death, a man is as conscious as when he was alive, as we see with the rich man and Lazarus in Luke 16. Man believes that because God clothed him with a body, so without this body, he cannot exist. Nevertheless, he is wrong. Man has forgotten that God is a spirit and knows everything and created everything. He has forgotten that the angels are conscious, and they are spirits; even so, his soul and spirit will be conscious after death. Moreover, his body will be raised from the dead and reunite with his soul and spirit to face God; so will you, my reader. So will you!

We have another power of terror that will join the Assyrian in its destruction of the land shadowing with wings; Meshech and Tubal are that power. This is a big surprise. We read about this power in Ezekiel 32:26-28. However, who is this power? We get the answer to that question in Ezekiel 38–39.

In Ezekiel 39, we read, "And thou, son of man, prophesy against Gog, and say, thus saith the Lord Jehovah: behold, I am against thee, O Gog, prince of Rosh, Meshech, and Tubal; and I will turn thee back and lead thee, and will cause thee to come up from the uttermost north and will bring thee upon the mountains of Israel" (Ezek. 39:1-2 JND). In Ezekiel 38-39, we know this is Russia, which will attack Israel after the Lord returns and restores Israel. The Lord will then destroy the Russian force.

Therefore, Meshech and Tubal in Ezekiel 32 represent Russia. This Russian power will support the terrorist group and make it very strong. Russia will be the strength of "the mighty," the Assyrian. This passage ties Russia as the power, which will strengthen the Assyrian. Unless Russia had supported the Assyrian, it would not have become so strong. "Slain by the sword, though they caused their terror in the land of the living" (Ezek. 32:26 JND). They will cause their terror all over the world - in the land of the living. However, they will be destroyed by the Lord Jesus Christ when He comes.

This event never happened in the past. There was never a link between Meshech and Tubal and Nebuchadnezzar. The Meshech and Tubal of Ezekiel 32 are the additional powers that will join the Assyrian to crush designated Egypt by the Euphrates River and terrorize the world. After the Lord comes, He will destroy the Assyrian. The Russian regime will then attack Israel but the Lord Jesus Christ will also crush that power. However, the Russian power is seen gathered with the Assyrian in Hades after death. They all will meet after death.

There is great significance in what comes next. We notice in Daniel 8 that the power of the Assyrian "shall be mighty ... and he shall destroy the mighty and the holy people" (Dan. 8:24). That is, one "mighty" destroys another "mighty." We find the same in Jeremiah 46. "The mighty stumbleth against the mighty" (v. 12). We have the same here. "They lie not with the mighty ... who are gone down into Sheol" (Ezek. 32:27 JND). The "mighty" that was gone down to Sheol was the land shadowing with wings, designated Egypt. That first "mighty" was seen associated with iniquity, whose iniquities were upon their bones.

We must remember that it is because of their iniquity that the land shadowing with wings will be destroyed. Now we read that Meshech and Tubal were the terror of another mighty in the land of the living. They were part of the terror of the Assyrian in the land of the living. There is no "but" in Ezekiel 32:27, as we notice in the J. N. Darby's translation. If we read it without the "but," then we get the sense of the passage. Let us understand the significance of these two names, Meshech and Tubal, since they represent the only European nation seen connected with terrorism. It is Russia that strengthened the terrorist empire with devastating results.

Please observe today how the West is snubbing Russia; they will keep isolating Russia until Russia will embrace the terrorist group called the Assyrian in Syria. A serious crisis will develop between Russia and the West which will cause the West to sanction Russia into the hands of the terrorist. The day Russia supports the terrorist power, this world as we know it will change. The terrorist kingdom will be emboldened and attack the West with devastating results. Nothing I write can make this happen; only God can bring this about. A European nation will support terrorism against other Western countries. If there is no God, it will not happen. Nevertheless, if God says it, it is surer to happen than the sunrise tomorrow. If my interpretation is correct, then and only then will these things come to pass. If I am wrong in my understanding, then none of this will happen. I am persuaded that I am not mistaken. It is necessary here to note, as this book was going to press, that Russia threatened the West to leave Europe over sanctions. This is a very serious development. It is not what it will leave, it is what it will embrace.

Furthermore, we read about the role of Edom and that all will be ashamed of the terror they cause. Edom has a crucial part to play, as we will see when we deal with the Assyrian. Edom was Israel's brother, but he is seen associated with the Assyrian. He, too, is slain by the sword - destroyed by the Lord Jesus when He comes. He has a grave with the others. We need to observe that Moab is not there, but Edom is present. Edom's presence will be explained later. Thus, returning to our passage, however, we find that all these powers are now in death - that is, they shall arise no more. This shows that all this happens at the end when the Lord comes. Then the scripture makes a critical statement. "There are the princes of the north" (Ezek. 32:30 JND). When we come to the Assyrian, we will see that the king of the North is the Assyrian. However, we are here told that these powers are the princes of the North. They form, guide, and support the king of the North. This is the Assyrian, a terrorist power, composed and sustained by these powers.

Lebanon, an ally of Israel during the reign of King Solomon, is also seen associated with the terrorist Assyrian. In the day of the great slaughter, Lebanon will be associated with the Assyrian because of its connection to the mosques on the temple mount. Then when the Lord Jesus completes His purpose concerning the Assyrian, He will cause the demise of the Assyrian's power. Nevertheless, in death, the members of the Assyrian will be ashamed of the terror they caused when they were "the mighty." When they realized their mistake, they will be greatly confused; this confusion they will have to bear. Their religion won't make a difference; they will be as confused as all the other dead. My readers, please turn away from your sins or end up in hell forever; you too will be confused. What you expect after death will not be. Christ died for your sins on the cross; receive Him as your Savior before it is too late.

Nevertheless, in Ezekiel 32:31-32, we are taken back to Pharaoh so we will know that the powers scripture is talking about, in verses 22-30, has to do with the future Assyrian, who will destroy designated Egypt. There is no Nebuchadnezzar here but a confederation of many nations glued together by their religion, which will eliminate Pharaoh. God now says, "I have caused my terror in the land of the living" (Ezek. 32:32 JND). This verse confirms what Isaiah 2 noted that there will be the terror of the Lord before the glory of the Lord (Isa. 2:10 JND). Here it is said to be His terror, regardless of who He uses. Therefore, though you might disagree with what is happening with this terrorism, God says that He is the one who will bring this on people because of their rejection of His Son, the Lord Jesus Christ. We now see that the destruction of this Pharaoh will be done by the Assyrian of the last days, not Nebuchadnezzar of the history books.

CHAPTER 10

THE FUTURE TYRUS: THE COMMERCIAL USA

W e need to observe another aspect of the land shadowing with wings presented in the Bible. This is the feature of its commercial activities. We must, therefore, ask, why is so much written on this land? The answer is simple. It is because of its close association with Israel. It is the association with Israel, God's earthly people, that makes a country significant in scripture. On my scale of difficulties, this topic is a nine.

In Ezekiel, there are three chapters on Tyrus before we have the four chapters on Egypt. These chapters are Ezekiel 26-28. These three chapters also develop the concept of the two-fold destruction of Tyrus, and therefore, Tyrus becomes a type of the destruction of the land shadowing with wings in its commercial activities.

First, Nebuchadnezzar destroyed the ancient city. Second, Alexander the Great conquered the new city the Tyrians had built.

In Ezekiel 26:1-5, we observe that Jerusalem was taken into captivity before Tyrus was attacked. Furthermore, we need to recognize the significance of what these prophecies unfold. The fulfillment of these prophecies is impossible without God. The probability that these prophecies could have been fulfilled by coincidence is zero. God says that the city of

Tyrus was going to be destroyed. However, the destruction of a city was common. The difficulties of the prophecies become evident when God said, "I will also scrape her dust from her, and make her like the top of a rock" (Ezek. 26:4). When we take verse 12 into consideration, we have impossible utterances that can never be fulfilled unless there is a God. We read, "And they shall make a spoil of thy riches, and make a prey of thy merchandise: and they shall break down thy walls, and destroy thy pleasant houses: and they shall lay thy stones and thy timber and thy dust in the midst of the waters" (Ezek. 26:12).

We need to grasp the scope of the prophecies presented in this portion. The houses in the city are going to be broken down. The towers are going to be destroyed. The walls are going to be broken down, and all materials are going to be laid into the sea. We even read that the city's stones, the city's timber, and even the very dust of the city are going to be laid in the water. Which madman was going to accomplish such devastation? How could such prophecies be fulfilled?

If there was no God, indeed, this could never happen. In Ezekiel 26:4, God's word states further that they will scrape the dust from Tyrus and make her like the top of a rock. Could this be literally fulfilled? Just imagine what these prophecies are saying. Could these things be true? If God can fulfill these prophecies, surely, He will fulfill all His word. Ezekiel wrote this around 595 BC. How could this event actually happen? Let us now put the Bible where it belongs, above everything man ever wrote.

Nebuchadnezzar first attacked the city of Tyrus in 586 BC, about nine years after Ezekiel prophesied. He besieged the city for thirteen years. This city was so formidable that the thirteen-year siege of Tyrus made the three-year siege of Jerusalem by the same Nebuchadnezzar fade in comparison. During this thirteen-year siege by Nebuchadnezzar, the Tyrians came up with an astonishing plan that prevented the capture of their precious wealth. They moved their valuables from the city and transported them by ships to an island about half a mile offshore. This island was quite rocky and capable of sustaining high city walls. There they began to build another city to protect their wealth. When the city finally fell to Nebuchadnezzar in 573 BC, the conqueror got nothing for his effort. He had no ships, so he couldn't get their wealth. The Tyrians had escaped with their riches.

This is the reason we read in Ezekiel 29 these select verses: "Son of man, Nebuchadnezzar king of Babylon caused his army to serve a great service against Tyrus: every head was made bald, and every shoulder was peeled: yet had he no wages, nor his army, for Tyrus, for the service that he had served against it: Therefore thus saith the Lord God; Behold, I will give the land of Egypt unto Nebuchadnezzar king of Babylon; and he shall take her multitude, and take her spoil, and take her prey; and it shall be the wages for his army" (Ezek. 29:18-19).

Here we are told that Nebuchadnezzar received no payment for his work against Tyrus, so God was going to give him Egypt as his wages. This conquest of Egypt will be 30 years after Jerusalem was taken captive. What a God who will pay man his wages! Please remember that the wages of sin is death. However, the gift of God is eternal life.

We must learn to appreciate the unique way in which the word of God is written. These two verses not only give us a historical perspective but also provide us with a sequence. Take a careful look at these verses, and you will see that Jerusalem was first going to be destroyed by Nebuchadnezzar. Next, the old city of Tyrus was going to be destroyed, then Egypt, and finally, the new city of Tyrus was going to be destroyed. This is how one must read the Bible and receive the necessary instructions. We must stick to God's word and seek to get a handle on the original words.

In verses 3-4, God broadens the attackers from "he" to "they." We now read,

"I am against thee, O Tyrus, and will cause many nations to come up against thee, as the sea causes his waves to come up. And they shall destroy the walls of Tyrus, and break down her towers: I will also scrape her dust from her, and make her like the top of a rock" (Ezek. 26:3–4).

Nebuchadnezzar wasn't the only nation that would attack Egypt, other nations would also do so. In Ezekiel 26:11-12 we are introduced to a "they" that would also attack Tyrus. The "he" is Nebuchadnezzar. The "they" is Alexander the Great and his army. We need to observe how the scripture moves from the "he" to the "they" in this passage. Note that it was the "they" who were going to cast the stones and timber into the sea. The "they" were going to scrape the dust off the rocks, and it is the "they" who were going to obtain the riches.

History records that the island city of Tyrus was even more formidable than the city on the mainland.[27] The wall opposite the land of the original city was 150 feet high. The channel between the new city and the old city was more than twenty feet deep. The city walls stood high above the sea.

Alexander the Great had many military campaigns. He wanted to conquer Egypt, so on his way, he took Sidon and then got to Tyrus. The Tyrians met him with goodwill, which was refreshing. However, he put their friendliness to the test. He informed their envoy that he would like to sacrifice at Heracles's shrine in their city. The Tyrians knew what that request meant, and they couldn't grant him that favor. They knew that if they allowed Alexander the Great into their city, it was no more their city. The Tyrians, therefore, refused his request.

Alexander's mind was focused on engaging and conquering Egypt; he didn't want to entertain a distraction. Therefore, he sent envoys of peace to Tyrus to persuade them to accept a peace treaty. However, the Tyrians, believing in their city's invincibility, killed the envoys, and with disdain cast their bodies into the sea; that's how confident they were about their island city. Alexander was infuriated, so he made plans to attack the city. He was quite aware of the difficulties of the challenge. How could he reach their city? How could he overcome their island's fortification?

The same situation confronted Nebuchadnezzar when he attacked the city of Tyrus, but Alexander wasn't Nebuchadnezzar. He was brilliant. In his ingenuity, Alexander the Great determined to build a walkway in the sea that stretched from the mainland to the island city of Tyrus. He calculated that the best width for his intended corridor was two hundred feet to get him and his troops to the island in the shortest possible time. Next, Alexander had to identify the source of the materials to be used in his project.

Here again, we see his cleverness. However, this time it was God's word that was going to be fulfilled. It is God's word that tells us how he was going to accomplish this task. He broke down the walls of the old city, the towers, and the houses. He took the timber and all the material

---

[27] Lucius F. Arrianus, "The Anabasis of Alexander, being, the History of the Wars and Conquest of Alexander the Great," Book 2, Chap. 15-25 in Edward J. Chinnock's translation (London, UK: Butler & Tanner 1884)

and laid them into the water to make his walkway to the island. He even scraped the dust from the city of Tyrus to complete his program because the materials were insufficient.

At first, the Tyrians laughed at Alexander and his army; they even sailed their ships close to his workmen to laugh at them. It was the same way men laugh at believers today when they speak of the Rapture and the coming of the Lord Jesus Christ, as they did in Noah's days. However, soon their laughter turned to concern when they saw the walkway getting closer and closer. Finally, the island city was in his grasp. Alexander the Great then conquered their unconquerable city and thus fulfilled the word of God. It took Alexander the Great just seven months, from January to July 332 BC, to capture this city. After only seven months, it was all over. The Tyrians lost eight thousand men, while Alexander lost only four hundred. Did God's word come to pass? You can be assured it did; even the dust was thrown into the sea. The impossible was now fulfilled.

We are aware that when we study these three chapters in Ezekiel on Tyrus, we find some strange expressions, which have their fulfillment only in the future. Moreover, the only country that could fulfill these prophecies is the land shadowing with wings.

First, in verses 15–16, Tyrus's fall, like designated Egypt, affected the whole world. Moreover, the trembling of the princes and the astonishment at Tyrus were the same posture taken when designated Egypt was destroyed. This directs us to believe that Tyrus represents designated Egypt in the last days.

Ezekiel 27:27 proves that this couldn't be the Tyrus of the history books. These things didn't happen when geographic Tyrus fell in the days of Alexander. For though eight thousand were massacred, Alexander spared all those found in the temple and even sold over thirty thousand as slaves.

Second, Ezekiel 27:28–32 presents the weeping and the fear that will prevail after the destruction of Tyrus, as will occur at Egypt's destruction. Therefore, Tyrus is seen as the land shadowing with wings in its wisdom, riches, and pride. We are then told in Ezekiel 26:20–21 that Tyrus wasn't going to rise again.

Third, those who traded with Tyrus are named, and there is a very long list. This shows that Tyrus was the land shadowing with wings in its commercial activities. Why was God interested in this list if this was all history? Why name all these countries that traded with Tyrus? The reason is, just as Tyrus was the central trading hub in that day, so is the land shadowing with wings today; all want to trade with it. Just as with the four chapters on Egypt, so we notice here that there was a past fulfillment, and there will be also a future accomplishment. Nevertheless, there is a time given here that ties this destruction to the future. We read, "And I shall set glory in the land of the living; I will make thee a terror, and thou shalt be no more" (Ezek. 26:20). The time when Tyrus will be in death is the time when the glory of the kingdom will be on display. It will be destroyed just before the glory of the kingdom. That makes Tyrus a type of the protective land.

Moreover, the same people who will destroy designated Egypt are said to have destroyed Tyrus in Ezekiel 28:4–9. We learn that Tyrus was prosperous. Tyrus had great wisdom. The city of Tyrus had great commercial activities. However, Tyrus's mistake was that it thought it was a god, the same error Egypt made in Isaiah 31. This pride brought judgment on Tyrus, and the same group that destroyed Egypt - the "strangers," the "terrible of the nations" - is the one scripture affirms will destroy Tyrus. Those who are "strangers" but claiming nearness to Israel's God are the ones who will destroy Tyrus.

What is even more critical here is that Nebuchadnezzar conquered only Tyrus's old city and didn't touch the new one. Who then are the "strangers," the "terrible of the nations"? This group of people will come directly from the division of Alexander's empire into the king of the North and the king of the South. It is for this reason that Alexander the Great is introduced in this scene. These chapters present the destruction of the land shadowing with wings as Egypt and Tyrus. I am repeatedly told that a religious group called the "Assyrian," the "strangers, and the "terrible of the nations" will be responsible for destroying the land shadowing with wings. Therefore, regardless of whatever the name the land shadowing with wings was given, I can proclaim only that the Assyrian will destroy it.

CHAPTER 11

THE FUTURE ASSYRIAN: A RELIGIOUS KINGDOM

W e have been taught that though many scripture passages speak of the Assyrian; the Assyrian before the prophet's eyes is not only the one of the past but, more so, the one of the future. Like the Roman Empire, the Assyrian has a historical and future component. As we study the scriptures carefully, we see the character that emerges of the future Assyrian as one of religious terrorism. We will seek to touch on the religiousness first, then on the terrorism. Moreover, we will want to know where the Assyrian will come from and of what countries it will be composed. These insights we will now seek to obtain. On my scale, the level of difficulty is a nine. The topic is complicated; therefore, great attention and focus are required.

This chapter will be slightly different from the previous one, in that we will not only study and develop one particular chapter in the Bible but also examine different portions of God's word. We will start with the book of Psalms; then we will meditate on other parts of scripture.

We have stated that the character of the Assyrian is religious. How do we know this? Let us begin to search God's word. The word of God must determine our thoughts. It is very dangerous to carry our thoughts to God's word and then seek scriptural support for them. This practice is responsible for the majority of errors Christian teachers make in their exposition of the Bible. We need to let the scriptures form our beliefs. God's word is complete; it has everything we need to facilitate the understanding of the future. What we need to do is search the scriptures—not only some favorite books but all the books of the Bible.

The evidence will show that as we develop many of these subjects, Psalms and the prophets seem to occupy a substantial portion of the scriptures we have advanced. Psalms is equally as crucial as other scriptures. Therefore, we need to find where Psalms is set. The early part of Isaiah 10 records the attack of the Assyrian on Israel. Then in the latter part of Isaiah 10, we have the Lord Jesus Christ's destruction of the Assyrian. In Isaiah 11, we see the coming and reign of the Lord Jesus Christ after the destruction of the Assyrian.

In Isaiah 12:1–6, the settings of Psalms are identified. In verse 6, we read, "Sing Psalms of Jehovah because he had done excellent things: this is known in all the earth" (Isa. 12:5 JND). The book of Psalms primarily gives us the Spirit of Christ's expressions in the Jewish remnant during their trial and deliverance in the last days. However, that is not all; we also have the expressions of Christ in Psalms. We must also appreciate that Psalms sprang from a partial fulfillment of those circumstances in the psalmist's days.

As we study the Bible, we see that the children of Israel in the last days are identified under three headings: 1) the rulers of Israel, 2) the people who follow the leaders, and 3) the godly remnant who follow Jehovah. The expressions of Psalms are primarily the words put in the mouths of the godly Jewish remnant in the last days. As an example, scripture presents the Antichrist, the ruler in Israel. It then shows the people who follow the Antichrist, and finally, it presents a godly remnant, which clings to Jehovah but is persecuted by the Antichrist and the Roman Prince. We need to grasp this to understand the settings of Psalms.

In Psalm 17, we read, "By the word of thy lips; I have kept me from the paths of the destroyer" (Ps. 17:4). The expression "kept me from the paths of the destroyer" is an important expression. This expression means that unless the Psalmist had known God's word, he would have been deceived and destroyed. The second consideration is the word *Destroyer*.

The Destroyer is the head of the Assyrian. He shall destroy spectacularly. "He shall destroy wonderfully" (Dan. 8:24). He is not a builder, and he is not a developer. He is a Destroyer - a terrorist, according to man - but used by God.

The Psalmist asked to hide under the shadow of Jehovah's wings, not under the Romans' wings or the land shadowing with wings. "From the wicked that oppress me, my deadly enemies, who compass me about" (Ps. 17:9). In the Psalms, the Assyrian is identified mostly under the term "the enemy," while the word "enemies" in the plural represents both the king of the North and the king of the South. "The wicked" here is the head of the Assyrian. When I was young, I read that "the wicked" was the Antichrist. That is true, but I had to learn more, a lot more; I had to learn that there were three persons referred to as "the wicked": the Antichrist, the Roman Prince, and the Assyrian head. It was also helpful to me when I saw that God would use those three persons to fulfill His plans.

"The wicked" in Psalm 17 is the Assyrian. "The wicked one" of 2 Thessalonians 2 is the Antichrist. What is before the psalmist in Psalm 17 is the attack of the Assyrian, not the attack of the Antichrist. The enemies are primarily the Assyrian to the northeast of Israel and the Egyptian alliance to the south. This is the reason why these nations are said to encompass Israel. They are all around Israel. When the word *enemy* is in the singular, it is the Assyrian, the stronger of the two powers.

We then read, "They are enclosed in their own fat: with their mouth, they speak proudly" (Ps. 17:10). We see this same boasting in Isaiah 10:15–16. Therefore, this passage in Psalm 17 is about the Assyrian. Having established this, let us observe what is said in verse 11. "They have now compassed us in our steps: they have set their eyes bowing down to the earth" (Ps. 17:11). Who are these people? They are the Assyrians; they come from the old Assyrian Empire. However, this attacker is religious; they "set their eyes bowing down to the ground" (Ps. 17:11).

This is a religious form of worship connected to the Iraqi/Syrian area and was seen displayed in Abraham's day. The only religious people who have this form of prayer today are the Muslims, who tie their religion to Abraham. In their mosques, they bow their heads to the ground. This is what distinguishes Israel's attackers. "They set their eyes bowing down to the earth." This is Islam; this is their religion. This is the way they pray.

They are the ones who have their mosques on the temple mount, whose mosques Israel will destroy. However, this passage alone can never prove their religious persuasions. We need to find more if we are to make that point, and we will see many more.

In the attack of the Assyrian on the future Roman Empire, seen under the aspect of Babylon in Isaiah 13, we read, "I have commanded my sanctified ones, I have also called my mighty ones for mine anger, even them that rejoice in my highness" (Isa. 13:3). In this simple verse, we have two expressions used to identify the Assyrian. These "sanctified ones" are jihadi fighters, since the word for "sanctified" is the word for "holy" in the passage. However, these are not Jews, so we may stretch the word *holy* to them; these sanctified ones belong to the Assyrian. The expression "my mighty ones" also identifies them with the Assyrian. However, Jehovah calls them His mighty ones. Now that we have established that it is the Assyrian, notice what they do. They "rejoice in my highness" (Isa. 13:3), Jehovah said. That is why there is the salutation "Allah Akbar," which is "God is great." They rejoice in God's greatness. Their greeting distinguishes them as rejoicing in God's greatness. In my discourse on the Muslims, I had great difficulty deciding whether to use uppercase or lowercase letter "g" for God, because of the way the Muslims are presented in the Bible. They are seen as embracing the God of Abraham; not a false god, but they are not seen in relationship to Him – He does not own them as His people. To understand this religious war, we must think of Cain and Abel. The story of those two brothers presents the characteristics of the religious war.

In Hosea 5 we notice a strange expression. We read, "They shall go with their flocks and with their herds to seek the Lord, but they shall not find him; he hath withdrawn himself from them. They have dealt treacherously against the Lord: for they have begotten strange children: now shall a 'month' devour them with their portions" (Hos. 5:6–7).

Who are these strange children we are reading about in Hosea? Let us read another passage in Hosea to appreciate the expression. "I will not have mercy upon her children; for they are children of whoredom" (Hos. 2:4). These are the strange children we read about in Hosea 5. They are not my children. He continued, "For their mother hath played the harlot; she that conceived them hath done shamefully: for she said, I will go after my lovers that gave me my bread and my water, my wool and my flax, mine oil and my drink" (Hos. 2:5).

This adulterous relationship here is Israel trusting designated Egypt for her protection and provision. Therefore, Israel produces children from this adulterous relationship - these children follow the advice and ways of the land shadowing with wings; they are not Jehovah's children. Israel goes after her lover, as we see today. Note again what God says in Hosea 5. "Because in self-will he walked after the commandment [of man]" (v. 11 JND). The commandment of man here are the dictates of the land shadowing with wings. Israel doesn't follow the commandment of God; instead, she follows the commandment of man. It is this advice of man that will cause Israel to degrade in her morality and become the house of the evildoers. Then, later, when she will follow the Antichrist's dictates, she will become a worshipper of the Roman statue. Yet men think this relationship between the USA and Israel will be blessed; they have no sense of the mind of a holy God.

In Jeremiah, we read, "For all thy lovers are destroyed" (Jer. 22:20 JND). God will subsequently remove all her lovers, and Israel will be left alone. God will act, and the lovers will be no more. This is what we are taught in the scriptures. He now continues. "I will hedge up thy way with thorns, and make a wall, that she shall not find her paths" (Hos. 2:6). There are two lovers; the first one is the land shadowing with wings, called designated Egypt. This is a sweet relationship of protection plus provision. This lover protects her and provides for her financially; she is given billions of dollars per year from this lover. Israel has produced children for this lover; the children follow the ways of this protective land so they will embrace all the practices of this land. We are now instructed that very soon God will act to put a rift between Israel and her first lover. God informs us that concerning this first lover, He will hedge up her way with thorns. The second lover is the Roman Empire; for this one, He will make a wall so Israel will not find her path. She rejected Christ, "the way," and now she cannot find her path. She will, therefore, fall into apostasy and idolatry.

We read further, "She shall follow after her lovers and shall not overtake them, but she shall seek them but shall not find them, then shall she say, I will go and return to my first husband" (Hos. 2:7). We need to observe that the lovers are called "them" - they are more than one. These lovers are the land shadowing with wings and the Roman Empire. It can be seen that ungodly relationships are carried on, by Israel, with these two lovers. These relationships will bring disaster.

Thus, to God, this relationship with the land shadowing with wings is an adulterous relationship, and He has already pronounced a woe on it. Israel's husband here is the Lord; therefore, Israel is seen as carrying on illicit relationships with these powers. Let us establish this point with a scripture. In Isaiah, we read, "For thy Maker is thine husband; the Lord of hosts is his name; and thy Redeemer the Holy One of Israel; The God of the whole earth shall he be called. For the Lord hath called thee as a woman forsaken and grieved in spirit, and a wife of youth, when thou wast refused, saith thy God" (Isa. 54:5–6).

It is clearly stated that Israel's husband is the Lord and this is stated in Isaiah; therefore, to trust in another person is to commit adultery. We herein perceive that only when the lover will be no more would Israel seek to return to the Lord. She will rebuild her temple only when the land shadowing with wings will be no more. These relationships will bring judgment. We are told that after the Assyrian destroys the land shadowing with wings - calling on Allah, their god - the Assyrian will then be sure that Allah is the real God. The Assyrian will believe that Jehovah destroyed the land shadowing with wings to establish it.

On the other hand, Israel will also know that God did act (that is the reason God will stretch out His hand, so that all will know He acted), but Israel will also be sure that it must be her God who did cause this destruction, or else this destruction could never have occurred. Furthermore, Israel will think God destroyed the land shadowing with wings so she might return to her God instead of trusting in that power. We read, "She shall follow after her lovers and shall not overtake them, but she shall seek them but shall not find them, then shall she say, I will go and return to my first husband; for then was it better with me than now" (Hos. 2:7). This is the sequence of events that will produce the defiling of the Muslim mosques and the rebuilding of the Jewish temple. This identical order is given in Isaiah 30; the wall is first broken in verse 14 then the subsequent defiling and rebuilding of the temple in verse 22. Therefore, after the first lover is destroyed, Israel will seek to return to her first husband, the Lord. She will do this by rebuilding her temple, the only way she thought she could return to her God.

However, despite all her desires, Israel cannot rebuild her temple, because on the temple mount stands two Muslim mosques, and one is situated on the temple site. This mosque on the temple site is called the Dome of the Rock and is separated from the temple location by only a wall. As a result, being faced with this difficulty, what will Israel do? Israel will defile and then break down the Muslim mosques (being assured that God will act for her protection) to rebuild her temple and return to her first husband. However, things won't work out that way; instead of Israel finding Jehovah, jihad will be declared. Jehovah, the Lord Jesus Christ, whom she already crucified, will not then come for her deliverance. At this juncture, no amount of diplomacy will prevail. The Muslims all over the world will be stirred up for Israel's destruction. We need to remember that the nations will all err.

We are now given the key; let us then open the passage. "They shall go with their flocks and with their herds to seek the Lord, but they shall not find him; he hath withdrawn himself from them. They have dealt treacherously against the Lord: for they have begotten strange children: now shall a month devour them with their portions" (Hos. 5:6–7). The Jews, having destroyed the Muslim mosques, will "go" with their sheep and their cattle to the temple they rebuilt in Jerusalem to worship Jehovah and offer sacrifices. Observe carefully that they don't "come" with their flock and their herd to seek the Lord, but they "go" because the Lord wasn't there in the temple. Nevertheless, for us believers, the Bible says, "Come boldly unto the throne of grace" (Heb. 4:16), for the Lord is there, and He invites us to come.

Nevertheless, they don't come to Him; they go away from Him because He isn't there. Moreover, they shall not find Him. They are strange children, not seen in a relationship with Jehovah, but children with ways of the land shadowing with wings. The Lord isn't there; the Lord whom they rejected is in heaven. As a result, "the month" shall devour them.

We must now endeavor to understand who "the month" is that shall devour Israel. Here again, J. N. Darby will have to help us; he translates this word *month* by the expression "the new moon." How shall "the new moon" devour Israel? Who is "the new moon" that shall devour Israel?

The new moon is a symbol of Islam. On the top of every Muslim mosque is the symbol of the new moon. This symbol is conspicuously displayed. How can the Bible be so right every time? The scripture doesn't have to say more. The religion of the Assyrian is Islam. The Assyrian will be a Muslim terrorist power. Nevertheless, the three passages aren't enough; hence, I will present more.

As early as Jeremiah 6, we began to read about an even stranger expression. "O ye children of Benjamin, gather yourselves to flee out of the midst of Jerusalem and blow the trumpet in Tekoa, and set up a sign of fire in Beth-haccerem for evil approaches out of the north, and great destruction" (Jer. 6:1). We are again in the very same place Isaiah 10 and Hosea 5 put us. Benjamin is again in the center of the storm. The evil is approaching out of the North, the very same direction we have in Isaiah 10. The Assyrian is seen coming in from the North. "The shepherds with their flocks shall come unto her: they shall pitch their tents against her round about, they shall feed everyone in his place" (Jer. 6:3). "Shepherd with their flocks" is a religious expression.

We now notice a significant expression in verse 4; here we have the expression "Prepare war against her; arise and let us go up at noon, woe unto us" (Jer. 6:4). We don't have to say much to establish that it is the Assyrian in this passage. It is the Assyrian and the king of the South attacking Israel during the tribulation. Nevertheless, I want us to notice the expression "prepare war" used here. If one thinks it is a simple expression to translate, then let him or her think again. The translators of the King James Version (KJV) don't know what to make of the Hebrew words. These words aren't in the translators' experience, and they are at a loss to understand the meaning of the expression. Yet, there are only two words. We need to turn again to J. N. Darby for help. He translated the expression as "prepare war," the same way as the KJV. Then one will ask, What is the purpose of J. N. Darby's translation in this instance? What help does this translation offer? He translated it in the same manner as the KJV. Yes, again because it is not in his experience. He knows the words, but he doesn't understand them.

However, this is what distinguishes Darby's translation. This is the difference! He wrote a note in his translation that explained that the word *prepare* used in this instance isn't the common word for "prepare" but the word for "hallow" or "holy" in the Hebrew - holy war, jihad. The same "sanctified ones" of Isaiah 13 we just mentioned are here again before us, since the word translated "sanctified" is the same one translated here as "holy" in this scripture. I love this translation, for although Mr. Darby may not have understood the meaning of the text, he faithfully gave what he saw in the original in his note. One will never learn these things by reading many of these modern-day translations.

However, lest one thinks it is an isolated expression, let me introduce a few more passages. In Joel, we read, "Proclaim ye this among the Gentiles: Prepare war, wake up the mighty men, let all the men of war draw near; let them come up: Beat your plowshares into swords and your pruning hooks into spears: let the weak say I am strong" (Joel 3:9–10).

This text presents the Assyrian's final attack on Jerusalem. Again, we find the same expression, "prepare war" - holy war, jihad. Here Muslims from all over the world are stirred up to come to Jerusalem. What brings them there? This "holy war" is because Israel defiled and broke down their mosques and rebuilt her temple. The defiling and destroying of their mosque are the reasons for the jihad. At that time, there will be no moderate Muslims; all will come to fight. This is what the word of God says, and this is what I believe. The breaking down of the mosques on Mount Moriah is responsible for the jihad. If you think the mosques on the temple mount are there for style, you are sadly mistaken. It will help if you think again.

We need to also notice the expression "There shall no stranger pass through them anymore" (Joel 3:17). Why is this expression here? This expression is here because the strangers are Muslims. The strangers here aren't ordinary but a religious group claiming nearness to Israel's God. This religious group will later discover they were strangers to Israel's God, though they say Israel's prophets are their prophets.

Another point of importance is found in the saying "Put in the sickle; for the harvest is ripe: come, get you down; for the press is full, the vats overflow" (Joel 3:13 JND). We need to see that when Israel is attacked and destroyed in this battle, the harvest is said to be ripe, but when the land shadowing with wings was destroyed, it was said to be "before the harvest." There is a big difference between the two expressions. The attack and destruction of the land shadowing with wings will occur before the tribulation, while Israel's invasion and destruction will occur during the tribulation. Finally, we read, "The Lord shall roar out of Zion" (Joel 3:16). When the Assyrian returns from Egypt for the final battle, the Lord would have already come from heaven, and He will come out of Zion and obliterate the Assyrian.

"Thither cause thy mighty ones to come down, O lord" (Joel 3:11). There and then is when the Lord Jesus Christ will return with His mighty angels and us. Primarily the angels are termed "the mighty ones" in this verse as we read in 2 Thessalonians 1:7–8. Note: the army is told to "come up" while "the mighty ones" are instructed to "come down." We are coming from heaven with our Lord Jesus Christ and the mighty angels to deliver Israel and to rule the universe.

One last passage on jihad will suffice. In Micah we read, "Then shall they cry unto the Lord, but he shall not hear them; he shall even hide his face from them at that time, as they have behaved themselves ill in their doing. Thus, saith the Lord concerning the prophets that make my people err, that bite with their teeth, and cry, Peace; and he that putteth not into their mouths, they even prepare war against him" (Micah. 3:4–5).

In Micah 3, Israel cries unto the Lord, but the Lord doesn't hear them; instead, He hides His face from them. The false prophets of that day will be saying peace, but they won't know what will be determined, even holy war - jihad. At that point, peace and safety will be declared, according to 1 Thessalonians 5:3, but jihad will be determined.

We, therefore, see that the Assyrian of the last days is a religious terrorist power. It is for this reason that we have terrorism today, but it will multiply exponentially tomorrow. What we have in 9/11 is the character of the Assyrian attack. At the time of 9/11, the Assyrian hadn't yet come, but God used it to show the nature of the case. The Assyrian was going to appear after 9/11.

Let it be observed that what I am presenting here is no speculation. We have in scripture even the fighters' character, and we may even have the suicide bombers. The writers in the *Bible Treasury* had written that just as much as there was going to be an apostasy in Christianity, there would be an apostasy in Islam. We will, therefore, need to study these prophecies carefully to grasp what they are declaring.

In Jeremiah 22, we read, "And I will prepare destroyers against thee, everyone with his weapons: and they shall cut down thy choice cedars, and cast them into the fire" (Jer. 22:7). Here again, the word for "prepare" is the word for holy - jihadi destroyers - not just destruction but destruction in the name of religion. This destruction in the name of religion is what we have today; however, it will worsen. We read the exact thing regarding Babylon, which is seen in Isaiah 13-14 as a type of the Roman Empire, the second protector, in the last days. In Jeremiah 51, we read, "Prepare nations against her" (Jer. 51:27 JND). The Roman Empire will seek to protect Israel during the tribulation, and the jihadi destroyers will come against it.

Consequently, these jihadi nations will attack Rome. We need to see that the jihadi fighters attack the Roman Empire. Still, we have holy war against Israel, not only jihadi soldiers, and this distinction is made because of Israel's defilement of the Muslim temples.

In Scriptural passages, there are only two nations apart from Israel, where the Assyrian is introduced without any explanation whatsoever. These nations are Babylon and Egypt. These two powers represent the Roman Empire and the land shadowing with wings. Moreover, there are only two nations that jihadi fighters attack. The reason is simple; these two powers will seek to protect Israel, but their protective posture will incite the Assyrian against them. Moreover, their protection will be ineffective. The Assyrian will destroy the first protector, Egypt; and the second one, the European Union, will break the treaty of protection with Israel.

I will now close this chapter with the belief that I have persuaded you that the Assyrian is a religious terrorist kingdom that will rise just before the Lord returns but after the towers fall. I can multiply the passages, but I think I have said enough on this matter. The Lord grants you understanding in all things.

CHAPTER 12

THE FUTURE ASSYRIAN: A TERRORIST POWER

We must now deal with this next aspect of the Assyrian, the element of a terrorist power. When the Assyrian is revealed, man will view it as a religious terrorist empire. If we came by evolution, then none of this that we are talking about will happen. Thus, if you believe in evolution, you don't need to worry. The things spoken about in this book won't just happen, because evolution cannot produce it. However, if God made the world - and I know God created the world - God will judge man for his sins and chastise him for what he did to His Son, our Lord Jesus Christ. Moreover, to accomplish this task, God will use a religious terrorist power called the Assyrian.

The powers that be, seek to restrain the ministers of God's word from speaking against evil. Moreover, the world is determined to dictate to the church what it should do and speak. Many church groups seek not to offend, so they preach miracles and money, and the world laughs at them and says, "You sure are frauds!" Nevertheless, the leaders of the world are committed that the church must not determine their moral values. What is evident is that the rulers today don't cater to God's response. What then is the divine response when men shut their ears to the gospel? God will send pestilences, famine, and earthquakes. And He will raise the Assyrian, which will deal with men's presumptuousness.

Therefore, we read, "O Assyrian, the rod of mine anger, and the staff in their hand is mine indignation. I will send him against an hypocritical nation, and against the people of my wrath will I give him a charge, to take the spoil, and to take the prey, and to tread them down like the mire of the streets" (Isa. 10:5–6). This presumptuousness of man will be the reason for the introduction of the Assyrian, and this introduction will produce the final crisis. On the scale of one to ten, this is a nine.

In Isaiah 2 we read, "Enter into the rock, and hide thee in the dust, for fear of the Lord, and for the glory of his majesty. The lofty looks of man shall be humbled, and the haughtiness of men shall be bowed down, and the Lord alone shall be exalted in that day" (Isa. 2:10 -11).

We cannot help but notice in God's word that there will be "the terror" before "the glory." The glory is when the Lord comes with us in glory and establishes His kingdom. However, before this glory, the scriptures tell us that there will be terror over and over again. We again will need Darby's help because he will consistently translate the word *fear*, used here in Isaiah 2 by the KJV, into the word *terror*. Therefore, in his translation we read, "The terror of the Lord and the glory of His majesty" (Isa. 2:10 JND). In verse 12, the scripture ties the terrorism to the day of the Lord.

In Ezekiel 32, we read, "For I have caused my terror in the land of the living" (Ezek. 32:32). The beauty of this verse in Ezekiel is that both the KJV and Darby translate the Hebrew word as "terror," which is the correct translation. My terror in the land of the living is the terror of Jehovah. Jehovah said He would cause His terror in the land of the living. Here again, the terror is in the land of the living. Every nation and country will suffer this terror. Why do you think we have terrorism today? Is it just by chance? The evolutionists deal with chance; we do not. Think again, my reader, think again; everything that is happening in this world is according to God's "determinate counsel and foreknowledge" (Acts 2: 23). This world didn't come by evolution; it didn't come by chance. It came by creation. God made it, and God will take it when He is ready. No power can stop Him.

Moreover, this terror isn't misdirected. The terror here will be directed on everything in which man takes pride, according to Isaiah 2:11–22.

What the scripture declares is that the Lord will use the Assyrian to destroy all that encapsulates the pride of man. There will be destruction upon destruction until the Lord accomplishes His purpose; then the Lord will destroy the Assyrian, and He alone will be exalted in that day.

We use the term "providential dealings" when we talk about divine things; these are events that look like normal occurrences - events for which there are typical explanations. Take, for instance, the present coronavirus pandemic. It seems like a normal disease trend; therefore, man will say we don't need to introduce God into this, since there is a cause and an effect. There is a normal explanation for this pandemic; however, how can there be a disease that affects the whole world unless God allows it? Therefore, these events are what we call "cause and effect" occurrences. Consequently, there is no reason to introduce God in the incidents as far as man is concerned.

We need to establish how these incidents will unfold. The Assyrian attacks man; it attacks his strengths - the countries he prides himself in. It attacks his cities, all his defenses, shipping, and all his works of art. This is the future of this world until the Lord Jesus Christ comes and deals with the Assyrian. It is for this reason that Daniel 8 states that the Assyrian will destroy spectacularly. He is the Destroyer, not a builder. He isn't developing anything; he is ruining everything. God declared in Isaiah 54, "I have created the destroyer to ravage" (Isa. 54:16 JND). God created the Destroyer for that purpose, and no one can stop Him from fulfilling that determination.

I need the significance of what is unfolding about the Assyrian to penetrate our hearts. The terror the Assyrian (if it is ISIS) will unleash on this world is beyond words. The scripture declares that there was never a time like it, and there will never be a time like it after. I want you to imagine the destruction by fire of Sodom and Gomorrah; it doesn't come close to the anguish the Assyrian will inflict on this world. Think about the destruction by water through Noah's flood; it doesn't come close to the agony the Assyrian will wreak on this world. I want you to believe me; it will be terrible, because I believe God. Repent and be saved before it's too late.

In Isaiah 2:10, the word of God declares, "For the terror of the Lord and the glory of his majesty" (Isa. 2:10). In verse 17, we read, "And the Lord alone shall be exalted in that day" (Isa. 2:17). In verse 19, we read, "For the terror of the Lord and the glory of his majesty when he arises to shake terribly the earth" (Isa. 2:19). In verse 21, it is the same declaration: "The terror of the Lord and the glory of his majesty" (Isa. 2:21). What is about to be unfolded is terror, real terror, so much so that God puts His name on it and declares, "My terror in the land of the living" (Ezek. 32:32) - the terror of the Lord. This is what is coming - the terror first, then the glory after, not the other way around. This simple coronavirus has caused such fear in men's hearts. What about when God introduces His terror in the land of the living? It's not the glory and then the terror; it is the terror and then the glory. This is what is coming on man, and that is the order. The terror is before the Lord comes; the glory is when He comes.

In Psalm 88:13–18, we hear the psalmist's entreaties. "But unto thee have I cried, O Lord; and in the morning shall my prayers prevent thee" (Psa. 88:13). He cried unto the Lord, he cried to no one else. "In the morning, my prayers cometh before thee" (Psa. 88: 13 JND). He then asked two questions of the Lord. Then he affirmed, "I suffer thy terrors ... thy fierce anger hath gone over me. Thy terrors have brought me to naught" (Psa. 88:15,16 JND). Here the remnant is going through this indignation, and he sees it as pure terror. It needs to be emphasized that both the KJV and the JND translate the Hebrew word here as "terror" in this passage. The "terror" of the Lord hath brought her to nothing. Here the word is in the plural because it's not only a great slaughter but also multiple terrorist attacks.

We then read, "They have surrounded me all the day like water: they have compassed me about together" (Ps. 88:17 JND). Who are the "they"? Indeed, they are the Assyrian and the king of the South. The terror is brought to bear on Israel, and the remnant expresses the depth of their circumstances to Jehovah. Here they surrounded her; they surrounded her like water - the water of the river, strong and many - Jehovah brings against her. Like the bee, the Assyrian swarms Israel; as a result, she is brought to naught.

We find the need for a question. Where are Israel's friends? Where are her associates, which she boasted about during their protection? The answer is given. "Lovers and associates hast thou put far from me: my familiar friends are darkness" (Ps. 88:18 JND). Though Israel looks to these lovers and friends today and speaks much of them, she will confess that her lovers and friends are darkness and no light. As we said before, these lovers and friends are the land shadowing with wings before the tribulation and the Roman Empire during the tribulation. Her familiar friends won't be there for her. Terror will surround her.

In Ezekiel 32, we read of the principal nations that will provide this terror. The first of them is the Assyrian; in Ezekiel 32 it is called the name Asshur. We read, "Asshur is there and all her company … all of them slain, fallen by the sword, which caused terror in the land of the living" (Ezek. 32:22–23). Asshur is Assyria; it is the Assyrian. When we interpreted Ezekiel 32, we had shown that this chapter describes the scene when the Lord will come and destroy the terrorist Assyrian. He looked back and highlighted the terror that it had caused in the world. Moreover, He showed how the warriors were confused after death.

Therefore, because we have interpreted this passage before, we will now deal only with the terror these nations will cause. They caused their terror in the land of the living. Asshur is first mentioned, which is the central terrorist power - it is the Assyrian. "We notice that Assyria is here with her company" (Ezek. 32:22), the company here are the nations in association with the Assyrian. Why not Babylon? Why not Rome? Why not Greece causing terror? Because in the revived Assyrian, we will have a religious terrorist kingdom, which will not be true of these other nations. This Assyria will cause terror all over the world. We already see this terrorism before our eyes, even though the Assyrian isn't yet present. God is slow to anger; He is warning us to turn away from evil. Nevertheless, He won't warn forever; He will unleash His judgment.

The next country that will export this terror is Iran, he is named as the first companion of the Assyrian. In Ezekiel 32, this companion is identified by the name of Elam which is the ancient name for modern day Iran. Iran is one of the countries America called the "axis of evil." However, here we read, "There is Elam and all her multitude round about her grave, all of them slain, fallen by the sword, which are gone down uncircumcised into the nether parts of the earth, which caused their terror in the land of the living" (Ezek. 32:24).

Iran is next seen; it is a support to the Assyrian and will cause terror in the land of the living in association with the Assyrian. However, something else is added. "They have borne their shame" (Ezek. 32:25) with them that go down to the pit. Now that they have been slain by the Lord Jesus when He comes, being then in death, they were ashamed of the terror they had caused, because they then realized it was all for naught. They had killed so many people for nothing; now they had to answer to God for their actions. This same confusion will all men experience, who say that there is no God; when they die, they will be confronted with the truth.

The second companion of the Assyrian is Russia. It is the main supporter of the Assyrian. We, therefore, read, "There is Meshech, Tubal, and all her multitude … they caused their terror in the land of the living. And they shall not lie with the mighty that are fallen of the uncircumcised, which are gone down to hell with their weapons of war: and they have laid their swords under their heads, but their iniquities shall be upon their bones, though they were the terror of the mighty in the land of the living" (Ezek. 32:26–28).

If you believe this event isn't going to happen, then explain to me why Russia goes down to Syria, where the terrorist group ISIS is located. Is Russia about to fulfill the explanation of both Darby and Kelly concerning what they wrote over one hundred years ago - that Russia was going to support the terrorist group that was going to rise out of Syria? Is this about to happen? We will wait and see. They never saw this happen; nevertheless, they explained what the scripture said would transpire. We are the eyewitnesses.

Moreover, the falling of the towers announces that the time of the terrorist attacks has come, and Russia, the scripture explains, is going to strengthen the terrorist to deliver those attacks. If everything is moving in that direction, then think, my friend, think. Don't worry about man and his explanation. Soon man will be astonished when these things begin to unfold; he will run and hide.

What we have for the first time is a European nation associated with this terror. This is the only European nation seen in scripture that is associated with terrorism, this European power is Russia. "Meshech" here is the ancient name for modern-day "Moscow." Therefore, the Meshech and Tubal here are the leaders and people of Russia seen associated with the Assyrian. Note carefully that Russia is given the same name here as in Ezekiel 38–39.

In Daniel 8, we read that the Assyrian "power shall be mighty, but not by his own power" (Dan. 8:24); that is, another power was going to strengthen it. We know that the power that will enhance it will be Russia. This verse proves conclusively that it is Russia with Iran that will support and strengthen the Assyrian. We will explain this association between Russia and the Assyrian when we develop the subject of the Assyrian.

However, note what is said here of Meshech and Tubal. First is "slain by the sword" (Ezek. 32:26); that will be when the Lord Jesus returns in glory and destroys the Russian army. That is the meaning of the expression. Then they being in death - they will then discover that death will not be the end of their existence; they will be as conscious as when they had their bodies.

The second thing we notice about Russia in Ezekiel 32 is that they will cause their terror in the land of the living. Note very carefully that a European nation was causing terror in the world. What is stated next is beyond belief. We read, "They shall not lie with the mighty" (Ezek. 32. 27). That is the first "mighty," the land shadowing with wings, the USA: they are not seen as associated with him, although they are a European power. The Hebrew words rendered "mighty" in verse 27 are identical to those in Jeremiah 46. The first word rendered "mighty" represents the USA; the second word rendered "mighty" speaks of the Assyrian.

However, Russia is seen associated with the second "mighty," which is the Assyrian. Please note the new expression: "Though they were the terror of the mighty in the land of the living" (Ezek. 32:27). The scripture here declares categorically that Russia will be the terror of the "mighty." Russia is the one that will support this second mighty and cause the terror. Russia will be the one that will make the Assyrian very strong, the one that will betray the West and arm this terrorist power. The West cannot keep isolating Russia and enclosing all Russia's allies in the European Union and NATO. The West cannot think that they can sanction Russia into conformity. Russia will react and embrace the Terrorist Assyrian. Russia will respond and support the terrorist king of the North, and the world will change forever.

In Isaiah 21, 24, and 33, Russia is called "the treacherous." The word for "treacherous" in Hebrew is the word *bagad*; it means "a betrayer." Russia will betray the West and join the terrorist empire of the East. What is playing out today with Russia in Syria will have severe consequences in the future. This is how all these problems with Russia today will end. This is not evolution; this is God's word, and everything is on schedule. You can see it in action; just look at Russia. Look carefully; it is all happening before our eyes.

Russia may reason that it doesn't need to fight the West but can support the Assyrian power to fight them. This is what will cause the terrorist group to become strong, very strong. Therefore, when this terrorist power, the Assyrian, becomes strong, it will attack the world with terrorist attacks. No writer can make this happen. Which one of us can make Russia forsake its traditional trading partners and support the terrorist? Only God can bring this to pass. Many men have tried to ignite jihad in the world, but they have all failed, yet at the right time, God will allow Russia to support the terrorist group, called the Assyrian, and all that will change.

We stand in awe at the perfection displayed in verse 29. We next read, "There is Edom, her kings, and all her princes, which with their might are laid by them that were slain by the sword: they shall lie with the uncircumcised, and with them that go down to the pit" (Ezek. 32:29). There is a particular reference to Edom. This is so because when Israel seeks to escape through Jordan from the Assyrian, Edom will be there to cut her off. Edom will act terribly toward Israel during the tribulation. When the Assyrian attacks Israel, the Jews will flee to all their neighbors to escape the Assyrian; in most of these nations, if the Jews are caught trying to escape, they will be handed over to Edom for destruction. The nations will believe Edom has the cruelest methods to deal with the escaping Jews. This is why the Lord Jesus Christ will deal with Edom when He returns, for its absolute cruelty toward Israel. Yet Edom was Jacob's brother - it is the Cain and Abel story all over again.

This family rivalry we will develop in another place. We need to grasp that Edom isn't necessarily part of the Assyrian, but it acts in cruelty against Israel in support of the Assyrian. If we scrutinize the language, we will understand what is said. "Which with their might are laid by them that were slain by the sword" and again, "they shall lie with the uncircumcised, and with them that go down to the pit" (Ezek. 32:29). We need to observe that scripture doesn't say Edom caused terror in the land of the living; however, the scripture notes its association with the Assyrian. It must be remembered that in Daniel 11:41, Edom is said to be one of the peoples who will escape out of the hands of the Assyrian. Consequently, the language is precise.

In Ezekiel 32:30, the scripture establishes that those powers caused the terror and also formed the king of the North. The king of the North is the Assyrian; the princes of the North are the individual powers that will establish this entity, called the king of the North. These associated rulers constitute the Assyrian power, but they are all about terror. This is like the future Roman Empire, which will be composed of ten kings.

The word of God then declares, "For I have caused my terror in the land of the living" (Ezek. 32:32). With this power, God will cause His terror in the land of the living. The power He uses will be the Assyrian, but here we see the countries that will be his companions. However, we must remember that there is another terrorist power in the south of Israel, but that is not what the scripture is speaking about at this time. It is the Assyrian that will be the greatest terrorist power to be manifested in this world.

We believe we have established that the Assyrian is a terrorist power. If, for instance, it is ISIS, though the nations today fight against it and seem to prevail, that power will rise again, and the victors today will be the vanquished tomorrow. They will all be defeated when the Assyrian arrives. God will accomplish His word. However, I need to be specific. I'm not saying that ISIS is the Assyrian. I am only mentioning a name, because ISIS could fulfill the scriptures. Yet I am not saying that it is ISIS in scripture; I don't want to say who that power will be. Remember that when the power rises at first, it isn't strong, but Russia's involvement with that entity will strengthen that power. Remember, too, that the Assyrian power rises after the falling of the towers and that it will establish its caliphate in Syria. Even J. N. Darby, writing over one hundred years ago, said that the Assyrian's capital would be in Syria, in the very place where we are witnessing all the turmoil today. In our day, we have therefore seen ISIS arriving after the falling of the towers and seeking to establish its caliphate in the same areas where scripture puts the Assyrian. As a result, we watch, and we observe.

What is so intriguing is that Syria's destruction is placed in Isaiah 17 between Moab being asked to be a cover for Israel in chapter 16 and the land shadowing with wings in Isaiah 18. What is so important is that we are today witnessing the very destruction of Syria. The capital city of Damascus is prophesied to be a ruinous heap. We read, "Damascus is taken away from being a city, and it shall be a ruinous heap" (Isa. 17:1). The other cities will, at the same time, be forsaken. We read, "The cities of Aroer are forsaken: they shall be for flocks, which shall lie down, and none shall make them afraid" (Isa. 17:2). Then the scripture asserts that "in that day it shall come to pass, that the glory of Jacob shall be made thin" (Isa. 17:4). The scripture declares that at that very time, the glory of Jacob shall dissipate. Let me ask a question. Is this what we are witnessing today: the capital reduced to a ruinous heap, the people of Syria forsaking the cities and seeking a better life in Europe and elsewhere? How can the Bible be so right? This is happening before our eyes. Yet men say there is no God. Man is wrong to the bone.

Interestingly, even the Golan Heights, which Israel captured during the Six-Day War in June 1967, seems to be in this passage. During that war, approximately one hundred thousand Syrians fled or were driven away by Israel. We read in verse 9, "In that day shall his strong cities be as the forsaken tract in the woodland, and the mountain-top which they forsook before the children of Israel; and there shall be desolation" (Isa. 17:9 JND). Here the mountaintop they forsook before the children of Israel clearly seems to be the Golan Heights. However, unmistakably the passage is teaching that after the capture of the Golan Heights, this abandonment of the cities will take place and not before. Note again that they won't be taken captives as in previous wars, but they will forsake the cities as they are doing today. These events clearly show we are very close to the return of my Lord Jesus Christ. Are you ready?

In Jeremiah 46, in the battle of the Assyrian against designated Egypt, we read of "terror on every side" (Jer. 46:5). All the companies fighting by the Euphrates River will unleash terror against designated Egypt until it is destroyed. In his pride, man speaks of the way to destroy an enemy. He says, "Kill the head, and the body will die." What man doesn't know is that no man would be able to kill the head of the Assyrian; only the Lord Jesus Christ will be able to destroy him.

In Psalm 9:1–5, we read that Christ will destroy the enemies when He returns. We observe that "mine enemies" are primarily the Assyrian and the king of the South. We are here told that the enemies fall and perish at His presence. Christ must come before the Assyrian is destroyed. He must be present before the Assyrian falls. It is when He returns that He will destroy the king of the South. In that day, He will rebuke the heathen. At that time, He will destroy the wicked. Again, the wicked in this psalm is the Assyrian head, not the Antichrist. Nevertheless, in verse 6, we read, "O thou enemy, destructions are come to a perpetual end: and thou hast destroyed cities; their memorial is perished with them" (Ps. 9:6). We have the Assyrian singled out and referred to as "the enemy" in verse 6. The Antichrist is never called "the enemy" in the Bible; he is "the adversary" as in Psalm 8. The enemy speaks of one outside Israel's land, while the adversary represents one in the land. The word of God then zooms in on the head of the Assyrian, the Destroyer, and proclaims that his destruction has come to a perpetual end. The scripture then tells us that the Destroyer destroyed cities so utterly that the Bible says their memories have perished with them.

It is painful to imagine what will happen when we contemplate what the scripture unfolds, when the word of God says the Assyrian will destroy wonderfully. The head of the Assyrian will destroy not only people and properties but also a whole city at a time. I didn't write these things; God's people wrote them. I didn't write the Bible; the Jews did. All I am doing is interpreting what their prophets have written. You can do like others and say, "I don't believe in the Bible." Nevertheless, I believe it with my whole heart.

CHAPTER 13

RUSSIA STRENGTHENS THE TERRORIST ASSYRIAN

W e said that the Assyrian is a religious terrorist power God will raise up to chastise this world and particularly Israel. We noticed that this Assyrian will come on the scene after 9/11 or after the falling of the towers. How long after that, it is not stated. We are now made aware that ISIS or any future terrorist power coming from around the Euphrates River area may qualify as the Assyrian.

In this study, we want to answer two of the most fundamental questions. One, is ISIS the Assyrian? Two, how did the Assyrian become so strong to defeat all other powers? These answers we will now seek to acquire from the scriptures. On my scale of difficulties, this is a ten.

In Daniel 8, we read the following:

And in the latter time of their kingdom, when the transgressors are come to the full, a king of fierce countenance, and understanding dark sentences, shall stand up. And his power shall be mighty, but not by his own power: and he shall destroy wonderfully, and shall prosper, and practice, and shall destroy the mighty and the holy people. And through his policy also he shall cause craft to prosper in his hand; and he shall magnify himself in his heart, and by peace shall destroy many: he shall also stand up against the Prince of princes; but he shall be broken without hand. (Dan. 8:23–25)

William Kelly wrote the following on Daniel 8:

The ram with two horns is explained to represent the kings of Media and Persia; and, in verse 21, the rough goat is the king of Grecia: "and the great horn that is between his eyes" (Dan. 8:21) is the first king. Then, in verse 22, we have the breaking up of the Grecian Empire; and in verse 23, it is added, "And in the latter time of their kingdom, when the transgressors are come to the full, a king of fierce countenance, and understanding dark sentences, shall stand up" (Dan. 8:23). This, I think, does not refer to Antiochus Epiphanes, but to the person whom Antiochus typified.

Mark the expression again, "In the latter time of their kingdom, when the transgressors are come to the full" (Dan. 8:23). "And his power shall be mighty, but not by his own power" (Dan. 8:24): a remarkable word, which is not said at all about the little horn of Dan. 7. There, I apprehend, it was by his own power. Satan might give him power, too; but in his own person he wielded the force of the Roman Empire. But, in the case of this ruler, though his power will be mighty, it will not be by his own power. He depends upon the strength given him by others. He will be the instrument of foreign policy and power, not his own.[28]

Edward Dennett wrote the following:

First, the fact of the establishment of the Grecian kingdom is given; then the death of Alexander in the midst of his triumphs - "when he was strong"; - the subsequent partition of his empire between four of his generals; and finally the rise out of one of these of "a little horn, which waxed exceeding great" (Dan. 8:9).

The four kingdoms, as pointed out in Daniel 7, into which Alexander's empire was ultimately divided, were Syria, Egypt, Greece, and Thrace. The two latter soon succumbed to the advancing Roman power; but the two former continued till about 50 BC. The one out of which the little horn arose was Syria, and for reasons which will appear in the course of the prophecy, this little horn was the king known as Antiochus Epiphanes. It will, therefore, be seen, if what was said of the little horn of chapter 7 be remembered, that the two little horns are entirely distinct; that the one of chapter 7, which subdues three kings, and finally wields the whole power of the empire, belongs to the west. It is the dominion of the revived Roman Empire which he possesses. The little horn of Daniel 8 has his seat and throne in Syria, and it is on this account that he becomes such a remarkable foreshadowing of the personage so often mentioned in the prophetic scriptures as the Assyrian, and as the king of the north.

Next, the actions of this fierce king are described: "He shall destroy wonderfully, and shall prosper, and practise, and shall destroy the mighty and the holy people" (Dan.

---

[28] William Kelly, *"Remarks on Daniel,"* The Bible Treasury, Vol. 3, ed. William Kelly (London, UK: George Morrish, 1860), *118.*

8:24). The location of this king, it must not be forgotten, like that of his prototype, will be in Syria, in the north of Palestine, and hence his designation in this book (Dan. 11) as the king of the north.[29]

We are explicitly taught that the Assyrian will arise from Syria, according to the word of God and expounded by Kelly, Darby, and Dennett over one hundred years ago. This is the same Syria where the battles are taking place today between the terrorist power called ISIS and the different nations. Also, having read the interpretations of men who have lived over one hundred years ago, who never saw the battles now taking place in Syria to bring in the Assyrian, but just interpreted the scriptures, we will now need to apprehend this expression -"not by his own power." Here we read, "And his power shall be mighty, but not by his own power" (Dan. 8:24).

The implication of this expression cannot be underestimated. We must grasp its importance. Therefore, we will first let Edward Dennett attempt an explanation. He wrote: "Two things are often put together in connection with this statement, viz., That the seat of the sovereignty of this king will be in Asiatic Turkey; and, secondly, that Russia, as plainly shown in Ezekiel 38 and 39, will be the final enemy of Israel, after their establishment in the land in blessing under their Messiah. The deduction is then made that the power behind this king of the north will be Russia."[30]

We need to identify the location Dennett presents: "That the seat of the sovereignty of this king will be in Asiatic Turkey."[31] Dennett already said that the Assyrian will arise from Syria. Nevertheless, Turkey had control of Syria and Iraq during the days of Dennett. Therefore, Dennett was speaking about Syria when he mentioned Asiatic Turkey. Furthermore, we need to follow this deduction that Russia is the one who will strengthen the Assyrian. This is very significant because it puts all these players right in the Syrian arena, as they are today. Let us develop this because it is essential. This also will help with the question: Is ISIS the Assyrian? We need to appreciate that Dennett was stating a belief that was prevalent in

---

[29] Edward Dennett, *Daniel the Prophet,* (London UK: A. S. Rouse 1893), 132.
[30] Dennett, *Daniel the Prophet,* 132.
[31] Dennett, *Daniel the Prophet,* 132.

his day. We can be helped by our beliefs, but we need scripture for our faith. Yet we need to remember that this brother was writing about this issue over one hundred years ago.

We notice further that after Alexander the Great died, his kingdom was divided into four main parts. Those parts were Syria, Egypt, Greece, and Thrace. The last two, Greece and Thrace, were soon conquered by the ever-expanding Roman power. They didn't last long as separate kingdoms. However, the first two, Syria and Egypt, continued till about 50 BC. These first two, Syria and Egypt, are the ones spoken of in Daniel 8 and 11 as the king of the North and the king of the South. It's needful to say that the history written by man expresses exactly the same thing.

It is the fact of history, as is stated here in the word of God, that on the death of this "mighty king," as so designated in Daniel 11:3, and after many contentions and battles, his kingdom was "divided toward the four winds of heaven; and not to his posterity" (Dan. 11:4) but by four of his generals. Two of these kingdoms soon disappeared, and two remained under the appellations of the "king of the North" and the "king of the South." The Syrian kingdom continued until 65 BC; then the Roman Empire conquered it. The Egyptian kingdom persisted until 51 BC, before the ever-conquering Romans extinguished it. Those two kingdoms represent the two famous dynasties of the Seleucidae (Syria) and the Ptolemies (Egypt). The two founders of these two dynasties were Seleucus and Ptolemy: one from Syria and the other from Egypt.

Moreover, to help in our understanding, we must remember in following the narrative that the king of the North and the king of the South don't always designate the same persons. They are titles like "duke" and "pharaoh." Moreover, this title "king of the North" or "king of the South" applies to all the monarchs of the same line. Therefore, when one king of the North died, his successor was given the same designation. Nevertheless, in Daniel 8:23–27, there is only one king spoken about, the Destroyer, the king of the North.

In this Daniel 8 passage, we read, "In the latter time of their kingdom" (v. 23). What is being emphasized in this portion of scripture is that these two empires will reappear. The revival of these empires was what ISIS was attempting to accomplish; it was trying to resurrect the king of the North and the king of the South, and believe me, these empires will be restored.

The king of the North will be revived in the northeast of Israel and the king of the South in the south of Israel. The king of the North will have his seat in Syria and occupy the territories around the Euphrates River in present-day Syria, Iraq, and Turkey. The king of the South will have his seat in Egypt and occupy the territories of Egypt, Libya, Tunisia, Ethiopia, and parts of other African countries. These revivals won't follow the pattern of the Roman Empire's revival, which is the European Union. The revival of the Roman Empire was without upheaval, as we also see in the fourth seal of Revelation 6. However, as the word of God declared, in contrast, the revival of the king of the North and the king of the South will be attained through bloody wars and the overthrow of established powers, as we see in the first two seals of Revelation 6.

Therefore, from what we have learned, we know that the king of the North - the Assyrian - will be a religious terrorist power, and so will be the king of the South. We also learn that the religious terrorist unit in the North will seek to establish an empire comprising Syria, Turkey, and Iraq; that is, it will conquer and unite the Euphrates River territories. What is exceedingly interesting is that we have observed ISIS attempting to establish these foretold empires in our day and before our eyes. According to the scriptures, the kingdom to the South must also be established. Therefore, we have observed another push by ISIS to establish another Islamic caliphate in the South as in the North.

How could men doubt that the Bible is God's word when its predictions are unfolding before our eyes? It is required of us to be the judge. Does one still think he or she came from evolution? In your answer, you decide. Therefore, is ISIS the Assyrian? I will answer that question in seven words: we will have to wait and see.

Let us go through the evidence of identification. According to Isaiah 30, the Assyrian will rise after the falling of the towers of Isaiah 30:25 - that is, after 9/11. The terrorist group ISIS appeared after the falling of the towers. The Assyrian will be a religious terrorist power; ISIS is a religious terrorist unit. The Assyrian will arrive suddenly; ISIS rose suddenly. Moreover, we learned that when the towers fell, the day of the multiple slaughters had come. Hence, ISIS is right on schedule. The Assyrian must come from the Turkey, Syrian, and Iraqi area - the territories of the ancient Assyrian Empire; ISIS originated from the same geographic designation.

Furthermore, we noticed that ISIS was endeavoring to establish the empires in the regions where scripture said the kingdoms would be established. With all these similarities, we could decide whether ISIS is the Assyrian, but I have reverence for scripture. I will make no pronouncement.

Nevertheless, one other point will suffice. When the Assyrian is revealed, at first it isn't strong; but it will show its real intentions, unlike the Antichrist and the Roman Prince, who will deteriorate later. In contrast, the terrorist power called ISIS acted, determined to establish its caliphate against all the odds. We need to ask now, Could ISIS be the Assyrian? Yes, it could. Could it be a type of the Assyrian? Yes, it could. Is ISIS the Assyrian? I will not answer that question. We will have to wait and see.

We cannot allow the significance of the following expression to evade us. We read, "When the transgressors are come to the full" (Dan. 8:23); a specific time is here given before some serious events unfold. We need, however, to identify the "transgressors" in this passage. The sinners are the Gentiles. The transgressors are the Jews. We are therefore taught that the sins of the nation of Israel were going to rise to the full. God doesn't judge until sin has come to the full. This we learn in Genesis 15. "But in the fourth generation they shall come hither again: for the iniquity of the Amorites is not yet full" (v. 16). Until their iniquity had come to the full, God didn't judge and displace the Amorites.

More is presented in Genesis 6; corruption and violence were what brought the judgment of water, since idolatry hadn't yet been present. In Genesis 19, it was sodomy that brought the judgment of fire. Therefore, the lifestyles and practices of those in Genesis 6 and 19 brought sin to the full. Similarly, the lifestyles and practices of the Jews will bring transgressions to the full.

The word of God tells us about "the days of Noe" (Luke 17:26), when there was the judgment by water: "So shall it be also in the days of the Son of man" (Luke 17:26). Moreover, God's word affirms that as it was "in the days of Lot" (Luke 17:28), when there was the judgment by fire, "thus shall it be in the day when the son of man is revealed" (Luke 17:30). Hence, when corruption and violence will be ripe, as "in the days of Noe," and sodomy has returned to Israel and will be ripe as "in the days of Lot," then God will raise up the Destroyer. In Isaiah 1, Israel is seen as fully embracing this lifestyle. We read, "Except the Lord of hosts had left unto us a very small remnant, we should have been as Sodom, and we should have been like unto Gomorrah. Hear the word of the Lord, ye rulers of Sodom; give ear unto the law of our God, ye people of Gomorrah" (Isa. 1:9–10). They had done the things of Sodom, and they had deserved the judgment of Sodom. It was only God's mercy that saved a remnant.

In Isaiah 1, Israel is addressed as Sodom and Gomorrah. The question we must ask is, how did Israel, the people of God, become Sodom and Gomorrah? How did she deteriorate to that depraved moral condition? The answer is attached to her relationship; she was following the counsels of the land shadowing with wings. What is essential to note is that Israel deteriorated to this condition because of her association with the land shadowing with wings. In Number 23:9, God had said Israel shall dwell alone. Israel said no; I will be aligned with the land shadowing with wings. Sodom and Gomorrah were then the result. Oh no!

Therefore, the day of the Destroyer's manifestation is near, since Israel is getting close to fully embracing all forms of evil practiced in the protective land. This is what will bring judgment. Nevertheless, man won't listen to the word of God; he prefers to listen to the evolutionist. Man doesn't want God. He is going on to what the scripture calls "the apostasy," the complete giving up of all divine revelation; therefore, it doesn't surprise believers that man has embraced his evolution. Man in his sinful state will accept anything else but God.

Nevertheless, God will judge him regardless of what he thinks. This judgment is so close, but man will not take heed. In Genesis 6, corruption and violence were of sufficient evil to invoke God's judgment; under grace, every form of evil will be present and necessitate God's expressed judgment.

"A king of fierce countenance, and understanding dark sentences, shall stand up" (Dan. 8:23). When Israel's iniquity rises to the full, then the Destroyer will stand up. He is the head of the Assyrian. This king is bold. This king is fierce. He isn't afraid. He will believe he is more righteous than the West. He will see the West as Sodom and Gomorrah, which must be destroyed, and he will believe that God has called him for that purpose.

Moreover, he understands "dark sentences" according to this passage. He is a Muslim, he understands dark sentences – what his religious book teaches. Christ is the light of the world; his views of Christ are different from what God's word says. What his book teaches about Christ is different from what the Bible teaches, but that is what he understands - dark sentences, not the light. The sentences of his religious book will lead him to attack the West and the USA.

"And his power shall be mighty, but not by his own power" (Dan. 8:24). We come now to this important consideration: when the Assyrian first appears, it isn't strong; it is a weak power. However, it will seek to establish its kingdom and display its real intentions, but its power will later become mighty because another power will strengthen it. The power we said will support it is Russia. Edward Dennett gave us a reason sound Bible teachers of his day believed Russia would strengthen the Assyrian. However, carefully note what Kelly wrote,

> Quite in its true prophetic place, whatever the date of separate delivery, stands Isa. 33 which appears to be the invasion of Gog (cf. Ezek. 38, 39) rather than the Assyrian. The mighty ruler still farther north, who will have strengthened in vain "the king of the north" of Daniel (i.e. the last Assyrian of the other prophets). It is therefore as easy to confound these two (for both express the same policy), as most also identify in error the last ruler of the Roman Beast with his political vassal but religious chief, the Antichrist who reigns over the apostate Jews in Palestine.[32]

Here Kelly clearly stated that Russia will strengthen the Assyrian. However, Kelly states more. He declares, "in the case of this ruler [Assyrian], though his power will be mighty, it will not be by his own power. He depends upon the strength given him by others. He will be the instrument of foreign policy and power, not his own."[33]

Now we have a new terrorist power that came up after 9/11 and is fulfilling the identification of the Assyrian. Moreover, this power is in Syria, and Russia has invaded Syria to protect its Mediterranean base and

[32] William Kelly, *"The Known Isaiah,"* The Bible Treasury, Vol. 19, ed. William Kelly (London, UK: George Morrish, 1893), 223.
[33] Kelly, *"Remarks on Daniel,"* The Bible Treasury, Vol. 3, *118*.

support President Assad. Nevertheless, Russia has lately threatened to leave Europe due to the sanctions. This threat has shocked the German chancellor. Moreover, in November 2021 President Vladimir Putin declared that the West was taking Russia's warnings not to cross its red line too lightly. Therefore, the question that must be asked is, is Russia about to embrace ISIS? The day Russia leaves Europe, the world will never be the same. Oh! The times we are living in are so exciting. Soon I will see my Lord, who died for me.

Nevertheless, I will now show you the scriptures that will clearly establish that the Assyrian supporter will be Russia and Iran. We should observe that former president Donald Trump courted the friendship of Russia, but Russia will be a snake in the bosom of America.

Russia is presented in Ezekiel 32 as the only European power associated with the terrorist empire. We learn further that Russia will strengthen the Assyrian. We read, "There is Meshech, Tubal, and all her multitude: her graves are round about him: all of them uncircumcised, slain by the sword, though they caused their terror in the land of the living. And they shall not lie with the mighty that are fallen of the uncircumcised, which are gone down to hell with their weapons of war: and they have laid their swords under their heads, but their iniquities shall be upon their bones, though they were the terror of the mighty in the land of the living" (Ezek. 32:26–27).

Ezekiel 32:26–27 highlights the primary point that Russia will cause terror in the land of the living. The next issue of interest is that Russia is presented as associated with the second mighty, the Assyrian. The third point of consideration is that Russia is introduced as the terror of "the mighty" (the Assyrian) in the land of the living. These three points tie Russia as the one who will strengthen, supply, and encourage the Assyrian terrorist group, according to the book of Ezekiel.

We also see this connection in Isaiah. "Woe to thee that spoilest and thou wast not spoiled; and dealest treacherously, and they dealt not treacherously with thee. When thou shalt cease to spoil thou shalt be spoiled: and when thou shalt make an end to deal treacherously, they shall deal treacherously with thee" (Isa. 33:1).

William Kelly's writings help us with this passage:

The Spirit of God, having given us a blessed picture of the King-Messiah reigning in righteousness, here contrasts with it a certain spoiler who is not expressly named by our prophet. But we need not find much difficulty in identifying him if we remember the last prophecy of Ezekiel that describes a hostile Gentile power. It is remarkable that he there describes Gog as one who had been predicted before. Hence it is certain that this marauding power is not peculiar to the later prophet, who tells us in Ezekiel 38, "After many days thou shalt be visited" (Ezek. 38:8) ... it is only Isaiah 33, which plainly connects itself in character with the northern leader of Ezekiel ... "Woe to thee that spoilest, and thou [wast] not spoiled; and dealest treacherously, and they dealt not treacherously with thee! When thou shalt cease to spoil, thou shalt be spoiled; when thou shalt make an end to deal treacherously, they shall deal treacherously with thee" (Isa. 33:1). This covetous foe appears to be the last which comes up, and so far distinct from "the king of the north," which title is not limited to the end. But assuredly, it is a ruler of the same sort, insatiable and treacherous.[34]

This power in Ezekiel 38–39 is Russia. In Ezekiel 38, we read, "Thus saith the Lord God, Art thou he of whom I have spoken in old times by my servants the prophets of Israel, which prophesied in those days many years that I will bring thee against them" (v. 17). We are thus told that other prophets had spoken about Russia before—not only Ezekiel but also other prophets. We believe this is the power Isaiah 21, 24, and 33 introduced to us.

Therefore, let us get some further help from J. N. Darby on these passages. When we obtain that help, we will be able to make the connection. He wrote in Isaiah 21-22 the following:

---

[34] Kelly, *Notes on Isaiah*, The Bible Treasury, Vol. 6, 1.

These two chapters introduce us to God's mind by showing the contrast between Babylon "the desert of the sea" and Jerusalem "the vision of peace." The idea of the Holy Spirit speaking of Babylon is that it becomes a "wilderness," the "sea" in prophetic language signifying the mass of peoples.

It is in Jerusalem that the Holy Spirit sees the glory and the peace of Christ, Salem, as is well known meaning "peace." The confusion is evident historically if one essay to consider the prophecy as a whole already accomplished, however visibly Babylon's fall is given. It is plainly here a question of God's ways in times to come. All the events are brought together here without any reference to the chronological order in the past, but in the relation that they will have among each other in the last days. For Jerusalem falls after Babylon, the inverse of history. We find here also instruction for ourselves now. In chapter 21, we see God preparing a rod of vengeance for Babylon, as of chastening in the following chapter for Jerusalem, where the power of evil was displaying itself after another way.[35]

What Darby said is that this Babylon is a future power, even though there might have been a partial historical fulfillment by geographic Babylon. Moreover, both Darby and Kelly showed from the scriptures that the Roman Empire represents Babylon in the future. Hence, from our studies, we know two things. First, the land shadowing with wings will endeavor to protect Israel. However, the Assyrian will destroy this power. Second, the Roman Prince, the head of the European Union, will sign a protection treaty with Israel, but due to the Assyrian's unrelenting attacks, he will break that treaty. Therefore, we find the power of the treacherous Russia against Rome and against the land shadowing with wings. Note carefully what Darby said in the quotation above. "In chapter 21, we see

---

[35] Darby, *Thoughts on Isaiah*, The Bible Treasury, Vol. 13, 131.

God preparing a rod of vengeance for Babylon, as of chastening in the following chapter for Jerusalem where the power of evil was displaying itself after another way."[36]

Therefore, we need to lay hold on this rod of vengeance for the Roman Empire, seen under the picture of Babylon. We need to also grasp that the same power that was going to chasten Babylon was going to chasten Jerusalem. Babylon here is the future Roman Empire. The fulfillment of what is prophesied here will have its accomplishment in the Roman Empire. We may call him "designated Babylon," just as we called Egypt "designated Egypt," since these two powers are seen as the two protectors of the Jews in the last days. These aren't literal Babylon or Egypt, but they are given Old Testament names contemporary to the Assyrian. However, this "designated Babylon" is easier to understand than "designated Egypt"; as a result, I will use the term "designated Babylon" only in a limited way to make some passages more understandable. Therefore, in some sections, I will retain the name Babylon instead of "designated Babylon." We accordingly need to understand who this rod of vengeance will be for designated Babylon.

In Isaiah 21, we read, "A grievous vision is declared unto me; the treacherous dealer dealeth treacherously, and the spoiler spoileth" (v. 2). Why was such a vision grievous to him if the speaker was a Jew? If it were in the past, the Jews should have rejoiced since Babylon would be defeated, and Israel would have been delivered. However, we find that Israel doesn't rejoice because this isn't the past but the future. Therefore, in the future, when "designated Babylon" will be spoiled, Israel will be left defenseless, since Babylon here is the Roman Empire, which breaks the treaty. It is for this reason that we read in the next verse, "Therefore are my loins filled with pain; pangs have taken hold upon me, as the pangs of a woman that travaileth: I was bowed down at the hearing of it; I was dismayed at the seeing of it" (Isa. 21:3).

This development wasn't joyous for Israel but painful. She heard, and she saw; it was happening before her eyes. It was the breaking of the treaty that caused Israel that tremendous pain. We must endeavor to comprehend the depth of Israel's trepidation as outlined in the following verse: "My

---

[36] Darby, *Thoughts on Isaiah*, The Bible Treasury, Vol. 13, 131.

heart panted; fearfulness affrighted me: the night of my pleasure hath he turned into fear unto me" (Isa. 21:4). We now clearly see that this Babylon isn't the one of the past but of the future. It is designated Babylon, the Roman Empire, but more importantly, it is Russia strengthening, supporting, and supplying the Assyrian to attack the Roman Empire until it abandoned Israel. This abandonment of Israel is what caused great consternation.

We must stress the impact of Isaiah 24. Again, we find the treacherous dealing treacherously, but this time it isn't the Roman Empire in focus but the land shadowing with wings. We read, "From the uttermost part of the earth have we heard songs, even glory to the righteous. But I said my leanness, my leanness, woe unto me" (Isa. 24:16). It is the same personage of Isaiah 33 and 21. We will, therefore, read it from Darby's translation to lay hold on its scope. "The treacherous have dealt treacherously; yea the treacherous have dealt very treacherously" (Isa. 24:16 JND).

The passages on Russia are complicated; therefore, we must seek Darby's help on chapter 24. He wrote, "Since chapter 13 we have in general judgments on the nations, and have seen the Jews given up for the Gentiles, the beasts of the earth, to winter upon them. Here we see judgment on Israel, and from verse 13 extending to all the earth and the isles of the sea. At that time, the resurrection will be, and after the judgment blessing."[37] Moreover, Darby made a note in his Bible for "land" in verse 1. He wrote, "The prophecy begins with the land of Israel, and the scene enlarges, embracing (verse 4) the whole world, of which the land is the center." When the beasts of the earth will winter upon Israel (Isaiah 18), it will be when the land shadowing with wings is already destroyed.

Therefore, what we have in Isaiah 24 is the effect on Israel and the world as a result of the destruction of the land shadowing with wings. In chapter 21, when Rome broke the treaty, Israel primarily felt the effect. However, when the land shadowing with wings was destroyed, the impact was felt not only by Israel but also by the whole world.

This verse emphasizes the effect of this destruction on the entire world. We read, "From the uttermost part of the earth have we heard songs, even glory to the righteous" (Isa. 24:16). What kind of song is this, and who is

---

[37] Darby, *"Thoughts on Isaiah,"* The Bible Treasury, Vol. 13, *132.*

singing it? The explanation is this: after the land shadowing with wings is destroyed by the Islamic terrorist group, calling on Allah, its god, the believers in the world will respond with glory to the righteous one - that is, glory to the Lord Jesus Christ. John N. Darby states that the word *righteous* is singular and could be translated as "righteous one." We must observe that the song of praise is tied to the treacherous dealing treacherously. The scripture associates the song to the activities of Russia.

Why are believers then saying glory to the righteous one at this destruction? The answer is that the Assyrian will be attributing the glory to its god. The Assyrian will be sure it was its god, who had given them the victory, and they will be singing his praises. We need to recall that these events cause everyone to err. The believers, who are informed, respond by singing glory to the righteous one, not Allah, and this is what is presented here. It's not a nation that responds with this song but saints all over the world. Therefore, in chapter 24, we have Russia strengthening the Assyrian to defeat the land shadowing with wings.

Moreover, this expression "From the uttermost part of the earth have we heard songs, even glory to the righteous" (Isa. 24:16) presents the response of believers all over the world to the exuberant praises of the Assyrian to their god, Allah, for giving them the victory over the land shadowing with wings. This destruction of the land shadowing with wings will bring two different responses: one from the Muslims and another from the believers. The Assyrians will praise their god, while the believers will respond by saying, "It is not Allah that needs to be honored, but the righteous one, the Lord Jesus Christ."

We need to remove the obscurity connected with this song. Isaiah 25:1–5 gives us a better understanding of this song of praise. This passage speaks of the Assyrian. This city here is the capital city of the Assyrian, the city "the mighty" in Jeremiah 46 said he was going to destroy. However, "the mighty" was destroyed instead. Yet, the Lord Jesus Christ, when He comes, will destroy this city.

Nevertheless, this city is said to be the palace of strangers. There is where the palace of the Assyrian will be located. The strangers here are those claiming nearness to Israel's God. This city of the terrible nations is the headquarters of their caliphate. The terrible ones are the ones that rain terror. "The blast of the terrible ones is as a storm against the wall" (Isa.

25:4) is the character of their attack on Israel's protector. This passage ties "the strangers, the terrible of the nations" (Ezek. 31:12), to the Assyrian and their capital in Syria.

In this scene, the Bible presents Christ as already come and has put everything in its rightful place. Therefore, verse 5 is very significant, but we cannot appreciate this significance because of how it is translated in the KJV. In the translation by John Darby, we get a better understanding of the text. We read, "Thou has subdued the tumult of strangers, as the heat in a dry place, as the heat, by the shadow of a cloud, so the song of the terrible ones is brought low" (Isa. 25:5 JND). It is only when the Lord comes that He will "subdue the uproar of the strangers" and "the song of the terrible ones will be brought low" (Isa. 25:5 JND). It now becomes clear that victory after victory, the Assyrians will celebrate with joyful songs of praise to their god. It is this celebration of praise the believers are countering in Isaiah 24.

This expression of praise to the righteous comes from the heavenly ones and may also indicate that the church might still be on earth when the land shadowing with wings is destroyed; this makes those who so express themselves the heavenly ones or those associated with Christianity. This scene seems to be the last time we have the heavenly ones present on earth.

Am I saying that the church is found in the Old Testament? No! I am not saying that. The church was formed on the day of Pentecost in Acts 2. Nevertheless, no one can doubt there are scenes in the Old Testament that include the saints that form the church. In Zechariah 14, for instance, we read, "And the Lord my God shall come, and all the saints with thee" (Isa. 14:5). Who will venture to say that the saints there don't include those of the church when Christ returns in glory? Especially when it is noticed that Jehovah comes with *all* His saints and not just some of His saints. Therefore, the expression of praise in Isaiah 24 comes from the heavenly saints.

This song, *glory to the righteous one*, couldn't be the appropriate response from the Jews since it will be their protector that will be destroyed. Their response to the destruction of their protector was already given in Isaiah 21. They declare, "Therefore are my loins filled with pain; pangs have taken hold upon me, as the pangs of a woman that travaileth, I was bowed down at the hearing of it; I was dismayed at the seeing of it" (Isa. 21:3).

This will be the response of the Jews to the breaking of the treaty by the Roman Prince.

Moreover, this verse indicates that it couldn't have been the Jews who were saying "glory" to the righteous. It could never have been the world either. Neither would the Jews own that "the righteous one" whom they crucified was the one who should be glorified. We must remember that God, who stretched out His hand, according to Isaiah 31, will cause the defeat of the land shadowing with wings. If God doesn't act, this defeat will not happen; but now the religious communities, not the heavenly ones, will be absolutely confused. The heavenly ones will know who caused the defeat.

More so, the religious communities will be sure that God did act. This is one reason God will stretch out His hand; then all will be sure that the destruction came from God. The problem will be to determine which God or god did act. The Muslims will be sure it was their god who acted on their behalf. This will stir them up into a frenzy to attack the land shadowing with wings at home and destroy it; this second destruction will strengthen their belief that their god acted on their behalf.

On the other hand, the Jews will be equally sure that their God acted; they will believe that the destruction was a clear message to them from their God, instructing them that they need to return and put their faith or trust in Him. They will surmise that the only way they can return to Him is to reestablish their temple worship - they must rebuild their temple. God has set this whole situation up perfectly. The trap is flawlessly set.

The Jews, however, cannot return to their temple worship, because the Muslim mosques are there. They cannot rebuild their temple - the mosques are in their way. What will the Jews do? They will, therefore, break down the mosques and rebuild their temple, assured that God will be on their side. Why do you think these mosques are there? Is it by mere coincidence? If you believe so, then you are seriously wrong. This world didn't come about by chance; neither are the mosques there by chance. We don't deal with chance. The evolutionists deal with chance; we deal with design.

What we read in the next verse further strengthens this point. "Fear and the pit, and the snare are upon thee, O inhabitant of the earth" (Isa. 24:17). This last word isn't "earth" in the original but "land," as Darby translates it. It is Israel, not the world. The word for "fear" is the same word Darby translated in Isaiah 2 as "terror"; hence, what do we have now for Israel?

We read, "Terror and the pit, and the snare are upon thee, O inhabitants of the land" (Isa. 24:17 JND). We are now told that Israel will have three things before her as a result of the destruction of the land shadowing with wings. "And it shall come to pass, that he who flees from the sound of the terror shall fall into the pit and he that comes up out of the midst of the pit shall be taken in the snare" (Isa. 24:18 JND). "It shall come to pass" is very significant because it means that it was a future event and a certain event. Man cannot stop it regardless of what he does. God will accomplish His word. Israel will seek to run from the terror, and when she tries to escape the terror, she will fall into the pit, which is the hole in which the trap is set. She will then be taken in the snare; the trap will snap. However, when we come to the topic of the trap, we will see this clearly. This is just what will happen after the destruction of the land shadowing with wings; Israel will try to avoid the terror but will fall into the trap. That is why we said earlier that Israel will break down the mosques after the destruction of the land shadowing with wings. When she breaks down the mosques, she shall fall into the trap. The options are terrible for Israel: terror, pit, and trap. She will get all three.

What we have proven is that Russia will support, supply, and strengthen the Assyrian. The actions of Russia will make the Assyrian very strong. We already see the problems between the West and Russia; the USA is sanctioning Russia for various reasons. They will keep isolating Russia until they will push it into the hands of the terrorist group. If the Assyrian is ISIS, then shortly Russia will embrace and support ISIS, which will make this power very strong. When this power becomes strong, it will shower this world with terror. This is sure to happen since God says so. If the Assyrian is another power, then Russia will support that other power.

Please be reminded that believers can never and will never support terrorism. What I am saying is what is recorded in God's word. God is the one who says He will bring terror on man. Therefore, I plead with you to turn away from your sins, my readers. Turn away from your sins. I have nothing to do with destruction; I have everything to do with salvation.

It is for this reason that the expression "the treacherous" is applied to Russia. "The treacherous" means "actors of betrayal." Russia will act in treason against the West. What does that mean? The prophet Jeremiah's writings help us understand that expression. He wrote, "Surely as a wife treacherously departs from her husband, so have ye dealt treacherously with me, O house of Israel, saith the Lord" (Jer. 3:20). What it means is that Russia will depart from the West and join with the terrorist group of the East - Russia will betray the West. The terrorist group will become its ally, since the West wanted to incorporate Russia's former allies into their scheme. Let us read another verse, and we will learn something more. In Lamentations, we read, "She weeps sore in the night, and her tears are on her cheeks: among all her lovers she hath none to comfort her: all her friends have dealt treacherously with her, they are become her enemies" (1:2). Here there is a change from being a friend to being an enemy. Russia will turn from the West to be a friend to the terrorist Assyrian.

What the word of God is saying is that Russia will be teaming up with a terrorist group to inflict untold sorrow on this world. God is so wise; He has determined that only when Russia joins this terrorist government will the terrorist group become strong. This action of Russia will cause the many slaughters of Isaiah 30:25. This prevents anyone from saying it is because of the writings of this person, or that book, or a sermon that a person preached, is responsible for the absolute terror that will flood this world. The responsible ones will be Russia and the Western leaders; they should have acted better, but then again, it will all be of divine doing.

What we see from the word of God is that the governments of those powerful nations will push Russia into the lap of the terrorist Assyrian. They will confidently implement their sanctions but they will be in total consternation when Russia, responding to their sanctions, embrace the terrorist. This is how this European power will team up with an Asian power to inflict terror on its European neighbors and the USA. This is how it will unfold, if my interpretation of scripture is correct; and I believe I am accurate. The treacherous will deal treacherously.

Nevertheless, there is one other thing in the Isaiah 24 passage that needs to be amplified. In Isaiah 24, we don't read of "the spoiler spoileth" as in the Isaiah 21 and 33 passages. Spoiling wasn't on Russia's mind when it teamed up with the Islamic terrorist power at first; this was to get even with the West, not to spoil its goods. However, like Judas, who betrayed the Lord Jesus Christ, Russia never imagined the results. Terror on every side! This is the reason there is terrorism today; it will shortly culminate with terrorist attacks all over the world.

In Isaiah 21, it is Russia that strengthens the Assyrian, the rod of vengeance for Babylon, to attack the Roman Empire with vicious terrorist attacks until the Roman Empire forsakes Israel. These are the same Russians we have in Isaiah 33, but this time they come with another group against Israel, according to Ezekiel 38–39; this is after the Assyrian has been destroyed. The one who will strengthen the Assyrian to defeat the Roman Empire is the one that will come against Israel after the return of our Lord Jesus Christ from glory, while in Isaiah 24, it is Russia that strengthens the Assyrian to defeat the land shadowing with wings. What we see is that in the Isaiah passages, we have Russia in support of the Assyrian, while in the Ezekiel passages, he acts in collaboration with others.

In Jeremiah 6:24–26, we see Russia supporting the Assyrian in its attack on Israel. At the time of that attack, both the land shadowing with wings and the Roman Empire would have been defeated, so Russia is presented as the spoiler, not the treacherous. In Jeremiah 6, Israel was waxed feeble. What had happened to her strength? Her protectors were gone. Israel was in pain as a woman in travail. We read of the most bitter lamentation. What a situation Israel would have to confront.

Again, in Jeremiah 15:6–8 we have the Lord using Russia to chastise Israel. In Isaiah, Russia is seen as the treacherous and the spoiler in the way it dealt with Israel and her protectors; while in Jeremiah, Russia is the spoiler, since Israel's protectors are no more. In Ezekiel, it is Gog, since Christ has already come. It is only a number to be destroyed.

There are three passages in Isaiah on Russia, but each gives a different aspect of the involvement of Russia in the last days. We need to note carefully that in all three passages, Russia is called the "treacherous that dealeth treacherously." Therefore, it is the same power. In Isaiah 33, it is when Russia will "cease to deal treacherously" that Israel "shall deal treacherously" with Russia. What Isaiah 33 highlights is that Israel will provoke Russia into attacking her, knowing that the Messiah is going to destroy the Russian force. In Isaiah 33, we have the reason for the attack of Russia on Israel in Ezekiel 38–39.

In Isaiah 21 and 24, in contrast, we have the occasions when Russia will deal treacherously. It becomes clear, therefore, that in Isaiah 21 and

24, Russia will act in support of the Assyrian, while in Isaiah 33, Russia will initiate the attack on Israel. In Isaiah 21 and 24, the Assyrian's acts are seen before the Lord comes, while in Isaiah 33, its actions are seen after the Lord comes. In Jeremiah, Russia comes to spoil. Nevertheless, when it shall cease to spoil, it shall be spoiled.

What we learn in Isaiah 33 is the reason Russia will attack Israel. Israel will betray Russia, which will cause Russia to attack her. Still, Israel wanted this development, since Israel knew any attack from Russia will be met with destruction from the Messiah. We read, "When thou shalt make an end to deal treacherously, they shall deal treacherously with thee" (Isa. 33:1). Here we are given the reason for the Russian attack in Ezekiel 38–39. It was a treacherous act on the part of Israel to provoke Russia to attack her. Nevertheless, Russia, which had dealt treacherously with Israel in the past, wouldn't be able to resist the temptation.

Therefore, it's Russia's involvement that will cause the Assyrian to be very strong. We will know who the Assyrian is when Russia embraces the terrorist group. We need to remember that when the Assyrian arrives on the scene, it won't be strong; it will become strong later when embraced by Russia. Already all the players are on the ground in Syria; the next move, if the Lord doesn't yet come, we will be right here to observe.

CHAPTER 14

ISRAEL: GOD'S EARTHLY PEOPLE

C hrist is the object of all God's counsels. He is the man of God's thoughts. The whole book, the Bible, is written about Christ, because He is God, the Creator, who became man. He is both God and man. If we miss that point, we lose the entire purpose of the word of God. Nevertheless, Christ came through Israel; thus, Israel is the subject of prophecy, and Christ is the object of all God's purposes. On my scale of difficulties, this topic is a five; it's not too difficult to grasp.

In this chapter, we will first trace man's history from Adam to Abram's call. Then we will trace the history of Israel from the call of Abram to the present day. We will see how God's word is fulfilled in every instant. We will read about the war with the ancient Assyrian empire, the war with Babylon, World War II, and the USA's protection of Israel. We will now begin our study on the children of Israel.

God tried the first man under the dispensation of innocence; an innocent man was placed in the Garden of Eden. He had no sin, but he could sin. The word *dispensation* in this discussion means "a defined period." That set period was when Adam was in the garden until he was cast out. However, the man failed, and the period was terminated. Man was put out of the garden and was prevented from reentering it. The dispensation couldn't be continued; it was over. Man could pretend to be in the garden, but in reality, he was an exile; he was out to provide for himself.

Second, after being cast out of the garden, man was guided by his conscience. God then tried man under the period of conscience; man was to let his conscience be his guide. Under this period outside the garden, Cain killed his brother, Abel. This was the guide of Cain's conscience and the consciences of so many others today. More so, man got worse until God destroyed the whole world. It was failure not only of one man but also of the entire human race; so, God destroyed "the world that was" and placed man in "the world that is." The ark brought man from "the world that was" into "the world that is." Without the ark, he couldn't move from "the world that was" into "the world that is." It was a completely different world into which man then entered. He couldn't go back to the conditions before the flood; he couldn't reverse the flood. He could pretend to be living under those conditions, but the conditions had changed entirely.

Third, God tried man under the period of human government. Noah was responsible for governing under these new conditions, but he couldn't rule himself and became drunk and brought a curse on his grandson. In the world that was, Adam brought a curse on the ground; now in the world that is, Noah pronounced a curse on a people. In the world to come, Christ would bring in the blessings. Man was told to explore the earth and multiply, but man did the opposite and stayed in one place. God then confounded man's language and scattered him abroad. Man was now divided along the line of his family; he then made a god of the head of his family, and idolatry was born. Man couldn't go back to the conditions before the flood; neither could he pretend to be living under those conditions. He spoke a different language, and was separated from the other families.

Fourth, we noticed in the book of Genesis that God chose a man called Abram. It was man who like Lot chose first and chose an idol. God chose afterward, and He chose a man named Abram. God allowed man to choose, but he didn't choose God, yet God chose man. Man could ask God why He chose Abram and not him. God could reply, *Why, you chose an idol instead of me?* The sad reality is that man left to himself will accept anything but a holy God. We must notice that each specified period was terminated because of man's failure, and there was judgment connected to the termination of each period.

We now come to the time of promise, where God was already given up for idols. Nevertheless, God won't be frustrated in His purpose. In Genesis 12:1–5, God chose a man named Abram. There we read, "Now the Lord hath said to Abram" (Gen. 12:1). We know that that couldn't have been the first communication to Abram. We need to read Acts 7:2–6 to get the original communication.

What is highlighted in Acts 7 is that the God of glory appeared to Abram before he dwelt in Charran. In Genesis 12, Abram was already in Charran, and later he departed out of Charran after his father had died. In Genesis 12, he was to leave his father's house, so we don't find his father going with him. However, in Acts 7, where we see his father going with him, he wasn't told to leave his father's house. What we find isn't failure but faith. Abram was told to go, and he left, walking by faith. He was to "go from" and to "come to." He was to leave the world and go to God. God called a man to Himself to separate from everything - his country, his kindred, and his father's house. Once he came by faith, God was there to direct his steps. He was to go to God and look to God.

God then gave Abram His promise: "I will make of thee a great nation" (Gen. 12:2). The first nation God told Abram about was Israel. He told Abram that if other nations came out of him, Israel was the one of His promise. God said that He will bless him, He will make his name great and make him a blessing. We read further, "in thee shall all families of the earth be blessed" (Gen. 12:3). Though Israel was to come through Abram, all the earth's families would be blessed in Him - that is in Christ. He was to be a blessing to all the families of the world. When God divided the nations at Babel, He distributed them by families, now in Abram; all these families in the earth were to be blessed. However, it was to be by faith - not by works but in Christ. The blessing wasn't on the principle of what they did but on the principle of God's grace.

God took Abram into the land after his father had died and showed Abram the land (Gen. 13:14 -18) after Lot separated from him. It was close to Hebron where this separation occurred, since Lot was seen journeying east to go toward Sodom, and Abram was seen at Hebron after the split.

It was close to Hebron where God showed Abram direction. This is the center from where we get east, west, north, and south in scripture.

Direction in scripture is taken from close to Hebron. Abram saw the land from this location, and God gave it to him. The promised seed was introduced at this point and was given the land. This seed was to be made like the dust of the earth. That was the Jewish seed. God gave the land to the Jewish seed. This seed is God's earthly people, the Jews, the dust of the ground. This is the first kind of seed Abram was going to have. This is the natural seed. However, there would be another kind of seed after this earthly seed - a heavenly seed.

In Genesis 15, we read, "And Abram said, Lord God, what wilt thou give me seeing I go childless, and the steward of my house is this Eliezer of Damascus? And Abram said behold to me thou hast given no seed and lo, one born in my house is mine heir" (Gen. 15:2–3). God told him that his seed was to be like the dust of the ground. Abram responded to God by saying that he had no seed. God told him that his seed was going to be given the land. Abram said to God, "The heir of my house is this Eliezer of Damascus." What excellent discourse between God and man!

Again, we read, "And behold, the word of the Lord came unto him, saying, this shall not be thine heir; but he that shall come forth out of thine own bowels shall be thine heir. And he brought him forth abroad, and said, look now toward heaven, and tell the stars, if thou be able to number them so shall thy seed be. And he believed in the Lord, and he counted it for righteousness" (Gen. 15:4–6). Without any pretension, what we notice is a heavenly seed. Abram was to look up, not around. He wasn't to look east, west, north, nor south but to look up. Abram was promised a heavenly seed, but this brought in faith and grace, for how can we possess heavenly things except by faith? What work can we do to possess heavenly things? It must be by grace.

We read further, "In the same day the Lord made a covenant with Abram, saying, unto thy seed have I given this land, from the river of Egypt unto the great river, the river Euphrates" (Gen. 15:18). We need to appreciate the God with whom we have communion. Here this covenant is seen as already accomplished. We now get the size of the land, from the Nile River to the Euphrates River. This designation of the land shows that

Egypt and Assyria were going to come into the blessing with Israel, as we read in Isaiah 19.

Moreover, we must observe the character of these promises. They are without conditions; that is, they are unconditional promises. They depended on God and God alone for their fulfillment. The effect of such promises was that what God had promised Abram, He would fulfill regardless of the ensuing circumstances. This point must be emphasized if we are going to understand God's restoration and dealing with Israel in the future. Look at this covenant with Abram; it depends on God alone. What happened at Sinai doesn't affect this covenant. There is no "if" as the Sinai covenant. God sees this transaction as already done: "have I given this land" (Gen. 15:18). There is no Abraham's part. There is only God's part. This is the same character of blessing for Christians today.

We have unconditional promises given to Abraham, Isaac, and Jacob. The fulfillment of these promises depends on God and God alone. Therefore, these promises cannot fail. Now, from Genesis 12 to the giving of the law in Exodus, we have 430 years. This time is reckoned from when Abraham was seventy-five years old. The period of Israel's history will entail three prevailing components: faith, promise, and the dispensation of the law. We will seek to take up this history from the giving of the law to the present day and see that all that has happened to Israel has happened according to the word of God.

What we have been discussing is the peculiar nature of the dispensation of promise. We have noticed that under this dispensation Abraham received righteousness by faith. He was declared a righteous man - not because of what he did but because he believed what God had said. The word of God declared that Abraham believed God, and it was counted to him for righteousness. The same is true of the Christian. The word of God states, "Believe on the Lord Jesus Christ, and thou shall be saved" (Acts 16:31).

Moreover, we saw further that Abraham was given unconditional promises of blessing, which God would fulfill. Israel has forfeited the benefits proposed under the law. Yet Israel will be blessed - not because of the law but because of God's unconditional promises. The same is true of the Christian position; we are said to be blessed with all spiritual blessings in the heavenlies in Christ Jesus without any condition attached to these blessings. Furthermore, because the law had penalties attached to failure,

Israel will fall under those punishments because she did not, or ever could, keep the law. The true Christians will never come into judgment.

Having stated these principles, we will now follow the history of Israel starting from Exodus 19:2–8. In this chapter, God first told Israel what He had done for them; then He said to them that if they obeyed His voice, they would be a peculiar treasure unto Him. Israel should have returned a word to the Lord that would have emphasized that indeed He had borne them on eagles' wings and pray God to continue to do the same. However, Israel didn't know herself and thus returned a word to the Lord that put her under the condition of obedience. This was a grave mistake. However, God was going to use the law to show how holy He was and, on the contrary, how sinful Israel was. Then she would see the need for a savior and, as a consequence, repent and accept Christ.

Before the law of Exodus 20, all the murmurings of Israel were met with grace, not judgment; but after the law was given, there was a completely different situation. The murmurings of Israel were met with punishment. Under the principle of the law, Israel was under a curse, and all who put themselves under that principle are under a curse. Consequently, Israel failed under judge, prophet, priest, and king. And finally, they did crucify their own Messiah - this crucifixion will bring the worst judgment on them - because the Messiah is God, the Son.

In Leviticus 26 and Deuteronomy 28, we have the prophetic history of the tribes of Israel. In Leviticus 26, we mainly have the prophetic account of the ten tribes until the Lord comes. In contrast, in Deuteronomy 28, we have the two tribes' prophetic history, primarily until the Second World War.

In Leviticus 26:1–13, we have the outline of Israel's responsibility. We saw blessings associated with her obedience and curses linked to her disobedience. We have stated here what Israel wasn't to do and what God would do for Israel if she did listen. However, if she didn't obey, we have what God was going to do to her. Moreover, in Leviticus 26:14–39, we notice that God was going to punish Israel if she didn't obey His word, because the law had penalties attached to it. Moreover, if she didn't change her course, she was going to go into captivity. We also observed something of even greater significance; that is, once Israel went into captivity in her enemy's land, she wasn't going to come out as a unit until Christ comes.

What is clear is that the passage didn't give a time or circumstance for her exit. Therefore, this passage presents the prophetic history of the ten tribes or the nine and a half tribes called Israel. We learn the Assyrian would take them into captivity. Once they were made captives, they weren't going to return to Palestine's land as a unit until the Lord Jesus returned in glory; this was to prevent confusion between the Assyrian of the past and the Assyrian of the future. The Lord, when He returns, will recover the ten tribes of Israel. We must ask ourselves this question. Has this event happened? Yes, it happened exactly as prophesied.

We notice further, in Leviticus 26:40–46, that even if the children of Israel confessed their iniquities and their fathers' iniquities, they still wouldn't come out of their enemy's land -moreover, also if they humbled themselves and accepted their punishment, yet this wasn't going to produce an exit. They weren't going to leave their enemy's land. However, God promised that He was going to remember the covenant of their ancestors, and He wasn't going to cast them away, abhor them, or destroy them. Nevertheless, coming out of their enemy's land wasn't going to happen until Christ returned.

Nevertheless, the history of the two tribes is entirely different. First, in Deuteronomy 28:1–14, we observe that like the ten tribes, the two tribes' blessings were connected with their obedience; if they obeyed God, what was going to happen to them. Second, we have, if they didn't hearken, what would be the result.

Moreover, in Deuteronomy 28:15–22 we note with alarm the curse that would come on the two tribes, called Judah, if she didn't obey. We know no one would write unpleasant things about himself; if the Bible was a man's book, who would write these things about himself? Who would write about all the curses that would come on him if he didn't obey? If you listen to talk show hosts, all they say is that God is love; so, we can do all the evil we want, and this God will love us. However, that doesn't even happen with the police and the lawbreakers. Let me say unequivocally that this same God, who is love, is holy. Therefore, for a holy God to allow a sinner with all his sins in His presence, He has to cease being God, which will not happen. God loves us so much that He gave His only begotten Son to die for us so the righteous requirement of a holy God would be met and the love of a wonderful God would be displayed. Therefore, if we reject

His love, we will have His judgment. We see Moses could write only what God told him to write and nothing else.

In Deuteronomy 28:23–35, we find that Israel would come into more severe judgments until finally she would go into captivity. Nevertheless, we here see the big difference between Deuteronomy and Leviticus. We read, "The Lord shall bring thee, and thy king which thou shalt set over thee, unto a nation which neither thou nor thy fathers have known; and there shalt thou serve other gods, wood and stone" (Deut. 28:36). In verse 36, we notice that Israel would go into captivity in Babylon but that she would be a captive with her king. This is a significant addition because she would again be conquered, but she would have no king at that second conquest. Therefore, the first captivity had to do with Babylon, as seen in verse 36; Babylon defeated her, and she was taken into captivity with her king.

Note how God gives signposts so we will know without a doubt what and who God was addressing. The signposts here let us know when the conqueror was Babylon and when it was Rome. These signposts are seen all throughout the Bible. In Babylon, she was going to go with her king and serve other gods. However, in Deuteronomy 28:49–52, Judah was conquered again but this time by the Romans, and at that time, she had no king. This is how it happened in history - just how the word of God said it was going to happen.

Nebuchadnezzar began the carrying away of Judah - the two tribes - to Babylon around 606 BC. In 588 BC, he destroyed the city of Jerusalem and the temple. He had then fulfilled this prophecy. There were 133 years between the ten tribes' captivity and the two tribes' captivity. The king of Assyria had taken the ten tribes captive, while the Babylonian king had taken the two tribes captive. In Babylon, Judah and Benjamin - primarily the two tribes - were going to serve the gods of wood and stone. God had said it; He recorded that it was done.

Moreover, in Deuteronomy 28:37–47, we are enlightened further as to the ways of the omnipotent God. Here God gives us the reason for His chastisement. "Because thou servest not the Lord thy God with joyfulness and with gladness of heart for the abundance of all things" (Deut. 28:47). If Israel was so dealt with for not serving the Lord with joyfulness and gladness of heart for the abundance of all things, then what would be the judgment for those who reject His very existence? If men won't have

God, they will have His judgment; so, it will be, and none can stop it. It needs to be emphasized that man will have either God's righteousness or His judgment.

In Deuteronomy 28:48–52, we notice that another nation would conquer Judah, and again she was going to be extracted from the land, but in this instant, there was to be no king in Israel. This reality wasn't so in the first captivity. When the Babylonians attacked Israel, there was a king, but when the Romans destroyed Israel, there was no king - just as it is stated here. God's word has real order. The nation that was to come against Judah at that time was the Roman Empire. A key point noted in this context is that this enemy came from far; this wasn't said in the first dispersion. Here, the enemy came from a different continent. He was supposed to come from the end of the earth and travel as swift as an eagle. The eagle was the very insignia of the Roman Empire.

Moreover, this enemy was a nation of fierce countenance and would show no mercy. He didn't regard the old or the young, but he would eat the fruit of Judah's cattle and the fruit of their land. This is just what the Romans did. Moreover, we find that everything was to be spent in the city of Jerusalem. The city would have nothing left to sustain it.

Additionally, in Deuteronomy 28:53–58, we read to what depth Israel was reduced. History informed us that when Rome besieged Judah in all her gates, there was no place for Judah to obtain food until finally the parents began to eat their children in the siege.[38] Did this happen? Sure, it did, just as it is stated. God said it, and God brought it to pass. Josephus, the Jewish historian, with sadness wrote about this event, and it pained him to record it as a Jew. However, God's word came to pass again, and it will forever come to pass. Let a man say what he may against it; he will live to regret it.

In AD 70, Titus, the son of Vespasian, the Roman Emperor, besieged and conquered the city of Jerusalem. At that time, Titus had Tiberius Alexander, a trusted friend, as his deputy.[39] Titus began to besiege the city a few days before Passover[40]. He surrounded the city with four legions: the

---

[38] Josephus, War of the Jews, book 5, chap. 1, para. 6.
[39] Josephus, War of the Jews, book 5, chap. 1, para. 6.
[40] Josephus, War of the Jews, book 5.

Fretensis X, the Apollinaris XV, the Macedonica V, and the Fulminata X11. Josephus, the Jewish historian, stated that Jerusalem was inundated with many people who had come to celebrate the Passover, just like when the church was formed on the day of Pentecost. There were many Jews there from the surrounding nations.

The Roman Titus built a wall to starve the Jewish population of the city.[41] Titus was well known for his efficiency; nevertheless, in this instant, Titus preferred negotiation rather than destruction, since he harbored some personal thoughts about Jerusalem. He, therefore, tried to use Josephus to negotiate with the Jews, but the Jews would have no negotiation.[42] Rather than negotiate, the Jews wounded the negotiator and thereby declared their message to the Romans. Titus also wanted to spare the temple at all cost, because Herod, who was his ally, had lately refurbished the structure. Titus also had a desire to transform the temple site into a place for the worship of the Roman emperor and their deities, but that wasn't realized.

Slaughter was everywhere. The majority of those who were butchered were unharmed citizens who craved for peace. Those who were weakened by the starvation that swamped the city of Jerusalem were easy prey to the sword of the Romans. The Romans slew the Jews wherever they were found. The Jewish corpses overflowed the altar[43]; the sanctuary steps splattered with blood and bodies. Finally, by September 7, AD 70, Jerusalem's city was entirely in the Romans' hands. This is what God's word said: "A nation of fierce countenance which shall not regard the person of the old, nor shew favour to the young." (Deut. 28:50).

Josephus noted that one million and one hundred thousand people were killed during the siege. The majority were Jews he declared. Ninety-seven thousand were captured and enslaved.[44]

---

[41] Josephus, War of the Jews, Book 5, Ch. 12, para. 1.
[42] Josephus, War of the Jews, Book 5, Ch. 9, para. 3, 4.
Josephus, War of the Jews, Book 6, Ch. 2, para. 1, 2.
[43] Josephus, War of the Jews, Book 6, Ch. 4, para. 6.
[44] Josephus, War of the Jews, Book 6, Ch. 9, para. 3.

There were more wars fought between Rome and Israel. There was a second Jewish Roman war called the "Kitos War"[45] or the exile's rebellion during AD 115–117. History records a third Jewish-Roman war fought during AD 132–136, which was led by a man named Simon Bar Kokhba.[46] This man proclaimed himself as the Jewish Messiah and the one to restore Israel. This Bar Kokhba managed to establish an independent state of Israel for two years. However, the Romans ended his rebellion with six whole legions and elements of another six legions. As a result of this war, the Jews were barred from Jerusalem. Additionally, even though the Jewish Christians weren't supporters of Bar Kokhba as Messiah, they were also prohibited. It was stated that this war and its repercussion helped to distinguish Christianity from Judaism.

Furthermore, the emperor Hadrian made every attempt to root out Judaism because he saw it as the cause of the empire's constant rebellion. As a consequence, he prevented the Torah from being read and prohibited the Hebrew calendar. Hadrian also executed many Jewish scholars and burned the sacred scroll on the temple mount. He erected two statues on the temple mount, one to Jupiter and another to himself. He removed Judah's and Israel's names from the province and replaced them with the name Syria and Palestine. He then reestablished Jerusalem as the Roman Polis of Aelia Capitolina. The Jews were also barred from entering the city except on one particular day. Another fundamental change that took place, from then on, was that the Jewish religion was more attached to the synagogue and not the temple and the Jews were scattered throughout the world.

Finally, it was stated that the Christians in Jerusalem at the time of the temple's destruction fled to Jordan, and not one was killed. They knew from God's word that Jerusalem would be destroyed, so they left the city. The others who remained in unbelief were either slain or enslaved. The Christian historian Eusebius wrote, "The whole body, however, of the church at Jerusalem, having been commanded by a divine revelation, given

---

[45] Eusebius Pamphilus, The Ecclesiastical History, book 4, chap. 2, para. 1-5 in Christian F. Cruse and Henry De Valois's translation 3d ed., 6 vols. (London UK: Samuel Bagster and Sons, 1842)

[46] Eusebius, The Ecclesiastical History, book 4, chap. 6, para. 1-4.

to men of approved piety there before the war, removed from the city, and dwelt at a certain town beyond the Jordan, called Pella."[47]

Besides, Adam Clarke wrote, "It is very remarkable that not a single Christian perished in the destruction of Jerusalem, though there were many there when Cestius Gallus invested the city; and, had he persevered in the siege, he would soon have rendered himself master of it; but, when he unexpectedly and unaccountably raised the siege, the Christian took that opportunity to escape…[That as] Vespasian was approaching with his army, all who believed in Christ left Jerusalem and fled to Pella, and other places beyond the river Jordan: and so, they all marvelously escaped the general shipwreck of their country: not one of them perished."[48]

We read further, "Then the Lord will make thy plagues wonderful, and the plagues of thy seed, even great plagues, and of long continuance, and sore sicknesses, and of long continuance" (Deut. 28:59). Here again we see how accurate the word of God is. We read about the destruction by the Romans. Now we are told that after this destruction, there was to be a long time when Judah (called "Israel" by the nations) wouldn't obtain anything else but plagues. She had no homeland; Judah had no king. She had no prophet; Judah had no temple. Did this happen? Indeed, it did. For nearly nineteen hundred years, Judah was out of Palestine's land—that's a long duration, and the scripture mentioned it; at that time, she had no homeland. However, there is more; the prophecy ends with World War II. William Kelly said this in his book on Zephaniah 2: "The captivity in the days of Nebuchadnezzar was nothing at all as extreme as their scattering to the ends of the earth, consequent on the Roman destruction of Jerusalem."[49] It was just how God said it would be, and so it was.

God communicated more information in Deuteronomy 28:60–67. Again, we must ask ourselves the question. Who would write these things about himself? There is only one answer. God communicated them to Israel. In verse 64, we are told that they would be scattered among all peoples from one end of the earth to the other. Did this happen? Indeed,

---

[47] Eusebius, The Ecclesiastical History book 3, chap. 5.

[48] Adam Clarke, *Commentary on the Bible,* 6 vols. (Nashville TN: Abingdon Press, 1960) 5:228-29.

[49] William Kelly, *"Lectures on the Minor Prophet:"* Zephaniah (London UK: George Morrish 1860), *364*

it did. The Jews are found in every continent of the world, just as the word of God said.

Please observe how God dealt with the Jews, since the way He has dealt with them has been a powerful witness of scripture's accuracy. Furthermore, the scattering of the Jews to all parts of the world has also been a silent testimony of creation in contrast to evolution. As a result of the dispersion of the Jews, we now have Jews of different nationalities and races. In Europe, the Jews are mostly white; they look like the Europeans. In Asia, they are primarily red; they look like Asians. In China, they look like the Chinese; you couldn't tell the difference between Chinese and Jews. In India, the Jews look like the Indians; you couldn't tell the difference between an Indian and a Jew. In Japan, they look like Japanese. In Africa, the Ethiopian Jews look like Africans, yet they are Jews. How could this have happened?

What is vital to remember is that the Jews are not like Americans, where people come from different parts of the world and become American citizens, and their descendants become American born. Jews claim parentage. Each Jew, not proselyte or converted, claims that he or she descended from Judah, and we widen the term to mean Israel. Therefore, each Jew is claiming that his or her grandfather was Jacob, whose name was changed to Israel, and that he or she descended from one of Jacob's sons.

When a Jewish community makes such a claim, their claim must be verified; a person can't just wake up one morning and claim Jewish parentage; his or her claim must go through a process of verification. A Jewish community could be isolated in Africa (like the Ethiopian Jews) or in India or in China and look exactly like the Indians or Chinese respectively yet decide to return home to Israel. Israel would then send a delegation to that community to verify that they are indeed descendants of Israel. If their genealogy isn't complete, then they would be rejected. They have to show proof that they indeed descended from Israel. The Jews are renowned for keeping records; that is why we have the Bible today, the Dead Sea Scrolls, and so forth.

The difficulty we face is, how did they become black? How did they become white? How did they become red? Furthermore, how is it that some look Chinese? How is it that some look Indian? How is it that some look European if they all came from the same father? The answer is simple;

the word of God says, "Look not upon me because I am black because the sun hath looked upon me" (Song of Solomon 1:6). Therefore, it is where they live relative to the sun or equator that determines the color of their skin and the intermarrying that defined their facial features. Instead of evolutionary considerations that say one came from monkeys, God's word has the right explanation. This makes me remember a story about one biology class at a particular university, where the professor was speaking about the steps of evolution from monkey to man. In that class, a student asked a crucial question. Sir, which species of monkey you came from? That question ended the discussion.

Deuteronomy 28:65–67 declares that when the Jews were in their enemies' land, they were smitten with all types of evil. We deduce further that things were unbearable in those foreign countries just before they returned to their land. We are also informed that the Jews suffered greatly in their enemies' lands.

This fear was particularly evident during World War II in the territory occupied by the Germans. It was primarily in Europe that this was going to happen, since Israel was taken captive by a European power, the Roman Empire. When it was evening, the Jews wished it was morning, and when it was morning, they wished it was evening. This chastening was so severe that both morning and evening were equally terrible to the Jews. Their lives hung in doubt; they had trembling hearts, failing eyes, and sorrowful minds. They experienced the very things the word of God declared. Yet men still doubt that the Bible is God's word. Stop and consider for eternity is at stake.

"And the Lord shall bring thee into Egypt again with ships, by the way whereof I spake unto thee, Thou shalt see it no more again: and there ye shall be sold unto your enemies for bondmen and bondwomen, and no man shall buy you" (Deut. 28:68). Thus, verse 68 shows that the passage still contemplates the events after the destruction by the Romans. After this destruction, the Jews were taken by ships to Egypt and sold as slaves, but no one was willing to buy them. Even Josephus mentioned that the Jews were sold in Egypt,[50] but no one was willing to buy them.

---

[50] Josephus, War of the Jews, book 6, chap. 9, para. 2.

Today, once one writes anything unpleasant about Israel, one is termed anti-Semitic; but it was Josephus himself, a Jewish historian, who gave us these details. This passage unfolded to us what was going to happen to the Jews after the Roman destruction but before they became a nation again. What is certain is that what the word of God declared happened.

Therefore, it must be restated that we didn't write the Bible. We didn't write the Jewish history. The Jews wrote the Bible and stated those things. They wrote their own account. The only thing believers do is highlight what they have written. Believers are not anti-Semitic, for they believe everything the Jews wrote in the Bible. I am personally indebted to the Jews for the gift of the word of God.

We need to notice that the idea of *captivity* isn't inferred with the Roman siege as with the Babylonian siege in the passage in Deuteronomy. Anyone acquainted with the Roman wars with the Jews knows that the Romans did different things to the Jews after those wars. After one war, the Romans cut down a whole forest to crucify the Jews. Many were sold in Egypt as slaves, and they had no buyers because they were so many. Some were taken to Rome to fight in the Roman Coliseum. This wasn't like what took place with the Babylonian captivity. The word of God is accurate in every situation and every time.

Once we approached World War II, three passages then speak about Israel being reestablished in the land of Palestine. The first passage is in Zephaniah. "Gather yourselves together, yea, gather together, O nation not desired; before the decree bring forth, before the day pass as the chaff, before the fierce anger of the Lord come upon you, before the day of the Lord's anger come upon you" (Zeph. 2:1–2).

This passage isn't dated "after" an event but "before" an event. Israel has suffered many terrible experiences. However, a worse one was yet to come. The distress to come is called "the day of the Lord." Moreover, their return is dated before the tribulation, because that event is in the future. These verses also help us with the context in which the passage is placed.

We read in Zephaniah that the great day of the Lord was near. We are told that, after the restoration of the Jews in the last day, the Great Tribulation would be near at hand. Therefore, Zephaniah 1:14–18 informs us that the Lord was going to bring a terrible time upon men, called the "day of the Lord." The word of God instructs us that the "day of the

Lord" was a day of wrath; it was a day of trouble and distress. God further stated that He would bring misery on men, and they would walk like blind men. He also instructed us that neither their silver nor their gold would deliver them in that day. Their riches wouldn't make a difference in the destruction that was coming. However, how could it affect the Jews in the land if the Romans had put them out? The Jews were going to return to the land of Palestine.

The prophet declared, "Gather yourselves together, yea, gather together" (Zeph. 2:1). However, God also gave us the time of this return. He didn't date the event after the Babylonian captivity; Cyrus didn't encourage it, but it was dated "before," not "after," the event. It wasn't after Babylon; it wasn't after Cyrus, but it was "before the decree bring forth, before the day pass as the chaff, before the fierce anger of the Lord come upon you, before the day of the Lord's anger come upon you" (Zeph. 2:2). The event that was closer to Judah's return wasn't the Roman captivity but the Great Tribulation. God connected the return of Israel (to Palestine) to a time before the tribulation. He lets us know that before the Great Tribulation, which was sure to come, Israel would return to the land of Palestine. In this instant, she was going to return by herself. She was returning to the land, not by the commandments of the Lord but by her national aspirations. Did this happen? Yes, it did. God's word is fulfilled again. However, because it is dated before the tribulation, it means that the Great Tribulation is looming.

A little history will suffice to show how Israel returned by herself and thus fulfilled God's word. In 1500 AD there were only about 5,000 Jews in Palestine and they were a mere 1% of the population. Yet, by 1550 AD the Jewish population had not increased, but their percentage had climbed to 3.2% of the population. Moreover, for the next hundred years the Jewish population had merely increased by a few thousand to a total of about 7,000 Jews. Furthermore, from 1650 AD to 1750 AD the number of Jews in Palestine practically remained the same. Yet, for the next hundred years the Jewish population began to show growth, but at a very slow rate.

However, as the time specified for their return got closer there was a stark increase in the Jewish population in Palestine. Things began to move faster, so that by 1850 AD, the Jews were one of the largest groups in Jerusalem. Moreover, this increase could be highlighted by the numbers, for by 1882 AD, the Jewish population had increased to 24,000 and they were now 8% of the country.

Furthermore, things were developing on another front, for by 1881, the Jews, mostly from Russia, were establishing villages in the land of Palestine. These Russian Jews made an outstanding contribution to the initial movement of the Jews back to their homeland. They started the "Love of Zion" movements to help fellow settlers and thus shaped many new communities' thinking. These Jews from Russia were differently oriented and sought to be self-sufficient instead of relying on overseas donations. Along with this new way of thinking, the Hebrew language was revived. This revival of the Hebrew tongue attracted many Jews from all walks of life. On another front, there was a desire to regain the land by collective farming and occupation.

Furthermore, according to the history of the Zionist movement, there was a name given for each wave of Jewish arrival. Each group of arrivals of Jewish immigrants was called an "aliyah,"[51] the immigration of Jews from the diaspora to the geographic land of Israel. The period between 1881 and 1903, saw the influx of over thirty-six thousand Jews. This was the first aliyah. Nevertheless, the country was mainly populated by Muslims. However, the Jews resolved to change the composition of the city. Therefore, by 1892, the Jews were the majority in the city of Jerusalem. Nonetheless, they were still only about 10 percent of the country. Why were the Jews in the diaspora resettling in Palestine? The word of God alone has the answer. They had to return to become a nation again, after World War II.

Thus, Theodor Herzl in 1896 began to suggest that a Jewish state be established. He felt that the solution to the rising anti-Semitism problems in Europe was to establish the Jewish nation. A year after his suggestion, the Zionist organization was formed. At its first congress, it stated its aim "to establish a home for the Jewish people in Palestine secured under public law." Israel was serious about her future.

However, new immigrants continued to arrive, so between 1904 and 1914 more than forty thousand Jews settled in present-day Israel - the

---

[51] Howard M. Sachar, *History of Israel from the rise of Zionism to our times*, Chap. 2, 3rd ed., Revised and expanded (New York: Alfred A. Knopf, 2007) 47.

evidence of the second Aliyah.[52] Consequently, because of the Jewish interest in returning to their homeland, the Zionist organization in 1908 set up a bureau to adopt an organized Jewish settlement policy.

It is important to note that most of the migrants were from Russia and Poland, seeking to escape persecution, as the scripture had said would happen to them. Again, just as the word of God stated, they were persecuted in those countries.

The Jews continued to arrive by their own will, according to the word of God, so much so that by 1910 the first kibbutz, a type of settlement that is unique to Israel, was established. Nine Russian Jews founded this kibbutz. The Jews were becoming more self-conscious. In 1909, Jaffa became the first city where people spoke only Hebrew. As a result, newsprints were then published in Hebrew. The country was on the move.

It is unbelievable that the Jews supported the Germans during World War I. This support was partly because Germany was fighting Russia, whom the Jews considered their main enemy. Russia so badly treated the Jews that the Jews wanted the Russians to lose the war at all costs; they didn't know Germany would turn out to be even worse than Russia. However, the British government sought to have the Jews support the war against Germany.

The Zionist movement got much sympathy from the British government, including the prime minister, Lloyd George. The British Army had driven the Turks out of Southern Syria in 1917. Hence, Lord Balfour, the British foreign minister, forwarded a letter to Lord Rothschild, a leading member of the Jewish community and a member of his party. That letter eventually became known as the Balfour Declaration of 1917. That letter stated that Britain viewed favorably the establishment in Palestine of a national home for the Jewish people. That declaration gave the British government a reason to claim and govern the country. Consequently, a set of new boundaries was decided by an agreement between the British and the French.

In the year 1922, this British directive, which in effect gave the British the right to rule over Palestine along with the Balfour Declaration, was subsequently confirmed by the League of Nations and became effective in

---

[52] Howard M. Sachar, *History of Israel from the rise of Zionism to our times*, Chap. 4, 89.

1923. The boundaries of Palestine were then settled. The United Kingdom then signed a treaty with the United States, which endorsed the terms of the mandate.

As a consequence of those developments, Jewish immigration began to accelerate. As a result, between 1918 and 1923, more than forty thousand more Jews arrived in Palestine. What was driving that resettlement? Let the critics of the bible give an answer. That became the third Aliyah. Most of those Jews came from Russia. That wave of Jewish migration was understandable since over one hundred thousand Jews were massacred in Ukraine and Russia alone. That was the treatment the Jews experienced, mainly in Europe, just as God had declared.

At that time, the vast majority of those immigrants were termed "pioneers" because they were experienced, or trained in agriculture. That designation meant they were skilled and could help in the establishment of autonomous communities.

As a result of the pioneers, the marches in the Jezreel Valley and the plain at Hefer were irrigated and transformed into model agricultural zones. Thus, more lands were bought by the Jewish National Fund from money collected abroad for that purpose. The Jews then established a militia to defend the Jewish settlements.

However, at the same time, there was the emergence of Palestinian nationalism. That national pride saw the Arab rioting in 1920–1921. Those riots were considered as a direct result of the French victory over the Arab kingdom of Syria. The British then responded to the riots by imposing immigration quotas on the Jews.

Nevertheless, more Jews were coming. This influx was so evident that between 1924–1929, over eighty thousand more Jews arrived; the fourth aliyah occurred. Those who came during that period were fleeing persecution in Poland and Hungary, since many were executed in those lands in the worst manner. Many who came were professionals who established businesses and industries.

In 1923, the first power plant was built in Tel Aviv. Then, in 1925, the Jewish Agency started the Hebrew University in Jerusalem. A technical university was also established in that year, in Haifa. Israel was on the move. Who could stop her? The year 1928 was no exception, the Jews established the Jewish National Council. This council became the foremost institute of the Jewish community. Its functions were comprehensive; it managed education, health care, and security. Moreover, the British permitted the council to raise its taxes and run autonomous services for the Jewish population. Those functions gave the council enormous influence.

The Wailing Wall came in for its share of problems. A significant problem arose over the Wailing Wall in 1929, and as a consequence, the elderly Jewish worshippers were prevented from using chairs or any furniture at the temple site. However, this hatred wasn't to go away any time soon, and again in August 1929, it exploded into more Palestinian riots. Although this riot brought to an end the Jewish community of Hebron, it caused the Zionists to establish their militia in 1931. This militia was called the National Military Organization.

The desire of the Palestinians at that time was to have majority rule. However, the British rejected the principle of majority rule. This rejection prevented the British from having to concede power to the Arab majority. However, the Jews continued to arrive, so from 1928–1938, over two hundred and fifty thousand more Jews came to Palestine - the fifth aliyah had come.[53] Furthermore, over one hundred and seventy-four thousand arrived between the short period of 1933–1936 alone, prompting the British to take steps to restrict immigration. This significant influx of Jews contributed greatly to the 1933 Palestinian riots. Most of the migration was from Europe, and they who came were very educated. The majority of them were doctors, lawyers, and professors from Germany.

However, as World War II approached, fascist regimes began to emerge all over Europe, and this meant more significant problems for the Jews. They were again persecuted in Europe. Moreover, they were stripped of their citizenship and deprived of civil and economic rights. They were then subjected to greater persecution from anti-Semitic governments which came to power in Germany, Hungary, Poland and Romania. The Jews were caught in Europe with no way out.

Circumstances were perilous for the Jews in Europe, so much so that the USA called an international conference to address their plight. The USA wanted a solution to the vast number of Jews in Europe trying to leave but could not. The British indicated that they were willing to attend

---

[53] Howard M. Sachar, *History of Israel from the rise of Zionism to our times*, Chap. 8, 200.

the conference providing that Palestine wasn't part of the discussion. The Jews weren't even asked to participate. However, the Nazis had their own plan to ship the Jews to Madagascar.

At that time, millions of Jews were trying to leave Europe, but every country in the world was closed to Jewish migration. As a result, Palestine was also closed off to the Jews by the British. This action was very unpopular among the Jews. They then had to resort to illegal immigration. They were now trapped in Europe with no way out. Things didn't get much better either; the month of March 1940 brought new problems. The British High Commission for Palestine issued an edict prohibiting Jews from purchasing land in most of Palestine. The Jews were in a dire strait. Consequently, not many managed to escape Europe during the period of 1939–1945. Those the British caught were dispatched to Mauritius. Those the Germans captured suffered the worst fate.

Therefore, in 1939–1945, the years of World War II, the Nazis, along with their supporters, embarked on a systematic effort to kill the Jews in Europe. This Holocaust caused the deaths of approximately six million Jews, with one-fourth being children.

We saw that the history of Israel's return to Palestine concurred with Zephaniah's prophecy. He stated that the Jews would return by themselves, they returned precisely that way. However, they were returning as they left; they had left in unbelief, and they were returning in unbelief; they still didn't believe Jesus Christ was their Messiah. The scripture noted that they would return before certain events, but those events were terrible. It must be emphasized that as bad as World War II was for the Jews, there will be some worse events to follow. These will come before us shortly.

The second scripture that records how the Jews were going to return to the land of Palestine is found in Jeremiah 16:14–18. We are now enlightened about another serious event. This passage enlightens us that the fulfillment of the prophecy would take place during World War II. The event wasn't when God brought Israel out of Egypt in the past, but it is an event that will occur after Jeremiah's day. It is essential to note what was stated: "It shall no more be said, the Lord liveth, that brought up the children of Israel out of the land of Egypt; But, the Lord liveth, that brought up the children of Israel from the land of the north, and from all the lands whither he had driven them" (Jer. 16:14–15).

The reference is now changed from the past to the future. It was a new "the Lord liveth." Here God will be known by what He did again at another time and another place. In this future gathering, He will bring them from the land of the North and from all the nations where He drove them. Here they are returning to Palestine after being scattered all over the world. This is, therefore, not the Babylonian captivity but the Roman captivity. When Judah was restored after the Babylonian captivity, she was returning from one location. However, after the Roman captivity, she was returning from different countries. However, God doesn't say to them to come. He doesn't give them a command - that is, their coming was as His providence will have it. It isn't by chance that they came but by design - yet not by command.

Nevertheless, He tells us how He was going to accomplish this. We read, "I will bring them again into their land that I gave unto their fathers. Behold, I will send for many fishers, saith the Lord, and they shall fish them" (Jer. 16:15–16). Here we are told that God was going to use many fishers to accomplish His task. They were going to return to the land because He would send for many fishers, and they would fish them. He doesn't say how the fishers were going to fish them.

What is the significance of the many fishers? How were they going to fish them? Here the fishing wasn't merely by net but primarily by hook. Therefore, the meaning is that they were going to be not only taken but also lined up as a fish caught on a line. They will be lined up for destruction. The Germans lined them up for destruction. We might not like the Bible, but we cannot deny its revelations. This is the way it happened in history. However, there is more. To cement this point, God said He was also going to do this by another means. He said, "I will send for many hunters, and they shall hunt them from every mountain, and from every hill, and out of the holes of the rocks" (Jer. 16:16). Here we clearly see that the Germans hunted them from all their hiding places, then lined them up for destruction. We now see that the fishing and hunting were to capture the Jews. Therefore, they were lined up to go on the trains. They were lined up to be gassed; we cannot help but remember the lines of World War II. The Bible said it, and so it was done. As a result of what happened to the Jews during the war, they became a nation shortly after that. The war ended in 1945, and Israel became a nation in 1948, just as the word of God had declared.

Finally, there is a third passage that deals with this matter; this passage is found in Isaiah 18. A powerful nation was going to help them be established in Palestine. This nation was going to shelter Israel after she became a nation. Under the protection of this country, Israel increased even further, but the primary focus of this land was Israel's protection and provision after she became a nation. This mighty nation is the USA.

We are then told that when Israel becomes a nation again, she will seek the shelter of a powerful country against her enemies instead of seeking God's protection. According to the direction given for this country's location, this country is the USA. Nevertheless, the Bible affirms that while this protection was going on, God will watch what man was doing until a particular time. At that predetermined time, an enemy would appear from the Syria, Iraq, and Turkey areas. This enemy would appear after an event called "the falling of the towers" and develop under Russia's protection and provision with Iran's assistance.

What the scripture highlights is that as the USA will protect Israel, so will Russia protect the enemy. This enemy will be called the Assyrian or the king of the North. The head of this Assyrian will attack this protective country with terrorist attacks on its homeland. These attacks will cause the protector to go down into the Syria, Iraq, and Turkey areas to fight against this Assyrian and kill its head. However, instead of being victorious, the protector will be defeated and destroyed by a two-fold destruction.

The destruction part of this protective country is in the future. Yet, the other parts are being fulfilled right before our eyes. After this destruction, Israel will be left without defense. At this present time, we know the USA protects Israel. However, just as God's word said this was going to happen, in the same way, it says that the head of the Assyrian will destroy this country. One part has come to pass; the other part is just as sure to happen.

This powerful country, the USA, is the leading country that protects Israel before the tribulation. Consequently, there is more written about this country than about the Roman Empire, which will protect Israel during the tribulation. Nevertheless, the scriptures that deal with the USA are very complex. Moreover, this present protector occupies a more extended period of defending Israel than the Roman power, which will sign a treaty to protect Israel for seven years but will break the agreement after three and a half years elapse.

Israel has returned to the land of Palestine, as the word of God said she would. Nevertheless, just 140 years ago, no Christian group believed in the restoration of Israel to their land except some simple believers like Kelly and Darby, who were meeting as believers "gathered unto the name of the Lord." Most Bible teachers of their days reasoned from what they were seeing instead of from what God's word said. Kelly, Darby, and others gathered to the Lord; as they did, they had an impossible task of convincing others that Israel had to return to the land of Palestine. Where was Israel in 1870? She was scattered all over the world. People couldn't see how Israel would be restored to the land. However, the word of God said she had to return, and so she did. Why is this so? The answer is simple; the Bible is God's word.

Let us read what William Kelly wrote in 1873 in the *Bible Treasury*, volume 9, about Israel's return to the land of Palestine. He expounded the following:

This had been feebly seen, nay, generally denied, throughout Christendom for ages. Scarcely any error is more patent throughout the Fathers than the substitution of the church for Israel in all their system of thought. Every Father, whose remains have come down to us, is a witness of the same allegorizing interpretations; not only the Alexandrian school of Clement and Origen, but Justin Martyr, Irenaeus, and the Pseudo-Barnabas. The Latins followed in the same wake, not Augustine and Ruffinus and Jerome only, but Tertullian, Cyprian, and Lactantius.

Not one held the restoration of Israel to their land, converted nationally; the millenarian portion expected that the risen saints would reign with Christ in Jerusalem rebuilt, adorned, and enlarged, not that the Jews would be restored and blessed in the land. The medieval writers naturally adopted the same view: so did the Reformers, as far as I am aware, without exception. All fell into the error of putting the church into the place of Israel, and so of leaving no room for His earthly people, besides His heavenly saints and glorified bride. They neglected the warning of the Apostle Paul and assumed that the Jewish branches were broken off that the Gentiles might be grafted in, and take their place gloriously and forever. They did not pay heed to the prophetic word, as Peter exhorts, but applied systematically the predictions of Israel's blessing in the last days to the Christian church: still less did they appreciate the day dawning or the daystar arising in the heart. Catholics, papists, Protestants, had no real light, no spiritual intelligence, as to the hopes of Israel as distinct from those of Christians.[54]

William Kelly, John Darby, and others wrote Israel would be restored to her land when all other church groups said no. Who was right? They didn't write from a position of what they were seeing but from what the word of God said. It is the same thing I seek to do now—nothing more and surely nothing less. Consequently, I expect to have critics, but I hope that my critics will search the scriptures to see whether the things I write about are expressed in God's word. They aren't my views that will come to pass, nor their opinions; it is God's word that will be fulfilled every time regardless of the critics.

---

[54] William Kelly, *Element of Prophecy*, The Bible Treasury, Vol. 9, ed. William Kelly (London, UK: George Morrish, 1866), 342.

CHAPTER 15

THE TRAP

The word of God is astonishing. The more we know, the more we realize just how little we know. We are told in God's word, "Then shall we know if we follow on to know the Lord" (Hos. 6:3). This subject of the trap has eluded most Bible teachers. But why has this subject been so difficult to grasp? As a matter of fact, it is so complicated that if you check Christian writers of all types and ages, you will hardly find a line on this topic anywhere in Christendom. The reason for this is simple: if one cannot see the Muslim mosques on Mount Moriah in the scriptures, then one can never see the trap, not one mosque but both mosques. I will say that the level of difficulty of this topic on my scale is ten.

We must observe that it is the Lord Jesus who is the cause of the trap. It is what Israel did to Him that will ensure that she is entrapped. I cannot reject the Christ of God without dire consequences. Worse yet, I cannot crucify the Son of God without calamitous consequences. This is an established principle. If I reject Christ, I will pay a severe price. We, therefore, read in Isaiah, "Sanctify the Lord of hosts himself; and let him be your fear, and let him be your dread. And he shall be for a sanctuary; but for a stone of stumbling and for a rock of offence to both the houses of

Israel, for a gin and for a snare to the inhabitants of Jerusalem. And many among them shall stumble, and fall, and be broken, and be snared, and be taken" (Isa. 8:13–15).

Here we notice that the Lord Jesus Christ as Jehovah was going to be "for a gin" and "for a snare" to the inhabitants of Jerusalem. The word *gin* here is the word *pach* in Hebrew, and it means a "metallic sheet with a spring" - that is, a trap. It is used twenty-seven times in the Old Testament. The word for "snare" here is the word *moqesh*, which means a noose or bait. It is also used twenty-seven times in the Old Testament. These words are so akin that they are used together and almost interchangeably in the translations. This is evident when we realize that the word *pach* is translated twenty-two times in the KJV as "snare" and two times for the word *gin*.

On the other hand, the word *moqesh* is translated in the KJV twenty times for the same word *snare* and three times for the word *gin*. Moreover, this word *moqesh* is used two times for the word *trap*. As a result, the question must be asked. When is it a trap, when is it a bait, and what is the difference?

However, we need to notice a distinct meaning God's word is placing on this word *snare*. This meaning will help us as we seek to consider this subject. Therefore, Amos 3 gives us a handle on the way scripture uses these two words. Thus, it reads, "Can a bird fall in a snare upon the earth, where no gin [is laid] for him?" (Amos 3:5 JND). The word for "snare" here is the word *pach*, which means a metallic sheet or trap. Here, the term *gin* is the word *moqesh*, which gives the meaning of "bait" in this scripture. We will, therefore, use this word *moqesh* for bait in our study. The question Amos is asking is this. Can a bird fall into a trap unless a bait is set for it? The answer is usually no. This verse shows why these two words are so closely attached. The bait is typically connected to the trap. It is going after the bait that causes the trap to activate. Therefore, we must have the bait and the trap. The snare is a trap for birds, and the temptation is what lures the birds. We need both the bait and the trap. The bait without the trap won't work, and the trap without the bait is ineffective.

We now have the tools to undertake this study and are ready for this subject. Let us take the psalms that will put us in the last days and let us listen to the Spirit of Christ in the remnant making expressions to God.

In Psalm 69, the Lord Jesus used these terms. We read, "They gave me also gall for my meat, and in my thirst, they gave me vinegar to drink. Let their table become a snare before them: and that which should have been for their welfare, let it become a trap" (Ps. 69:21–22). We have the two words again. The first one is "snare," and the other one is "trap." The word for "snare" in the Hebrew is the word *pach*, which means a spring net or a metallic sheet with a spring; we will use this word for "trap" since it describes the instrument. The word translated "trap" in the passage is the Hebrew word *moqesh*, the word we will use for "bait." The translator uses the word according to his spiritual judgment. We will consistently use these words for one thing and one thing alone.

We have noticed that the meaning of the word *trap* also involves a spring net; we will need to investigate the term *net* to grasp this important concept. The word translated "net" is the word *resheth* in Hebrew. Let us, by God's grace, now proceed.

We will now seek to understand these three words: the snare, the net, and the trap. These three words come together in Psalm 140. "The proud have hid a snare ["pach," trap] for me, and cords; they have spread a net by the wayside; they have set gins ["moqesh," bait]—baits for me. Selah" (Ps. 140:5). Here the proud wanted to trap Israel. The first word, *snare*, is the word for "trap." The term *net* literally means "net"; it describes the kind of trap. The word for "gin" is the word for "bait," which is the bait to entrap the animal. The word for "gin" is here in the plural, which means more than one. What we need now is the pit.

In Psalm 35, we have the pit. We read, "For without cause have they hid for me their net in a pit, which without cause they have digged for my soul" (v. 7). According to the passage, this trap also is to catch men. The trap is described as a typical trap used to catch animals. A pit is dug; a spring net is set in the hole in the pathway of the animal. The bait is set to entice the animal. In this picture, the pit is covered with objects of similar appearance and color to that of the environment so the impending danger isn't perceived. Therefore, when an unsuspecting animal walks on the path leading to the pit to obtain the bait, it falls into the hole. The trap is then activated, and the animal is secured. The animal also entangles itself in the net and is held captive. However, the trap here isn't to catch animals but to catch Israel.

Lennox F. Hamilton

In Psalm 9, we read, "The heathen are sunk down in the pit that they made: in the net which they hid is their own foot taken. The Lord is known by the judgment which he executeth: the wicked is snared in the work of his own hands. Higgaion. Selah" (Ps. 9:15–16).

What we are told is that the heathen made the pit. The net here is in the hole. We aren't told where it is set, but we will be notified. We are told, moreover, that the heathen are caught in their trap. They set the trap, but they are caught in their own trap. Besides, we need to identify the time frame for this occurrence. The time is when the Lord is known by the judgment He executes. This is, therefore, in the future when the Lord comes; the heathen will be taken in their own trap.

We are, furthermore, told that the wicked is snared in the work of his hand. We said there are three persons the scriptures call the wicked: the Antichrist, the Roman Prince, and the head of the Assyrian. This is why all three persons are cast into hell alive; there is no need for any trial. Once they come on the scene, no one will be able to kill them. In this scripture, the Assyrian head is "the wicked"; here we find that he is entangled in the work of his own hands.

Most importantly, we now learn that the trap is connected to the Assyrian; but where is the trap set, and what is it? We still don't know the answers to these questions. Nevertheless, we will definitely know.

Psalm 9:3–6 confirms that the Assyrian is "the wicked." Furthermore, we know that the future enemies are primarily the king of the North and the king of the South. The king of the North is the Assyrian; please carefully note that the king of the North isn't Syria but Assyria. There is a vast difference between the two names. The future capital of the Assyrian Empire will be located in Syria. Syria will be part of Assyria, but it isn't Assyria. We have Syria today, but we don't have Assyria as yet; Assyria will soon be established. We had Assyria before, but that was destroyed. We now know that the old Assyrian empire will be restored. An Islamic power will create a country called Assyria. Moreover, the king of the North isn't Gog but the Assyrian. The Gog of Ezekiel 38 comes from the extreme North; the Assyrian comes from north of Israel. Gog is Russia.

We see here that "the wicked" is associated with the heathen; he isn't the Antichrist. The Antichrist, who is also one of the wicked, is seen associated with Israel. Therefore, "the wicked" here is the Assyrian head.

"O thou enemy, destructions are come to a perpetual end" (Ps. 9:6). When the word *enemy* is used in the singular in prophecy, it primarily refers to the Assyrian. Here the Assyrian head is the Destroyer, but his destruction has come to a perpetual end. There will be no more destruction, but that state of no destruction will be realized only when the Lord destroys the enemy; until then, destruction will increase.

Psalm 9:7–12 tells us that when the Lord comes, He will prepare His throne for judgment. He will judge the quick. The quick are those who are alive when the Lord comes. He will judge the world in righteousness. He will then be dwelling in Zion. This is all future, but it alerts us to the time when the heathen will be caught in the trap.

Moreover, we learn from Psalm 9:13–20 that the trap will be activated during the end-times. Therefore, the time of the trap is just before the Lord returns in glory. In Psalm 31, we read, "Pull me out of the net that they have laid privily for me: for thou art my strength" (Ps. 31:4). We know that verse 5 speaks of the Lord Jesus, who commits His spirit to His God and is delivered, but the rest of the psalm shows us why morally this verse is here. We see Israel in Psalm 31 caught in the trap because she killed the Lord Jesus Christ. Israel has no way out but to trust the very Lord she killed. The Lord isn't caught in any trap; Israel will be entrapped. Again, we see that the enemy had laid the net, but Israel is now caught in the web. "Pull me out of the net," Israel cries. She cannot get herself out. She is doomed unless the Lord comes to her rescue.

In Psalm 25, she asserts with confidence that the Lord will pull her out of the net. She declares with assurance, "Mine eyes are ever toward the Lord; for he shall pluck my feet out of the net" (Ps. 25:15). Again, we read in the psalm, "Blessed be the Lord, who hath not given us as a prey to their teeth. Our soul is escaped as a bird out of the snare of the fowlers: the snare is broken, and we are escaped. Our help is in the name of the Lord, who made heaven and earth" (Ps. 124:6–8).

Israel is seen as a bird, so the word is translated "snare," though it is the one for *trap*. She is delivered from the trap; it was the fowler's trap. The head of the Assyrian trapped her. The Lord gave the deliverance. Israel was caught like a bird, she couldn't fly away; she was trapped like an animal, she couldn't run away; she was caught like a fish; she couldn't swim away. Israel was trapped by the net, she was caught in the pit, she couldn't get out of. The Lord alone would have to deliver her. What are we discussing? Why is it important? This is most important, and we will deal with "the why" and "the what" immediately.

In Psalm 69:20–25, the Lord Jesus was so reproached that he said his heart was broken. He looked for some to take pity. He looked for comforters, but there were none. He then told us about the two tables. "On my table, they gave me gall for my food, and in my thirst, they gave me vinegar for my drink." He responded to their insults, "Let their table become a snare ["pach," spring net, trap] before them and that which should have been for their welfare, let it become a trap [bait]" (Ps. 69:22). What was their table, and where was their table located? What they had done to Him wasn't going to go unpunished. Israel was going to pay and pay dearly for the crucifixion of the Son of God.

In 1 Corinthians 10, we read, "The cup of blessing which we bless, is it not the communion of the blood of Christ? The bread which we break is it not the communion of the body of Christ?" (v. 16). In verse 21, we read, "Ye cannot drink the cup of the Lord, and the cup of devils: ye cannot be partakers of the Lord's Table, and of the table of devils." In 1 Corinthians 11, we read, "When ye come together therefore into one place, is it not to eat the Lord's Supper" (v. 20). We, therefore, have the purpose, the practice, and the place. The Lord's Table is the place of communion. Their table is their place of communion, their temple.

If we are going to understand this topic, it is crucial that we stick to the original words in Hebrew instead of the translated words. We have also said that we will let the word *pach*, which refers to the metallic sheet with a spring, denotes the "trap," the equipment, and the word *moqesh*, the "bait."

Therefore, what the Lord requested was that the Jewish table, their place of communion, become a trap. Moreover, that which should have been for their welfare, the temple, become the bait to draw them into the trap. This is what the original Hebrew words are saying. Their place of communion is the temple site on Mount Moriah. The request of the Lord, therefore, was that the temple site would become a trap and that their drive to rebuild their temple would become the bait to cause their entrapment. These aren't my words; I am just giving you the meaning of the Hebrew words the Jews wrote. Please remember that the bait is tied to the trap. The Muslim mosques are there on the temple mount, not by chance but by design; they are there to entrap the Jews. We will now prove this assumption. We know that the mosques are there. God knows that too; He saw to it that they were placed there. He answered the request of the Lord Jesus Christ. We will now put another piece of the puzzle in its assigned location.

First, let us establish without a doubt that God wrote in His word that this mosque, the Dome of the Rock, was going to be there close to the original Jewish temple. Once we establish this fact, we will clearly see that the mosques aren't there by chance. Moreover, we will see the purpose of God in allowing these mosques to be built there.

In Ezekiel 43:4–9, the prophet was transported into the future and shown the temple during the kingdom. There will be four temples built by the Jews on Mount Moriah. The one Ezekiel was shown was the last temple that will be built. The Lord then told Ezekiel that this temple was the place of His throne, where He will dwell amid the children of Israel. Moreover, He said that His holy name will the house of Israel no more defile. These expressions show that the time of this temple is during the millennium, during which time Christ, my Lord, will reign for a thousand years. The man who stood by the prophet in the temple is the Lord Jesus Christ, who is the speaker.

In Ezekiel 43:7–9, we have the most profound statement concerning the Muslim's mosque on the temple site. We must grasp the implications of these verses. First, let us note that the word *defile* is used here regarding Jehovah's temple just as it is used in Isaiah 30 regarding the Muslim mosques. "The house of Israel shall no more defile my holy name" (Ezek. 43:7 JND). It is when Jehovah speaks of His dwelling place that He speaks of this defilement. It is the same thing we have in Isaiah 30. "And ye shall defile the silver covering of your graven images and the gold overlaying of your molten images thou shall cast them away as a menstruous cloth: Out! Shall thou say unto it" (Isa. 30:22 JND). In Isaiah 30, Israel defiled the Muslim mosques located on their temple mount and cast them away as something unclean. Israel will violate both places of worship and remove them from those locations.

Second, we observed that after the words the "carcasses of their kings" (Ezek. 43:7), there is no run over to the next expression but an abrupt change before this essential expression, and after this expression, the Lord uses the word *fornication*. The expression about Israel ends with their kings. We now see that because of Israel's unfaithfulness - her fornication or whoredom, leaving her husband (the Lord) for another (to go a whoring after another) would cause another - a *they* to build two high places of worship on the temple mount. Moreover, at least one of these high places was so close to where God's house was located that God's word says that "their threshold by my threshold" (Ezek. 43:8 JND).

This word here for "threshold" is the Hebrew word *saph*, which is used in the KJV twelve times for "door," eight times for "threshold," four times for "basin," three times for "post," two times for "bowls," two times for "gates," and once for "a cup." When this is so expressed, it means the door of their mosque was close to the door of His temple, their posts were close to His post, their gates were close to His gates, and their basin, bowls, and cups were close to where His things, in His temple, were located.

The nearness of the Muslim mosque to Jehovah's temple is what the word of God here expresses. The door of the Muslim mosque was close to Jehovah's temple door, their post was close to Jehovah's post. Moreover, lest one thinks God's word is referring to another object, it records, "And there was only a wall between me and them" (Ezek. 43:8 JND). That "wall" we all know today is called the "Wailing Wall." The Roman Emperor Titus left it there when he destroyed Jerusalem in AD 70. That wall is the only thing presently standing between the Muslim mosque - the Dome of the Rock - and the location of the Jewish temple. It needs to be emphasized that how the scripture declares it, so it is precisely.

In Isaiah 26, we find the Wailing Wall again. We read in Darby's translation, "Jehovah, in trouble they sought thee; they poured out [their] whispered prayer when thy chastening was upon them" (Isa. 26:16 JND). Darby has a note for prayer - "lisping or secret speech." This is what is going on today at the Wailing Wall, where the Jews insert their prayers on paper into the wall.

Moreover, in the familiar and precious passage, Isaiah 6:1–5, we have in verse 4 the expression "And the posts of the door moved at the voice of him that cried." In John Darby's translation, the passage is expressed this way: "And the foundations of the thresholds shook at the voice of him that cried" (Isa. 6:4 JND). We have observed that instead of the word *posts*, Darby translates this word as "thresholds," which is the same word as in the Ezekiel 43 passage. Furthermore, those who have a KJV with notes will perceive that the word *threshold* is listed in the margin for the word *post*. What is expressly taught, therefore, is that this word *threshold* is used regarding the temple, as both passages in Ezekiel and Isaiah confirm.

Nevertheless, Isaiah 30 shows two mosques, not just one located on the temple mount. In contrast, Ezekiel 43 shows the closeness between one of the mosques and the former Jewish temple wall.

Moreover, because there is so little written about the trap by Christian writers, we need to develop it further. In Psalm 69: 22-28, we read about the sixfold judgment the Lord Jesus requested to fall upon Israel because of their crucifixion of Him. These six things aren't put in chronological order of priority but in a moral order of preference. First, that the Jewish's table, the temple site, becomes a trap; and instead of the temple being for their good, it will become a bait to draw them into the trap. We are looking at this now, the place of their worship is to become a trap to them. This is the item of the highest moral priority, yet we know so little about it. Second, that their eyes be darkened - that is, "let them be blinded." This truth is primarily developed in Romans 9 -11. Third, that God pours out His indignation upon them and let His wrathful anger take hold of them. The Assyrian will accomplish this; this idea is primarily developed in the book of Isaiah.

William Kelly wrote the following on the indignation in his exposition on Zephaniah 2: "By the 'indignation' is meant God's wrath, which will be poured out on the nations, and more particularly on the apostate Jews. The indignation of God takes in both; but it is very evident that the Christian has nothing to do with either. He is called out from the earth and man's portion here, and is entitled to wait for heavenly hopes with Christ."[55] Fourth, that Israel be out of the land for a long duration. This judgment was executed by the Romans and is developed in Deuteronomy 28. Fifth, that God will add iniquity to their iniquity and let them not come into His righteousness. Sixth, that they be blotted out of the book of the living and not be written with the righteous.

---

[55] William Kelly, *"Lectures on the Minor Prophet:"* Zephaniah, (London UK: George Morrish 1860) *364*.

Psalm 69 is quoted in Romans 11:8–10, where we observe that God has acted already on the requests of the Lord Jesus Christ. God has already given them the spirit of slumber, eyes that they couldn't see. God acted immediately at the request of His Son. The first request is being fulfilled presently. Thus, regarding the fulfillment of the blindness, it has already begun and will end only when the Lord returns. Nevertheless, there is more: in the prophecy in Psalm 69, there was nothing said of their ears. In Romans 11, however, we notice that Israel was not only to be blinded but also be deafened. Israel cannot see, and they cannot hear, so they will turn to the Land shadowing with wings and the Roman Empire for help, which will cause significant problems for them and this world. In their deafness, they will not hear God's word and will eventually apostatize.

Their deafness was also another event so important that it couldn't be left out, and though the scripture is speaking about blindness in Romans, it still included this other event. However, some additional points have been made, so if a person didn't understand the passage in the psalm, that person couldn't misunderstand this one in Romans. "And David said, let their table be made a snare, and a trap, and a stumbling block, and a recompense unto them: Let their eyes be darkened, that they may not see, and bow down their backs always" (Rom. 11:9–10). These things will come on Israel because of their rejection and crucifixion of their Messiah. These requests were made by their own Messiah against them.

In Romans 11, it became clear that their table was their place of communion; the temple was to become a trap and bait for their entrapment to prevent their escape. Additionally, the table was also to become a stumbling block. It was to become a stumbling block to them so God may repay them for what they did to His Son. For this to be accomplished, God would darken their eyes so the judgment determined may be fulfilled. If men think God has forgotten what they did to His Son, they are sadly mistaken. He will repay them for sure. This is God's word; it will be accomplished.

We need to see that this trap was carefully set. There was no escape. Therefore, to see how purposefully it was set, let me give you a piece of history. Julian (Flavius Claudius Julianus Augustus),[56] who was born in AD 332 and died on June 26, AD 363, sought to advance the Jewish religion because he was jealous of the spread of Christianity. He wanted to impede the perceived progress of the Christian faith. To accomplish this aim, Julian encouraged the Jews to rebuild their temple.[57] He opened the Roman treasury and gave every encouragement to see the task accomplished. The Jews were enthusiastic and felt that that was the day and time. *We will soon have our temple again*, they thought. *We will soon be privileged to carry our rams and lambs to worship our God. Nothing can stop us now*, they imagined. *The Romans, the greatest power on the earth, are on our side. Our Jewish brethren, from far and near, are on our side. All we need to do is start and finish.* This was one time when the Jews agreed with the Romans.

The Jews had come in their numbers; they all gathered on Mount Moriah. They began with zeal to move the stones and clear the place for their beloved temple. The weather was fine, and it seemed as if God was also in this project, orchestrated by man. They encouraged one another; perhaps they said similar words like these: "This is the day which the Lord hath made; we will rejoice and be glad in it" (Ps. 118:24). Yes, the day had come, and the work had begun, but what looked so promising soon began to crumble. The weather changed; a storm was coming. This wasn't expected. *Run, hide yourself, a hurricane is upon us,* the Jews may have expressed. God brought a hurricane and chased the Jews away.

What a chance happening, they thought. *Let us clear the stones and begin again.* They encouraged themselves again. *Up to the work, we will overcome. We have removed the rubble. We have cleared the rocks; we will now see the building rise.* Nevertheless, this wasn't to be. *What was that?* They inquired. *What was that shaking? Run, it is an earthquake.* Suddenly, another event interrupted their progress and chased the Jews away. This time it was an earthquake.

[56] New World Encyclopedia contributors, "Julian the Apostate," *New World Encyclopedia,* https://www.newworldencyclopedia.org/p/index.php?title=Julian_the_Apostate&oldid=1012286 (accessed February 11, 2022).
[57] Theodoret (Bishop of Cyrrhus), *Ecclesiastical History: A History of the Church,* Book 3, Chap.15 (London, UK: H. G. Bohn, 1854)

This can't be happening, they thought. *This isn't real; something strange is happening. We must work harder. Why do you think God will be against us?* They thought. *To the work - let us do this for our God. Difficulties only come to make us strong. Don't worry; things will be fine.* They encouraged themselves with similar words. Do I not sound like the motivational speakers of today? Those who think they can force God to do what He doesn't want to do? What was that? What was that cracking sound? *Fire! Fire! Everywhere! Where is it coming from, my brother? It is coming from under the earth. Perhaps it is a gas leak. I don't know; what I know is that I cannot stay here. What I know is that there is fire everywhere, and it isn't stopping. Let us run. Let us save ourselves; let us abandon this place. This whole place is against us. No more! No more!* You can let me tell you the story, or you can read the account given by the historians. This is no imagination; this was the display of a holy God.

What did God do? He sent a hurricane; after that, He sent an earthquake, and finally, He sent fire and chased the Jews away. If you think this was all by coincidence, then think again because when the Muslims came to build the mosques, there was no wind. There was no earthquake; there was no fire; all was calm. The mosques are there now for all to see. The trap is set. We will now wait. What will happen when the trap snaps? Terrible things. Terrible things.

The official history will read like this: Julian in AD 363, prior to his battle with Persia, engaged and encouraged the Jews to rebuild their beloved temple at Jerusalem. He appointed Alypius of Antioch, his trusted associate, to supervise the task. Julian had stopped at the ruins of the temple site on his way to fight against Persia; however, after he saw the ruins, he endeavored to rebuild the temple. In his simple mind, he thought that if he could rebuild the temple, he would thereby prove the fallacy of Christianity. He then officially praised the Jews to encourage them to perform the intended mission. He also eased their tax burden and provided the funds needed, to rebuild the temple, from the treasury of the Roman Government. The Jews were ecstatic. They attended to the matter with diligence. They came in their thousands. Their stones were on their shoulders and their joys were in their hearts. They thought the project was going to usher in the reign of their Messiah. However, this project was a gigantic failure. First, fierce storms broke out on their noble endeavor. Second, a serious earthquake in 363AD flattened the area. Third, and most decisive, strange fires kept igniting from under the temple site destined the project to disaster. The workers became very discouraged and abandoned the project. With all that effort, with all that money, with all that power, they had accomplished nothing. This is what is recorded in the history books. This is what God did. Hence, there is no Jewish temple on the site, instead, there are two Muslim mosques. The trap is set. God doesn't play.

Therefore, these two Muslim mosques constitute the baits, but the Dome of the Rock is also the bait and the trap. However, a reader who has paid particular attention to this discussion would ask a more fundamental question. How could the temple site be the trap? And you now say the Muslim mosque is the trap? The answer is simple; the trap is looked at from both sides: from the Jewish side and the side of the Assyrian. Therefore, from the Assyrian side, the heathens set the trap by building the mosque on the temple site, while the mosque - the Dome of the Rock - is the trap. When the Jews break down the mosque, they activate the trap. God's word speaks of both "baits" and "bait" - the plural and the singular, but the plural is used regarding only the heathen. We have to interpret God's word we cannot change it. The baits are the two mosques on Mount Moriah, but the Dome of the Rock is also the bait and the trap. Please remember that the bait is connected to the trap.

Moreover, from Israel's side, the temple site is the trap, and the drive to rebuild their temple is the bait to activate the trap. This is the same distinction we had in Isaiah 18:1-2, where we got direction from Israel's side and the side of the land shadowing with wings. It is giving us the information from both sides. We also have the king of the North and the king of the South as "the enemies," but "the enemy" is the king of the North.

According to Hosea, the trap is activated when Israel has lost her lovers and seeks to go back to her former husband, which is the Lord. Yet she couldn't go back to worship the Lord. Something was preventing her. It was the Dome of the Rock, and her only recourse was to break it down; she had to rebuild her temple. This hindrance had to be removed. It became necessary to break down the mosque. Israel then will fall into the trap.

Once she falls into the net, the repercussion becomes unimaginable. This event opens the door to unparalleled suffering.

We are conscious of the immaculate order displayed in Isaiah 30. The wall of protection was first destroyed, then the images on the temple mount will then be broken down. The sequence of events is obvious. The wall of protection is the land shadowing with wings. God's hand in destroying the land shadowing with wings will cause all to err. The trap was set. God had intervened, and now all were caught in the trap. First, Israel was caught in the trap; then all the nations will be caught later.

If one thinks this is beyond belief, then let him or her be aware that numerous scriptures speak about this matter. In Isaiah 30, we are told that there would be two religious objects on Mount Moriah that were going to be defiled. One was covered with silver, and the other was covered with gold. The mosques on Mount Moriah are similarly covered; one is covered with silver, and the other is overlaid with gold, just as the word of God declared in Isaiah 30:22. The Dome of the Rock is overlaid with gold, while the Al Aqsa Mosque is covered with silver.

Furthermore, one was of graven silver and the other of molten gold; so are the mosques. The dome was covered in gold in 1920, and that event fulfilled the word of God. Nevertheless, there is another crucial point; even the order given in Isaiah 30 is correct. The silver Al Aqsa Mosque was built first, then the Dome of the Rock; the gold-covered mosque came later.

Islamic scholars agree that Rashidun Caliph Umar commissioned the building of the Al Aqsa Mosque, and that the Dome of the Rock Mosque was built by order of Umayyad caliph Abd al-Malik and his son on the temple mount.[58] The construction of the Dome of the Rock was started in AD 687 and was completed in AD 691. It was commissioned in AD 692.

Islamic teachers state that the Al Aqsa Mosque, in contrast, was at first a small prayer house built by Umar, the second caliph of the Rashidun caliphate. However, this structure was rebuilt and expanded by the Umayyad caliph, Abd al-Malik in AD 690 along with the Dome of the Rock. It is important to note, that one testimony claimed that Abd

---

[58] Guy Le Strange, *Palestine under the Muslims* (Boston and New York: Houghton Mifflin and Company, 1890)

al-Malik used materials from a particular Christian church, which was destroyed to build the mosque.

Eventually, Abd al-malik's son, al-Walid, finished the Al Aqsa Mosque in AD 705. Furthermore, an earthquake in AD 746 destroyed the mosque, but the Abbasid caliph al-Mansur entirely rebuilt it in AD 754. Moreover, it was again destroyed, but the new caliph, Al-Mahdi, rebuilt it in AD 780. An earthquake also destroyed the Al Aqsa Mosque in 1033, but the Fatimid caliph Ali Az-Zahir rebuilt it two years later. This is the structure that is currently there.

In Joel 3:4–8, we have the Muslim mosques again in focus. Three names are singled out: Tyre, Zidon, and the coast of Philistia, Israel's close neighbors. These three nations weren't singled out for scattering Israel, not even for destroying her but for using God's silver and gold in association with their temples (mosques). The silver and gold are what will distinguish these Muslim Temples (mosques). I am using the word *temple* here because Joel 3 is using that word. One of the mosques is called today *the silver dome*, and the other is called *the golden dome*.

Tyre was very instrumental in building Solomon's Temple, but now he was seen in association with others in the construction of the two temples, on the temple mount, not far from Israel's place of worship. In one temple they used God's silver, and in the other temple, they used His gold. That is, God's things were used in the construction of their temple and in the worship of their god. His beautiful, pleasant place was being used for the display of their temple and their god. This is what is displayed on the temple mount.

We must appreciate that it's the destruction of the mosques on Mount Moriah that will ignite the holy war, the jihad. In Jeremiah 6, we find, "Holy War against her" (Jer. 6:4). We have said before that the word translated "prepare" is the same word for "holy" in Hebrew. We, therefore, have "Holy War" in Jeremiah 6, the same we have in Joel 3. "Proclaim you this among the Gentiles; Holy War, wake up the mighty men, let all the men of war draw near; let them come up" (Joel 3:9). We have the same thing in Micah 3. "Holy War against her" (Mic. 3:5). The holy war is clearly a religious war; it is a war in the name of religion. There is also a reason for it; the Jews had defiled and cast out the Muslim mosques, according to Isaiah 30; this is what generated the holy war. We must remember that the Muslims didn't violate the Jewish temple when they built their mosques; even the Wailing Wall was left standing. This wall was so close to their mosque, yet they didn't touch it. Therefore, the defiling of the Muslims Mosques will generate the holy war.

We will now take a glimpse at this "Holy War." We will notice the Assyrian attack on Israel in Psalm 74:1-10 as a result of the destruction of their mosques on Mount Moriah. This is the attack after the Roman Empire will break the treaty. We learn from the expression "there is no more any prophet" that this is in the future. In verse 3, the enemy was the Assyrian. The temple was rebuilt, but the Assyrian attacks it with vengeance. "When you rise up, lift up your feet - look down at all that the enemy has done wickedly in the sanctuary," they said to God. It is the temple that is being attacked. The sanctuary here is the temple. The enemy has done wickedly in the sanctuary - they defiled the temple. They wanted to return the favor to the Jewish temple what was done to their mosques. In Psalm 79, the Islamic Assyrian defiles the temple. In Psalm 74, he destroys it.

In verse 6, the Assyrian breaks down the carved work at once in the temple with axes and hammers. Here it isn't guns and bombs but axes and hammers. They will be so infuriated by what Israel will do to their mosques. They will defile the sanctuary, then burn it to the ground. The Assyrian will retaliate to the Jewish defilement of their mosques by defiling the Jewish temple even worse. They will then have in their minds, and only in their minds at that moment, to destroy Israel also with the temple. Later on, Psalm 83, they will agree to this destruction of Israel, in the second Assyrian attack; but the Lord won't allow it, and instead, He will destroy them.

Nevertheless, they don't stop there; they then attack all the synagogues. The synagogues are the places where Israel prays today. They will attack these also. Every symbol of Israel's religious worship will be greeted with utter disdain. Why is this so? Do you think it is because some earthquake destroyed the Muslim mosques? No! No! No! Holy war. They then will burn down all the Jewish synagogues in the land of Israel. The Assyrians will be enraged with fury. Israel will be in dire straits. She will have none to help. She can cry to God only, and the remnant will plead with Him, as we find in the rest of the Psalm. There is no protector to help; he has been destroyed. There is no Roman Prince to help; he has broken the treaty. Only God is there, and the remnant will cry to Him.

The remnant then pleads with the Lord in Psalm 74:11–23. We are privileged to hear their intercessions. In verse 18, the remnant pleads with God to remember that the enemy reproached and blasphemed His name. The enemy will begin to speak derogatory things against Israel's God, having now believed that its god was the right God. Moreover, we have a clear indication in verse 19 that "the wicked" here is the Assyrian. It is the multitude of "the wicked" that have attacked Israel. The multitude belongs to him. The last verse states clearly that the army is increasing continuously. The Assyrian will be getting bigger and bigger. Who will be providing all these fighters? Not a country but an ideology.

In Psalm 79:1–13, we are told even more. Again, Israel is under attack by the Assyrian. The attackers are those round about; they are Israel's neighbors. The first object of their attack will be the temple. The trap has generated this fury. There is nothing like it in the whole history of humankind. *Do you defile our mosque? We will defile your temple to such an extent that you will not believe it.* That is why, regarding the table in Romans 11:10, it was said a second time, "Let their eyes be darkened." How could Israel not see that if they defiled and broke down the mosques that this would have been the result? It was, for this reason, that their eyes were blinded a second time; that they may defile and break down the Muslim mosques without thinking about the consequences. They were sure that when they broke down the mosques and rebuilt their temple, God was going to help them. Nevertheless, they will be so wrong; what a terrible mistake.

Moreover, we find that the whole city is laid in heaps. The dead bodies are given to the birds of the heavens. The flesh of the saints is given as meat to the beast of the earth. They have shed blood like water around Jerusalem. There is no one to bury the dead. Who are the people who have done this? They haven't come from far; they are Israel's neighbors. They are those round about Israel. They are the Assyrian. What destruction. What a catastrophe.

Carefully notice Psalm 79. "Pour out thy wrath upon the heathen that have not known thee, and upon the kingdoms that have not called upon thy name. For they have devoured Jacob, and laid waste his dwelling place"

(vv. 6–7). Pay particular attention to the words: *the kingdoms that have not called upon thy name* (Ps. 79:6). These kingdoms are the kingdoms of the king of the North and the kingdom of the king of the South, which shall be revived. Daniel 8 declared that "in the latter time of their kingdoms" (Dan. 8:23); therefore, in Psalm 79, we have the kingdoms restored and causing havoc in Israel and the world.

Furthermore, as we meditate on Jeremiah 7:1–4, we note God's warning to Israel concerning false words about the temple. He said in verse 4, "Trust ye not in lying words, saying, The temple of the Lord, The temple of the Lord, The temple of the Lord, are these" (Jer. 7:4).

We need to be clear as to this and other similar passages in the prophets, as Darby and Kelly have indicated; we aren't saying that there might not have been a partial fulfillment in the days of the prophet. In most cases, there were, but what we are saying is that there is a future component that is of vital importance.

Therefore, if we accept this translation as it is, what is it saying to us? Can we say that the temple of the Lord was those buildings? Then, if we say so, are those words of falsehood or words of truth? This is the first problem with this interpretation. We must confess that these are the words of truth. This same truth is verified in Matthew 24:1 when the disciples showed our Lord Jesus Christ the buildings of the temple; He never said that the words they spoke were words of falsehood.

What, therefore, make those expressions the words of falsehood? What was the meaning of the terms? Therefore, we must see that this passage directly bears on the destruction of the Muslim mosques. Therefore, "the words of falsehood" was the belief that once they rebuilt the temple, everything was going to be well. Let us, then, look at the expression again. "Trust ye not in lying words, saying, The temple of the Lord, The temple of the Lord, The temple of the Lord, are these" (Jer. 7:4).

Moreover, not only was the expression "words of falsehood," as we have it in J. N. Darby's translation, but God was also telling them not to trust in those words. Not only were they words of falsehood, but Israel was trusting in those words as gospel truth. Therefore, we are in a position to understand the expression "Trust ye not in words of falsehood, saying, the temple of the Lord, the temple of the Lord, the temple of the Lord, are these" (Jer. 7:4 JND). This scripture enlightens us that the Jews will all be chanting, "The temple of the Lord! The temple of the Lord! The temple of the Lord!" The word *they* is there in the original Hebrew, but the word *are* isn't there. Since the word *they* is there in the original, it merely means "they [cried]," which will give us the sense of the passage.

We have something similar in Acts 19. "All with one voice about the space of two hours cried out: Great is Diana of the Ephesians" (v. 34). Here they cried for about two hours, "Great is Diana of the Ephesians! Great is Diana of the Ephesians! Great is Diana of the Ephesians!" This is what religious fury produces. This is what we have here. The temple of the Lord! The temple of the Lord! The temple of the Lord!

What they are saying is that the temple of the Lord is the answer to all their problems. Name the problem, and the temple of the Lord will fix it. Let us build back the temple, and all our problems will disappear. That is what they will be saying, but they were words of falsehood. They didn't know that rebuilding the temple was going to cause them to fall into the trap.

Now, look at what is said subsequently. "For if ye thoroughly amend your ways and your doings ... then will I cause you to dwell in this place, in the land that I gave to your fathers, for ever and ever. Behold, ye trust in lying words, that cannot profit" (Jer. 7:5–8).

As Israel trusts in the land shadowing with wings, which is of no profit to them, so are they doing here likewise. It wasn't in a place but in a person, they needed to trust, just as in the olden days, when the Philistines took the ark of God. Israel thought that if they brought the ark into the battle, they were guaranteed victory; but instead, they were guaranteed defeat. We also often make the same mistake.

We notice in Jeremiah 7:12–16 that what the Lord did at Shiloh was the type of what He was going to do to the temple. However, to which temple was He going to bring such devastation? What He did to the temple then is typical of what He is going to do to the future temple in the day of the trap. Here, for instance, He says, "Therefore pray not thou for this people, neither lift up a cry nor prayer for them, neither make intercession to me: for I will not hear thee" (Jer. 7:16). This is an important signpost. He said to Jeremiah that He wasn't going to hear the prophet's request about Israel. "Pray not thou for this people ... neither make intercession to me: for I will not hear" (Jer. 7:16). This couldn't be in the prophet

Jeremiah's days when Babylon destroyed the temple, since the Jewish remnant asked Jeremiah to make intercession for them, which He did.

Moreover, God heard and answered the prayer of Jeremiah. Nevertheless, the people refused to obey the voice of the Lord, because they were determined to go to Egypt. Also, we see a similar response with King Zedekiah in the days of Jeremiah; God answered all the questions he asked, but Zedekiah refused to hear the word of the Lord. Therefore, the time of this event is in the future.

However, during the tribulation period is when God will refuse to hear them. Thus, though the passage had a partial fulfillment in the prophet Jeremiah's days, yet it awaits a future day for complete fulfillment. This is how scripture is written, and if one doesn't see this, one is in line to make significant mistakes in the interpretation of God's word. We need to grasp this aspect of the word of God. Let's take another well-known passage. In Matthew 24, we read, "And Jesus said unto them, See ye not all these things? Verily I say unto you, there shall not be left here one stone upon another that shall not be thrown down" (Matt. 24:2). Which temple was He talking about? "Why sure," you may answer, "the temple destroyed by the Romans." However, are you sure? What is sure is that the temple destroyed by the Romans was a partial fulfillment of the prophecy.

In Jeremiah 7:20, God informs us that His anger and fury will be poured out on that place. Therefore, when these mosques are broken down, then these passages will have their complete fulfillment. Then no amount of diplomacy will help, and the time will also be right, for it is then that one religion will be sure that their God is the true God.

This becomes a Cain and Abel story all over again. This is what causes the holy war and ignites the jihad. From then on, the Assyrian will seek the destruction of Israel. It must be remembered that the land shadowing with wings must first be removed before the Jews seek to rebuild their temple. We know that the Jews will rebuild their temple because the Antichrist will sit in the temple and declare that he is God according to 2 Thessalonians 2. It is only when this help is gone that they want the protection of the Lord, at least nominally, for they cannot seek the shelter of the land shadowing with wings and that of the Lord at the same time. It is when "their lover" is no more that they seek to return to their first husband. "Therefore, behold, the days come, saith the Lord, that it shall no more be called Tophet, nor the valley of the son of Hinnom, but the valley of slaughter: for they shall bury in Tophet, till there be no place. And the carcasses of this people shall be meat for the fowls of the heaven, and for the beasts of the earth; and none shall fray them away" (Jer. 7:32–33).

There is no way one can say all these scriptures are fulfilled. The total fulfillment awaits the events of the day when the trap will snap. Then and only then will these things apply.

Therefore, one final passage from Hosea 5 will help. "They shall go with their flocks and with their herds to seek the Lord, but they shall not find him; he hath withdrawn himself from them. They have dealt treacherously against the Lord: for they have begotten strange children: now shall a month devour them with their portions ... among the tribes of Israel have I made known that which shall surely be. The princes of Judah were like them that remove the bound: therefore, I will pour out my wrath upon them like water" (Hos 5:6–10).

We need to appreciate that in verse 6, Judah, or present-day Israel, is the one seen going with their flock and herd to seek the Lord. They had broken down the mosques and rebuilt their temple. They then will go with their flocks and their herds to sacrifice in their rebuilt temple. Nevertheless, instead of the temple being the answer to all their problems, as they thought, we then read, "But they shall not find him, he hath withdrawn himself from them" (Hos. 5:6). The Lord isn't there. Consequently, the Lord will not hear them.

Nevertheless, there is more. God says, "They have dealt treacherously against the Lord: for they have begotten strange children: now shall a month devour them with their portions" (Hos. 5:7). We are told that they dealt treacherously against the Lord. The word treacherous means to betray; they had betrayed the Lord. Judas betrayed Him to the leaders for 30 pieces of silver. Moreover, we read, "Surely as a wife treacherously departs from her husband, so have ye dealt treacherously with me, O house of Israel, saith the Lord" (Jer. 3:20). They departed from Him. They trusted in the land shadowing with wings. Not only did Israel depart from the Lord and commit adultery, but her infidelity produced children -"strange children"- as the word of God says here. These strange children are the Jews who listen and take the advice of the land shadowing with wings. They are brought up and guided by the land shadowing with

271

wings. Israel wants to return, but it is too late; her return will not be on her terms.

Observe what is declared in this scene: "Now shall a month devour them" (Hos. 5:7). Who or what is the month that will devour Israel? The new translation by J. N. Darby gives us a better rendering: *The new moon shall devour you.* You can now see why it is translated as the *month* because the new moon begins the month. Anyhow, we still have a problem. Who is the new moon? Just take a look at the top of every Muslim mosque and tell me what you see. You will see the symbol of the new moon. It is the very symbol of Islam. It now makes sense. Instead of Israel finding God, they will find the new moon, and the new moon will devour them for destroying their mosques. This is the religion of the Assyrian, and sad to say, the Assyrian will devour Israel for breaking down their mosques.

CHAPTER 16

THE EUROPEAN UNION AND THE ROMAN PRINCE

T he more we study the Bible, the more we are convinced that the church is seen as a parenthesis - not only theoretically but actually. That is, when the church is raptured, the ways of God regarding the earth, and Israel, will flow smoothly from the past to the future. The parenthesis doesn't affect the sentence but only introduces additional details. The church is seen as a parenthesis, because contrary to the views of many, the church isn't earthly but heavenly. Therefore, it becomes evident that the political structure that was before the church's formation must return after the church is raptured.

Hence, because the church is heavenly, no prophecy needs to be fulfilled before the church is raptured. The eyes of the saints are heavenly, not earthly. Israel, on the contrary, is earthly and, as a consequence, the subject of prophecy. Christ is the object of it all; without Christ, nothing matters. On my scale of difficulty, this topic is an eight. Therefore, we need God's help to apprehend the future Roman Empire.

We need to comprehend that because the church of the living God (Matt. 16:18) is a parenthesis, the powers preceding the church formation must reappear before the tribulation and be present after the rapture.

Moreover, because Israel is the subject of prophecy, she had to return before the other horses and riders of Revelation 6.

First, when the church was established, the political power in control was the Roman Empire. This power must return. When the Lord Jesus Christ was present on earth, the Romans crucified Him; therefore, before He returns in glory, the Roman Empire must return. The Roman Empire has a vital part to play in the last days. The Lord will deal severely with the government that crucified Him. This power has reappeared in our day, before our eyes, in the form of the European Union. Let there be no illusion; the European Union is the revised Roman Empire, and it is so according to prophecy. We see not only the preparations in our days but also the reappearance of the Roman Empire, according to Daniel's declaration.

Second, before the formation of the church of God, the Roman power had destroyed the king of the North. The king of the North, which was before the church was formed, must reappear before the tribulation. The Romans put an end to that kingdom in 65 BC. This king of the North will reappear as the Assyrian. This event is about to happen.

Third, before the church's formation, the Romans destroyed the king of the South. The Romans subjugated this power around 51 BC. This power must also reappear; this fulfillment is also to be accomplished shortly.

Fourth, preceding the formation of the church, Israel was in Palestine's land; she had to return to the country before the Lord appeared. Faithful to scripture, she returned to that land.

Fifth, besides, the nations around Israel, when the church was formed, were all in their lands; they all had to return. They have all returned.

Sixth, before the church's formation, there was no land shadowing with wings; it must disappear. It will soon disappear.

Seventh, when the church was formed, Rome was the most significant power on the earth. Rome must reappear as the dominant power on earth. For this reason, we don't find the land shadowing with wings in the book of Revelation, but we find the Roman Empire.

Therefore, in Revelation 6, after the church's Rapture in chapter 4, we don't see the land shadowing with wings because it disappeared. However, we find the Assyrian, the king of the North, as the white horse. We see the king of the South as the red horse. The Israel of God is pictured as the black horse, and the Roman Empire, as the pale horse, completes the picture. These powers had all returned and will become the leading players during the tribulation. The land shadowing with wings is the main player before the tribulation, and Russia, the Gog of Ezekiel 38, is the dominant player after the tribulation. God's word has order, stringent order.

In history, Rome defeated both the king of the North and the king of the South. However, the future battles will be different, very different.

We will therefore commence our study on the Roman Empire by studying the image presented in Daniel 2:31–35. We need to clearly state that this image represents the times of the Gentiles, from Nebuchadnezzar's Day until the establishment of the kingdom of Christ. Moreover, it is only one image, and that image is of a man. This image, therefore, represents human government as seen in Adam's posterity. However, though the image is one, we find that it is yet separated into four different parts: 1) the head of gold 2) the breast and arms of silver 3) the belly and thighs of brass 4) the legs of iron, and its feet and toes partly iron and partly clay.

Therefore, according to the metals used, we have deterioration of the head to the feet. There was another point of great importance; the image was smitten by a stone "cut out without hands," and all its several parts were "broken to pieces together, and became like the chaff of the summer threshing-floors; and the wind carried them away, that no place was found for them: and the stone that smote the image became a great mountain, and filled the whole earth" (Dan. 2:35). The image, which represents man on the earth, was crushed by another man, the man from heaven, our Lord Jesus Christ, from which there was no recovery. Thus, the government man establishes will be replaced by the government God will establish. There will be a complete change.

However, before the kingdom of God would be established, the word of God lets us know that there would be four world empires. The establishment of those empires would directly affect the Jews, the subject of prophecy. These four empires were the Babylonian Empire, ruled from Iraq; the Medes and Persian Empire, ruled from Iran; the Grecian Empire, ruled from Greece, and the Roman Empire ruled from Rome in Italy. Two of these empires were in Asia and two were in Europe.

However, the word of God enlightens us from Daniel 2 and Revelation 17, that the Roman Empire will rise, then be destroyed; then rise again when Israel is returned to the land in the last days. Therefore, the former Roman Empire will revive and return in the last days after the return of Israel to her land. This revised Roman Empire should be visible at present since Israel is in the land. True to God's word, the Roman Empire is rising in the form of the European Union.

The scripture further instructs us that when the Roman Empire reappears in the last days it will be different from the ancient Roman Empire. In this revived form, the future Roman Empire would be composed of individual countries aligned in a common federation. True to God's word the Roman Empire has reappeared exactly so.

We are instructed that the empire will increase in size above ten countries; then a crisis will occur, which is the destruction of the land shadowing with wings. Consequently, Israel will be targeted for destruction by the Islamic Empire, the Assyrian. As a result, Israel will desire the protection of the European Union. Israel will then negotiate a treaty with the European Union representatives, but when that treaty will be presented to the European parliament for ratification, that treaty will cause a division and near break-up of the union and only ten nations will remain.

We will now ask a question; do we have such a union today? The answer is a resounding yes. This power was established, in our day before our eyes, as the European Economic Community by the treaty of Rome in 1957. The name of Rome was inextricably bound to this treaty. The original members of this European Community were Belgium, France, Italy, Luxembourg, the Netherlands, and West Germany. Yet, the agreement was called the treaty of Rome.

The number six speaks of the number of a man, so it is no surprise that six members formed the power. Eventually, everyone in the Roman earth will have to show allegiance to this power by having the number 666.

Furthermore, from the initial six members, the first increase of the European Community took place in 1973 when Denmark, Greenland, Ireland, and the United Kingdom joined the union. Greenland, however, left the European Communities in 1985 because of disputes over fishing rights. Norway had negotiated to join in 1973, but the Norwegian people rejected European Community membership. The European Community was composed of 10 nations when it held its first direct election for the European Parliament in 1979. This was significant because the Roman

Empire would be reduced to ten countries, at the end, when the Roman Beast will preside over the empire. Therefore, these highlighted numbers are important.

Furthermore, in 1981 Greece joined the European Community. Then, both Portugal and Spain joined in 1986. Also, in that same year, the European Flag began to be used. The Schengen Agreement came into force in 1985. Consequently, from that point, passports were no longer required to travel between most member states. When East Germany was reunited with West Germany in 1990, East Germany became a member of the union as a united Germany. What was even more significant was that to expand further, a new treaty had to be negotiated. The new agreement was the Maastricht Treaty. That treaty established the European Union in November 1993, and the movement was then called the European Community. Almost immediately after that treaty, in 1995, Austria, Finland, and Sweden joined the European Union.

There was further development in the Union in 2002. The euro bills and coins became the standard currency in the European Community and replaced national currencies in twelve Community member states. To date, the euro has increased in popularity and is now used in 19 member states. This euro has become the second-largest used currency in the world.

Then in 2004, ten new members joined the European Union. Those countries were, in alphabetical order: Cyprus, Czech Republic, Estonia, Hungary, Latvia, Lithuania, Malta, Poland, Slovakia, and Slovenia. Then in 2007, Bulgaria and Romania joined the union. Finally, Croatia became the 28th and final member of the European Union in 2013.

There was not only an enlargement in the union but also greater popularity of the euro. Slovenia embraced the euro in 2007. Cyprus and Malta welcomed it in 2008. Slovakia followed this in 2009. Then in 2011, Estonia also adopted the euro. Latvia would follow in 2014 and Lithuania in 2015. The currency was getting stronger and more popular as the years progressed. Is this all of man, or is this of God? You will have to answer that question. Your answer will determine how you will order your life.

Moreover, there was a significant development in 2009; the Lisbon treaty came into force. This treaty transformed and redefined many aspects of the European Union. For one, it created a permanent president of the European Council. Secondly, it provided High Representatives of the Union for Foreign affairs and Security Policy. This President is a forerunner of the Beast who will be the head of the European Union during the tribulation.

Furthermore, the unity of the European Community had been tested by many issues over the years. The withdrawal of the United Kingdom from the European Union will also be a significant test for the union. The Exit of Britain from the league, which was slated to take effect on March 29, 2019, has not broken up the union but has put a tremendous strain on the European Community's cohesion, as did the debt crisis and migration from the Middle East. Nevertheless, this Brit Exit is vital for another reason; it gives us a glimpse into the future, to enable us to understand how the other nations will leave the European Union over the matter of the protection of Israel. When these nations leave, ten countries will remain. These ten nations will form the ten toes of the prophecy.

Yet again, we are confronted with the accuracy of the word of God. It states clearly that there will be a united group of countries in Europe, just before the tribulation begins. At the time of the distress, the number of countries in the confederation will be 10. Before the tribulation, the number of countries in the league will be higher than ten. Already this power is in place, just as the word of God states. How close must the coming of the Lord Jesus Christ be? How can a man say the Bible is irrelevant? It is the only book that can give us direction.

In Daniel 2:36–43, the Spirit of God gave us the interpretation of Nebuchadnezzar's dream. Nebuchadnezzar was declared the representative of the head of gold. However, let us observe that it is not only Nebuchadnezzar personally that the gold represented but also his successors until Belshazzar, his grandson. This we will see as we consult other scriptures. In Jeremiah 25, we have the epoch of the seventy weeks of captivity. Moreover, in Jeremiah 27, we have the succession of the Babylonian Empire. "All nations shall serve him, and his son, and his son's son, until the very time of his land come" (Jer. 27:7). Did this happen? Sure, it did.

We are astonished again, concerning the absolute accuracy of scripture. What is so remarkable about this prophecy is that after Nebuchadnezzar died, his son Evil-Merodach, according to God's word, took the throne. However, after Evil-Merodach died, the succession became very interesting.

The next person who took the throne wasn't Nebuchadnezzar's grandson; instead, the new ruler was his son-in-law.

Nebuchadnezzar's son-in-law wasn't in the line of succession, according to scripture, but he took the throne because he loved power and wanted to rule. The people of Babylon also fancied him and wanted him to be their king. He was married to Nebuchadnezzar's daughter and reigned for a while. After he died, his son then reigned. It seemed as if the succession would have gone in a different direction, and God's word would have failed. According to the sequence, we had Nebuchadnezzar, his son, his son-in-law, and his grandson through his daughter.

Still, God's word in Jeremiah 27 said it would be Nebuchadnezzar, his son, and his son's son; and there the kingdom would be terminated. What would happen now? How would the word of God be fulfilled, especially in a strange land? It seemed as if the prophecy had failed. However, that couldn't happen because the Bible is God's word. Therefore, just a few months later, another of Nebuchadnezzar's grandsons came to the throne, but this time it was through his son and so again established the accuracy of scripture. The word of God says, "Nebuchadnezzar, his son, and his son's son," and so it was.

Nevertheless, the way I have stated this history seems so peaceful and sublime, but that is far from the reality; it was vicious and violent. Nebuchadnezzar reigned for 43 years before his death. After he died, his son Evil-Merodach, 2 Kings 25:27-30 and Jeremiah 52:31-34, succeeded him. He reigned for only two years before his brother-in-law Nergalsharezer, Jeremiah 39:3, 13, called Neriglassar of secular history, murdered him. Nergalsharezer managed to reign for only four years before his demise. When he died, his son, Laborosoarchod, who was still a child and mentally challenged, ruled for only nine months before he was beaten to death by a gang of conspirators. Nabonidus, was then appointed king and ruled conjointly with Belshazzar his eldest son until Cyrus the Persian conquered Babylon. Belshazzar, was stationed in Babylon while Nabonidus, his father, was in Arabia. Nebuchadnezzar grandson, therefore, reigned for twenty years before the kingdom came to its end. Belshazzar reigned conjoinedly with Nabonidus for 17 years. When we sum the years, the kings of Babylon ruled the empire; from Nebuchadnezzar to Belshazzar, we confirm the 70 years of Jeremiah's prophecy.

As usual, historians and archaeologists were quick to challenge the accuracy of the scripture because they knew that Nabonidus was said to be the last king to reign over Babylon and they did not notice the name Belshazzar in the Babylonian history. To them, this was another evident contradiction of the Bible. However, this so-called discrepancy soon dissipated when evidence was uncovered indicating, not only that Belshazzar was Nabonidus eldest son, but that he was associated with him in governing the kingdom. Moreover, the evidence clearly showed that during the last part of his reign, Nabonidus lived in Arabia while his eldest son, Belshazzar, conducted the affairs of the kingdom in Babylon.

Men are usually very quick to accuse scripture of inaccuracies but only to the display of their ignorance. They prefer to believe any other source than the Bible because they desire no God. Therefore, men accused the Bible of contradiction until the *Nabonidus Cylinder* was discovered by John George Taylor in 1854. This Cylinder is now displayed in the British Museum for all to see who was right, God or man. Therefore, according to Babylonian records, Belshazzar became co-regent in 553 BC, the third year of Nabonidus's reign, and continued as co-regent until the fall of Babylon in 539 BC.

What is most important to grasp is that it wasn't only the succession God had spoken about; He also talked about the length of time the kingdom would last. What became evident, when it seemed as if the prophecy had failed, was that God was also accomplishing the time of the existence of the Babylonian Kingdom, according to His utterance. All must be fulfilled; all will be fulfilled. It was, therefore, in Nabonidus, the grandson of Nebuchadnezzar, with his co-regent Belshazzar that the whole succession terminated. This wasn't by chance; this was by design. God's word will be fulfilled, regardless of the circumstances.

In Daniel 2:31–38, the Babylonian Empire is presented as the head of gold. We then read, "And after thee shall arise another kingdom inferior to thee;" this second kingdom is that of the Medes and Persian. The next kingdom is then presented, "And another third kingdom of brass, which shall bear rule over all the earth" (Dan. 2:39). The third kingdom is the Grecian kingdom. Therefore, we know from Daniel 2, that there were going to be three kingdoms before the arrival of the Roman Empire. Did this happen? We know it did.

In Daniel 2:40–44, we have the presentation of the Roman Empire. The iron is presented as strength. The breaking and subduing of all things are presented as the character of the iron. However, we see that there were going to be two parts to the Roman Empire. The legs which give us the longer ancient Roman Empire and the shorter revived Roman Empire, as the feet and toes. Therefore, the future Roman Empire will revive as the feet by man and the toes by the Devil.

Now, it is only when we get to the feet of the revived Roman Empire, that we find this mixture of iron and clay. Daniel 2:40 states that the fourth kingdom shall be as strong as iron. This entire kingdom was presented to be strong as iron. Thus, this mixture of clay comes into the discussion only when we consider the feet and toes. When the Lord Jesus Christ smote this image, He smote it upon its feet, according to verse 34. Therefore, the feet and toes are the latter parts of the empire. The legs are the historical part of the empire. We, therefore, need only to account for the clay in the future part of the empire. This clay is the most central element in the mixture. This clay isn't a passing expression but a critical component.

We need to see that there are two parts to this future Roman Empire: first, "the feet"; and second, "the toes." These are the future parts of the empire. Additionally, there are two revivals of this future empire. One is revived by man, the feet - the Dragon will revive the toes. The toes are the final part of the empire. During the tribulation, the empire will be seen as the toes; before the tribulation, the empire will be regarded as the feet. However, when the Lord judges the empire, He judges the feet. If we don't see this difference, then it will be difficult for us to accept the present European Union as the Roman Empire. Nevertheless, it is the Roman Empire, and it is unfolding just as the scripture depicts its rise. When our interpretation is suspect, we have difficulty identifying even the power that is clearly rising, according to the information given to us in God's word.

Yes, it is when the empire is in the form of the ten toes or ten kings that it is seen as coming from the Dragon or the bottomless pit. That point is reached only after the Rapture of the church of God and just before the tribulation. During the time of grace, when the empire is larger than the ten toes, when it is presented as the feet, the Roman Empire isn't seen as coming from Satan.

If we think of the apostasy, we will get a better handle on this. During the time of grace, when the church is present on the earth, we will have some who will apostatize according to the book of Timothy; however, the apostasy cannot take place until after the Rapture. We might have *some who apostatize*, but we cannot have *the apostasy*. We must see that during the time of grace when the church is present on earth, the European Union, which is the Roman Empire, is seen as the feet, larger than the ten toes. It is not at this time regarded as coming from the bottomless pit.

However, after the Rapture, when the Dragon will be cast down, he will strengthen the Beast and the ten nations. As a result, the empire will be seen as coming from the bottomless pit; Satan is the one who will empower the empire. One part of the Roman Empire is now, the feet; another part is in the future, the toes. One part is before the tribulation; the other part is during the tribulation.

Today we see the feet; during the tribulation, the toes will be seen. We, as believers, won't see the toes, but we see the feet today. Today the power is seen as ordained of God; during the tribulation, the influence will be seen as coming from the bottomless pit. What causes this change in the source of power in the same empire? The only thing that can create this change in the source of power is that Satan will be cast down, and as the Dragon, he will give his power, throne, and great authority to the Beast and the Roman Empire.

If we see the complete Future Roman Empire as coming from the bottomless pit, then we will be tempted to view the present European Union as coming from the bottomless pit, if we accept it as the Roman Empire. This will have profound implications because one may be tempted not to submit to this power. Nevertheless, the scripture is clear; once the church is on earth, "the powers that be are ordained of God" (Rom. 13:1). After the church is removed to heaven, then and only then can the empire be presented as coming from the bottomless pit; and at that time, the empire will be composed of ten nations.

Furthermore, if we see that the clay is introduced only into the Future Roman Empire, then we will quickly know the meaning of the clay. When we put the clay in the historical part of the empire, where it is not, we speculated, without a proper foundation, as to what the clay represents. Some think it means capitalism, and others believe it is communism. They are those who think it denotes the Barbarians who invaded the empire and so on. However, the true meaning of the clay can be grasped only when it is seen that the iron always represents what crushes and destroys.

The introduction of the clay suggested a new meaning in addition to that of the iron. The empire was taking on a new role. Therefore, instead of its old function of crushing and destroying, it was now protecting and preserving. This new function will be on display when the empire decides to protect and preserve Israel. This is the purpose of the introduction of the clay. This clay is mentioned nine times in this chapter, and in three distinct ways, it is no passing feature.

Let us observe the changing features of the clay. First, in Daniel 2, we read, "His feet part of iron and part of clay" (v. 33); that is, one part of the empire will want to protect Israel, and the other part didn't. In verse 34, we read, "Which smote the image upon its feet that were of iron and clay." Until now, we don't read about the toes. The feet were of iron and clay. The problem arose when the empire was seen as the feet as it is today. The division took place in the feet before it came into the toes. When the empire was seen as the feet, the land shadowing with wings was destroyed, necessitating this protection. It is this division in the feet that will produce the toes. It is only when Daniel gives the interpretation that we read of the toes. In the prophecy, we learned only of the feet. The problem came up when the empire was larger than the toes.

After the Assyrian destroys the land shadowing with wings, the Assyrian will attack Israel at home. As a consequence of this attack, the Jewish leaders will want the European Union to protect them, but this will cause a split in the union.

In Daniel 2, we read, "Then was the iron, the clay ... broken to pieces" (v. 35). Now note carefully what verse 40 says, "And the fourth kingdom shall be strong as iron: forasmuch as iron breaketh in pieces and subdueth all things: and as iron that breaketh all these, shall it break in pieces and bruise" (Dan. 2:40). The fourth kingdom is the Roman Empire, it was strong as iron. Furthermore, both the ancient Roman Empire and future Roman Empire will be strong as iron. This is the feature of the Roman Empire; it is strong and it is called *the strong*. In contrast, the land shadowing with wing is never called the strong, but is called the mighty, as is the Assyrian. These are important signposts that we might not make mistake with God's word. Here in verse 40, we get the meaning of the iron; the iron breaks all.

However, in verse 41, we read, "And whereas thou sawest the feet and toes, part of potters' clay, and part of iron, the kingdom shall be divided; but there shall be in it of the strength of the iron, forasmuch as thou sawest the iron mixed with miry clay." It is clear from the description that the clay will be the element that will introduce the division. The iron didn't introduce division. We need to grasp that though the clay is introduced, God's word indicates that the strength of the iron remained. It never said there should be in it the strength of the clay but only the strength of the iron. It is never said that the clay reduced the empire's strength. The clay didn't affect the strength. The clay instead will cause division. Note the expression "The kingdom shall be divided" (Dan. 2:41) - not weakened, but divided. The clay didn't weaken the empire; it divided the empire. What will be dividing the empire? It is simple: the protection of Israel. Some will want to protect her, and others won't; it was the confirmation of the covenant that was causing all the problems.

The Assyrian will therefore be so big and powerful before the tribulation that most of the members of the union won't want a confrontation with it. The land shadowing with wings will be already destroyed, and Israel will need protection from this Assyrian, which will be targeting her.

The first time the toes are mentioned with the feet, the word of God calls the clay by a new name: potters' clay. This potters' clay fixed the meaning of the clay. The definition of potters' clay hinges on what builds instead of what destroys, as in the iron. The potter's role is to make; even if he wrecks it later, he must first build it. The purpose of the iron is to crush. The strength of the kingdom won't change, but the roles will be reversed. The purpose of the Roman Empire will be changing from a destructive power to a protective one, similar to the land shadowing with wings.

In the second place, the moment the clay is introduced as the potters' clay, the Bible then states that the kingdom shall be divided - not weakened but divided. Here the clay will introduce division in the empire, not weakness. The empire will still be as strong as iron. This division will be the reason the protection treaty won't be confirmed. There will be division among the members.

Moreover, in the third place, the clay will be both in the feet and the toes. This stated fact lets us know that the European Union we have today will be divided in the future over the protection of Israel. This must be so since it is presently bigger than ten. Once we understand the clay, then we may see why Satan needs to be cast down at the beginning of the seven-year period and not in the middle.

There is one other expression in the verse that is of primary importance. We see a further change in the clay. It started as being "clay," then it became "potters' clay," but then, the clay changed even further to "miry clay." It is to be observed that the iron wasn't changing. The iron hadn't been weakened or strengthened; the only change that was taking place was in the clay. The clay will then turn to miry clay; the whole empire will now be caught in a dilemma. This matter of protecting Israel will cause chaos in the empire. There will be great confusion and no progression; the mire will cause the empire to split into two parties: those who will want to protect Israel and those who won't want to protect her. It is only after this split that we will have the toes, because the toes will be the product of the separation.

The clay will start in the feet but will spread to the toes. The toes will become prominent because of the division in the empire. The feet will no longer be noticeable; the emphasis will now be on the toes. In other words, the union's size will be reduced to ten nations. Nevertheless, all will not be well; there will still be clay in the toes. This clay in the toes indicates that there will be further conflict in the empire. There will still be a division in the toes. What will take place in the Roman Empire clearly shows why it cannot be the first seal of Revelation 6. The Roman Empire cannot be the power seen as conquering and to conquer, since it will need a rescuer itself at this point. That is why Satan will need to come down at this moment, since the scene is all providential; there is a cause and an effect. The Dragon must be cast down at this point to rescue the empire and become the source of its power.

In that day, the ten nations will manage to salvage part of the empire; however, three members of that ten-member union will be still sympathetic to the other side's cause. Those three members wanted to stay in the league as ten nations, but they will still believe that protecting Israel wasn't in the empire's best interest. That situation will explain why; when the

Dragon will be cast down to earth, he will strengthen the Roman Empire to prevent it from disintegrating. This situation is similar to Daniel 10 regarding the prince of Persia. This matter is providential—there is a reason for the event. There is a cause, and there is an effect.

Once we grasp this process, it becomes easy to see that the European Union of today is the future Roman Empire of tomorrow, but it will go through a particular crisis to get to the number ten. That will explain why the European Union today is bigger than the ten nations of the tribulation, because it is the feet and not the toes.

Everything is happening according to God's word and not our speculation. If we speculate on this, we will never get it right. We read further, "And as the toes of the feet were part of iron, and part of clay, so the kingdom shall be partly strong, and partly broken. And whereas thou sawest iron mixed with miry clay, they shall mingle themselves with the seed of men: but they shall not cleave one to another, even as iron is not mixed with clay" (Dan. 2:42,–43).

Here we have the diplomatic efforts to prevent the total collapse of the Roman Empire. There will be discussions among all the members of the empire to prevent the division. Why do we then have the two parts - one partly strong and one partially broken? Why doesn't the scripture say one part was strong, and one part was weak? Weak is the opposite of strong, yet scripture doesn't say so. The clay didn't weaken the empire. It said one part was strong and that the other part was broken. That is what the division will cause, the breaking up of the empire into two factions, one strong and one broken. The strong part will be the one composed of ten nations, while the broken part will be the part that will separate and will never become a unit again. That part will completely break up. However, when the Lord will judge the empire, He will smite it on the feet. He will destroy the whole empire - not only what it will be during the seven-year tribulation but what it was before the tribulation. He will destroy those who were united and those who were broken.

Let it be observed that from that point onward, we don't read of the feet but only of the toes. The ten nations were the remnant of the feet. In Daniel, we have the empire's history, so we have the feet and the toes. In Revelation, we have the things that shall be hereafter or after the Rapture. As a result, we have only the ten kings or toes because the feet were before the Rapture. Moreover, because there is no mention of the land shadowing with wings after the Rapture, we can conclude that it was destroyed before.

Despite the split, there will still be sympathy with the other side's position among the three members of the ten nations. The word of God is telling us that the diplomacy to prevent the split wasn't going to be successful. "They shall mingle themselves with the seed of men: but they shall not cleave one to another, even as iron is not mixed with clay" (Dan. 2:43). The mingling still had to do with the matter of the clay and not something new. They will have discussions among members of the two sides, but the diplomacy won't work. Nothing was going to keep the whole empire together. Once we grasp this, then the other scriptures become simple.

It is during the time of these ten nations or toes that the Lord Jesus shall establish His kingdom. Thus, we read, "And in the days of these kings shall the God of heaven set up a kingdom, which shall never be destroyed: and the kingdom shall not be left to other people, but it shall break in pieces and consume all these kingdoms, and it shall stand forever" (Dan. 2:44). This will be the kingdom of God that our Lord Jesus Christ will establish. Nevertheless, the verse also makes it clear that there will never be a time when the empire will be seen as seven countries; it goes from a large number to ten. These ten countries will remain for the coming of the Lord Jesus Christ.

Therefore, as we study the Roman Empire, we will observe that from the Roman Empire the Roman Prince will emerge. The Roman Prince is different from the Antichrist. He is the head of the European Union. He is one of the three wicked men of the end-times.

However, having been shown the Roman Empire we will observe the way the Roman Prince is portrayed before us. Yet, before we see his actions, we will see his rise to power in Daniel 7:7–8. In this fourth Beast, we have the Roman Empire again. However, it is seen when it emerges as the ten horns after the split. Upon the ascension of the Roman Prince, called here the "little horn," to the position of the head of the reshaped European Union, he will be immediately confronted with the division among the ten countries – the clay in the toes. There will be a significant problem in the empire. The ten members will disagree as to how they should proceed. We must remember that the ten horns are the same as the ten toes; the horn shows their individual power; the ten toes show their collective relationship. An important point to grasp is that the Roman Prince will come after the ten horns. However, he isn't an eleventh horn. He isn't the head of a new country. He will be the new head of the European Union.

When he arrives on the scene, three-member countries will still not be convinced that the decision to protect Israel will be in the empire's best interest. These three countries will want to stay in the union of the ten nations, but they won't be convinced that Israel's protection will be the role of the empire. As a result, the prince's first task will be to remove that doubt; this he will do skillfully. Here the word of God says, "Before whom there were three of the first horns plucked up by the root" (Dan. 7:8). Here we see that there will be three countries embracing the clay and will be the reason there will still be a division in the empire. The Roman Prince will then uproot the foundation of the three horns. He will erode their footing.

There are three expressions used regarding the subduing of these kings, just like the three expressions used in connection to the description of the clay. These expressions are vital to the understanding of the matter. Using his skills, the prince will convince the three members to protect Israel for a limited time. He will not fight with them militarily. He will have no army but he will have great authority and ability. The strength of the Roman Empire will be his strength. He cannot start a war with his members, and there is a mighty enemy, the Assyrian, just outside his borders. His eloquent speech will cause the three kings to give up their position. What he will want is unity not rivalry.

The Roman Prince has "eyes of a man," which represent his intelligence. He has a "mouth speaking great things" (Dan. 7:8); that is, he is a great speaker. We learn more about his speaking ability in Psalm 55, where we read, "He hath put forth his hands against such as be at peace with him: he hath broken his covenant. The words of his mouth were smoother than butter, but war was in his heart: his words were softer than oil, yet were they drawn swords" (Psalm 55:20–21). He will use his eloquence to defeat his opposition; his words will be smoother than butter. He would then outline his vision for the empire. At that moment, he hadn't yet shown his true colors; he had just come on the scene. Here, however, is not the breaking of the covenant but the profaning of the covenant. Here the word in the Hebrew Language is profane and not break. He will profane the covenant before he breaks the covenant. He will despise the covenant that he will make.

The first leader, will preside over the empire before the coming Roman Prince. He will face a grave problem. He will negotiate the treaty of protection with Israel, but he won't get it endorse. He will be unable to convince the European Union to pass the new legislation because there will be division. He will be a democratic leader; as a consequence, he couldn't force them to protect Israel. Therefore, he won't get the European Parliament to ratify the treaty. However, the coming Roman Prince, the second leader, will first remove the division; then he will get the agreement confirmed.

We now see in Daniel 7:19 - 21 that the treaty will be the cause of the division. We see from this description that these ten nations will then represent the Roman Empire. The former members will no more be recognized as a part of the union; then the empire's head will be introduced. The word of God then says, "Before whom three fell" (Dan. 7:20). The first expression used was "plucked up by the root" (Dan. 7:8); now the term is "before whom three fell" (Dan. 7:20). This Roman Prince will be a strong leader. He will be an absolute dictator; he will understand politics. The position the three members will hold, will be given up for the empire's common good. They will fall before him; his wisdom will be too much for them. This ability will come from the devil. The prince will first erode their foundation - plucked up by the root; then he will remove their visible position. It is like a tree. You pluck up the root; then the tree falls.

The second point stated here is that he will make war with the saints. Lest we think he will subject the three kings by war, the scripture says, "He made war with the saints" (Dan. 7:21), not the kings. Observe that he will not make war with Israel; he supported Israel. He will not make war with the ten kings; they were his strength. He will not make war with the three kings either. It will be with the Jewish saints that he will make war, since they wouldn't submit to his policies. The rest of the nation of Israel, however, will support him.

In Daniel 7 we read that he shall "subdue three kings" (v. 24). This is a new expression. Instead of keeping the empire divided, they will give up their convictions because of the skill of the Roman Leader. He subdued them; they gave up. He is seen as a wrestler who subdues his opponents. It will be a fierce fight in the legislature, but he will win. Why highlight this incident with the three kings, three times, if it were merely a matter of military defeat? It isn't a matter of defeat; it was a matter of differences of opinion. The opposition of these three kings will be the last obstacle preventing the confirmation of the covenant. With this obstacle removed, the covenant will then be confirmed – and the time of the tribulation will start.

The Roman Empire is now unfolding before our eyes, and as we see it, it is larger than ten nations. This is precisely what the word of God says, because the feet are first displayed, which are larger than the toes. The empire is precisely following the course presented in God's word, so much so that some are in doubt as to whether this is the Roman Empire, since they are looking for the toes, which are the future part of the revised empire.

In the same way, some doubt whether the USA is the land shadowing with wings, which is so because we haven't understood the sequence. We must follow the course; then we will see that all things are on schedule. All we need to do is stick to scripture, and we will never go wrong. Leave the opinions of men; cling to God's word. I don't mean disregarding good Bible teachers, but leave the speculations alone and search God's word.

The Roman Prince will then direct his words against the Most High. He also will wear out the saints of the Most High. He will not get to the Most High, so he will attack His saints. They will be following the Most High, but he will want them to follow him. He will then think to change times and laws, and these times and laws shall be given into his hands. These will be Jewish times and laws he will seek to change to appease the Assyrian—because these events are providential. He will want the attacks, by the Assyrian, on the empire to cease. The things he will want to replace will directly have to do with temple worship. Here again, he will be antagonistic to the saints of the Most High. These will be Jewish saints since the church would have already been raptured.

Daniel 9:26–27 is quite significant; however, we will limit ourselves to the Roman Prince. We note that after the Messiah is cut off, or put to death, the people of this coming prince will destroy the city of Jerusalem. The Romans destroyed the city in AD 70 after the death of the Lord Jesus Christ. This makes the coming prince a Roman, as we were saying. The people of the prince shall destroy the city. The Antichrist isn't a Roman. This prince is a Roman, and his people were going to destroy the city.

Daniel 7 states that the prince has a single horn, that is, he will only be a political leader. In Revelation 13, the Antichrist has two horns, he will be both a political and religious leader. Moreover, the Antichrist will lead two forms of apostasy: a Jewish and Christian apostasy. When we read 1st and 2nd John, the only books in which this man is called antichrist, he is presented as a religious leader and deceiver because of his miracles. The Roman Prince will neither do miracles nor is he a religious man. He will make war with the saints and stop the temple worship; he will want nothing to do with religion.

In contrast, the Antichrist will be a Jew and will perform miracles; the Roman Prince will do no miracle. The Antichrist, according to 2 Thessalonians 2, will sit in the temple because he will be the ruler in Jerusalem and is religious; while the statue of the Roman Prince, which is called the abomination of desolation, the Antichrist will place in the temple. The Antichrist will *sit* in the temple, while the statue of the Roman Prince will *stand* in the temple. I know many Christian teachers portray the Roman Prince as the Antichrist, but that isn't correct. In my next book, if the Lord allows, I will deal extensively with the Roman Empire where I will prove that the Roman Prince is not the Antichrist and the Antichrist cannot be a Roman.

Moreover, the Roman Prince of Daniel 9 hasn't yet come. His people are the ones who destroyed the city. The prince is then introduced in the next verse. The moment he is introduced, he is presented as confirming the covenant with the many. This covenant will be negotiated by his predecessor but will not be approved or ratified. The process to ratify the covenant will not only cause the splitting up of the empire but will even introduce division among the remaining ten nations. Three of the ten nations will still be unconvinced that the protection of the Jewish state will be in the best interest of the Roman Empire. However, with his eloquence and skill, the Roman Prince will convince these three kings to give up their position and unite them in the protection of the Jewish state. The Roman Prince will arise when there will be a crisis, but he will overcome the problem with his skill and ability.

We now see the change he will introduce to get the covenant confirmed. He shall establish the agreement with the mass of the Jews for one week. Therefore, instead of an open-ended agreement, he will put a time limit on it. The covenant shall be for one week. In the original language, it means a week of years or seven years. This covenant, therefore, will be limited to seven years. However, as we see here and in other scriptures, he will break the covenant after the middle of the week. Therefore, in Isaiah 33, we read, "Behold, their valiant ones shall cry without: the ambassadors of peace shall weep bitterly. The highways lie waste, the wayfaring man ceaseth, he hath broken the covenant, he hath despised the cities, he regardeth no man" (Isa. 33:7–8).

Isaiah 33 is essential, because it shows Russia strengthening the Assyrian, who will viciously attack the Roman Empire until the prince breaks the covenant, and forsakes the cities. However, we note that the prince will seek to negotiate a peace treaty with the Assyrian, but the Assyrian will have none of it. As a result, when the prince will see that war will be the only option, and his troops will not be disposed to fight, he will break the covenant. The prince will then withdraw his forces from Israel's cities and leaves Israel to the Assyrian. We should note that this will happen after there will be no hope for peace. We read, "The ambassadors of peace shall weep bitterly" (Isa. 33:7). All the diplomacy will end in failure and tears. We also read, "Behold, their valiant ones shall cry without" (Isa. 33:7). The valiant ones represent the defense force of the Roman Prince.

The Roman Prince will try to negotiate a peace treaty with the Assyrian, having had success with the ratification of the Jewish peace treaty. He will attempt the same with the Assyrian, but to no avail. Therefore, when the Roman Dictator will see that his only recourse was war and that his army will not want to fight, he will break the treaty because he will not want to be destroyed.

We, therefore, read, "Because ye have said, We have made a covenant with death, and with hell are we at agreement; when the overflowing scourge shall pass through, it shall not come unto us: for we have made lies our refuge, and under falsehood have we hid ourselves: Therefore thus saith the Lord God, Behold, I lay in Zion for a foundation a stone, a tried stone, a precious corner stone, a sure foundation: he that believeth shall not make haste" (Isa. 28:15–16)

Isaiah 28:15–16 is most instructive because it shows how Israel had forsaken the Lord Jesus Christ and sought protection in the Roman Empire. The Lord Jesus Christ is the foundation stone; He is the tried stone. He is the precious cornerstone, but Israel doesn't want Him. Instead, she will make a covenant with death. She will have an agreement with Hades. This will be the Roman Empire under Satan's control—this will be her protector.

We now understand why she will make this covenant. There will be a power at her border, called the Assyrian, who will seek to destroy her. This power is termed the overflowing scourge, and Israel feels that when the overflowing scourge shall "pass through" - that is, to attack the king of the South - it shall not affect her. She believes that her protector will be able to defend her. However, God lets her know she is wrong in her assessment.

It shows further that the Assyrian will be a mighty power before the tribulation begins. This is evident because Israel will sign this treaty of protection with Rome at the beginning of the tribulation. This treaty will commence seven years of troubles. Unless the Assyrian will be a significant threat, why will Israel sign this treaty? We must see that it is the Assyrian that will cause pandemonium in the last days. This is of paramount importance.

> Judgment also will I lay to the line, and righteousness to the plummet: and the hail shall sweep away the refuge of lies, and the waters shall overflow the hiding place. And your covenant with death shall be disannulled, and your agreement with hell shall not stand; when the overflowing scourge shall pass through, then ye shall be trodden down by it. From the time that it goes forth, it shall take you: for morning by morning shall it pass over, by day and by night: and it shall be a vexation only to understand the report. For the bed is shorter than that a man can stretch himself on it: and the covering narrower than that he can wrap himself in it. (Isa. 28:17–20)

Isaiah 28:17–20 tells us that Israel's covenant with death shall be disannulled, and her agreement with Hades shall not stand. Israel said one thing, but the Lord had something else planned. We are also told that "the hail shall sweep away the refuge of lies, and the waters shall overflow the hiding place. And your covenant with death shall be disannulled, and your agreement with hell shall not stand" (Isa. 28:17–18). In the sequence, "the hail," the Assyrian, first sweeps away "the refuge of lies" (Isa. 28:17). The Roman power is the refuge of lies. Second, as a result of this sweeping away, the Roman Prince will break the covenant and abandon Israel. The Roman Prince would have had enough. He will not take more. The Assyrian will then swoop in for the kill, but the Lord Jesus Christ will stop it in its endeavor.

In this passage, both "the hail" and "the waters" represent the Assyrian. The "refuge of lies" and "the hiding place" represent the Roman protection. Man looks at natural strength for protection and forgets God, but God will triumph every time.

We need to perceive that when the scripture states, "In the midst of the week, he shall cause the sacrifice and the oblation to cease" (Dan. 9:27), that doesn't mean the breaking of the covenant. The breaking of the covenant will be a political matter, while causing the sacrifice and oblation to cease will be a religious matter. The breaking of the covenant will affect the nation of Israel; the causing of the sacrifice and oblation to cease will affect the Jewish remnant. When the Roman Prince will cause the sacrifice and oblation to cease, the covenant will not yet be broken. He will cause the sacrifice and oblation to cease so that the Antichrist could introduce the worship of the Roman statue called "the abomination of desolation." However, the introduction of the abomination of desolation will be the precursor to the breaking of the covenant. As a result of the installation of the abomination of desolation, the Assyrian will raise the level of the terrorist attacks, which will cause the prince to break the covenant.

In Revelation 13, we observe two Beasts. The first Beast is the Roman power, and the second Beast is the Antichrist. Here, as in other passages, they are seen together, but they are distinct. However, many mistakes have been made between these two in Christian circles, and many teach that the Roman Prince is the Antichrist. We must not make this mistake, for if we make such a simple mistake, how will we comprehend the Assyrian and the land shadowing with wings, which are much more complicated subjects. How will we grasp designated Egypt?

In Revelation 13, we again behold the Roman Prince. The sea speaks of nations in turmoil. This truly will depict the chaos from which this Beast will arise. The European Union is bigger than ten nations today, as we all are aware, but in this passage, it is reduced to ten. It is seen as ten, because in the book of Revelation we have only the toes and not the feet. Furthermore, it is reduced to ten because of chaos in Europe over the protection of Israel, so much so that the whole empire will be engulfed in a quagmire. This mire will cause most members to leave the European Union rather than agree to protect Israel against the Assyrian. However, even though reduced in size, the organization will still arise and become the most significant power in the future Roman earth. Why is this so? The reason is that even though the European Union will lose strength from its reduced numbers, the empire will gain more strength from its association with the devil.

It is necessary to see something important here: "One of his heads, as it were wounded to death; and his deadly wound was healed" (Rev. 13:3). This wounded head was not only the imperial head, which is true, but notably the first head of the Roman Empire when reduced to ten nations -or the seventh head. Under this head, the empire will suffer a wound that will nearly kill it; but the deadly wound will be healed in the new head, the Beast. This wound in the first head was brought over to the Roman Prince, the second head. This wasn't an event that happened in the ancient Roman Empire; it is an event that will occur in the future Roman Empire.

This event is stated in Revelation, which deals with events after the Rapture. Three times we have this matter recorded in chapter 13. Therefore, again we read, "And he exerciseth all the power of the first Beast before him, and causeth the earth and them that dwell therein to worship the first Beast, whose deadly wound was healed" (Rev. 13:12). Here the word of God ties the healing of the wound to the Roman Prince, the Beast. We read again, "And deceiveth them that dwell on the earth by the means of the miracles by which he had power to do in the sight of the Beast; saying to them that dwell on the earth, that they should make an image to the Beast, which had the wound by a sword, and did live" (Rev. 13:14). The Roman Prince is seen as the one who will resurrect the empire after receiving it with a wound. The empire will suffer a wound that will nearly kill it, but the wound will be healed.

It isn't the cessation of the empire that is the wound. The wound will occur in the head, not the empire, according the Revelation 13:3. It is the

Dragon that will give the Beast his power, his seat, and great authority according to Revelation 13:2. These actions of the Dragon will heal the wound. It isn't the revival of the empire, as we see today, that will heal the wound. The Roman Empire is already revived, as the European Union, and the Dragon hasn't yet given it his power, seat, and authority.

The wound will occur during the seventh head, when the empire will split into two factions, because of the protection of Israel. The empire will nearly disintegrate, as a result of the wound; then the Dragon will be cast down to earth, and will resuscitate the empire by the Roman Prince. It is this revival that is seen as coming from Satan. The empire has only a ceremonial head at present. The authoritative heads will come into focus only when the empire enters the crisis. The empire as the "feet" has no such head; only when the empire will be seen as the "toes" will there be such a person.

Moreover, it will be Satan's intervention that will succor the empire. It will be Satan's involvement that will heal the wound. There are two revivals of the future Roman Empire: the revival as we have today and the revival that will follow the crisis. Therefore, the future rise will be seen as coming from Satan. The Beast will then be presented in its final form with seven heads and ten horns. This empire will come from the Dragon. The present empire doesn't come from the Dragon. It is to be noted that both the empire and the head are termed the Beast. This is similar to the Assyrian, where the leader and the power are termed the Assyrian. It is for this reason that we have in Revelation 6 the rider on the horse. The understanding is that the Beast, the Prince, will usurp all the authority of the empire. He will be an absolute dictator. He will ride the horse; he will dictate the policies of the empire.

There are two parts to the revived Roman Empire - the feet and the toes. The portion of the empire designated as the "feet" is before the tribulation, while the part called the "toes" will be during the tribulation. The "feet" are before the tribulation, and the "toes" are after the Rapture. Moreover, there are two revivals to the future Roman Empire - one by man and the other by the Dragon. What man revives Satan will take over.

In Revelation 12, Satan is the one seen with the seven heads and the ten horns. He is regarded as the source and the ruler of the Roman Empire. We read, "And there appeared another wonder in heaven; and behold a great red dragon, having seven heads and ten horns, and seven crowns upon his heads" (Rev. 12:3). We note that when the empire will be seen in this final form, of seven heads and ten horns, it will be seen as coming from the Dragon. Satan was seen as its source and ruler - the crowns are on the Dragon's head. Notice that it was the Dragon that had the seven heads and ten horns. Also, pay special attention to Revelation 13: "And the dragon gave him his power, and his seat, and great authority" (v. 2). This will happen when the dragon will be cast down.

Satan is seen only as a Dragon regarding being cast down from heaven. Moreover, the Dragon couldn't give the Roman Prince his seat unless his seat was now on earth. Therefore, when the empire was seen with seven heads and ten horns, and ten crowns upon the horns, it was so seen after the Rapture and just at the beginning of the tribulation. Today the empire is more extensive than ten nations. However, at the dawn of the tribulation and during the tribulation, it will be seen as ten nations. The Roman Empire will never be seen as seven nations in the union during the tribulation.

The seven heads speak of the different forms of government the Roman Empire will experience, as explained in Revelation 17:10–11. The horn speaks of power. Therefore, the ten horns speak of the ten nations that will make up the empire. These horns correspond to the ten toes of the image in Daniel 2. We should note that when this Beast was seen in Daniel 7, we don't see the seven heads. What we noticed was that the horns were in the head. However, here in Revelation 13, we have the seven heads. When Satan was seen as leading the empire in Revelation 12:3, the crowns were seen on his heads. However, in Revelation 13, where we see the imperial system's revival, the crowns are on the horns. Satan will give his power to the Roman Beast. In Revelation 17, where we see the false church associated with this power, the mystery Babylon the Great, there were no crowns; she, the false church, wanted to wear the crowns.

Moreover, "upon the heads the name of blasphemy" (Rev. 13:1) - that is, none of these forms of government had anything to do with glorifying God; all they had to do with God was to dishonor Him. That is why Christ must come and rule for the glory of God. Here it is more daring; it is the different forms of power, speaking more and more monstrous things against the Lord. What a sad picture of human government! The

Lord Jesus Christ will change man's order of government and govern for the glory of God. No lawlessness would be allowed.

In Revelation 13:5–9, we notice that the Beast will control the future Roman Empire. As we see today, there is a head of this European Union, but he has limited powers. This head is responsible for guiding the union. However, the leader in Revelation 13 will usurp all the authority of this Beast, so he is the Beast. He will have unlimited powers. He will be the empire. He will open his mouth in blasphemy against God, against His name and His tabernacle. It is of great importance to detect a new company in heaven called here "them that dwell in heaven" (Rev. 13:6). The church is now seen as the heaven dwellers. Nevertheless, when the church is so seen, it is in reference to the fall of the Dragon. When the church is seen in heaven, the Dragon is seen as cast down.

Therefore, the Rapture takes place, and the church is seen in heaven. This we see again in chapter 12 when Satan is cast down. We read, "Therefore rejoice, ye heavens, and ye that dwell in them. Woe to the inhabiters of the earth and the sea! For the Devil is come down unto you, having great wrath, because he knoweth that he hath but a short time" (Rev. 12:12).

The "ye that dwell in them" (Rev. 12:12) again represents the church. Once the church is raptured, I believe we will see that Satan is cast down shortly after. We need to carefully note that Satan's fall is referenced to those who dwell in heaven. There is no time the church is seen in heaven and the Dragon is seen in heaven. I have no problem with those who believe the Dragon is cast down in the middle of the week. I once embraced that view myself; however, as I study this matter carefully, I cannot see the providential reason for the casting out of the Dragon in the middle of the week. I see more reason for him to be cast down at the beginning of the week.

Moreover, it seems clear to me that Revelation 12:14 gives us more of the miraculous preservation of Israel, even though the Dragon was targeting her, during the Great Tribulation. This to me is a better explanation than the time the Dragon was cast out. Therefore, I present another side to consider on the teaching of the casting down of the Dragon. I'm not discrediting others; far be the thought, I have learned from them. But I am presenting what I have gleaned and leave others to judge what may be more scriptural.

The next thing we read about the Roman Prince is that he will be worshipped. Satan also will be worshipped. The Antichrist will also be worshipped. We are here told, "They worshipped the beast, saying, Who is like unto the beast? Who is able to make war with him" (Rev. 13:4)? However, the Assyrian will make war with him and cause him to flee. Finally, he will make war with the saints. Thus, since the saints wouldn't own him as an object of worship, then he will make war with them. There is more to this. The Roman Prince will make war with the Jewish remnant because he will want them to stop preaching the gospel of the kingdom. The Roman Prince will not tolerate the doctrine of the coming king.

The remnant's connection to the temple worship will cause the Assyrian to constantly attack the Roman Empire. This attack had to stop. Therefore, the future head of the Roman Empire, whom Israel will choose as her protector, will make war with the saints. This prince will be the Roman head; he isn't the Antichrist, and he is also distinct from the Assyrian head.

Edward Dennett wrote the following on the Roman Empire in his book on Revelation. He presented these thoughts for our consideration:

> This beast, the imperial head of the revived Roman Empire, has seven heads, or forms of government, and, as pointed out in Rev. 12, therein completeness; and he has ten horns, on all of which are diadems, indicating the fact repeated again and again (see Daniel 2, 7; also Revelation 17:12), that the dominion of the beast is composed of ten kingdoms, having their respective sovereigns, but allied together in a common federation under his imperial sway ... The moral character of this last representative of Gentile sovereignty is exhibited in one word - he has upon his heads the names of blasphemy. We have next the source of his dominion unveiled. "And the dragon gave him his power, and his seat, and great authority" (Rev. 13:2). He is therefore characterized by Satan's inspiration and energy. Such is the picture presented to us, delineated

by an infallible hand, of the last governmental power on
the earth, before the coming of Christ to establish His
kingdom.[59]

We need to notice how perfectly Edward Dennett presented the rise of
the future Roman Empire, which he never saw. He clearly stated that the
future Roman Empire would be composed of respective sovereigns allied
together in a common federation. This was the complete opposite of the
historical Roman Empire. How could he be so right unless the Bible is
the word of God?

Moreover, in Revelation 17:7-13, we are given greater details. "The
woman" here is the Roman Catholic Church, which is seen connected
with the Roman Empire and the city of Rome. There is only one city on
seven hills, and that city is Rome. The church, which has its headquarters
in Rome and is seen connected with the Roman Empire, is before the
prophet's eyes. We now get the understanding of how the Roman Empire
will reappear. The Roman Empire will have three distinct phases: a past
empire when the book of Revelation was written, a time when there will
be no empire when the Roman power was destroyed, and a reemergence
of the empire in the future. "The beast that thou sawest was, and is not;
and shall ascend out of the bottomless pit, and go into perdition: and they
that dwell on the earth shall wonder, whose names were not written in the
book of life from the foundation of the world, when they behold the beast
that was, and is not, and yet is" (Rev. 17:8).

The beast that thou sawest "was" - that is, it existed at that time of
the writing of the book of Revelation. We are instructed further, "And
is not." It will disappear for a time, that is, it shall be destroyed. We are
given more information: "And shall ascend out of the bottomless pit, and
go into perdition" (Rev. 17:8). The Roman Empire will reappear. However,
this reappearance here is not the feet, as in Daniel 2, but as the toes.
Furthermore, this future rise of the empire is seen as coming from the
Dragon, because it is the toes. In Revelation, we do not have the feet since
we are dealing with events after the rapture. In Daniel, we have the history
of the empire, so we have both the feet and the toes. Still, the reemergence

---

[59] Dennett, *The Visions of John in Patmos*, 179.

of the empire will be as a result of satanic influences, which ties the fall of Satan to the beginning of the tribulation. The empire will then go into perdition; that is, it will be completely and permanently destroyed.

We now see that the seven heads represent seven forms of government; five already passed during the time of the prophet: "one is" - that is, number six, who was ruling during the time of John. The seventh form was yet to come, and when he was come, he must continue a short space. The one who was to come would be the first head of the revived Roman Empire when it will be reduced to ten nations. That head will be of a democratic form. This is the reason he had problems confirming the covenant. He will be the one reigning when the European Union will be reduced in size. The Roman Prince will be the eighth and was of the seven. It was the imperial head that had revived. These eight heads seem to be the following:

1. The Kings
2. The Consuls
3. The Dictators
4. The Decemvirs
5. The Military Tribunes
6. The Caesars
7. The Democratic Leader (the first leader of the ten-headed Beast)
8. A Democratic Ruler (at first, then an absolute dictator controlled by the Dragon—the Roman Prince)

These seem to be the governmental heads of the Roman Empire until the Lord Jesus Christ appears.

What this means is that the Beast will be the second leader of the Roman Empire when reduced to ten nations. The leader before him will preside over the empire when it will experience the split and will be unable to confirm the treaty since three of the ten nations will be unwilling to change their positions. Daniel 7, confirms this detail: "And the ten horns out of this kingdom are ten kings that shall arise: and another shall rise after them, and he shall be diverse from the first, and he shall subdue three kings" (Dan. 7:24). These ten kings will first arise from the quagmire. It must be noted that the Roman Prince will arise after the ten kings. When he appears, the empire will already be in the form of ten kings; the split would have already occurred. When the Roman Prince emerges, the empire would have already changed from the feet to the toes. Satan isn't seen connected to this empire as the feet; neither is the Roman Prince. Satan and the Roman Prince are simultaneously related to the Roman Empire just after it becomes ten nations.

Next, we are told that the prince shall be diverse from the first. "The first" is the first leader of the empire when it will be seen as ten nations. The first ruler will preside over the transition of the empire from the larger size to the smaller one. He will then lead the kingdom for a short time when reduced from the feet to the toes. This second head, the Beast, will then be elected as the head of the European Union and will immediately receive power from Satan at the same time with the Roman Empire. With the power he will receive from the devil, he will convince the other kings to give up their position for the empire's good. At that juncture, Satan will be seen related to the empire and its head. Therefore, the empire will then be seen as coming from the Dragon.

This doctrine we will see unfold in the next verse: "And the beast that was, and is not, even he is the eighth and is of the seven, and goeth into perdition. And the ten horns which thou sawest are ten kings, which have received no kingdom as yet; but receive power as kings one hour with the beast. These have one mind, and shall give their power and strength unto the beast" (Rev. 17:11– 12).

The Beast will be first seen connected to the empire as its seventh head, a democratic leader. However, he will become an eight form - an absolute dictator under satanic control. He will be presented as a distinct form because the things he will do, under the control of the Dragon, no human would even dare to do. He will be a seventh and an eight form. If, therefore, Satan was cast down in the middle of the week, Satan would have to be seen connected to the eighth form and not the seventh; for by the middle of the week, the Roman Prince will be fully developed.

The scripture unfolds more; it states that "the ten horns which thou sawest are ten kings, which have received no kingdom as yet" (Rev. 17:12). In the day of the prophet, these kings had received no kingdom as yet. They will receive it in the future. Therefore, the Roman Empire was going to change from an empire with no individual king to a state of distinct kings but no empire, then to an empire with distinct kings. We read, "But receive power as kings one hour with the beast." We are told that these kings will receive power simultaneously with the Beast. The scripture isn't merely stating they are receiving their kingdoms at the same time with the Beast but are receiving power from the devil at the same time with the head of the empire "one hour with the beast" (Rev. 17:12). What does that mean? They all received authority from the Dragon at the same time. Remember, the scripture said that the Roman Prince would arise after the kings. The scripture now states that they receive power at the same time as the prince.

Let us look at the empire as it is emerging today; even currently, the European Union is seen as composed of twenty-eight individual kings or rulers of their different countries, with one, Britain, making plans to leave the union. However, even this sensitive issue of leaving the union had happened in the past to show us what will happen in the future. For example, even Greenland, who joined the league in 1973, left the union in 1985; so, what the United Kingdom would like to do in our day is a further demonstration of what will happen just before the tribulation. When Greenland left, she left because of fishing rights, so when these other countries leave, they will leave because they don't want to be part of Israel's protection.

Please note that even today, the twenty-odd kings are already leaders of their countries. Therefore, what the scripture is saying is that these kings and the Roman Beast will receive power from Satan at the same time. It seems clear, when Satan will give his power to the kings and the Beast, he will be confined to earth. What the scripture does is tie the power Satan gives to the Beast to his fall from heaven. Note again, "the beast that thou sawest was, and is not, and shall ascend out of the bottomless pit, and go into perdition" (Rev. 17:8). This Beast will have its origin in the bottomless pit; this is when Satan will strengthen it. This detail is further confirmed by what we read next. "These have one mind, and shall give their power and strength unto the beast" (Rev. 17:13). The ten kings received power from the Dragon, but now they give it to the Beast. To me, this is clearly when Satan is cast out, which will be at the beginning of the week. Why would the Dragon invest everything in an empire unless he was confined on earth?

However, this scripture highlights one other point; they now have "one mind." Before, there was division; now there is none. They are now totally united. When does this take place? This takes place when Satan will give them his power, which will unite the empire and prevent the breakup. This will not be in the middle of the week but at the beginning of the week.

In Revelation 12, Satan is the one seen with the seven heads and the ten horns. We read, "And there appeared another wonder in heaven; and behold a great red dragon, having seven heads and ten horns, and seven crowns upon his heads" (Rev. 12:3). The Dragon will be ruling the empire. We need to observe that according to this verse, the seventh head will already be in place when Satan will be seen with the crowns on his head. This seventh head will be the Roman Prince, but he will not yet have developed into the character of the Beast - the eighth head - which will come later.

If it were in the middle of the 70th week of Daniel's prophecy, that the Dragon was cast down, Satan would have been associated with the eighth, since at that time the Roman Prince would have displayed his true character. Remember what the scripture says: "And the beast that was, and is not, even he is the eighth, and is of the seven, and goeth into perdition" (Rev. 17:11). The Roman leader will deteriorate into the eighth - he will become a different form - but when he will be given the power from the devil, he will be seen as the seventh. Satan will not be seen connected to the first leader of the empire. The first leader will be the seventh form. When the prince comes, he will also be of the seventh form - a democratic form - but will quickly degenerate into a new form, called the eighth. It is later that the prince becomes a terror and becomes the eighth. It is the same process with the Antichrist, who will later manifest his real character.

When the Beast ascends out of the bottomless pit, the empire is seen as coming from Satan. This is when Satan is cast down. In Revelation 12, where Satan is seen associated with the Beast, the empire is presented as "seven heads" then "ten horns." In Revelation 17, where the false church is seen associated with the Beast, the Beast is again seen as "seven heads" and "ten horns." This, I believe, is telling us time, the Roman Prince would have just assumed power. Remember the Beast is depicted as a *he* and an *it;* the Beast is a power and a person. The Roman Empire is called the Beast and the leader of the empire is also called the Beast. When the Beast is presented as the *he*, the head is prominent, when mentioned as the *it,* the empire is prominent.

However, in Revelation 13, where the empire is seen as rising, the empire is seen in the reverse, as ten horns and seven heads. Let us hear from William Kelly: "But besides these seven heads and ten horns, there were upon the latter ten crowns." Let me just say that I have no doubt the ten horns ought to be mentioned before the heads: "having ten horns and seven heads and upon his horns ten crowns, and upon his heads names of blasphemy (Rev. 13:1 WK). Not that one would attach undue importance to the order, save that we ought always to be right; but the two clauses of the verse agree in putting the horns first."[60]

This order shows that when Satan will be cast down and associated with the Beast, the seventh head will be then in power, not the eighth, which is of the seventh, which will be in the middle of the week. If the Roman Empire, in the form of the European Union, is seen as already revived and isn't seen as coming from Satan, because Satan has access to heaven, then the only time it can be so seen as coming from Satan will be when Satan will be cast on earth and has no access to heaven. If we put the casting out of Satan in the middle of the seventieth week of Daniel's prophecy, then all these details will make no sense; in my judgment, the scriptures will seem to contradict.

It is clearly stated that at the time when the Roman Prince will come on the scene, Satan will strengthen the Roman Prince and the ten kings. The scriptures clearly say that Satan isn't seen connected to the first head. Yet it must be noticed that at this strengthening by Satan, the second head is seen as usurping all the authority of the empire, since the ten horns give their power and authority to the Beast. He doesn't strengthen the Beast alone, nor the empire alone; he strengthens both the Beast and the empire. Both will need to be strengthened at that time. He will strengthen them to accomplish a particular task. If it were the first ruler of the empire that was so empowered, he would have achieved the task. It is like Judas, whom Satan entered to strengthen him to betray the Lord Jesus Christ. This strengthening prevented the empire from deteriorating into chaos. Therefore, this final form, of seven heads and ten horns, will be seen as coming from the Dragon.

---

[60] Kelly, *Remarks on the Revelation*, The Bible Treasury, vol 2, 213.

CHAPTER 17

THE WICKED AND THE ANTICHRIST

T his chapter will identify the three evil men of the tribulation and the governments they will control. We will, therefore, see the attachment of the Destroyer to the Assyrian power. We will view the control of the Roman Prince over the Roman Empire, and we will observe the power of the Antichrist over the apostate Jews and Christians. Moreover, we will explore the relationship between the Rapture and the tribulation and the casting down of Satan relative to the tribulation.

The scripture enlightens us that three wicked men will occupy their space on the earth in a coming day. These are the Antichrist, the Roman Prince, and the Assyrian head. These three are the trinity of evil. Each is as wicked as the other. The Antichrist and the Roman Prince are confederates, while the Assyrian is an antagonist of them both. These three men will arrive at different times, but they are all contemporaries. These three men will be so wicked that they will be cast alive into hell a thousand years before Satan. They will be so evil that no man or power will destroy them; only the coming of the Lord will stop them.

Think of the worst men of history; they cannot come close to these three. These are the first residents of hell; all others come after. Scripture calls these three "the wicked." When they appear, they will set the world on fire. Each will be as wicked as the other. They need no trial. Hell is the only place for them. On my scale of difficulty, this topic is a nine.

The first to arrive on the scene is the Assyrian head. The second to be manifested is the Roman Prince. The last one to be revealed is the Antichrist. There is an Assyrian power, and there is an Assyrian head, just as there will be a Beast, which is the Roman power, and the Beast who will be the Roman head. The actions of the leader will be the actions of the empire. He will supersede all the authority of the empire. Moreover, there is an Antichrist, and there is the spirit of Antichrist.

We need to be careful not to confuse "the powers" with "the persons." As for powers, the first to arrive is Israel. She has already been restored in part and still in unbelief. The second to arrive is the Roman Empire; this power will take the place of the land shadowing with wings after its destruction. This power has already been revealed in part and is now displayed as the European Union. The third power to arrive is the Assyrian power northeast of Israel. It hasn't yet arrived but will soon be manifested, for Russia, the one who will strengthen the Assyrian, has already established itself in the Euphrates area. It has gone into Syria to help President Assad. Still, Russia will control Syria and eventually support the terrorist power. The last power to arrive is the king of the South. He will come soon after the Assyrian.

As a person, the Assyrian will be the head of the terrorist power northeast of Israel, called "the enemy." Please note the scripture calls both the person and the power the Assyrian, because the person is seen as usurping the authority of the power. The Roman Prince, who is also called "the Beast," will be the head of the Roman Empire, seen today under the flag of the European Union. The Antichrist will be the head of the Jews. Christian writers often mistake the Antichrist for the Roman Prince or the leader of the Roman Empire, but the Antichrist will be a Jew from the land of Israel. He will be the king of Israel, not the leader of the Roman Empire. The Romans never expected a Christ; therefore, they will never get the Antichrist as their leader. The Jews expected a Christ, but they have already killed Him. Consequently, they will receive the Antichrist, who is a false Christ.

We have stated that there will be three wicked men who will be in the place of authority during the tribulation. These are the Assyrian head, the Roman Prince, and the Antichrist. In Psalm 140, these three men are all seen together. "Deliver me, O Lord, from the evil man: preserve me from the violent man; which imagine mischiefs in their heart; continually are they gathered together for war" (Ps. 140:1–2). In this psalm, we are going from within Israel to without the land. The first person we have introduced is called the "evil man." The psalmist asks the Lord to deliver or free him from the evil man. The evil man wants to defile him. This evil man is near; he is within Israel. The evil man is the Antichrist, and he is religious.

The psalmist then asks to be preserved from the "violent man." This man is seeking to kill him, and the psalmist wants to be protected from him. This man is a man of violence. This violent man is the Roman Prince, the head of the Roman Empire, and he isn't religious. He will make war with the Jewish saints to kill them. The Jewish remnant is calling on the Lord to preserve them from this man. Though this man is seen in a friendly relationship to the Jewish mass, he will be antagonistic to the godly Jewish remnant. This man will declare war on the Jewish remnant and treat them with utter disdain; this position must be understood. He will be in favorable terms with Israel as a nation but totally against the pious remnant. The nation of Israel will trust him, but the godly remnant will cling to the Lord. This cry isn't a cry of Israel but of the faithful remnant.

We read further, "They have sharpened their tongues like a serpent; adders' poison is under their lips. Selah. Keep me, O Lord, from the hands of the wicked; preserve me from the violent man; who have purposed to overthrow my goings" (Ps. 140:3–4).

We need now to note that there are two distinct persons, pointed out by the pronouns "they" and "their" in this passage. We know there are two because one is the evil man, and the other is the violent man. However, they are seen as confederates; they are associates of evil. Notice that the king of the South is not in their league. He is not as wicked as these three. What makes these men wicked is not only what they will dare to do but also what they will dare to say. The remnant asks to be kept from the hands of the wicked. We need to appreciate the progression; they are "deliver me" and "keep me," the psalmist indicated. We also need to discern that the wicked wanted to get his hands on the remnant. However, the cry against the violent man remains the same, but a purpose is given. "He wants to overthrow my steps." We must notice their lips and tongues. Their utterances are coming clearly from the devil, and poison brings out their dangerous doctrine. These two men, as stated before, are seen as associated with a common purpose.

There is one other point of great importance. We read, "Continually are they gathered together for war" (Ps. 140:2). There will be talk of war. This will be continuously before the Beast and the Antichrist because the Assyrian will be constantly attacking them. Moreover, there will be the war that the Roman Prince will wage against the saints. There will be consideration of war primarily against the Assyrian, which will be continually assaulting the Roman Empire with terrorist attacks that it might forsake Israel. This the Roman Empire will finally do. The Roman head and the Antichrist will be gathered continuously for war but they will not go to war with the Assyrian. The Assyrian will be too powerful for their liking. Nevertheless, they will carry on a war against the saints.

Further, we read, "The proud have hid a snare for me, and cords; they have spread a net by the wayside; they have set gins for me" (Ps. 140:5). We have a new introduction; another person is introduced here, called "the proud." However, mention is made of the people rather than the head. How do we know this person? Simple. Just look at what he did. He hid a snare for the remnant; that is, he set a trap for Israel, but Israel isn't aware of it. The word for "snare" in Hebrew is the word for "trap." The Assyrian is the one who sets the trap. This trap is a net in their path. Their path to Jehovah is a trap set. We read, "They have set gins for me." The word *gins* represents more than one since it is now in the plural. The word for "gin" is the word for "bait." Without the bait, who will fall into the trap? These baits are representative of the two mosques on the temple mount. Two speaks of adequate testimony. It wasn't a chance happening that we have two Muslim mosques on Mount Moriah. The Jews will activate the trap when they break down the Muslim mosques and rebuild their temple.

"I said unto the Lord, Thou art my God: hear the voice of my supplications, O Lord. O God the Lord, the strength of my salvation, thou hast covered my head in the day of battle" (Ps. 140:6–7). In the day of battle, the remnant will look to Jehovah to cover or protect his head. This battle is primarily against the Assyrian, even though the Roman Prince will also wage war against the remnant, which will refuse to worship the Beast's image.

"Grant not, O Lord, the desires of the wicked: further not his wicked device; lest they exalt themselves. Selah. As for the head of those that compass me about, let the mischief of their own lips cover them" (Ps. 140:8–9). Here the remnant pleads with Jehovah not to grant the desire of the wicked. The question is, which one of the wicked? "Further not his wicked device" (Ps. 140:8), he pleads, but against which wicked is he pleading about? We further read, "Lest they exalt themselves" (Ps. 140:8). What we find, therefore, is that everyone is called "the wicked." It isn't only the Antichrist who is "the wicked"; each of these three men is referred to as "the wicked." We don't have only the character of the wicked; we have all the wicked.

Moreover, we need to note that special attention is now cast on the head of the Assyrian. "As for the head of those that compass me about" (Ps. 140:9). The ones who compassed the Jews about are the Assyrians. The Destroyer, therefore, is the head of the Assyrian. The psalmist specifically identifies the head, then ties the head to the other two and shows that their destruction will be the same.

These three men are thrown into hell together. We, therefore, read, "Let burning coals fall upon them: let them be cast into the fire; into deep pits that they rise not up again" (Ps. 140:10). Therefore, the Assyrian head and the Antichrist will both be cast into the lake of fire, according to Isaiah 30, and the Roman Dictator and the Antichrist will be cast into the lake of fire, according to Revelation 20. The scripture clearly states, that these three men will be thrown into the lake of fire together, even before the devil.

Nevertheless, in Christian circles, of the three wicked men who will walk on this earth, the Antichrist is the most known. By far, he is the one the majority of writers describe, and he is the most spoken about in discussions. Yet much said about the Antichrist is true only of the Roman Prince. There is much confusion between the Antichrist and the Roman Dictator. The Antichrist comes from Israel; the Roman Prince comes from Western Europe. The two are confederates but aren't the same. We must not make a mistake as to their identity. We must carefully examine scripture to make sure we get it right. Scripture doesn't make mistakes;

men do. The word of God is perfect. There is no possibility of error in it. We will now examine what the word of God says about the Antichrist.

The first hint we have of the Antichrist is in the book of Genesis 49:16–18. We are told that Dan was going to rule Israel. He was going to judge his people as another of the tribes of Israel. However, we aren't told when he was going to rule in this verse, but in Genesis 49:1, we read, "And Jacob called unto his sons, and said, gather yourselves together, that I may tell you that which shall befall you in the last days" (Gen. 49:1). In Darby's translation, the last part of the verse is translated "the end of days." So, we know the time this prophecy was addressing.

Moreover, the people are his people. He has been in complete control over them. When he rules, we learn that he shall be a serpent by the way and an adder in the path or "a horned snake in the path" as J. N. Darby's translation puts it. The way is to Jehovah; the path is to the Lord. But he occupies that place as a serpent and a snake. We have already learned that those who seek to worship Jehovah will find themselves in the presence of the snake. Those who like to consider the Roman Prince as the Antichrist will have to define for me the period when Dan ruled as one of the tribes of Israel in the last days and was a horned snake in the path.

Furthermore, lest men say that this ruling of Dan is past, we read the following: "The burden of the beasts of the south: through a land of trouble and anguish, whence cometh the lioness and lion, the viper and fiery flying serpent, they carry their riches upon the shoulders of asses, and their treasures upon the bunches of camels, to the people that shall not profit [them]" (Isa. 30:6 JND).

We know that the fulfillment of Isaiah 30 is in the future; therefore, the fulfillment of this prophecy concerning Dan must be in the future. The "beasts of the south" is Egypt seen as the land shadowing with wings, in its multiple components. The land of trouble and anguish is Israel. The lioness and the lion represent Christ as seen in Genesis 49:9. The viper and the fiery flying serpent represent the Antichrist as seen in Genesis 49:16, 17. He is not yet come, he is still to come. We need to notice that both the lion and the serpent come from Israel's land. You cannot say Satan comes from Israel's land; it is Christ, the rejected Messiah, and the Antichrist, who is received as Messiah. These two personages come from the same land. Christ came first, but He was rejected; afterward the Antichrist will

311

come, who will be accepted. The majority of the people rejected Christ, but a remnant received Him. In the future, when Antichrist comes, the situation will be reversed. The majority of the people will receive the Antichrist, and a remnant will refuse him. Christ came first, and the Antichrist will come later.

What is even more pointed is that in Revelation 7, where we have the twelve tribes of Israel sealed to preach the gospel of the kingdom to all the world during the tribulation, we don't have the tribe of Dan listed. He is conspicuously absent. Instead, Joseph has his two sons represented. Why is this so? The reason is simple. Instead of preaching about the coming king, Dan, is ruling as the false king. He has no interest in saving souls; he misleads them.

Therefore, as the serpent he deceives them. As the snake, he bites them and poisons them with his doctrine. He is very active in the positions of deception and destruction. Here he bites the horse to get at the rider. If the horse speaks of strength, as it does, even the strong will not be protected from the Antichrist - so much so that the only protection and deliverance the writer sees is to wait for the salvation from Jehovah. Thus, the time of Dan's rule will be immediately preceding the Lord's coming. He alone can bring deliverance from this deceiver. This is the Antichrist, an Israelite who will come from the tribe of Dan; but he will be a deceiver and yet the ruler in Israel. Even the strong shall fall backward. He isn't the Roman Prince, but he will be allied with him; he is a Jew in Israel's land.

We would also like to observe the Antichrist from 1 John 2. We read, "Who is a liar but he that denieth that Jesus is the Christ? He is antichrist, that denieth the Father and the Son. Whosoever denieth the Son, the same hath not the Father: he that acknowledgeth the Son hath the Father also" (1 John 2:22–23).

We have said before that the Antichrist will lead two forms of apostasy - a Jewish and Christian apostasy - which will take place after the Rapture. During this period, the Antichrist will be manifested. We may see the Assyrian and know him; we may see the Roman Prince, but we will not know him; we may not see the Antichrist, and for sure, we will not know him. This all depends on when the Rapture takes place. If the Rapture takes place close to the tribulation, we will see the Assyrian and know him; because he is the first to be manifested. If the land shadowing with wings is destroyed in our days, the one who does it is the Assyrian head. We could, therefore, see him and know him.

We may observe the Roman Prince, but we will not know him, because he is manifested only as the Beast during the tribulation. He is the one who will confirm the treaty with the mass of the Jews, and he comes to power only just before that event. The Antichrist we may see, but we will not know him, because he will be manifested as the Antichrist only during the tribulation. However, if the church is still present when the European Union will be split into two parts, then the new leader will be the Roman Prince. The Antichrist and the Roman Prince may grow up before our eyes, but we will never know them as those characters. Judas, in the presence of the Lord Jesus Christ, is a case in point. He was with the other disciples, yet even John didn't know who the betrayer was. The Beast and the Antichrist are manifested only during the tribulation, but they will grow up with their neighbors before the tribulation.

Permit me here to give Darby's translation of 1 John 2. "Who is the liar but he who denies that Jesus is the Christ? He is the antichrist who denies the Father and the Son" (1 John 2:22 JND). It isn't merely "a liar" but "the liar" we have before us. What we have is "the liar" and "the Antichrist"; we have, therefore, a Jewish denial and a Christian denial. We see immediately that the Antichrist is a religious man, while the Roman Prince isn't a religious man. The Antichrist denies that Jesus is the Christ. This makes him the liar.

We must distinguish these two men: the Antichrist is the False Jewish Christ in Jerusalem; the Roman Prince is the protector of the Jewish State in Rome, they are confederates but not the same person. The Antichrist, according to Revelation 13, has two horns or forms of power; since horn speaks of power. He is both a religious and political leader. He works miracles because he has to duplicate what Christ did. He is called a king, Daniel 11, and he is like a lamb, Revelation 13; because Christ is both the King and the Lamb of God. In Revelation 19, 20, the Antichrist is called the false prophet since Christ is the prophet of Deuteronomy 18. When Christ comes the Antichrist, false prophet, will be found with the Roman Prince in Rome; since as the hireling, he will flee from the Assyrian; but Christ as the good shepherd gave his life for the sheep. The Roman Prince, in contrast, has one horn, according to Daniel 7. He has one form of power;

he is a political leader. He is never called a king, but a prince. He is not seen as a lamb because he wants to deceive no one. In Revelation 20 the devil is said to join both the Beast and the false prophet in hell. Since we know that it is the Antichrist and Roman Prince that are cast into hell together; then the false prophet is the Antichrist, the false religious leader in Israel.

Take note that most Jews today deny that Jesus is the Christ. This denial makes them ripe for the Antichrist. We also have another rejection; this time, it is a Christian denial. The Antichrist denies the Father and the Son. Many people today, religious and irreligious, deny the equality between the Father and Son. Let us confess today that Jesus Christ is the Son of God and God the Son. However, many deny this equality; this rejection makes them ripe for Antichrist. Let us be clear: what the word of God teaches is that Jesus Christ is the Son of God in three ways. He is the Son of God in eternity. He is the Son of God in time, and He is the Son of God in the resurrection. Today, even many church leaders deny that He is the Son of God, coequal with the Father and the Holy Spirit; they prefer to believe what they think instead of what the word of God declares. However, we confess loudly and clearly that Jesus Christ is the Son of God and God the Son.

In fact, those who deny that He is the Son of God should take note of what the word of God states. "For the Father judgeth no man, but hath committed all judgment unto the Son: That all men should honor the Son, even as they honor the Father. He that honoreth not the Son honoreth not the Father which hath sent him" (John 5:22–23).

Here the Father states clearly that the same honor given to the Father must be given to the Son, and if this isn't so, then that person doesn't honor the Father. I say to those who deny that He is God the Son, "You wait until you get before Him as the Judge. Then you tell Him that He isn't God."

Moreover, the Father has made it very clear that if one doesn't honor the Son, he or she doesn't honor the Father. The Father desires no honor that doesn't honor His Son. Moreover, the Father will see to it that everyone honors His Son. That is guaranteed.

Nevertheless, 1 John 2 lets us know that already there are many religious leaders who are Antichrist. They command great following, but their doctrine identifies them as Antichrist. We read, "Little children, it is the last time: and as ye have heard that antichrist shall come, even now are there many antichrists" (1 John 2:18).

First, the scripture tells us that it is the last hour. Second, it informs us that the Antichrist shall come, but he isn't yet come. Third, "even now are there many antichrists" (1 John 2:18). Today there are many Antichrists, so the word of God states, and so it is. I need you to advise me as to which religious leader is willing to say he or she is an Antichrist. Nevertheless, so he or she is who denies the equality between the Father and the Son. Therefore, those who deny Jesus Christ is the Son of God, coequal with the Father, are Antichrist. The Antichrist will take all of them down the slippery road of destruction, like the piped piper. Carefully note that the Jews deny that Jesus is the Christ before the Antichrist comes, and there are many Antichrists in Christendom before the real Antichrist comes. Let it be stated that those who deny that Jesus is the Son of God are Antichrists.

Moreover, the Jewish denial is the spirit of Antichrist. In 1 John 4 we read, "Hereby know ye the Spirit of God: Every spirit that confesseth that Jesus Christ is come in the flesh is of God: And every spirit that confesseth not that Jesus Christ is come in the flesh is not of God: and this is that spirit of antichrist" (1 John 4:2–3). Thus, the Christian denial is the sign of Antichrist.

Let a few verses touch our hearts before we continue this subject. In 1 John 2, we read, "Whosoever denieth the Son, the same hath not the Father: he that acknowledgeth the Son hath the Father also" (v. 23). Also, in 1 John 5, we read, "Who is he that overcometh the world, but he that believeth that Jesus is the Son of God" (v. 5)? In 1 John 5, we read again, "He that hath the Son hath life; and he that hath not the Son of God hath not life." Then we read, "These things have I written unto you that believe on the name of the Son of God; that ye may know that ye have eternal life and that ye may believe on the name of the Son of God" (1 John 5:12–13). We also read in 1 John 5, "And we know that the Son of God is come, and hath given us an understanding, that we may know him that is true, and we are in him that is true, even in his Son Jesus Christ. This is the true God, and eternal life" (v. 20). Then in John 3, we read, "He that believeth on the Son hath everlasting life: and he that believeth not the Son shall not see life, but the wrath of God abideth on him" (v. 36).

Finally, let us clearly state that no one can know Christ above a prophet except by revelation. Therefore, man can never know Him as Son of God unless man accepts the revelation God has given of His Son. If people reject God's word, they will reject God's Son. We aren't surprised when men reject the glorious person of our Lord Jesus Christ: but for us, He is too precious to deny.

We will now enlarge the subject of the Antichrist. We read in Revelation 13, "And I beheld another beast coming up out of the earth; and he had two horns like a lamb, and he spake as a dragon" (v. 11). This second Beast of Revelation 13 is the Antichrist. He has two horns like a lamb; he is both a religious and a secular leader. While the first Beast of Revelation 13 is the Roman Empire and its head is the Roman Prince, He has a single horn. This we read in Daniel 7, for instance: "And of the ten horns that were in his head, and of the other which came up, and before whom three fell; even of that horn that had eyes, and a mouth that spake very great things, whose look was more stout than his fellows" (v. 20). The Roman Dictator is a single horn. He is a secular leader. The Antichrist has two horns; he is both a religious and secular leader.

Hence, having two horns like a lamb, he leads both the Jewish and Christian apostasy. He is, consequently, both the Jewish secular leader and religious leader. As the secular leader, he is their king and is called "the king" in scripture, both in Isaiah and Daniel. Christ was rejected as king; the Jews will accept the Antichrist as king. John 5 states, "I am come in my Father's name, and ye receive me not: if another shall come in his own name, him ye will receive" (v. 43). The Antichrist will be received. He will come in his own name. The Lord Jesus did the Father's will; the Antichrist will do his own will. He will not come to honor any god; he will praise himself. He will present himself as God, and yet he will own the Roman Prince as his god.

In John 19, the Lord is rejected as king. We read, "But they cried out, away with him, away with him, crucify him. Pilate saith unto them, shall I crucify your King? The chief priests answered we have no king but Caesar" (v. 15). The Lord is rejected as king. Their king is Caesar; that is why they will accept the Roman Dictator.

The king in Daniel 11:36–40 is the Antichrist; he is the one who is called the king. He isn't the godly king but the wicked king. The Lord

Jesus Christ did His Father's will; this king will do his own will. The Lord Jesus Christ humbled Himself. This king exalted himself and magnified himself - not only above every man but above every god. He then speaks evil things against the God of gods. We are then told about his history. He shall prosper until the indignation is accomplished.

When is the indignation, and how can the Antichrist prosper until the indignation is accomplished? The indignation is the destruction the Assyrian brings. The rod in the Assyrian's hand is Jehovah's indignation. The end of the indignation or the accomplishment of the indignation is when the Assyrian leaves Israel to go to Egypt. This is the end of the tribulation and the end of the indignation. If we interpret the indignation to be accomplished after the destruction of the Assyrian, then the king cannot be said to prosper until the indignation is accomplished, because the Antichrist is destroyed with the Roman Beast when Christ is revealed from heaven before the Assyrian is destroyed. Hence, the Antichrist is destroyed before the Assyrian is destroyed. When Christ comes, the Assyrian is in Egypt and hears the tidings of Christ's coming. The Roman power is terminated before the Assyrian. Therefore, since the Antichrist shall prosper until the indignation shall be accomplished, that means the indignation's accomplishment must be at the departure of the Assyrian from Israel to Egypt to fight against the king of the South.

In Daniel 11:36, a person is abruptly introduced into the scene. However, we aren't told who this person is, nor where he came from; but what is said of him and the place that he occupies all declare that he is the Antichrist, the ruler from the tribe of Dan, the serpent and snake. He is in the land of Israel as a personal antagonist to Messiah. In Isaiah, we read, "For Tophet is ordained of old; yea, for the king also it is prepared; he hath made it deep and large: the pile thereof is fire and much wood; the breath of the Lord, like a stream of brimstone, doth kindle it" (Isa. 30:33 JND).

We need to see that when the Antichrist is introduced as "the king," we see him as the embodiment of sin. He is the man of sin. Sin at that time will exceed all bounds. At that time the Rapture would have taken place, and the church and the Holy Spirit would have departed to heaven. God will then remove the restraints to evil so the three evil men who step on the world's stage will be unshackled. The providential checks God put on men will be removed after the Rapture so Satan will have his free reign.

However, what is even worse is that the Antichrist will do his own will - not only in the land on which God's eyes rest continually but also in the very place where God had put His name. In the place where Jehovah was worshipped, the Antichrist will demand worship.

It is at this juncture that we are told, "The king shall do according to his will, and he shall exalt himself, and magnify himself above every god" (Dan. 11:36). The Antichrist will exalt and magnify himself not only above every man but "above every god." More than that, it isn't only that he takes his place above the idols or these so-called gods, but "he shall speak marvelous things against the God of gods" (Dan. 11:36). Yet though the Antichrist displays all this evil, God still allows him to continue until the end of the tribulation. "He shall prosper till the indignation be accomplished; for that that is determined shall be done" (Dan. 11:36).

"Neither shall he regard the God of his fathers, nor the desire of women" (Dan. 11:37). The fact that he doesn't regard the "God of his fathers," shows by that expression that Antichrist is an apostate Jew. The next phrase "the desire of women" refers to Christ as the expectation of all the Jewish women. They looked for the coming of the one whom all Jewish mothers expected. But it was more than that; each Jewish woman wanted to be the mother of the Messiah. Each Jewish wife desired that the baby she was carrying was the Messiah.

Furthermore, the passage shows that the Messiah was a divine person because the expression occurs between "the God of his fathers" and "any god." Christ is here distinguished from "the God of his fathers." He, the Son, was to become incarnate. Christ, in the expression "the desire of woman," is given equal importance as the expression "the God of his fathers." The scripture then lets us know that "he shall magnify himself above all." What he does is that he magnifies himself above God and Christ.

Nevertheless, this isn't all; not only does he reject the God of Israel and the Messiah, but he also doesn't honor any of the gods of the Gentiles either. Yet though he sets himself up as the true God on the earth, he will honor the god of forces. The "god of forces" is the Roman head, whom he honors. This is the one to whom he bows and causes others to bow along with himself. This is similar to the situation with Nebuchadnezzar, who didn't bow to any god, yet he made himself a god and made others also bow to it. This is what we have here. The Antichrist will make a god as well as set himself up to be God. "A god whom his fathers knew not shall he honor with gold, and silver, and with precious stones, and pleasant things" (Dan. 11:38). He will invent this god. This god is the Roman Prince. It is his statue the Antichrist will place in the temple. This statue what is called the "abomination of desolation," the idol that causes the destruction of the city. The Jews will then worship the Roman Ceasar that they declared was their only king. We have no king but Ceasar will become a reality.

"And at the time of the end shall the king of the south push at him" (Dan. 11:40). This expression causes us to know the time. The time is at the end. This confirms that "the king" is found "at the time of the end." Then "shall the king of the south push at him: and the king of the north shall come against him like a whirlwind, with chariots, and with horsemen, and with many ships" (Dan. 11:40). God's word told us about the king of the North and the South earlier; now we see them at the time of the end. This shows that these ancient powers must be revived. These past events have a future component. Moreover, they attack the king because he will sit at the site of their former mosque, declaring himself to be God.

The Antichrist will still go further with his scheme. He then will regulate even commerce. He will cause "all, both small and great, rich and poor, free and bond, to receive a mark in their right hand, or in their foreheads: and that no man might buy or sell, save he that had the mark, or the name of the beast, or the number of his name" (Rev. 13:16–17).

A significant security company paid a million dollars for research to find out the best place on the human body to insert their computer chip for their wealthy clients. The company wanted to insert their chip at the best location, just in case one of their clients was kidnapped so he or she could be quickly located. After all their research and the million-dollar investment by those who had commissioned the study, the researchers issued their verdict: "Insert the chip in either the hand or the forehead," just as the word of God foretold. Are you going to tell me the Bible isn't relevant? I could have told them the answer; they didn't have to invest all that money.

Finally, in 2 Thessalonians 2, the Antichrist is presented concerning Judaism. He will seek to set aside Judaism and claim divine honors for himself. The seat of his power will be Jerusalem. At the time of the

Antichrist, the Jews would have returned in unbelief and would have rebuilt their temple. The book of 2 Thessalonians 2 declares that the "man of sin," who is the Antichrist, will sit "in the temple of God, showing himself that he is God" (2 Thess. 2:4). This temple will be in Jerusalem. It isn't a Roman leader but a Jewish leader who goes into God's temple and declares himself God. Moreover, it needs to be clear that these events occur after the Rapture of the church of God.

The word of God mentions four temples. King Solomon built the first temple about 957 BC, on the temple mount. King David wanted to build that temple, but God said his son would make it. God clearly instructed how it was going to be built, who would build it, and where it was to be built. When it was finished, God stamped His approval on it with His presence in the form of the Shekinah glory. Nebuchadnezzar destroyed that temple around 588 BC.

After that destruction, God instructed the building of the second temple. This building began about 536 BC and was completed on March 12, 515 BC. When this building was dedicated, there was no Shekinah glory evident. However, a promise was given that Adonai, Adonai Jehovah, was going to come to this temple before it was destroyed.

Thus, we read in the book of Malachi, "Behold, I will send my messenger, and he shall prepare the way before me: and the Lord, whom ye seek, shall suddenly come to his temple, even the messenger of the covenant, whom ye delight in: behold, he shall come, saith the Lord of hosts" (Mal. 3:1). We here learn that before the Romans would destroy this temple in AD 70, the Lord Jesus Christ as Adonai Jehovah had to come. So, it was said, and so it was done. This book proves over and over again that it is God's word. When a man says the Lord Jesus faked His death, then that man has a more significant problem explaining how the Lord Jesus Christ decided His birth, since His birth had to take place within a very short window.

Moreover, we know the third temple will be built (2 Thess. 2:4), but we have no instruction from God's word for its building. We do, however, have guidance concerning the fourth. Consequently, because God hasn't sanctioned the construction of this third temple, the Antichrist will sit in that temple and declare himself to be God. In the second temple, Jehovah was to come to it, but in the third temple, the Antichrist will come to it. It is always Christ, then Antichrist. If Christ is rejected, then we get Antichrist. When God doesn't instruct us to do something, even the best we do may invoke the worst display of satanic activities. This temple is where the Antichrist will come and sit and declare that he is God.

Zechariah 6:12 declares that the Lord Jesus will build the final temple, and He was going to bear the glory. Moreover, He was going to sit and rule upon His throne. In Matthew 24, we read, "And Jesus went out, and departed from the temple: and his disciples came to him for to shew him the buildings of the temple. And Jesus said unto them, See ye, not all these things? Verily I say unto you; there shall not be left here one stone upon another, that shall not be thrown down. And as he sat upon the mount of Olives, the disciples came unto him privately, saying, tell us, when shall these things be? And what shall be the sign of thy coming, and of the end of the world?" (Matt. 24:1–3)

We must ask ourselves, Which temple was the Lord indicating? Was it the second temple, when the Lord was there? Alternatively, was it the third temple? It couldn't be the first, and it definitely couldn't be the last. The answer must be either the second or the third. If it was the second, then it was the temple Titus destroyed. If it is the third, then it is the temple the Assyrian will destroy.

Take another passage, the one in Mark 13. "And as he went out of the temple, one of his disciples saith unto him, Master, see what manner of stones and what buildings are here! And Jesus answering said unto him, seest thou these great buildings? There shall not be left one stone upon another that shall not be thrown down" (vv. 1–2). Consider even the passage in Luke 21, which some have insisted was wholly fulfilled in the destruction of the temple by Titus in AD 70; was it completely fulfilled? Was this the second temple or the third?

I have stated before that anything we do without instruction from God's word can bring the worst consequences. The answer to the question is the third temple, the temple where the Antichrist will sit. The destruction of the temple by Titus in AD 70 was an illustration of a future destruction. The secret to understand these verses is found in the expression "There shall not be left here one stone upon another that shall not be cast down" (Matt. 24:2). When Titus destroyed the temple in AD 70, he said he would leave a wall, emphasizing to the Jews that they couldn't rebel against the

Romans. This wall Titus left is still standing there today; it is called the Wailing Wall. God preserved it for us. Titus had one purpose in mind when he left that wall; however, God had another purpose, and that purpose was to enable us to interpret these verses correctly.

We need to appreciate that all these scriptures in the Synoptic Gospels speak about the "stone upon another." He left this wall so we might not misinterpret the scriptures. I have shown earlier that even in Ezekiel, this wall is noticed. The second temple, which Titus destroyed, has many stones upon another. There was not only one stone upon another, but there is a whole wall. There were stones upon stones upon stones; how could this be the fulfillment of this prophecy? The temple the Assyrian will destroy is the fulfillment of this prophecy. In the future attack on Jerusalem, the Muslims will thoroughly pour out all the temple stones when they recapture the temple site. The Jews would have broken down their mosques to rebuild their temple, and the Antichrist will sit in that temple and demand worship, declaring that he is God.

Moreover, the abomination of desolation will be placed there - that is, the Roman idol that will bring devastation to the city. That idol is the statue of the Roman Prince. Every stone will then be poured out because of the defilement to their temple site; then this scripture shall be fulfilled. The Assyrian will be so angry because of the Jewish defilement of their mosque and the holy place that they didn't want even a stone left standing at the temple site - they will pour out all the stones. When the Muslims built their mosque, even though it was so close to the temple wall, they didn't even touch the Jewish temple wall Titus had left standing. This is how carefully God preserved that structure. However, when the Jews will defile the Muslim mosques, the Assyrian will wreak their vengeance on the Jewish religious structures.

In the book of Lamentation, we read, "How is the gold become dim! How is the most fine gold changed! The stones of the sanctuary are poured out in the top of every street" (Lam. 4:1). Here Jeremiah is in agony over the destruction of the temple by Nebuchadnezzar, the king of Babylon. As he expressed his sorrow, the Spirit of God put words in his mouth like Psalm 45. The Spirit of God takes him forward to the destruction of the third temple, and he expresses words that will be fulfilled only in the destruction of that future temple by the Assyrian. Here note that they take the stones of the temple and pour them out at the top of every street. This didn't happen in the days of Nebuchadnezzar. This didn't occur in the days of Titus. There was a fundamental reason for this. That is why we have emphasized again and again that these scriptures have a partial fulfillment in the past but await the complete fulfillment in the future. Moreover, these things are providential.

In Psalm 74:3–7, we observed that the Assyrians will break down the carved work in the temple with axes and hammers. They attacked the temple with axes and hammers. When did this happen in the past? This is all future when the Jews will say, "The temple of the Lord; the temple of the Lord; the temple of the Lord" (Jer. 7:4) is all our salvation. We have to trust God, not things, even if that thing is the temple of the Lord.

We have the order of events in 2 Thessalonians 2:3–8. Before the day of the Lord could come, the Antichrist had to come; and before the Antichrist could appear, the apostasy had to come. Consequently, what we have is apostasy, then Antichrist, then the day of the Lord. These are the three events discussed here.

Nevertheless, before these three events, we must have the Rapture of the church of God, as stated in 2 Thessalonians 2:6–8. What is so touching is that the mystery of lawlessness was already working to bring in the lawless one; nevertheless, there were two who were restraining the evil. The "what" that withholds is the church of God, and the "He" who now restrains is the Spirit of God. What we therefore learn is the Spirit of God and the church of God being present were restraining evil from reaching its zenith. When the church of God is taken away and the Spirit of God, who indwells this church, is gone, there will be no restraint on evil, and Satan will manifest his full power. Once the church is on earth, the Antichrist cannot be displayed. Therefore, though the mystery of iniquity is already working, the restraints will restrain the manifestation of the evil one in the person of the "son of perdition" until the church departs. Then, and only then, will room be made for the revelation of the man of sin. He will then have his way until the Lord destroys him with the brightness of His coming. We find, though, that the Antichrist will have already abandoned the Jews and taken refuge with the Roman Prince in Rome when the Lord comes.

As a consequence, both the Antichrist and the Roman Prince will be taken together and cast alive into the lake of fire. This period between the Lord's coming for His saints and His coming with His saints is the period of the manifestation of the Antichrist. When the Antichrist comes, the church is absent, the Spirit of God is absent as resident in the church, and the Lord Jesus Christ is absent, but at the same time, Satan is present. He will be the company for man, a companion for man on the earth; I will have the fellowship of a wonderful God in heaven.

CHAPTER 18

THE ASSYRIAN CONFLICTS

The Assyrian will fight many battles. He will be mostly victorious in his struggles until he comes up against the Lord Jesus Christ. We will now investigate those battles and their results. The level of difficulty of this topic is nine out of ten.

We will now proceed with the consideration of this topic. In Daniel 8:22–25, we have the presentation of the Assyrian. This power is the main antagonist in the last days. It is the one who will terrorize the world, and it will soon be revealed. Most capable Bible expositors agree that Daniel 8 speaks of the Assyrian.

The first point to note in this passage is that the kingdoms of the king of the North and the king of the South will be revived. These are the two kingdoms, from Alexander the Great's Empire, that had a direct impact on Israel. The other two kingdoms in Europe did not have a direct bearing on Israel. We read, "In the latter time of their kingdom" (Dan. 8:23) - that is, the Assyrian kingdom - will be restored and the kingdom south of Israel. These phenomena will astonish the world. A huge Islamic kingdom to the northeast of Israel will cause great trepidation. We need to know how this kingdom will be established. The scripture explains to us that a mighty terrorist group will overthrow the countries along the Euphrates River and forge them into the Assyrian Empire.

The establishment of this empire was what ISIS was attempting to do, but it will be done. This event will further demonstrate to all that the Bible is the word of God. This development will undoubtedly take place. Already we know that ISIS has this in mind, since it tried to accomplish it; the world went to war against ISIS to prevent its realization. How could ISIS seek to do the very thing the word of God said would be done? The only reason is that there is a greater power driving it to accomplish what God has declared. ISIS doesn't believe in the Bible, but it is the Bible that says the kingdoms north and south of Israel will be restored. Why, then, has ISIS tried to restore them in our day before our eyes? What is even more astonishing, just as the word of God said, is that the power won't be able to accomplish that task because it will be weak at first, but when strengthened by Russia, it will restore these empires.

The second point is the time. "When transgressors are come to the full" (Dan. 8:23) - that is, when Israel embraces the lifestyle of the land shadowing with wings altogether. This declaration of their state is seen as early as Isaiah 1. We read, "Except the Lord of hosts had left unto us a very small remnant, we should have been as Sodom, and we should have been like unto Gomorrah. Hear the word of the Lord, ye rulers of Sodom; give ear unto the law of our God, ye people of Gomorrah" (Isa. 1:9–10). God addressed Israel as Sodom and Gomorrah. Her association with the land shadowing with wings had produced this degraded moral state. Furthermore, the word *transgress* is used regarding Israel or one disobeying a direct command like Adam. The nations are sinners, not transgressors; the Jews are transgressors because they were given the law.

The third point to note is that the head of the Assyrian will then appear on the scene. He will be a terrorist. He is called the Destroyer. He will build nothing; he will destroy everything valued in the West. We read, "A king of fierce countenance, and understanding dark sentences, shall stand up" (Dan. 8:23). He will stand up against the whole world and terrorize it.

However, when the Assyrian head stands up, his power shall be mighty. We read, "And his power shall be mighty, but not by his own power: and he shall destroy wonderfully, and shall prosper, and practise" (Dan. 8:24).

Here we are told that the Assyrian power will be mighty. The land mass of its territory will be the countries of Syria, Turkey, and Iraq. The people who will make up the empire will be Muslims attracted from all over the world to this caliphate. Then the governments of Russia and Iran will support the Assyrian.

We have already seen that Russia has established itself in the Syrian area, since it will support the terrorist government, and the Assyrian capital will be in Syria. The head of the Assyrian will come from Syria and lead the empire. The events that caused Russia to go down into Syria are providential; there is, however, a greater purpose behind why Russia is in Syria, if this is the time. He is there to strengthen the terrorist; however, this is terrible news for the world, those who don't believe in the Son of God.

We need to observe that the moment the Assyrian becomes strong, it will carry out terrorist attacks worldwide. Nevertheless, there is something even more alarming; the word of God declares, "And shall prosper, and practise" (Dan. 8:24) - that is, no one can stop the Assyrian, and no one can kill him. These attacks are before the tribulation. It then will attack "the mighty" - which we proved already is the land shadowing with wings. Also, these attacks on the mighty are before the tribulation. "The mighty" will then go down by the Euphrates River to fight the Assyrian in its kingdom, but "the mighty" will be destroyed. This is what we read next: "And shall destroy the mighty" (Dan. 8:24). There are two powers represented by the word "mighty" here and other places; one is the Assyrian, who defeats the second mighty, represented by the land shadowing with wings. All these events until this point must take place before the tribulation. This must be so since, at the beginning of the tribulation, Israel will sign a treaty with the European Union for protection. The ratification of this treaty will commence the tribulation. Therefore, the land shadowing with wings must be destroyed before the tribulation. This is the declaration of God's word.

Fourth, he then destroys "the holy," which is Israel. This destruction will take place during the tribulation but after the middle of Daniel's seventieth week. This destruction takes place after the Roman Empire breaks the treaty of protection.

Fifth, after the destruction of Israel, we find that the Assyrian will destroy again, this time a group with whom he shared an association.

We read, "And through his policy also he shall cause craft to prosper in his hand, and he shall magnify himself in his heart, and by peace shall destroy many" (Dan. 8:25). The group it attacks here is located in the Egyptian, Ethiopian, and Libyan areas, the king of the South, a fellow terrorist power.

The word for "craft" in Hebrew is *mirmah*, which means "deceit," "feigned," "false," "guile," and "treachery." The Assyrian will deceive the king of the South, who would have helped it defeat the land shadowing with wings, but then the Assyrian leader will treacherously seek to destroy this rival power, because "he shall magnify himself in his heart" (Dan. 8:25). He will want to become the greatest power on earth, who will entertain no rival. Nevertheless, before he could complete this destruction of the king of the South, he will have to return to Jerusalem to stand up against the Lord Jesus Christ.

Sixth, after defeating Israel, the Assyrian leader will think he can defeat the Lord Jesus Christ. The Assyrian leader will believe that the Lord Jesus was only a prophet, so he will venture to stand up against Him. This we read next: "He shall also stand up against the Prince of princes, but he shall be broken without hand" (Dan. 8:25). He then will come up against the Lord Jesus Christ, but the Lord will crush him. The only King of kings and Lord of lords will stop him in his endeavor. This will be the end of the Assyrian.

However, the Assyrian will be the power that will have the world on edge. The life of the Assyrian leader spans from before the tribulation to after the tribulation. This man's life shows that the Rapture and the tribulation are closely related. There is no other power that will cause the world so much distress. My readers, believe me; it will all happen. Turn to the Son of God before you are lost forever.

Let us, therefore, develop a little more about the activities of the Assyrian. The Assyrian leader, as we noticed, will mainly fight (not destroy) six opponents. First, when he comes on the scene, he will have to fight to establish his empire. Second, he will fight against the land shadowing with wings. Third, he will fight against the Roman Empire. Fourth, he will fight against Israel. Fifth, the Assyrian head will war against the king of the South. Sixth and finally, he will desire to fight against the Lord Jesus Christ.

The Assyrian head will come on the scene after the falling of the towers as a religious terrorist power. He will come out of the Syria/Iraq area, the former territories of the old Assyrian Empire. He will not be strong at first, but Russia will turn against the West and embrace it. This support will make the Assyrian very strong. The Assyrian head had first to establish his empire to the northeast of Israel. We know from Isaiah 19 that when the Lord returns, there will be a land called Assyria.

However, there is no such country called Assyria today. To establish Assyria, this religious terrorist power will have to go to war with many powers trying to prevent its establishment. Even though these powers were going to fight against the Assyrian head, he would still conquer and control Syria. He was going to establish in Syria the capital of his empire. He was going to capture and control Iraq, this country he was going to incorporate into his realm. He was going to conquer and control Turkey. This country also he was going to forge as part of his kingdom. This is how the Assyrian Empire will be established.

Here we see that Isaiah is complete and outlines each battle. It was said that the Egypt of Isaiah 30–31 is the land shadowing with wings. Notice how out of nowhere, God introduces the Assyrian into both passages. This is how the Assyrian head will suddenly appear on the scene. He seems to appear out of nowhere.

Moreover, we never read about a battle between the ancient Assyrian and Egypt, because Egypt was the most significant power in the day of the Assyrian Empire, and the Assyrian wasn't going to fight Egypt. We read that Egypt, in contrast, went to fight with the Assyrian by the Euphrates River. Instead of being informed about the result of that battle, we learned that Nebuchadnezzar, the king of Babylon, attacked Egypt and destroyed Pharaoh. That wasn't by chance; that was by design.

That destruction of Egypt sets the stage for God to introduce the future Assyrian in the passage with the future Egypt, without having to state a battle. This Egypt of Isaiah 30-31, as the land shadowing with wings, will be in the future, and the war will also be in the future. God, therefore, gave the land shadowing with wings, Egypt, a name contemporary with the ancient Assyrian, but the result of the struggle wasn't stated. However, what Nebuchadnezzar did to Pharaoh, king of Egypt, by first destroying his army - and then his country - will become the type of the future battles.

The future Assyrian will first destroy the army of the land shadowing with wings, the future Egypt, by the Euphrates River, then he will proceed to destroy the homeland of that power.

In Isaiah 30:30–33, God states that He will destroy the Assyrian. Designated Egypt won't defeat the Assyrian. With all its pomp and glory, Egypt will be conquered. The Assyrian will smite him with a rod. Moreover, where Egypt will be defeated, the Lord will triumph. In Isaiah 31:4–9, God declared that the mighty man won't defeat the Assyrian. The mighty man is the land shadowing with wings - as is Egypt; the Lord alone will defeat the Assyrian.

The next Assyrian battle will be the one against the Roman Empire. This battle won't get to the stage of a direct confrontation, but the Assyrian will escalate his attacks on the Roman Empire by repeated terrorist attacks, until the Roman Empire will break the protective treaty with Israel. These constant, intense, attacks on the Roman Empire, will serve to intimidate Rome to break the covenant with Israel. In Revelation 8, we have the attacks of the Assyrian on the Roman Empire. The Roman Prince will not want to break the protective treaty with Israel. He will first try to negotiate a peace treaty with the Assyrian; as is highlighted in Isaiah 33:7-8. However, when that attempt fails, and war will be his only option, the Roman Prince will break the covenant with Israel. We have highlighted this development before, so we will deal with the next battle.

The Assyrian will then fight against Israel. We have said much about that already. In Daniel 11:40–45, the Assyrian, the king of the North, and the king of the South will attack the Antichrist in Israel just after the middle of the tribulation.

The next power the Assyrian will attack is the king of the South. The king of the South will be another Islamic terrorist power. He will be the first power to attack Israel in the last days when the Roman Empire will break the treaty. This power will be composed of Islamic countries south of Israel, such as Egypt, Libya, and Ethiopia. This Assyrian attack on Egypt will take place shortly after the Assyrian will invade Israel. This will occur a short while after the middle of Daniel's seventieth week. We notice from God's word that when the Assyrian invades Israel, the leader will be subsequently absent after the initial invasion. The Assyrian head will leave the main part of his invading army in Israel and invade Egypt.

He will attack his confederate Islamic power, who helped him destroy the land shadowing with wings and Israel, by the Euphrates River. The Assyrian head will betray his fellow terrorist power and subjugate Egypt, according to Isaiah 20:2–6.

Now notice in Isaiah 20 that the prophet speaks to us of geographic Egypt in the last days; Assyria will lead Egypt and take Ethiopia captive. Even the length of three years is essential, because they are the three years of the last half week of Daniel's prophecy. This clearly shows that the invasion doesn't occur long after the middle of Daniel's seventieth week. Assyria will fight against Egypt and Ethiopia in the last days. This battle wasn't in the past but will be in the future. Assyria never ventured so far south to fight Egypt in the past, much less to go further and invade Ethiopia. We now see why God caused the Assyrian emissaries, who came to the wall of Jerusalem in the days of Hezekiah, to list the territories they had conquered. This was vital information, for we have neither Egypt nor Ethiopia on that list. God had a reason He wrote everything, so we might not confuse the past with the future.

The king of the South will be the terrorist power south of Israel, which will be composed of the African countries, of which three are here mentioned: Egypt, Libya, and Ethiopia. Note the time: the word of God calls it, "the time of the end" (Dan. 11: 40). The king of the North will be the terrorist power north of Israel. The Antichrist will be the one the Assyrian head will attack. Nevertheless, the Antichrist will be the head of Israel, therefore, Israel will be under attack.

The Antichrist will become the object of the Assyrian attack, because he will sit in the temple, on Mount Moriah, at the site of the Assyrian former mosque, declaring himself to be God. The king of the South, headquartered in Egypt, will attack the Antichrist first; then the king of the North, headquartered in Syria, will attack him afterward. However, as a hireling, the Antichrist will flee to Rome for protection and leave Israel to the Assyrian. The fleeing of the Antichrist to Rome will be a critical, providential development. The fleeing of the false Messiah, who declared he was God in the temple of God, will have a pronounced effect on the Assyrian. Therefore, when the Lord comes, the Assyrian head will also think he can make the true Messiah flee; but he will be wrong, so wrong. The Antichrist will display all power, even performing all miracles; he will declare that he is God in the temple. Nevertheless, he will flee from the Assyrian. The Assyrian head will think he can do the same to Christ, but he will be deceived.

However, after the rebuilt Jewish temple is destroyed by the Assyrian, the Islamic leader will summon his main force in Israel to Egypt, to hasten the conquest of the king of the South. The Assyrian desire will be to become the unrivaled and undisputed champion in both the North and the South. It is during this time, when the Assyrian will be away in Egypt, that Christ will return from heaven with His raptured saints. At that time, the Lord will come back to deliver Israel and will descend on the Mount of Olives, which is declared to be east according to Zechariah 14. Jerusalem is said to be north according to Psalms 48.

Therefore, the tidings out of the east and north (Daniel 11:44) that the Assyrian will hear will state that Christ has returned on the Mount of Olive and destroyed that part of the Assyrian all-conquering force that was located at Jerusalem. The Assyrian will hear these tidings from the mouths of Edom, Moab, and Ammon. The Mount of Olives, on which Christ will descend, is located east of Hebron; therefore, it is the news of Christ's return that the Assyrian will hear. It is for this reason that we must embrace scripture and not speculation.

If we make Jerusalem the geographic center of Israel, then we cannot locate the direction of the report and will be unable to interpret the report. If, however, Hebron is the geographic center of Israel, then north will take us to Jerusalem, where the Assyrian force is located, and east will take us to the Mount of Olives, where Christ has descended, and everything will line up perfectly.

Moreover, God allowed the nations of Edom, Moab, and Ammon to be spared for this purpose. These nations will then encourage the Assyrian to return for the destruction of Israel according to Psalm 83. We then notice that these nations will return with the Assyrian but only to be destroyed by the Lord Jesus Christ at the intercession of the psalmist. It is also necessary to see that the past attack of the Assyrian on Judah was a type of the future attack.

In 2 Kings 18 and Isaiah 36, we have the historical attack of the Assyrian on Judah. We need to observe the distribution of the Assyrian army. The head of the Assyrian wasn't there in Jerusalem; he was in another place, away from his army. He then sends "Rabshakeh from Lachish to Jerusalem unto King Hezekiah with a great army" (Isa. 36: 2). The king of Assyria had invaded the whole territory. We read, "Sennacherib king of Assyria came up against all the defenced cities of Judah, and took them" (Isa. 36: 1). However, he was occupied with another aspect of the war. He wasn't in Jerusalem when his army was destroyed by the angel, a type of the Lord Jesus Christ, coming out of heaven and destroying the future Assyrian army.

This will be repeated in the future when the Assyrian head invades Israel, which is, in fact, Judah; he goes to Egypt and lets his main force proceed with the invasion. However, after he takes control of Jerusalem, he withdraws part of his force from Israel to Egypt and leaves a smaller unit in Israel to capture the remaining Jews. When he withdraws this main force, this act will end the tribulation. He will then be in the Egyptian, Libyan, and Ethiopian corridor with his additional force. While there, Christ will come out of heaven and crush the Roman Empire, which will make war with Him, and at the same time the smaller Assyrian force in Jerusalem. The Assyrian chief will then hear this significant piece of information and will hastily return to Jerusalem, only to be destroyed by the Lord Jesus Christ.

In Isaiah 37:7–13, we have the fall of the historic Assyrian. We noticed that the Assyrian's fall will be a type of the fall of the Assyrian in the future. There, in Egypt, the Assyrian leader heard the rumor that Tirhakah, king of Ethiopia, was come to make war with him, so he departed. The same thing will happen in the future. The Assyrian head will hear that the Lord Jesus, the king of Israel, has returned and destroyed his force; as a result, he will depart from Egypt and return to Israel, convinced that Allah, his god, was going to secure for him the victory. As far as he was concerned, Christ was only a prophet. He will learn differently in his confrontation with Him.

Psalm 18 is a beautiful psalm of this period; it will open our eyes to the Assyrian's confrontation with the Lord Jesus Christ. In Psalm 18:3–9, we have the remnant crying to God to address their needs. We then notice the Lord Jesus Christ coming for their deliverance as a result of their intercession.

In verse 6 the Jewish remnant calls on the Lord, and the Lord hears him and delivers him. However, another group here will also call on Jehovah, but Jehovah won't hear. Who is this person who will call on the Lord, but the Lord won't answer?

In Psalm 18:16, the remnant was delivered from his strong enemy. Here "enemy" isn't in the plural but the singular. There is only one strong enemy since the other isn't strong. The strong enemy is the Assyrian. Here Israel acknowledges that this enemy hated her and was mightier than her. The psalmist also informs us when this will take place; it will be in the days of his calamity; that is the day of the Great Tribulation.

The Lord Jesus Christ is then introduced in Psalm 18:37–40. He will come as a result of the intercession of the Jewish remnant. Yes! It is a psalm of David, but David's experience was only a small portion of what is displayed in this encounter. Here the Lord crushes the enemy. Here the deliverance of Israel is tied up with the coming of the Lord Jesus Christ.

"They cried, but there was none to save them: even unto the Lord, but he answered them not. Then did I beat them small as the dust before the wind: I did cast them out as the dirt in the streets" (Ps. 18:41–42). Yet pay particular attention to these verses, and you will see something remarkable. Now the Assyrian head, as he comes back from Egypt, will not think much of my Lord Jesus Christ; as far as he will be concerned, Christ is only a prophet, so he feels his big army is capable of dealing with Him.

However, as the Lord begins to beat down the Assyrian army, note carefully that the Assyrian head calls on the same God as the Jewish remnant, but God doesn't answer him. We read, "They cried, but there was none to save them: even unto the Lord, but he answered them not" (Ps. 18: 41). The Jewish remnant did call on Jehovah in verse 6 and He did answer them. In contrast, the Assyrian called on Jehovah but He didn't answer them; likewise, when the Assyrian head did call on Jehovah, He didn't answer him.

This development is very significant because it underscores the point that the Assyrian will be calling on Abraham's God; he was calling on Jehovah. He wasn't calling on a false god, but the passage highlights that God wasn't seen in relationship with the Assyrian. It is like the Canaanite woman in Matthew 15, who cried, "Have mercy on me, O Lord, thou son of David; my daughter is grievously vexed with a devil, but he answered her not a word" (Matt. 15: 22). As Son of David, He wasn't sent to the Canaanites. It was at that instant that the Assyrian will realize he was a stranger to Israel's God. He realized then that he was deluded, and he couldn't reverse his position. He was subsequently caught and cast into the lake of fire. He will not only be religious, but he will also claim the same God. Here he calls even to Jehovah, but Jehovah doesn't answer him. The word in Hebrew for Lord in Psalm 18:41 is the word for Jehovah.

There is another significant point here. The Assyrian head will realize that the person he was confronting was more than a man, and consequently, he will need divine intervention. Therefore, he will call on God, but the God he will call on will be the same God he was opposing, though, presented as a man – the Lord Jesus Christ.

In Psalm 18:43–48, we see how things will change when the Lord Jesus Christ returns. He will take absolute power and reign; then all will obey and submit to Him. Furthermore, we notice that the strangers appear again - they are the Muslims - claiming closeness to the God of Israel. They now submit to Him and are even afraid to be associated with their places of worship. What a change from what we have today.

Then the truth of Isaiah 25 will apply: "He will destroy in this mountain the face of the covering cast over all people, and the veil that is spread over all nation. He will swallow up death in victory; and the Lord God will wipe away tears from off all faces; and the rebuke of his people shall he take away from off all the earth: for the Lord hath spoken it" (Isa. 25:7–8).

Then all the nations will see clearly, when the veil is removed, they will know who the Lord Jesus Christ really is - God blessed forever. Finally, at the end of all these battles, when the Lord returns, things will change.

Then Jeremiah 16 will also apply. "O Lord, my strength, and my fortress, and my refuge in the day of affliction, the Gentiles shall come unto thee from the ends of the earth, and shall say, surely our fathers have inherited lies, vanity, and things wherein there is no profit. Shall a man make gods unto himself, and they are no gods? Therefore, behold, I will this once cause them to know, I will cause them to know mine hand and my might, and they shall know that my name is the Lord" (Jer. 16:19–21).

What is so precious in this passage is that when the Lord Jesus comes, the people who were made to believe in the different religions of the world will say, "Our fathers have inherited lies" (Jer. 16:19). Instead of "Go you into all the world and preach the gospel to every creature" (Mark 16:15), we find that the nations from all over the world will come and say, "Our fathers have inherited lies" (Jer. 16:19). They will then characterize the religions of their fathers as lies. This is a significant change that is about to take place in this world. However, we cannot say that to these religious people today, but tomorrow, when the Lord returns, they will say it to all, *Our fathers have inherited lies*: whether it be religion, evolution, or philosophy; they are all lies.

CHAPTER 19

JORDAN: THE ESCAPE ROUTE

T he more we study scripture, the more we find that when God allows a trial, He makes a way of escape. It is no wonder that three peoples are said to escape out of the hands of the Assyrian; these are Edom, Moab, and the chief of the children of Ammon. These three peoples are those who make up the country called Jordan today. This king of the North will leave this country unconquered - not because it is mighty, but it is left as a passage for the Jewish remnant to escape and for these nations to inform the Assyrian of the return of Christ. Edom is the son of Isaac, the brother of Jacob. Moab and Ammon are the sons of Lot. This topic is a nine on my difficulty scale. Let us now seek to understand the matter at hand. In Matthew 24, we read, "When ye therefore shall see the abomination of desolation, spoken of by Daniel the prophet, stand in the holy place, (whoso readeth, let him understand:) Then let them which be in Judaea flee into the mountains: Let him which is on the housetop not come down to take anything out of his house: neither let him which is in the field return back to take his clothes" (Matt. 24:15–18).

There will be a time to preach. There will be an hour to flee. During the first three and a half years of the tribulation, the faithful Jews will preach the gospel of the kingdom, though persecuted by the Roman Prince. However, just after the middle of the seven years tribulation, the Antichrist will place the statue of the Roman Prince in the future temple at Jerusalem. This statue, the Antichrist will cause the Jews to make (Rev. 13: 14,15), he will place in the rebuilt temple and demand that the Jews worship it. This image is what is called the abomination of desolation. The Jewish remnant are told in Matthew 24: 15-18 that when they shall see, the statue placed in the temple, they must run. They should no longer stay in Jerusalem. The time to run is specified. When the Jewish remnant see the Antichrist place the statue of the Roman Prince in the future temple at Jerusalem, and command Israel to worship it, the Jewish remnant must run, run, run as fast as possible and don't look back. Why must the Jewish remnant flee? They must flee because the Assyrian will then invade the land to destroy the holy of Daniel 8. It is the coming of the Assyrian that begins the great tribulation and the departure of the Assyrian that ends it.

It is essential to observe that when the Assyrian invades Israel, the Jews will flee to their neighbors. However, as the Jewish remnant flees into Jordan, where they go will determine their fate. It will be necessary not only to flee but also to know where one was going. If Israel enters into Jordan, where Edom will be located, there will be no hope for her; she will be slaughtered.

Let us find the remnant in Jordan as they flee the Great Tribulation. Psalm 42 puts the remnant in Jordan. We need to discern from these verses that the godly remnant will be in Jordan for safety and on the mountain in the North. The soul of the psalmist was cast down; he went with the other Jewish worshippers to the house of God, but now he had to run to the land of Jordan, and the land of the Harmonite, and the hill Mizar for safety. However, in these places, he will find no rest; the neighbors will taunt him, saying, "Where is your God?" The locals reproached him daily because they were all Muslims. He will have no peace.

If Israel flees west from Hebron, she will enter into the land of the Philistines, and if she is caught, the Philistines will deliver her up to Edom for destruction. Moreover, if Israel flees northwest from Samaria, she will enter Lebanon; if she is found, she will be taken to Edom and delivered for slaughter. Furthermore, if Israel escapes east from Shechem, she will come into Ammon's land; if Israel is caught, Ammon will deal with her.

However, if Israel flees south from Beersheba, she will enter the land of Edom and will be destroyed most savagely. There is only one way, with some measure of safety - that is, for Israel to flee east from Hebron, which will take her into the land of Moab. There God will provide a way of escape. *Flee Israel and escape into the land of Moab; God may show you mercy.*

In Isaiah 16, we read, "Let mine outcasts dwell with thee, Moab; be thou a covert to them from the face of the spoiler: for the extortioner is at an end, the spoiler ceaseth, the oppressors are consumed out of the land" (Isa. 16:4). Moab had a part in Judah through Ruth the Moabitess, from whom came David the king of Israel. However, in the future God will commit the care of the remnant into the hands of Moab. Here Moab is told to "let mine outcast dwell with thee" (Isa. 16:4). The outcasts are the ones who will flee from Israel for safety, the rest of the Jews will seek to fight the Assyrian. This scenario is similar to the destruction of Jerusalem in AD 70, the Jewish Christians fled the city and went to Pella in Jordan; the rest of the Jews stayed to fight the Romans. However, in the future, Moab will be a covert for the remnant from the face of the spoiler. The spoiler is Russia, seen associated with the Assyrian. Moab is to protect those who will escape from Israel, but Israel needs to pray that she receives mercy.

In Psalm 83:5-8, we perceive that Moab will become tired of Israel's presence in her land and will take part in an evil confederacy. Moab will then encourage the Assyrian to return to Israel from Egypt for Israel's destruction. However, the Lord will put an end to this vicious purpose. Observe that all these ancient nations will be back in their lands when the Lord returns.

In Amos 1:6-14, God stated why He will judge Israel's neighbors. The reason is their treatment of Israel during the tribulation. In this passage, Moab is conspicuously absent because it was asked to be a shelter for the remnant of Israel. All the other neighbors are seen here in their hatred toward Israel. The person who will be totally infuriated against Israel is Edom, Jacob's brother. He will deal with Israel to the extreme, so much so that the other nations will deliver up to Edom the outcast of Israel they will capture. He will deal with Israel with full hatred.

In Amos 1:6, we notice that as a result of the attack by the Assyrian, Israel will flee to all her neighbors. However, God told Moab to show Israel mercy. Hence, when Israel will escape to the west, to the Philistines' land, the Philistines will deliver her up to Edom to execute his cruelty against her. Though the Philistines, who are today the Palestinians, have fought so many battles with Israel, they will still believe that the brutalities of Edom exceeded their hatred for Israel; so, they will deliver up the captive Israelites to Edom.

When Israel will run north to Lebanon, though Lebanon and present-day Israel have fought so many battles, still Tyrus will deliver up the captives to Edom for destruction. In verse 11, Edom comes up for special mention, and her hatred for Israel is on display. Edom is said to "pursue his brother with the sword, and did cast off all pity, and his anger did tear perpetually, and he kept his wrath forever" (Amos 1:11). When Ammon comes up for consideration, He is said to have "ripped up the women with child of Gilead, that they might enlarge their border" (Amos 1:13). Therefore, the best place for Israel to run is Moab. It is something to be noted that Moab isn't present in this passage.

The attitude of the nations towards Israel, as she flees the great tribulation, will be the premise for the judgment by the Lord Jesus Christ in Matthew 25: 31- 46. In the following two scriptural passages, we will get a sample of this judgment. However, all of these nations will be judged for their attitude towards Israel's future plight.

In Ezekiel 25:12–16, we are given the reason for Edom's judgment. His hatred for Israel is highlighted by the Lord Jesus Christ. This passage shows the complete judgment on Edom for his hatred toward Israel during the tribulation. Don't worry about the peace that seems to exist today between Israel and Jordan; very soon, those old wounds will open up for destruction. However, Moab, it seems, will remain truly neutral until the end of the tribulation. We now have the reason for this famous scripture in Isaiah 63:1–6, where the Lord deals with Edom for his cruelty toward Israel.

We must bear in mind that there will be two attacks by the Assyrian on Israel. In the first, the Assyrian will be entering Israel from the North, his homeland. In the second, he will be returning from the South, from Egypt. In the first attack, his purpose will be to recover the site of his mosques; in the second, his goal will be to obliterate Israel's name from the earth altogether. God will allow the first but will prevent the latter.

This sequence helps us to understand the passage in Matthew 24: "For then shall be great tribulation, such as was not since the beginning of the world to this time, no, nor ever shall be. And except those days should be shortened, there should no flesh be saved: but for the elect's sake, those days shall be shortened" (Matt. 24:21–22).

How were the days shortened? We have struggled to answer this question over the years. This we have been unable to explain. Unless we have all the pieces of the puzzle and seek to put the parts together as a whole, we will never fully understand the puzzle. That is why we have so many difficulties with the dates, stated in God's word, relative to the tribulation. These dates are given in years, months, weeks, days and times, time, and the dividing of time or half a time. Without the Assyrian, we cannot solve the puzzle. Moreover, the dates are there to prevent mistakes. If the numbers don't correspond, our interpretation is wrong.

In Matthew 24 we read,

> Immediately after the tribulation of those days shall the sun be darkened, and the moon shall not give her light, and the stars shall fall from heaven, and the powers of the heavens shall be shaken: And then shall appear the sign of the Son of man in heaven: and then shall all the tribes of the earth mourn, and they shall see the Son of man coming in the clouds of heaven with power and great glory. And he shall send his angels with a great sound of a trumpet, and they shall gather together his elect from the four winds, from one end of heaven to the other. (Matt. 24:29–31)

We need to grasp the sequence. Here the tribulation of those days is said to be over, yet the Assyrian isn't yet destroyed, the Roman Empire isn't yet subjected, and Christ has not yet come. How could this be? We know Christ hasn't yet arrived because the same passage states that after the tribulation of those days, then shall appear the sign of the Son of man in heaven, and they shall see the Son of man coming. What will bring the tribulation to an end?

Moreover, if Christ hadn't yet arrived, how can the Roman Empire and the Assyrian be destroyed? How can we solve this mystery? Unless we understand the Assyrian, we cannot understand these passages. After the Assyrian head will accomplish the destruction of the Jewish temple and synagogues, he will remove his main force from Israel, to intensify his attack in the Egyptian, Libyan, and Ethiopian areas. His objective will be to conquer the king of the South, to become the undisputed king of the North and the South

The departure of the Assyrian from Israel to Egypt will cause the end of the tribulation of those days. Once the Assyrian head removes his large army from Israel and primarily relocates it in Egypt, there will be an ease of the terror that will be taking place in Israel. It is this reduction of the terror that signals the end of the tribulation. If the main Assyrian army was still in Israel, the terror would have continued, and the tribulation couldn't have been said to be ended. While the Assyrian head will be in Egypt, the Lord Jesus Christ will come and destroy the Roman Empire and the smaller Assyrian force in Israel, as in the days of Hezekiah. The head of the Assyrian will then hear the tidings of the Lord's return. He will then be encouraged to return to Israel to obliterate Israel's name from the earth and stand up against the Lord Jesus Christ. When the Assyrian head responds to that request, the Lord Jesus Christ will come forth from Zion, confront the Assyrian, and destroy him.

The Lord Jesus, when he returns from heaven will destroy the Roman Empire and the small Assyrian force in Israel. At that point, the Assyrian, with his mighty army, will be in Egypt. Then, when the Assyrian returns from Egypt to Israel, the Lord Jesus will come out of Zion and crush him. There is, therefore, a gap between the first invasion of Israel by the Assyrian and the second. This gap between the two Assyrian attacks is very important. The shortening of the days of Matthew 24 is the limiting of the great tribulation to the first attack. It is for this reason the Assyrian attack will be divided into two parts and the carnage will be confined to the first part. Therefore, except the days of the Assyrian attack was limited to the first part no flesh would have been saved according to Matthew 24: 22. This verse is confined to the Jews and does not extend to the Gentiles.

God will not allow one continuous attack, or else, no flesh would be saved. The days will not be less than twenty-four hours, and the time will be three and a half years. However, the attack will be divided into two parts. The days of the severe Assyrian conflict will be shortened to the first part of the war, until the Assyrian will leave for Egypt, though the Assyrian will not yet be destroyed. When the Assyrian head returns from Egypt to obliterate Israel, he will be crushed. If the days are not shortened to the time the Assyrian will remain in Israel, before he leaves for Egypt, then the Assyrian would have exterminated every Jew in the land, because that will be the purpose for his return to Israel. The days were shortened to the duration of the first attack and not to the length of the war with the Assyrian. The shortening of days to the first attack prevented Israel's total destruction; if the Assyrian had stayed in Israel, the Jews would have been completely destroyed. Therefore, unless I understand the Assyrian, I will never solve the puzzle of the last days.

CHAPTER 20

CHRIST'S FIRST COMING

The Bible teaches us that a wonderful God made man from the dust of the ground. He provided everything for the man He had made, and the first man enjoyed sweet fellowship with that blessed God. Then we read that man disobeyed God and became a sinner. When God came looking for the man, Adam, who was then a sinner, cowered before God's mighty presence and hid when he heard his Master's voice. How could a holy God come and save a poor sinner? This topic is a three on my scale of difficulties so all may understand. God loved the man, whom He had made; God loved him so much that He was willing to save him at great cost.

In Genesis 3:7–9, we notice that God did everything for Adam; He created him. He provided for him food and water. He provided him with gold and precious stones; He provided him with plants and animals. All things were his, since there was no one else to claim them. God saw that he lacked one thing, a helpmeet, and God gave him that also; Adam was then complete.

For all His goodness to man, God desired one thing from Adam; He desired that man would obey Him. One commandment God gave to

Adam so the man would live an obedient life. He gave him this command even before He gave him the helpmeet. This wonderful God wanted the man to guide his family according to His instructions stated in Genesis 2:16–17. Nevertheless, the man didn't obey God but listened to the devil instead. As a result, man became a sinner. He became a transgressor. Now we need to ask ourselves an important question. Would a sinful man go to God and confess his sins and repent of those sins? No, he wouldn't go to God, even if he had done only one sin.

However, we find that though the man didn't seek after God, God came searching for the man. Nevertheless, in Genesis 3:8–11, we see that man in his sins could not stand in the presence of a holy God like before. We observed that Adam and his wife were taking a stroll in the garden in the cool of the day when they heard the Lord God's voice. Adam knew that voice, but this time he was afraid of his Creator. Adam couldn't go to God; he was now a sinner. He couldn't have fellowship with this holy God as before, so he hid himself. The man declared plainly that he was afraid of God. What caused the first man to hide from God when before he had such excellent fellowship with Him? Sin was what made Adam hide from God, and sin is what continues to cause men to hide from this wonderful God. It must be noted that when Adam sinned, he didn't go looking for God, but God came looking for Adam. However, as we have noticed, if He comes as God, His mere voice will cause the man to be afraid and hide. God will have to come in a different way to save the sinner.

When we get to Exodus 20, we read, "And all the people saw the thunderings, and the lightnings, and the noise of the trumpet, and the mountain smoking: and when the people saw it, they removed, and stood afar off. And they said unto Moses, Speak thou with us, and we will hear: but let not God speak with us, lest we die" (Ex. 20:18–19).

God spoke to the children of Israel at Mount Horeb, and they were so terrified that they said, "Let not God speak with us, lest we die" (Ex. 20:19). They said to Moses that he should speak to them and not let God speak with them, lest they die. We learned the painful truth that a man in his sins can never stand in the presence of a holy God. However, if his sins are removed, he will be at home in God's presence. Israel couldn't stand in God's presence, and they couldn't stand His words. The sins of the man needed to be removed. How will God then speak to the creature He made?

How will He come to rescue the creature from his or her sins? The people suggested a solution, and God had the same thing in mind.

In Deuteronomy 18:15–19, Israel declared that she didn't want to hear the voice of the Lord again. Therefore, a prophet was going to go to Israel like Moses; him they were going to hear. This prophet was the Lord, but came as a man. "According to all that thou desiredst of the Lord thy God in Horeb in the day of the assembly, saying, Let me not hear again the voice of the Lord my God, neither let me see this great fire any more, that I die not" (Deut. 18:16). This great prophet is Christ Himself.

In Deuteronomy 18:15–18, the fullness of truth was to be made known by Jesus alone with the greatest danger of slighting Him. "It shall come to pass that whosoever will not hearken unto my words which he shall speak in my name, I will require it of him" (Deut. 18:19). This prophet was going to speak Jehovah's word. He was Jehovah, yet He came as a man on earth.

In Acts 3, the apostle Peter clearly showed that this prophet is the Lord Jesus Christ, and so does Stephen in Acts 7. He was to come to speak to Israel as a man, yet He was God blessed forever. They were to hear God's word from a man without being terrified by His presence. Nevertheless, when He came this way in humility, man crucified Him and denied He was God.

In Daniel 9:24-27, we are given the time when Christ was to be seen in Israel. He had to appear 483 years after the commandment by Artaxerxes to restore and build Jerusalem. Moreover, He had to put in His appearance 434 years after the rebuilding of the walls of Jerusalem, as we notice in the seventieth week of Daniel's prophecy.

As the prophet, He was to bring God's word to Israel; as Messiah, He was the fulfillment of all God's counsel regarding the Jews. Nevertheless, the time of His coming and the indignity He was going to suffer are recorded in Daniel 9.

We need to define the period indicated by the seventy weeks. Let us now seek to understand the prophecy. Immediately, we are confronted with the date of the commencement of the seventy weeks. This date is provided with precision, as we have it in verse 25. Additionally, we need to grasp that the word *weeks* in this passage isn't merely weeks of days. In Hebrew, the word for "week" means something divided into, or consisting of, seven parts. Daniel had inquired about the seventy years of the captivity in Babylon. God gave him an answer concerning seventy periods, which in the KJV are called "weeks."

However, the word *weeks* doesn't necessarily mean periods of seven days but seven parts, though the word is most often used for a week, which is similarly divided. The Jews, as we know, use a septenary scale as to time. We reckon time by tens. The Jews reckon time by sevens; hence, we have the sabbatical years and the jubilees. We need to notice that the understanding of the term, therefore, hinges on the prayer of Daniel. He prayed about the seventy years of captivity, and God answered him about periods of seven years - the recurrence of sabbatical years - so the weeks in this passage signify periods of seven years.

The angel Gabriel gave the commencement of this period to be "from the going forth of the commandment to restore and to build Jerusalem" (Dan. 9:25). If we check the book of Ezra, we have two decrees: one by Cyrus and one by Artaxerxes. However, neither of these could be the point indicated in the prophecy, because they both dealt with the temple and not the city of Jerusalem.

When we come to Nehemiah, we have something about the city. We notice that in the twentieth year of Artaxerxes, he responded to Nehemiah's request, permitting him to go up to Judah unto the city of his fathers' sepulchers that he might build it.

In Nehemiah 2:4-8, we have the date the angel Gabriel referred to, and because there is no other communication concerning the "commandment" as to the restoration and building of Jerusalem in the word of God, the date is therefore certain. Now when was this? The twentieth year of Artaxerxes is approximately 455 BC.

In Daniel, we are told that seventy weeks, or 490 years, "are determined upon thy people and upon thy holy city, to finish the transgression, and to make an end of sins, and to make reconciliation for iniquity, and to bring in everlasting righteousness, and to seal up the vision and prophecy, and to anoint the most Holy" (Dan. 9:24). These expressions, therefore, clearly look forward to the full blessings of Daniel's people and city in the millennium.

The transgression would now be finished, for which they have been scattered and have received of the Lord's hand double for all her sins, according to Isaiah 40:2. Moreover, everlasting righteousness - not self-righteousness but God's righteousness - will be brought in according to Isaiah 51:4–8. The vision and prophecies will be sealed up forever according to Zechariah 13. Finally, the holy of holies will be anointed and set apart for the glory of Jehovah according to Exodus 40:9.

In Daniel 9, we have the period of seventy weeks divided into three parts with one week left out. "Know therefore and understand, that from the going forth of the commandment to restore and to build Jerusalem unto the Messiah the Prince shall be seven weeks, and threescore and two weeks: the street shall be built again, and the wall, even in troublous times" (Dan. 9:25).

The seventy weeks are divided into three portions - seven weeks (49 years), threescore and two weeks (434 years), and one week (7 years). The one week (7 years) isn't spoken of here. The first period is identified with the rebuilding of Jerusalem and its wall. The end of the verse gives us an understanding of what was being undertaken. The "troublous" times marked the period during the building of the walls.

We then have the second period of sixty-two weeks (434 years), which reach "unto" the Messiah, the Prince. Therefore, from the time the city was finished building to the Messiah was 434 years. When we add the forty-nine years engaged in the restoration of the city, we have another time frame for the Messiah. Therefore, from the commandment to build Jerusalem to the Messiah, the Christ, would be 483 years.

As a result, for us to understand the precise time of the expression "unto Messiah," we must remember that one week of years is seven years. Once we recall that fact, we will notice that Christ's life spans nearly five weeks of years, since Christ died at thirty-three years old. If it were, therefore, His birth that was in question, the word of God would have expressed it differently. The word of God would have subtracted the approximately five weeks of the life of the Messiah. Nevertheless, the scripture didn't subtract the roughly five weeks (thirty-three years) of His life but added them. The scripture then took us to Messiah's presence at the sixty-ninth week - that is, just before His death.

The Bible then states that after the sixty-ninth week (483 years) shall Messiah be cut off. I say sixty-ninth week (483 years) because God's word is adding two periods: the seven weeks (49 years) and the sixty-two weeks (434 years). The scripture enlightens us that from the year the city was finished building to the Messiah would be sixty-two weeks or 434 years. Nevertheless, there were two projects going on at the same time: the rebuilding of the city and the reconstruction of the temple.

Christ came just on time and entered the city of Jerusalem and the temple according to Matthew 21. Two projects were being undertaken at the same time: the rebuilding of the temple and the rebuilding of the city. In Malachi 3, we read, "Behold I will send my messenger, and he shall prepare the way before me: and the Lord, whom you seek, shall suddenly come to His temple, even the messenger of the covenant, whom ye delight in: behold, he shall come, saith the Lord of hosts" (Mal. 3:1). Those who have calculated the dates have found that the time of the coming of Messiah is fulfilled in Christ entrance into Jerusalem on the ass. This particular incident is recorded in each gospel being the fulfillment of God's promise to the Jews.

Therefore, in Matthew 21 the Lord Jesus Christ presents Himself as the long-expected Messiah. He was therefore seen in both Jerusalem and the temple. The coming of Christ to Jerusalem, according to Matthew 21:4-13, and His subsequent entrance into the temple was the time indicated for Messiah's presence in Israel. The Lord had to come sixty-nine weeks (483 years) after the commandment to restore and build Jerusalem, or sixty-two weeks (434 years) after rebuilding the city, and He had to die shortly after that.

If the Jews had received their Messiah, they would have ushered in the kingdom promised to their fathers. Moreover, even if He were received after the crucifixion when Peter spoke of the times of refreshing coming from the Lord's presence, Christ would have returned, as we read in Acts 3:9–21, but they wouldn't have Him. Yet all things happened according to His determinate counsel and foreknowledge. The Messiah was cut off after the sixty-ninth week (483 years) and didn't receive the kingdom. The Jews wrote that the Messiah was going to be cut off before the destruction of the temple and the city of Jerusalem, yet today the Jews say Christ isn't their Messiah; when Daniel 9 calls Him Messiah. Their Prophet, Daniel, calls the Lord Jesus Christ the Messiah when he wrote that Messiah was going to come and die before a specified time.

Therefore, as a result of His rejection, the kingdom and its associated glory were all suspended. Furthermore, the last week (seven years) of the seventy weeks of Daniel needs to be fulfilled. This period of the last week (seven years) is the period of the tribulation, and the last half of the week (three and a half years) is the period of the Great Tribulation. Bible teachers have noticed that the Lord's ministry encompassed the first half (three and a half years) of the seventieth week, and therefore only the remaining half week is yet to be fulfilled. This last half week is the period of the Great Tribulation.

It is necessary to make one last point before we leave this passage. It states, "And the people of the prince that shall come shall destroy the city and the sanctuary; and the end thereof shall be with a flood, and unto the end of the war desolations are determined" (Dan. 9:26). The scripture gives us not only the time when the Messiah was going to be in Israel - "unto the Messiah the prince" (Dan. 9:25) - but also when the Messiah was going to die. We read, "After threescore and two weeks shall Messiah be cut off" (Dan. 9:26). We then notice something even more sobering. The Messiah had to come and die before the Romans destroyed the city. More than that, He had to present Himself in the temple before the temple was destroyed, according to Malachi 3:1 prophecy. These two objects are stated in the prophecy: the city and the sanctuary are brought together in Matthew 21.

If men with their perverted minds accuse the Lord of forging His death, please tell me, how did He forge His birth? Which man could decide when he would be born and what age he would be to forge His death? Moreover, according to Psalm 102:24, Christ had to be approximately thirty-five years old at the time of his death: furthermore, He had to be at that age on the sixty-ninth week. Christ had to be born and die during the days of the temple and the city of Jerusalem, before their destruction. More than that, the people who were going to kill Him were also going to destroy both the temple and the city of Jerusalem not long after His death, and they had to be Romans. Please explain to me how a man can forge all these details. Nevertheless, Christ came and died just as the word of God declared. This can never be man's word. The Bible is the word of God.

CHAPTER 21

CHRIST PRESENTED IN ZECHARIAH

In the book of Zechariah, we see the Lord Jesus Christ presented to Israel. However, as John says, "He came unto his own, and his own received him not" (John 1:11). He was rejected and crucified. This truth and its consequences are presented in the book of Zechariah. The level of difficulty is five out of ten.

In Zechariah 9, we read, "Rejoice greatly, O daughter of Zion; shout, O daughter of Jerusalem; behold, thy King cometh unto thee: he is just, and having salvation; lowly, and riding upon an ass, and upon a colt the foal of an ass" (Zech. 9:9).

In Matthew 21, we read, "Tell ye the daughter of Sion, Behold, thy King cometh unto thee, meek, and sitting upon an ass, and a colt the foal of an ass" (Matt. 21:5). Israel was indifferent to the king; she didn't even know He had arrived and had to be told.

> And I said unto them, if ye think good, give me my price; and if not, forbear. So they weighed for my price thirty pieces of silver. And the Lord said unto me, Cast it unto the potter: a goodly price that I was prized at of them. And

> I took the thirty pieces of silver and cast them to the potter
> in the house of the Lord ... Woe to the idol shepherd that
> leaves the flock! The sword shall be upon his arm, and
> upon his right eye: his arm shall be clean dried up, and
> his right eye shall be utterly darkened. (Zech. 11:12–17)

In Matthew 26, we read, "Judas Iscariot, went unto the chief priests, and said unto them, What will ye give me, and I will deliver him unto you? And they covenanted with him for thirty pieces of silver" (vv. 14–15). However, in Zechariah 11:12–17, we read the incident in the first person. "I said unto them." But in Matthew, Judas spoke to the chief priests.

In Zechariah, the Lord is presented as going through the rejection in His own soul, and we get a deep sense of how it affected His heart. He was rejected as king, and the nation had a price for Him; so, they weighed for His price thirty pieces of silver. That was His price, the price for God the Son. Thirty pieces of silver were what Israel thought the Son of God was worth.

However, thirty pieces of silver was the price paid for a slave killed by a beast, according to Exodus 21:32. This is what Israel thought of their King, the Son of God. They declared plainly for all to hear, "Away with him, away with him, crucify him. Pilate says unto them, Shall I crucify your King? The chief priests answered, we have no king but Caesar" (John 19:15). The only king they had was Caesar.

Moreover, Jehovah felt the rejection of His Son. We are then told that the Lord said unto Him, "Cast it unto the potter in the house of the Lord" (Zech. 11:13). We are aware that Judas was going to do this, but what we see in Zechariah is that Jehovah felt the insult men heaped on His Son and instructed His Son to cast it unto the potter in the house of the Lord. Both the Father and the Son felt the rejection meted out to the Son of God. The Lord felt it personally and spoke about it. He then commented on the price. "A goodly price that I was prized at of them" (Zech. 11:13). The words "I was prized" give His intense feelings, while the expression "of them" shows that the whole nation was now guilty of this act.

We are confronted with the consequences of the rejection of the Messiah in Zechariah 11:16–17. Therefore, we read that after rejecting Christ, Israel was going to get the Antichrist. After rejecting "thy king," they were going to get "the king," the willful king, who is the Antichrist. He won't be interested in the good of anyone; he will be interested only in himself. He will be an idol shepherd. Therefore, he will seek divine honor. The rejection of Christ will bring in the acceptance of the Antichrist. It is a dangerous thing to reject Christ. We see also that the Antichrist was going to leave the flock; when attacked by the Assyrian, he was going to flee to Rome for protection. Just imagine the trap Israel will fall into; within seven years of the establishment of God's kingdom, which was the very hope of the Jews, they will accept the Antichrist, who will guarantee their destruction.

The King, whom Israel rejected and sold for thirty silver pieces, was put to death. We read in Zechariah 13 the following: "Awake, O sword, against my shepherd, and against the man that is my fellow, saith the Lord of hosts: smite the shepherd, and the sheep shall be scattered: and I will turn mine hand upon the little ones" (Zech. 13:7).

In Matthew 26, we read, "When they had sung a hymn, they went out into the mount of Olives. Then saith Jesus unto them, all ye shall be offended because of me this night: for it is written, I will smite the shepherd, and the sheep of the flock shall be scattered abroad" (Matt. 26:30–31). The sword here is a type of the judicial stroke that fell on Christ when He died on that cross. This is made plain in Jeremiah 47, where we read, "O thou sword of the Lord, how long will it be ere thou be quiet? Put up thyself into thy scabbard, rest, and be still" (Jer. 47:6).

However, instead of rest, we find the command to smite. Yet this smiting shows that though the Jews crucified and slew Him, He was "delivered by the determinate counsel and foreknowledge of God" (Acts 2:23). The expression "smite the shepherd" (Zech. 13:7) brings in God's side. "Wounded in the house of my friends" (Zech. 13:6), brings in man's side. Both sides are essential. As my shepherd, He is the one provided by Jehovah. The term *shepherd* indeed points to His place as the King, but "the man that is my fellow" (Zech. 13:7) undoubtedly refers to His divinity. This could be said of no other man.

However, because the Jews rejected and crucified Him, all God's counsels regarding the wellbeing of the Jews were suspended. Christ is now in a position to establish a new relationship. The association regarding God's earthly people is suspended; God now establishes a relationship with His heavenly people. This new affiliation is with the church of God. This church is seen as the body of Christ, the bride of Christ, and the house of God. Yet, the church is heavenly in contrast to Israel who is earthly. Furthermore, during this time of the rejection of Christ and His acceptance by the Jews, this church is being formed. The church is sandwiched between the sixty-ninth week and the seventieth week of Daniel's prophecy. When the church is complete, the Lord will rapture the church to heaven. This church is heavenly, while Israel is earthly; therefore, the church doesn't replace Israel. The Lord will resume His dealings with the Jews after the rapture; they will come under a severe judgment called the Great Tribulation. This period of the tribulation is the last week of Daniel's prophecy. After their repentance, they will be accepted by the Lord and enjoy the blessings of the millennium.

In the book of Revelation, the church is seen as a testimony on earth. Nevertheless, even there, in Revelation 2–3, because the church is heavenly and can be raptured at any time, that testimony is presented as "the things that are." Therefore, there is no event to take place before the Lord raptures the church to heaven. Yet there is a prophetic history of the church from the apostles' days to the coming of Christ. This prophetic history is seen under the figure of the seven churches of Asia. In this scheme of things, we are presently in the last church, the church of Laodicea. Therefore, we are soon to go home.

CHAPTER 22

CHRIST RETURNS IN POWER AND GLORY

W e believe the Rapture of the church of God is imminent. However, after the church of God is raptured and we approach the last part of the tribulation, we will have the conditions depicted in the book of Zechariah. "And it shall come to pass, that in all the land, saith the Lord, two parts therein shall be cut off and die; but the third shall be left therein. And I will bring the third part through the fire, and will refine them as silver is refined, and will try them as gold is tried" (Zech. 13:8–9). This subject is an eight on my scale of difficulties.

As a result of the death of Christ, two things happened to Israel. First, Israel was scattered all over the world. Second, God was going to secure for Himself a remnant of the Jews, who were going to believe in Christ during the period of His rejection. These conditions were going to go on until Israel returned to the land of Palestine in unbelief. When Israel resettled, she would then be protected by the land shadowing with wings, which will eventually be destroyed. Israel will then be protected by the Roman Empire, which will ultimately break the treaty of protection. She will consequently be exposed to the Assyrian attack, which will cause the situation described in Zechariah 13:8-9.

We need to appreciate that the present interval of grace is interposed between verses 7-8. God was then dealing with Israel, given her sins in rejecting and crucifying the Messiah. The attack that will cause the conditions depicted in Zechariah 13:8-9 is the Assyrian attack on Israel. In "all the land," of Israel, we are here told of every three Jews; two shall die. It is the most crucial point that the Spirit of God interjects. The one-third was tried most excruciatingly. With two out of every three persons deaths in the land, this point was the most critical for this reason; it is the point at which the Assyrian head leaves Israel to go to Egypt. It isn't two out of three soldiers but Jews as a whole. As far as the Assyrian head was concerned, he had Israel destroyed; two out of three were dead. One out of three remained but not so much as warriors but as those trying to hide from the Assyrian. What three couldn't do, one certainly couldn't do; at least, so the Assyrian calculated.

The Assyrian will then have possession of the temple mount, and he will station a force there to guard against any resurgence of the Jews. Nevertheless, the rest of the Jews will be struggling just to survive. The Assyrian head, therefore, will take his leave from Israel to push deeper into the Egyptian and Libyan corridor, to conquer the king of the South in battle. Though the king of the North and the king of the South would have both fought the land shadowing with wings and Israel together, the Assyrian will want to be the unrivaled king in the area. Still, there will be a remnant of one out of three Jews who will remain in Israel. Nevertheless, there will be a remnant of one out of three Jews who will remain in Israel. This remnant will be tried severely, but they will call on the Lord and He will deliver them.

However, in Zechariah 14, we find no power trying to oppose the Assyrian on Israel's behalf. This is further confirmed by what we read in Isaiah 10. "And my hand hath found as a nest the riches of the people: and as one gathers eggs that are left, have I gathered all the earth; and there was none that moved the wing, or opened the mouth, or peeped" (Isa. 10:14).

No one "moved a wing." No one even said a word in opposition to what was happening. No one even wanted to see what was going on. No one tried to protect Israel from the Assyrian; all her protectors were gone, and Israel will be left on her own; like Jacob with God.

Lamentation 4:12–17 highlights Israel's hopeless condition. Here we are told that neither "the kings of the earth" nor "all the inhabitants of the world" believed the adversary and the enemy would have entered into Jerusalem's gates. The world will think that the Assyrian will not invade the Jewish state. Israel will feel the same way as declared in Isaiah: "We have made a covenant with death, and with hell are we at agreement; when the overflowing scourge shall pass through, it shall not come unto us" (Isa. 28:15). This is the same situation we have today. Man believes in man's power instead of God's word, yet I know who will triumph. God will succeed every time.

In Lamentation 4, we notice the reception Israel will receive when she will flee to the surrounding nations. We read, "They cried unto them, Depart! Unclean! Depart! Depart, touch not! When they fled away, and wondered about it was said among the nations, they shall no more sojourn [here]. The face of Jehovah hath divided them; he will no more regard them. They respected not the person of the priest they favored, not the aged" (Lam. 4:15–16 JND). This is the position even Moab will come to finally: "They shall no more sojourn [here]" (Lam. 4:15 JND). Moab finally came to the same position and wanted Israel out of her land.

We need to notice the reason for the attack and the fact that this attack had nothing to do with the past. We read, "For the sins of her prophets, and the iniquities of her priests, that have shed the blood of the 'just' in the midst of her" (Lam. 4:13). The sins of her prophets were like "Caiaphas," the high priest, who prophesied, "That one man should die for the people, and that the whole nation perishes not. And this spake he not of himself: but being high priest that year, he prophesied that Jesus should die for that nation" (John 11:50–51). Here we are told that they shed the blood of the just amid Jerusalem. Do we need to ask who the just is? We know who He is, and it was for His blood that was shed that God inflicted this judgment on Israel. In J. N. Darby's translation, He is called "the Righteous" instead of "the just." Christ is the righteous, whom they crucified.

"As for us, our eyes as yet failed for our vain help: in our watching, we have watched for a nation that could not save us" (Lam. 4:17). They watched, but they couldn't believe what they were seeing. They watched for a nation that couldn't save them. Their help was in vain. In the new translation, it is better rendered, "Our eyes still failed for our vain help; in our watching we have watched for a nation that did not save" (Lam. 4:17 JND). The nation they were watching for to help them in their crisis was the Roman Empire. However, the Roman power refused to get involved. Egypt was going to help in vain and so also the Roman Empire - both of them were going to help in vain.

Next, instead of the enemy taking the spoils, he divides them there. Furthermore, we need to notice that this battle was taking place against Jerusalem. Moreover, we need to see that all these forces were coming against her, and she had no help. In Zechariah 14, we see the condition in the city. The city was already taken. The houses were rifled. The women were ravished. Half of the city was already taken as captives. Half of Israel was already prisoners, and that half was half of the one-third that remained (remember that two-thirds of the country was already dead; only one-third was still alive). The Assyrian head was seeking to capture the other half of the city. With this thought in mind, he withdrew the major part of his force from Israel to Egypt, leaving the lesser part in Jerusalem to capture the remaining Jews. He knew that both the city and the county were in his hands. However, he didn't anticipate the coming of the Lord Jesus Christ for Israel's deliverance.

In Joel 2, we see how the attack was divided. "Yea, the Lord will answer and say unto his people, Behold, I will send you corn, and wine, and oil, and ye shall be satisfied therewith: and I will no more make you a reproach among the heathen: But I will remove far off from you the northern army, and will drive him into a land barren and desolate, with his face toward the east sea, and his hinder part toward the utmost sea and his stink shall come up, and his ill savour shall come up, because he hath done great things" (vv. 19–20).

When the Lord answers the remnant's intercession, He will do two things. First, the Lord will remove the northern army far off. Second, He will drive it into a land barren and desolate, with its face toward the east sea and its hinder part toward the utmost sea. The northern army is the Assyrian, the king of the North. When the Lord will remove the northern army far off, where will He be removing it from, and where will He be moving it to? Indeed, it is from Israel to Egypt the Assyrian will be moving. This movement will take place when the majority of the soldiers of the northern army will leave Israel for Egypt. Why will God need to remove the northern army? The reason is simple; it was causing absolute havoc in Israel, fueling the great tribulation.

The Lord will then bring the northern army back from Egypt to Israel for its destruction. When the Assyrian's face is towards the east sea and his hinder part towards the utmost sea, the northern army is pictured as returning to Israel from Egypt. This event will be during the second attack; this attack will initiate its destruction.

The Assyrian will desire to capture all Israel so that he could do to them whatever he desires. However, he will let that wait until he returns from Egypt. He will then go to Egypt to subjugate the king of the South, but he didn't read Isaiah 49. "Shall the prey be taken from the mighty, or the lawful captive delivered?" (v. 24). He didn't know Isaiah 49. "But thus saith the Lord, Even the captives of the mighty shall be taken away, and the prey of the terrible shall be delivered: for I will contend with him that contendeth with thee, and I will save thy children" (v. 25). The "mighty" is the Assyrian. The "terrible" is the Assyrian. The prey will be taken from him. He never could imagine that eventuality. How accurate is the word of God! Once it is rightly divided everything will line up perfectly.

Isaiah 10 states, "And it shall come to pass in that day, that his burden shall be taken away from off thy shoulder, and his yoke from off thy neck, and the yoke shall be destroyed because of the anointing" (v. 27). We see that the yoke of the Assyrian will be destroyed because of the anointing. Christ is the anointed. Now very carefully notice the "he" and the "they." The "he" is the Assyrian head with his army; the "they" is the army alone without the leader.

The Assyrian will be invading Israel from the North, this is the first attack, which is before Christ returns. The second attack is after Christ comes. Consequently, in verse 28, we read, "He is come to Aiath, he is passed to Migron; at Michmash he hath laid up his carriages" (Isa. 10:28). The Assyrian head is seen with his army, causing great havoc in Israel. Now notice in what we read next, that the "he" isn't there; the army alone is in the land. "They are gone over the passage: they have taken up their lodging at Geba; Ramah is afraid; Gibeah of Saul is fled. Lift up thy voice, O daughter of Gallim: cause it to be heard unto Laish, O poor Anathoth. Madmenah is removed; the inhabitants of Gebim gather themselves to flee" (Isa. 10:29–31). We perceived that in verses 29-31, the Assyrian head will be absent, and his army's activity will be prominent. At that time, the Assyrian head will be in Egypt.

However, in verses 32–33, he will return from Egypt and will be destroyed. Remember that his army is over two hundred million strong. He feels he can do anything. "As yet shall he remain at Nob that day: he shall shake his hand against the mount of the daughter of Zion, the hill of Jerusalem. Behold, the Lord, the Lord of hosts, shall lop the bough with terror: and the high ones of stature shall be hewn down, and the haughty shall be humbled" (Isa. 10:32–33). In these verses, we notice the Assyrian will be returning to Israel from Egypt for his final attack on Jerusalem, only to be obliterated by the Lord Jesus Christ. Observe again the "he" in verse 32, the Assyrian's head, and the route he is traveling; we know he is returning from Egypt.

Further, in Zechariah 14, we read that the Lord will fight against the nations.

> Behold, the day of the Lord cometh, and thy spoil shall be divided in the midst of thee. For I will gather all nations against Jerusalem to battle; and the city shall be taken, and the houses rifled and the women ravished; and half of the city shall go forth into captivity, and the residue of the people shall not be cut off from the city. Then shall the Lord go forth and fight against those nations, as when he fought in the day of battle. And his feet shall stand in that day upon the mount of Olives, which is before Jerusalem on the east ... and the Lord my God shall come, and all the saints with thee. (Zech. 14:1–5)

In this passage, the Lord declares that He will gather all nations against Jerusalem to battle. This declaration makes the battle future and it will be fought just after the middle of the tribulation. During the battle, we are told that half of Jerusalem's city will be taken captives, and the whole city would be captured. The city will fall. Half of the inhabitants will be captives. However, the other half the Assyrian will seek to capture, but the Lord will not allow it. We, therefore, read, "Then shall the Lord go forth, and fight against those nations, as when he fought in the day of battle" (Zech. 14:3). Man says that God helps those who help themselves, but here we see that God helps those who cannot help themselves. This is how God acts.

At that juncture, the Jews will not expect a deliverance. The Assyrian will expect no further fight from Israel. However, it is at this stage that the Lord will enter the battle. We read, "then shall the Lord go forth and fight against those nations" (Zech. 14:3). He will come out of heaven and crush the Assyrian army which will be around Jerusalem. In this scripture, it is the Assyrian that is before us; so, He will destroy the Assyrian force near Jerusalem. However, bear in mind that the Lord's destruction of the Assyrian will be twofold: the smaller part first, then the larger part after.

Furthermore, in Revelation 19, where the Roman Empire is before us, the Lord will come and crush the Roman Empire. It must be understood that the Roman Army will fight no battle in Israel. The Romans will break the covenant of protection and remove their troops from Israel. They will never return. In Revelation 16, 17 and 19 the Roman army is in Europe. The European troops are gathered to fight the Lord as He comes down from heaven. When the Lord comes down from heaven, He will crush the Roman Army in Europe. Armageddon is a battle in Israel, therefore, it does not include the Roman Army. If we are careful with scripture, we will not make mistakes.

Notice carefully what Matthew 24 declares: "Immediately after the tribulation of those days shall the sun be darkened, and the moon shall not give her light, and the stars shall fall from heaven, and the powers of the heavens shall be shaken: And then shall appear the sign of the Son of man in heaven: and then shall all the tribes of the earth mourn, and they shall see the Son of man coming in the clouds of heaven with power and great glory" (Matt. 24:29–30)

We need to comprehend that Christ is coming after the tribulation. His coming doesn't end the tribulation. At the Lord's coming, the tribulation would have ended already because the Assyrian head would have summoned his main force that was in Israel into the Egyptian, Ethiopian, and Libyan corridor. While he will be in Egypt, the Lord will come.

However, we find something special about the Roman Empire. First, they see the sign of the coming of the Son of man. Then they see the Son of man coming with power and great glory. What does the Roman Prince do? He will see Christ coming down with his saints, and he will seek to make war with Him. However, he will lose before he starts.

In Revelation 19:11–21, Christ will come from heaven with the saints. Christ is the one seated on the white horse. He is called the Word of God, "the Word" of John 1. "The armies" that follow Christ aren't angels, though there will be angels when Christ comes; they are the saints, and we know this from their garments. How can the saints come from heaven unless they were first taken to heaven? It is the answer to this question that shows the necessity for the Rapture.

When Christ takes the saints in the air, that event is called "the Rapture." When He comes with the saints, that event is called "the revelation;" so, what we have here isn't the Rapture but the revelation of Jesus Christ. However, some are opposed to the word *Rapture*. They tell us that the word isn't in scripture. True, the word isn't there, but the idea is indeed there. The term *Rapture* is Latin, so it couldn't be there in a Greek New Testament. Why do they think we cannot borrow a word from another language to adequately express an idea? The English language has already borrowed so many words, and no one complains; another word won't make a difference. However, "caught up" is definitely there; so, also, is "translated."

Nevertheless, this Latin word *Rapture* expresses the idea perfectly. We then read, "He treadeth the winepress with the fierceness and wrath of Almighty God" (Rev. 19:15). It isn't "like" the almighty God but "of" the almighty God. Jesus Christ is the almighty God.

Therefore, in Revelation 19, we read further, "And I saw the beast, and the kings of the earth, and their armies, gathered together to make war against him that sat on the horse, and against his army" (Rev. 19:19). Ironically, the Roman army, which ran from the fight against the Assyrian, will be ready to fight the Lord. Nevertheless, there is no fight. "And the beast was taken, and with him the false prophet that wrought miracles before him, with which he deceived them that had received the mark of the beast, and them that worshipped his image. These both were cast alive into a lake of fire burning with brimstone" (Rev. 19:20).

In Revelation 17, we have the identical war, where the Roman kings make war with the Lamb. However, this war is stated only to highlight their destruction. We read, "These shall make war with the Lamb, and the Lamb shall overcome them: for he is Lord of lords, and King of kings: and they that are with him are called and chosen, and faithful" (v. 14). This Roman power makes war with the Lamb, but the Lamb crushes it. Here again, when He comes, the saints are there with Him, seen as the chosen and faithful. The Roman Army does not fight in Israel. The Roman Army does not attack the Assyrian. Armageddon is a battle between the Assyrian and Israel, with the intervention of the Lord who destroys the Assyrian. If we do not know the Assyrian, we will make endless mistakes.

In Revelation 19, the Beast is the Roman Prince. The false prophet is the Antichrist, who escaped to Rome to protect his life from the Assyrian. He is found with his companion of evil, the Roman Prince. We notice that the European armies are still in Europe. These Roman kings will see the Lord Jesus Christ descending from heaven; they then will turn their weapons of war against Him as He descends, but there will be no fight. They will lose before the battle gets started. The Beast will be taken - that is, the Roman Prince. Then we read, "And with him, the false prophet that wrought miracles before him" (Rev. 19:20). The false prophet is the Antichrist. He will be found with the Roman Prince in Rome because he will flee from Israel. Moreover, the Antichrist will have no governmental power, because he will run away from his government in Israel, so he is called the false prophet in this instance. He will leave all and flee to the Roman Prince for protection, so he is only the false prophet. The Antichrist will leave just before the Assyrian invasion.

Let us get some help in John 10. We read, "I am the good shepherd: the good shepherd giveth his life for the sheep. But he that is a hireling, and not the shepherd, whose own the sheep are not, seeth the wolf coming, and leaveth the sheep, and fleeth: and the wolf catcheth them, and scattereth the sheep. The hireling fleeth, because he is a hireling, and careth not for the sheep" (John 10:11–13).

The Lord Jesus is the good shepherd, who gave His life for the sheep. The Antichrist is the hireling, and when the Assyrian head invades, he will leave Israel and flee to the Roman Empire. It is evident that since the Roman Empire will not come to his defense, he will go to the Roman Prince for protection. The wolf in the passage above speaks of the Assyrian.

We read, moreover, "Within a year, according to the years of a hireling, and all the glory of Kedar shall fail" (Isa. 21:16). It seems that the time in which the Antichrist, as the hireling, will stay in Israel after the Abomination of Desolation will be short. As a hireling, he will flee to Rome early and will leave Israel on her own.

Further, in Revelation 19:20–21 the Roman Prince is captured, and so also is the Antichrist. My Lord Jesus Christ will cast both alive into the lake of fire. Next, we are told that "the remnant was slain with the sword of him that sat on the horse, which sword proceeded out of his mouth" (Rev. 19:21). The remnant is the rest of the armed forces and the kings of Europe. The coming of Christ will demolish the whole of Europe. It isn't merely the ten nations but the whole European force. This will explain why the stone fell on the feet of the image in Daniel 2, and not on the toes. The Lord Jesus will decimate the troops in Europe. History records that the Roman Empire crucified the Lord Jesus Christ. This time it will be the Lord Jesus who will destroy the Roman Empire and all of it.

We read in Zechariah 14 that the Lord demolishes His enemies. "Then shall the Lord go forth, and fight against those nations, as when he fought in the day of battle. And his feet shall stand in that day upon the mount of Olives, which is before Jerusalem on the east … and the Lord my God shall come, and all the saints with thee" (Zech. 14:3–5). At this coming, the Assyrian Army will be in Egypt.

It must be emphasized that it is Jehovah who goes forth and fights against those nations, but from the New Testament, we know it is the Lord Jesus Christ who will come. We see clearly that the Lord Jesus Christ is Jehovah, but as was stated before, the Father is Jehovah, the Son is Jehovah, and the Holy Spirit is Jehovah. Here it is Christ who is presented as Jehovah. We have more: "His feet shall stand in that day on the mount of Olives" (Zech. 14:4). Here Jehovah has feet, not figuratively, but actually, because He is a man and will forever remain a man. This is my Lord Jesus Christ, who will return on the Mount of Olives as was promised.

Additionally, we read, "And the Lord my God shall come, and all the saints with thee" (Zech. 14:5). Note that in the original Hebrew, the word for "Lord" is the word for "Jehovah" or "Yahweh," so it is "Jehovah my God shall come." The Jews rejected Him at His first coming as Messiah, but now He will come back as Jehovah, my God. Zechariah says that He is "Jehovah, my God." I say He is Jesus Christ, my God. What a wonderful Savior!

However, there is something more; He comes with all His saints, not some of the saints. Therefore, when we read in the New Testament that Christ comes with all of the saints, it must be the Lord Jesus as Jehovah who comes with all the saints. All the scriptures must agree. How could the saints come with Jehovah from heaven unless they were first taken with Jehovah to heaven? The saints must first be raptured before they could be revealed with Him. We are first raptured, then we are revealed with the Lord Jesus Christ. When the world sees Him, then we will also be seen by the world. The word of God declares, "When Christ who is our life shall appear, then shall ye also appear with him in glory" (Col. 3:4).

In 1 Thessalonians 3, we are told, "To the end, he may establish your hearts unblameable in holiness before God, even our Father, at the coming of our Lord Jesus Christ with all his saints" (v. 13). In Zechariah 14, we read, "And ye shall flee to the valley of the mountains; for the valley of the mountains shall reach unto Azal: yea, ye shall flee, like as ye fled from before the earthquake in the days of Uzziah king of Judah: and Jehovah my God shall come, and all the saints with thee" (v. 5 JND).

In 1 Thessalonians 3, it is Jesus who comes from heaven with "all his saints," but in Zechariah, it is Jehovah, my God, who comes from heaven with "all his saints." If Jesus comes from heaven with "all the saints" and not some of the saints, and Jehovah comes from heaven with "all the saints" and not some of the saints, then Jesus must be Jehovah. Therefore, both the New Testament saints and the Old Testament saints must be raptured. This must be true, since neither Jehovah nor Jesus comes with some of the saints but with all the saints. Jesus Christ is Jehovah, my God. All the scriptures must agree, and they do.

We have seen that the Lord will come down from heaven and deal with the nations. First, He will decimate the nations gathered around Jerusalem. Second, He will capture the Roman Prince and the Antichrist and will crush the European forces. With his main army in Egypt, the Assyrian leader will hear the tidings that Christ has come down from heaven and has destroyed part of his all-conquering force. He will then return to Israel from Egypt to deal with the Lord Jesus Christ, as we read in Daniel 8, "He shall also stand up against the Prince of princes, but he shall be broken without hand" (Dan. 8:25). He will stand up against the Lord Jesus Christ, but he will be broken without human intervention. The Lord Jesus Christ, therefore, will crush the Assyrian head - his army also will be decimated. The Assyrian head will then be taken alive, like the Roman Prince and the Antichrist, and these three men who will make the earth their playground of evil will be cast alive into the lake of fire. These three men will go into hell, even before Satan. Here we find the Lord Jesus Christ beginning to subjugate all His enemies.

However, He doesn't deal only with the nations; he must also deal with Israel. Israel must own that she crucified her own Messiah and repent of this horrible deed. This we will presently see in Zechariah 12. In Zechariah 14, Jehovah will come for the destruction of the nations, but here in Zechariah 12, He comes for the deliverance of the Jews.

First, in Zechariah 12:1–9, it is essential to notice that the horse and rider of Revelation 6 are presented here as rival powers connected to the battle of the last days. The Lord, when He comes, will destroy the horse and rider. As was stated earlier, those four powers were the king of the North, the king of the South, Israel, and the Roman Empire. These four powers are seen connected with the battle when the Lord returns, and the Lord will destroy them. Here in Zechariah 12, this battle is in Israel, therefore, the horse and rider that the Lord will destroy will be the king of the North and the king of the South.

In this passage, we see the Lord coming for the deliverance of His earthly people, Israel. His heavenly people, the church, will have already been raptured. They will have been raised from the dead. They will have been changed from mortality to immortality and from corruptibility to incorruptibility. They will now have spiritual bodies that could move from earth to heaven in an instant of time, but they will still look the same way. We don't read about travel when we are raptured. He says the word, and we are there! The lord Jesus said the word to Lazarus, and Lazarus returned from the dead. He will say the word to us, and we will be alive forever, nevermore to die. If the Lord puts us to sleep, He will wake us up, and then we will be conformed to His image and likeness. "Come up here" (Rev. 4:1 JND), and we are there. This is the power of God, the power that made the world from nothing, the power that will raise us from the dead, not Mother Nature, as a man speaks, but divine power.

He says in the following passage that He is the one who created all things, and He is also the one who will redeem all things. There is no evolution. There is only creation. He is the Creator. He says, "The Lord, which stretches forth the heavens, and lays the foundation of the earth, and formeth the spirit of man within him" (Zech. 12:1). Here He presents Himself as the Creator. The Lord Jesus Christ has a right to this world in three ways. He has a right as Creator, He has a right as Heir, and He has a right as Redeemer; He will now establish that right as Redeemer.

We need to go a little deeper. "I will make Jerusalem a cup of trembling unto all the people round about when they shall be in the siege both against Judah and against Jerusalem. And in that day will I make Jerusalem a burdensome stone for all people: all that burden themselves with it shall be cut in pieces, though all the people of the earth be gathered together against it" (Zech. 12:2–3). He was going to make Jerusalem "a cup of trembling" to all the people round about Israel. Those round about Israel are the Assyrian army. They will all tremble when He appears. They will not expect Him, but He will put in His appearance.

There is no solution to the present conflict between Israel and the Palestinians. This is how it is all going to end. Just imagine the difficulties man faces. The Jews were out of the land of Palestine for nearly two thousand years. The Romans had put them out and scattered them abroad. During that time, the Palestinians were living there. I am giving you history in general terms. However, Israel had to return, because God said so; this very God who man says doesn't exist is yet fulfilling all He said. He told us how Israel would come back; they were going to return by themselves and by their experience in World War II. As He said it, so it happened, because there is a God.

What can the peacemakers do? They cannot remove Israel, and the Palestinians won't give up their claims to the land they have been living in for so long. As a result, all who will burden themselves with this matter will be broken to pieces. This is the declaration of the word of God. Nevertheless, many countries burden themselves with it, trying to arrive at a political solution, but they cannot find one. They will find none until the world will be thrust into a crisis, when the land shadowing with wings will be destroyed. No man can stop what the word of God declares; all will come to past.

We then read, "Though all the people of the earth be gathered together against it" (Zech. 12:3). From this expression, we get an idea of the size of the Assyrian force. It is as if the whole world will be gathered against Jerusalem. The Assyrian force was so vast that no one wanted to fight it. No one will be willing to engage that force, but when the Lord comes, He will destroy it as a thing of naught.

In Zechariah 12:4–6, it is all about Judah, since Israel is still seen as in captivity; though Judah is called Israel today, yet there are pockets of all the tribes in Israel. We see again how the Lord will destroy all human power. All man's strength will be destroyed. When Israel sees how the Lord will destroy all her enemies, then Israel herself will join in the battle. This we are here told. However, when this enemy round about Israel is destroyed, the jubilant Israelites will surround the Lord Jesus Christ. The Jews will be so joyful after being delivered from certain death that they will have a reason to celebrate. In Lamentations, they said that their end had come. But now God had sent one from heaven for their deliverance. How privileged was Israel? They were ecstatic.

In Psalm 126, we read, "When the Lord turned again the captivity of Zion, we were like them that dream. Then was our mouth filled with laughter, and our tongue with singing: then said they among the heathen, The Lord hath done great things for them. The Lord hath done great things for us; thereof we are glad" (Ps. 126:1–3).

The deliverance that the Lord will bring will be like a dream to the Jews. They never expected it. They will be glad, and it will resound all over the world. Nevertheless, the Jews will not yet recognize their Deliverer, though they will be in His presence; like Joseph's brethren in Egypt. Nonetheless, the Jews will all be excited. They will be asking questions. "Are you a prophet?" They will ask the Lord. They cannot know Him higher than a prophet except by revelation. He will answer them, "But he shall say, I am no prophet, I am a husbandman; for man taught me to keep cattle from my youth" (Zech. 13:5).

Then another person near Him will see the wounds in His hands, the nail prints, and asked another question. "What are those wounds in thine hands" (Zech. 13:6)? This question has to do with the meaning of the wounds; nevertheless, the Lord's answer will address the place where He got the wounds. "Then He shall answer, those with which I was wounded in the house of my friend" (Zech. 13:6). In their present condition, they could only comprehend the place of the wound and not the meaning. Therefore, to apprehend the meaning of the wounds, He will have to prepare them to receive that information. Consequently, for them to "look," he had to "show" them. The Lord Jesus will do something that would change their disposition. He will show them His side; but before He does that, He will have to prepare them.

In Zechariah 12, we read,

> And I will pour upon the house of David, and upon the inhabitants of Jerusalem, the spirit of grace and of supplications: and they shall look upon me whom they have pierced, and they shall mourn for him, as one mourneth for his only son, and shall be in bitterness for him, as one that is in bitterness for his firstborn. In that day shall there be a great mourning in Jerusalem, as the mourning of Hadadrimmon in the valley of Megiddon. And the land shall mourn, every family apart; the family of the house of David apart, and their wives apart; the family of the house of Nathan apart, and their wives apart. The family of the house of Levi apart, and their wives apart; the family of Shimei apart, and their wives apart; All the families that remain, every family apart, and their wives apart. (Zech. 12:10–14)

What we are dealing with in Zechariah 12 isn't so much about the prints of the nails but the spear in His side. He will have to show them this. They couldn't see it unless He showed it to them. They never asked about the hole in His side; they never saw it, they asked about the wounds in His hands, because they could see those. The hole in His side will break them down into wailing. In His heart there is a hole. They made it in their hatred of Him, who only had love for them. When this verse: "They shall look upon me whom they have pierced" (Zech. 12:10) is quoted, it isn't cited regarding the nails in His hands but the spear in His side. The nails in His hands went in before He had died; the spear in His side went in after He was dead. He might have wounds in His hands yet live, but the hole in His heart declared that they had murdered Him. Yet the one they had crucified had come back for their deliverance. Who could conceive of such a thing? Only a holy God could think and so act.

In John 19, we read, "But when they came to Jesus, and saw that he was dead already, they brake not his legs: But one of the soldiers with a spear pierced his side, and forthwith came there out blood and water. And he that saw it bare record, and his record is true: and he knoweth that he saith true, that ye might believe. For these things were done, that the scripture should be fulfilled, a bone of Him shall not be broken. And again another scripture saith, they shall look on Him whom they pierced" (vv. 33–37).

The word here for "pierce" which is *ekkenteo* in the Greek, is used only twice. We find it here in verse 37 and again in Revelation 1. "Behold, he cometh with clouds; and every eye shall see him, and they also which pierced him: and all kindreds of the earth shall wail because of him. Even so, Amen" (v. 7).

In Revelation 1, we see that not only Israel but all kindreds of the earth were going to wail. Instead of the joys of Christmas, there will be the wailing of His piercing. Instead of the celebrations of His birth, there will be the wailing of His death. All humanity must go through the consequences of the death of the Son of God. He did no wrong, yet men just took the Son of God and crucified Him. There will be great wailing in this world.

Let me express the following thoughts shared with me by Alfred Bouter on "me whom they have pierced" (Zech. 12:10). He said, "This is amazing, 'Me' refers to Yahweh (see context) and in front of whom there are two Hebrew letters, *Aleph* and *Tau* (as in the Greek alpha and omega). This indicates to whom this refers. God cannot die (the 'Me' who speaks), but as a man, He was pierced, and He died, yet, He is the Same, God blessed over all."

They will see His hands, but then He will show them His side. Every family will begin to mourn. The family of the king is first mentioned. Here the wives are separated in their mourning—not just the women but the wives. The family of the prophet is second, and their wives are apart. The family of the priest is next, and their wives are apart. "The family of Shimei apart, and their wives apart" (Zech. 12:13); Shimei is the man who cursed King David when He was rejected, then returned in repentance. This name Shimei is essential because it represents all the Jews who despised and rejected the Lord Jesus Christ but then will return in repentance. All the families that remained - every family apart and their wives apart - will mourn the Son of God's crucifixion. The wives are separated because there will be loud public mourning. This will indeed be a solemn occasion.

Those who will not be there to mourn will be in death, to be raised from the dead: some to be raised shortly, and others a thousand years after. Nevertheless, the Assyrian head will not yet be destroyed. He will then return from Egypt, after the mourning of Israel is over, to be crushed by the Lord. The Lord Jesus will then bring down the Russian force from the extreme north (Ezek. 38, 39) and will destroy it. With all powers destroyed, He will reign as King of kings and Lord of lords, and thanks be to God, I will be there to share it all with Him. Where will you be? I pray to God that you will accept His grace and mercy. I don't ask whether there is a God. I know there is a God, and without Him, you will be lost forever.

Finally, God has given us the highlighted history of His earthly people, Israel, from the days of Abraham to the coming of Christ; even to the end of the kingdom. I have sought to outline just a sample of this history. What is past, has been completely fulfilled, what is present is being fulfilled before our eyes and what is future will be fulfilled. I hope you will believe God and receive His salvation. The evolutionist may look for his aliens, but I will look for Christ. I know He will come and take me to glory.

There are many other subjects I would like to take up, but they will have to wait, if the Lord wills, for another occasion. To God be the glory for all eternity.

CHAPTER 23

THE PRAYER

I greet you in the wonderful and precious name of our Lord and Savior, Jesus Christ, who loves us and gave Himself for us. It is with great desire that I pen you this letter because you have been one of the many readers who have continued through this book and have seen that the Bible is indeed God's word and it is the truth. My reader, I desire that you might be in the place where the Lord Jesus will be eternally.

Therefore, the first thing I would like to say to you is that God loves you. John 3 declares, "For God so loved the world that he gave his only begotten Son, that whosoever believeth in him should not perish, but have everlasting life" (v. 16). This is God's love to the whole world, of which you are a part. God not only made you but also loves you. He loves you so much that even though He had only one Son, He gave Him to die for you, because you are precious in His sight.

Further, in 1 Corinthians 15 we read, "Christ died for our sins according to the scriptures; and that he was buried, and that he rose the third day again according to the scriptures" (vv. 3–4). He died for you on that cross, but God raised Him from the dead. By raising Him from the dead, God assured us that He has accepted the work of Christ on our behalf and that this work has satisfied all God's righteous demands concerning the sinner.

In 1 John 1, we read, "The blood of Jesus Christ his Son cleanseth us from all sin. If we say that we have no sin, we deceive ourselves, and the truth is not in us. If we confess our sins, He is faithful and just to forgive us our sins, and to cleanse us from all unrighteousness. If we say that we have not sinned, we make him a liar, and his word is not in us" (vv. 7–10).

The word of God states what I need to do to be saved and have my sins forgiven; that is, confess my sins to God and repent of my sins. Romans 3 declares, "For all have sinned, and come short of the glory of God" (v. 23). We have all sinned against a holy God.

Moreover, in Romans 6, we have this declaration: "For the wages of sin is death, but the gift of God is eternal life through Jesus Christ our Lord" (v. 23). We can see that there is life in Christ as a gift from God - not as a reward for good works but as a gift from a wonderful God. You cannot pay for it, and you cannot work for it.

In Acts 20, we read, "Testifying both to the Jews, and also to the Greeks, repentance toward God, and faith toward our Lord Jesus Christ" (v. 21). What we are reading in Acts is what is being said to everyone. He is telling this to the Jews, and He is telling the same to the nations. I had to do it, and you will need to do it. There is no other way. "Repentance towards God and faith towards the Lord Jesus Christ" (Acts 20:21); that is, there are two things. Hence: 1) I need to own that I am a sinner, then confess my sins to God and tell Him I am sorry for my sins. 2) I need to believe that the Lord Jesus died for my sins and receive Him as my Savior.

Finally, if, after careful consideration of what I have said to you, you now believe in your heart that you are ready to receive Christ as your Savior, then I have included here a prayer just for you. I would also like to say to you that if you express similar words to God, meaning them in your heart, then God will save you and give you eternal life. The prayer is below.

> Oh God, I am a sinner. You know all the sins I have committed. You know all the wrong things I have done. I am sorry for my sins. I repent of all the wrongs I have done. I am sorry, O God. I am sorry. I ask you to forgive me of my sins and to wash away my sins in the blood of

your Son, Jesus Christ. I believe that He died for my sins, and I receive Him now as my one and only Savior. O God, please save me for Christ's sake. Amen.

Please be assured, my friend, that if you genuinely said those words from your heart and meant them, God has saved you as He said in John 6. "All that the Father giveth me shall come to me; and him that cometh to me I will in no wise cast out" (John 6:37). Once you come to Him in repentance, He will never reject you, because of what He said in Luke 19. "For the Son of man is come to seek and to save that which was lost" (v. 10). He came to save you. Receive Him and be saved. To Him be glory for all eternity.

BIBLIOGRAPHY

Arrian, Lucius F. *"The Anabasis of Alexander, Being, the History of the Wars and Conquest of Alexander the Great."* Book 2, Chap. 15-25, in Edward J. Chinnock's translation. London, UK: Butler & Tanner, 1884.

Bellett, John G. *Musing on the Apocalypse: Being Meditation on the Revelation.* London, UK: James Carter, 1895.

Clarke, Adam. *Commentary on the Bible.* 6 Vol. Nashville, TN: Abingdon Press, 1960. 5:228-29.

Darby, John N. *"Thoughts on Isaiah the Prophet."* In The Bible Treasury, Vol. 13, edited William Kelly. London, UK: George Morrish, 1880.

Dennett, Edward. *Daniel the Prophet. London, UK: A. S. Rouse, 1893.*

Dennett, Edward. *The Visions of John in Patmos: Being Notes on the Apocalypse.* London, UK: George Morrish, 1919.

Grant, Federick W. *The Revelation of Christ.* New York: Loizeaux Brothers, 1894. https://www.stempublishing.com/authors/FW_Grant/FWG_Revelation00.html

Josephus, Flavius. *War of the Jews.* Book 5, Ch. 12, Para. 1, 2 in Whiston's translation. Carol Stream, IL: Tyndale House Publisher, 1980

Kelly, William. *Element of Prophecy*. In The Bible Treasury, Vol. 9, edited by William Kelly. London, UK: George Morrish, 1866.

Kelly, William. Lectures on the Minor Prophet: Joel. London, UK: George Morrish, 1860. https://www.stempublishing.com/authors/kelly/1Oldtest/joel.html

Kelly, William. *Lectures on the Minor Prophet: Zephaniah*. London, UK: George Morrish, 1860.

Kelly, William. *"Notes on Isaiah."* In The Bible Treasury, Vol. 5, edited William Kelly. London, UK: George Morrish, 1865.

Kelly, William. *Notes on the Book of Daniel*. London, UK: George Morrish, 1865.

Kelly, William. *"Notes on the Epistle to the Colossians."* In The Bible Treasury, Vol. 6, edited William Kelly. London, UK: George Morrish, 1866. https://www.stempublishing.com/authors/kelly/2Newtest/REV_PT2.html

Kelly, William. *"Remarks on Daniel."* In The Bible Treasury, Vol. 3, edited William Kelly. London, UK: George Morrish, 1860.

Kelly, William. *"Remarks on the Revelation: Being Lectures on the Book of Revelation."* In The Bible Treasury, Vol. 2, edited William Kelly, London, UK: George Morrish, 1858.

Kelly, William. *"Remarks on the Revelation."* In The Bible Treasury, Vol. 2, edited by William Kelly. London, UK: George Morrish, 1858.

Kelly, William. *"The Known Isaiah."* In The Bible Treasury, Vol. 19, edited William Kelly. London, UK: George Morrish, 1893. https://www.stempublishing.com/authors/kelly/7subjcts/ISA_KNOW.html.

Kelly, William. *The Revelation Expounded. London UK: T. Weston, 1901. https://www.stempublishing.com/authors/kelly/2Newtest/Rev_expo. html#a6*

Le Strange, Guy. *Palestine under the Muslims.* Boston and New York: Houghton Mifflin and Company, 1890.

New World Encyclopedia contributors, "Julian the Apostate," *New World Encyclopedia,* https://www.newworldencyclopedia.org/p/index. php?title=Julian_the_Apostate&oldid=1012286 (accessed February 11, 2022).

Pamphilus, Eusebius. *The Ecclesiastical History.* Book 4, Chap. 2, Para. 1-5 in Christian F. Cruse and Henry De Valois's translation 3d ed., 6 vols. London, UK: Samuel Bagster and Sons, 1842.

Sachar, Howard M. *History of Israel from the rise of Zionism to our times.* Chap. 2, 3rd ed., Revised and expanded. New York: Alfred A. Knopf, 2007.

Scott, Walter. *Exposition of the Revelation of Jesus Christ and Prophetic Outlines.* London, UK: Pickering & Inglis, 1920. https://www. stempublishing.com/authors/Walter_Scott/WS_Revelation05.html

Theodoret of Cyrus. *Ecclesiastical History: A History of the Church.* Book 3, Chap.15. London, UK: H. G. Bohn, 1854.

Westcott, William H. *"A letter on New Birth and Eternal Life."* In Scripture Truth Magazine, Vol. 16, London, UK: Central Bible Truth Depot, 1924. https://www.stempublishing.com/authors/westcott/New_ Birth_and_Eternal_Life.html

Printed in the United States
by Baker & Taylor Publisher Services